hitler
&
AMERICA

hitler
&
AMERICA

Klaus P. Fischer

PENN

University of Pennsylvania Press
Philadelphia

Published by
University of Pennsylvania Press
Philadelphia, Pennsylvania 19104-4112
www.upenn.edu/pennpress

Printed in the United States of America on acid-free paper

10 9 8 7 6 5 4 3 2 1

Library of Congress Cataloging-in-Publication Data
Fischer, Klaus P., 1942–
    Hitler and America / Klaus P. Fischer. — 1st ed.
        p. cm.
    Includes bibliographical references and index.
    ISBN 978-0-8122-4338-3 (hardcover : alk. paper)
    1. Hitler, Adolf, 1889–1945—Political and social views. 2. Hitler, Adolf, 1889–1945—Psychology. 3. Germany—Foreign relations—1933–1945. 4. Germany—Foreign relations—United States. 5. United States—Foreign relations—Germany. 6. World War, 1939–1945. I. Title.
DD247.H5F525 2011
327.4307309'043—dc22

                                                                                    2011011167

CONTENTS

INTRODUCTION

A book about Hitler and America? The brief title calls for an explanation. Half a dozen books have been written about Hitler and the United States, most of them dealing with German-American foreign policy between 1933 (the year Hitler came to power) and 1941 (the year he declared war on the United States). Diplomatic relations between Germany and the United States between 1933 and 1941 should, of course, play an important role in any discussion of Hitler and America, but not at the expense of exploring the origins and development of Hitler's views. Many things in America during the 1930s caught his attention and influenced his decisions. They include American isolationism; the activities of Nazi sympathizers in America, especially the German-American Bund; American public opinion; American Jewish reactions to anti-Semitic events in Germany; and American-German business connections. Did Hitler have rigid prejudices against the United States that he never modified? Or did his perceptions change over time? Historians who have dealt with the subject of Hitler and the United States have often argued that Hitler was either ignorant or misinformed about America.

I hope that mine may be a fresh approach to this subject. It is now more than sixty years ago that Hitler committed suicide in his bunker beneath the Reich chancellery, sufficient time to permit us to assess his intentions with a greater degree of clarity than was possible a generation ago. The vast amount of material now available may be sufficient to fill out the record on almost any aspect of World War II. It is highly unlikely that many "new" documents will be found. What may be valuable now are reconsiderations of certain crucial issues.

One of these issues is Hitler's view of America and its role in world affairs. Most historians have argued that Hitler did not pay any attention to the United States in the 1930s, that if he thought of America at all, he did so through the prism of his ideology, which necessarily compromised his vision. Many have claimed that Hitler felt contempt for Americans because they were a mongrel people, incapable of higher culture or great creative achievements. Yet Hitler had considerable respect for the industrial power of the United States and its people's capacity for work. Whatever his distorted perceptions may have been, it is wrong to think that Hitler paid no attention to the United States. Indeed, he was better informed about political developments in America than has been customarily assumed.

Hitler did not want a war with either Britain or the United States; he believed that he could achieve his continental ambitions without drawing them into a direct confrontation. He hoped that his reach for hegemony in Europe would not have to lead to the loss of empire for the British. What did he think America would do if he dragged Britain and France—America's allies in World War I—into a general European war? Hitler hoped that the United States, militarily unprepared and officially neutral, would not intervene before he won his, necessarily short, European war. People close to Hitler said that he had everything calculated beforehand (*hat jede Möglichkeit von vornherein einkalkuliert*).[1] He did have a very astute judgment of his opponents and a fine sense of timing. Yet a major (and perhaps the prime) cause of his defeat was the power of the United States. Another cause was the greater tenacity of the Russian soldier as compared to the German soldier; yet another was the staying power of the British. In fighting against the three greatest powers in the world, Hitler had overextended himself, but—like Frederick the Great—he still hoped that the unnatural American-Russian-British alliance ranged against him would break up sooner or later. Hitler's efforts to split this unnatural alliance have received insufficient treatment by historians. In 1934 Hitler's chief deputy, Rudolf Hess, told a cheering mass of party members at Nuremberg that Germany was Hitler, and Hitler was Germany. This accolade was an extreme expression of faith in the führer's leadership. Yet many Germans believed that Hitler embodied the will of the nation and that his decisions reflected their true interests. The recent German historian Klaus

Hildebrand declared that "one must not speak of National Socialism but of Hitlerism."[2] If Hildebrand intends this to mean that the movement we associate with National Socialism is unthinkable without Hitler, he is wrong. Ideas about National Socialism existed well before Hitler ever became active in politics. What Hitler did was to give voice to beliefs, frustrations, hopes, and grievances in a way that no German politician had been able to before (or has been able to since). His ability to appeal to a large number of Germans and to persuade them that they could become a great power became reality in 1940. Hitler needed the Germans for the fulfillment of his conception of German greatness, but the Germans did not really need him to be great. The Germans are an old people with a long historical memory, which more often than not has failed them when they have given in to one of their main weaknesses, that of rendering unconditional loyalty to their leaders. Yet they have survived even the worst of them, including Hitler, who admitted on one occasion, "A man once told me: 'Listen, if you do that, Germany will be ruined in six weeks.' I said: 'The German people once survived the wars with the Romans. The German people survived the people's migrations (*Völkerwanderung*). The German people survived the great wars of the early and later Middle Ages. The German people survived the wars of religion of the modern age. The German people survived the Napoleonic wars, the wars of liberation, even a world war and a revolution—they will also survive me.'"[3]

When Hitler purportedly said that either Germany would be a world power or there would be no Germany,[4] he was almost but fortunately not quite right. The German people gave him their support to the very end—a remarkable loyalty if one considers the extent of the suffering he had visited upon his nation by that time. This subject of German loyalty to Hitler has still not been fully understood, least by the Germans themselves. Here my purpose is to remind the reader that for a long time Hitler justly saw himself as speaking for the majority of the German people. The notion of Hitler as an unpopular tyrant is misleading. The majority of the German people cheered him on during his triumphs, and they stood by him, for the most part, to the very end.

When Hitler spoke for Germany he therefore spoke with the support of his people in a way that few leaders of other nations could claim. But if Hitler spoke for the Germans, was there anyone who spoke with the same force and credibility for the United States? The title of this book, after all, is

Hitler and America. Did Franklin D. Roosevelt speak for America with the same popular support that Hitler did in Germany? Roosevelt was elected to the presidency four times, a unique event in America before or since, but his powers were not like Hitler's. Roosevelt faced considerable opposition in Congress and among isolationists throughout the nation. The economic crisis, which had brought him into office, went on in varying degrees of intensity well into the early 1940s, restricting a more active foreign policy backed by great military power. He was also fenced in by strict neutrality laws that were carefully monitored by vocal isolationists who did not want the United States militarily involved in any shape or form in Europe.

Thus, when Roosevelt spoke, he did so in very careful terms, aware as he was of various strong countercurrents in the form of popular opinion, congressional opposition, press criticism, or even dissension within his own administration. Hitler obviously had a freer hand than Roosevelt had. Still, Roosevelt must be considered the most important voice of the United States during this twelve-year period, but not at the expense of other voices or forces in America. For this reason alone, the book is not principally about Hitler versus Roosevelt, even though their contrast is unavoidable.

Hitler was well aware of the importance of Congress and of American political parties. He knew the machinery of democracy; after all, his rise to power took place within the democratic multiparty system of the Weimar Republic. Following his failed coup in Munich in 1923, which resulted in his imprisonment at Landsberg, he decided to reestablish his party and destroy the Weimar Republic using its own weapon of majority rule. He had plenty of time while he was in prison to plot his strategy. After 1924 the mission of the party was to exploit the methods of democracy to destroy democracy. This obliged Hitler, among other things, to monitor public opinion carefully, because one of the surest ways to power in a democratic system was to capture the hearts and minds of the people. Hitler knew that Americans were particularly susceptible to public opinion, which could be manipulated by the press and other mass media.

Although Hitler knew little about the American media, suspecting that it was under the control of Jewish interests, he realized its importance in influencing public policy. He was particularly interested in isolationist sentiments in America, and he thought about ways and means by which Germany could reinforce the isolationists. This interest has a direct bearing on this book, namely, what were the things about America that Hitler really wanted to know? The question he probably asked himself was, "How might the United States become a serious obstacle to the expansion of German power in Europe?" He thought that U.S. involvement in Europe was highly unlikely as long as its political and economic interests were not directly threatened. Hitler knew that the United States had tipped the scales in favor of the allied powers in World War I. Would history repeat itself? What could he do to keep America out of European affairs?

Throughout the 1920s, long before Hitler became chancellor, the United States was in relative isolation. The Senate had refused to ratify the Versailles treaty and join the League of Nations, thereby depriving that institution of the support it needed to enforce the peace settlement and prevent future wars. It had fallen to the Western democracies, chiefly Britain and France, to support and enforce the peace settlement that just about every German politician wanted to revise or undermine. British and French statesmen knew that in case of conflict with Germany over the provisions of the Versailles treaty, they could expect little save moral support from the United States. Some historians have concluded that Hitler knew this and decided that he could ignore the United States. Yet behind the Western democracies—at least potentially—loomed the American giant. Americans were always interested in supporting the cause of democracy in Europe. At what point would the United States take a more active role in Europe? Hitler knew that this depended on how German hegemony in Europe would develop. Once France was defeated, what would England do? Perhaps negotiate with him.

As this book illustrates, Hitler tried to calculate when the United States would take concrete actions such as supplying his opponents with armaments or even direct military intervention. He turned to certain people who could tell him the truth about America. Hitler had few trusted advisers who could furnish reliable information about what he called the "gigantic American State Colossus."[5] Of his early followers, only two had firsthand knowledge of the United States: Kurt Lüdecke and Ernst "Putzi" Hanfstaengl. Lüdecke was a footloose and opportunistic young follower who had gone to America in 1924 to drum up wealthy donors for the party. Hanfstaengl was the son of a well-to-do Munich art dealer who had established a branch of the Munich business on Fifth Avenue in New York. Hanfstaengl's father sent him to Harvard, where he met Franklin Roosevelt, and then encouraged him to manage the New York branch of the family business. Putzi Hanfstaengl's role in serving Hitler and freely offering advice on America is treated at length in the following pages. Hitler had several other America "experts" he periodically consulted after becoming chancellor: his commanding officer in the List regiment in World War I, Fritz Wiedemann, who spent time in America in the 1930s; Colin Ross, the well-known German globetrotter and author of popular travel books; and General Friedrich von Bötticher, the only German military attaché who served in Washington, D.C., from 1933 to 1941. There were others who periodically informed Hitler about America, including Sven Hedin, the Swedish explorer who knew America well, Joachim Ribbentrop, his foreign minister, and various diplomatic officials, notably Hans Luther, Hans Dieckhoff, Ernst von Weizsäcker, and Hans Thomsen.

Compared to Franklin Roosevelt's knowledge and firsthand experience of Germany and Europe, Hitler was at a considerable disadvantage. He had limited travel experience and spoke no foreign languages. Whatever travels Hitler undertook were dictated by political, or later military, circumstances. In early 1933 Roosevelt invited Hitler to America to discuss economic issues. Hitler declined, sending his economic minister, Hjalmar Schacht, in his place. It is interesting to speculate what these two leaders would have discovered about each other and how this might have changed their relationship. Often Hitler deliberately avoided face-to-face meetings with his major adversaries. Perhaps this is why he did not go to Washington or later to Moscow. He also deliberately turned down a meeting with Winston Churchill that Hanfstaengl had arranged in Munich in 1932. Hitler had a tendency to refrain from contact with people who held opposing views. The company of first-rate intellects made him uneasy; it brought out insecurities that stemmed from his obscure social origins in Austria. He frequently compensated for these insecurities through aggressive posturing or displays of his technical knowledge. Historians have had no trouble collecting many strange statements made by Hitler, including some about America and Americans. But this should not blind us to his brilliant political skills, including his ability to think and act pragmatically. He was far more unpredictable than historians have reported. Ernst Weizsäcker, state secretary in the Foreign Office, said that it was difficult to "see through" Hitler (*schwer zu durchschauen*) because he had an astonishing gift for dissimulation, making it difficult to tell whether he believed his own rhetoric or merely played a role, which he varied to fit particular people or occasions.[6] Historians must be extremely careful when trying to distinguish between rhetoric and conviction, between Hitler's visionary idealism and his brutal realism. In the case of America, he often employed the worst distortions, calling the United States a feeble country with a loud mouth while at the same time referring to it as an industrial colossus worthy of being imitated. He could belittle America in the vilest terms while at the same time eagerly looking at the latest photos from America, watching American films, and amusing himself with Mickey Mouse cartoons.

I intend to provide a more detailed and balanced account of Hitler's view of the United States than the few older accounts we have on this subject. So many Hitler studies leave us feeling uncertain about the man's character and convictions. Often the more we probe, the more elusive Hitler seems to become. He once told his close entourage that if he succeeded in his great plans, his name would be praised throughout the ages, but if he failed, his name would be cursed. Since the first possibility did not occur, we do not know whether it would have resulted in the apotheosis of the führer. It is highly unlikely. The fact that he failed led to exactly the outcome he feared; his name has not only been cursed but is associated with the embodiment of evil in history. The popular stereotype that depicts Hitler as a villainous character in a cheap melodrama, however, is misleading. For the sake of historical accuracy, it is important to steer clear of the snare of reductionism, of reducing all of Hitler's actions to some common demonic denominator. No one is evil personified, except the devil, and even if someone were, it would not follow that such a person could not be extraordinarily gifted or brilliant. For historians, a degree of detachment, open-mindedness, and the awareness of existential contingencies are necessary elements in viewing the past.

Hitler was not a noble character. He was malignantly destructive. For this reason, Joachim Fest, citing an ancient dictum, denied that Hitler was a great hero, because repulsive moral beings are unfit to be called either great or heroic.[7] Although Hitler may not have been a hero, he was a brilliant political Svengali who fundamentally shaped the twentieth century. His grandiose visions of establishing a Greater German Reich almost came to fruition in 1941. His hope was to match the industrial power of the United States, for in all other respects he thought that Germany was already superior. How he planned to do so, and what he thought of the United States, its people, leadership, culture, and way of life, is the subject of the following story. In this regard, it is important to mention that the book has deliberately been cast in narrative form because of my strong conviction that history is a storytelling art form rather than a social science that must imitate the natural sciences. All too many books about history nowadays are little more than retrospective sociology, front-loaded with theories and academic fads that are outmoded as soon as the books roll off the presses. I have a story to tell about Hitler and America, and I invite the reader to follow me through the narrative with as little distraction as possible. I believe that the narrative itself has cognitive value. Readers can make up their minds from the story itself, from the way I have cast it and from the explanations embedded in it. My own position about Hitler's split image of America/Amerika serves as a guiding theme and is summarized at length in the conclusion. Along the way, readers will find surprising and even disturbing material about Hitler, Roosevelt, and the German-American relationship.

CHAPTER 1

Hitler's Split Image of America

In February 1942, barely two months after he had declared war on the United States, Adolf Hitler praised America's great industrial achievements, admitting that Germany would need some time to catch up. The Americans, he said, had shown the way in developing the most efficient methods of industrial production.[1] This was particularly true in the iron and coal industries, which formed the basis of modern industrial civilization. He also touted America's superiority in the field of transportation, especially in the automobile industry. Hitler loved automobiles and saw in Henry Ford a great hero of the industrial age. His personal train that took him from Berlin to his retreat at Berchtesgaden and later to the various military headquarters was code named "Amerika."

It was not just America's achievements in technological or industrial fields that made it a major world power, but also its superior workforce drawn from highly skilled Nordic immigrants. The European continent, he believed, had given its "best blood" to the New World, thus providing the growth gene for its civilization. In his view, it was a tragedy that the South had lost the American Civil War because it was in the Confederate states that racial policies had been more strongly institutionalized than in the Northern states. Hitler made favorable references in both *Mein Kampf* and a second, unpublished book to various racial policies pursued by the U.S. government. For example, he spoke highly of immigration quotas, racial segregation laws, and sound eugenic measures that he thought were more advanced in America than in Germany.

Hitler believed that America's strength rested on two pillars: its powerful industrial capacity and its creative Nordic stock.[2] On the one hand, as long as the United States preserved its Nordic blood, and even continued to replenish itself through European immigration, it would continue to be a major power in the world. If, on the other hand, America abandoned its racial policies, becoming an "international mishmash of peoples"[3] it would quickly disintegrate as a unified nation. Until Hitler found himself seriously at odds with the United States in the late 1930s, he toned down grave doubts and prejudices he also harbored about "Amerika."

This darker side of the American equation was an old European prejudice that multiethnic nations, lacking inner racial cohesion, could not function for long. Hitler doubted that the United States could fuse so many people of alien blood, because they were "stamped with their own national feeling or race instinct."[4] This was the accusation that America was a "mongrel nation," as racially polluted as it was decadent and materialistic. Both prejudices were deeply rooted in European consciousness; and as Hitler came to blows with America, the negative stereotypes began to predominate. With the coming of World War II Hitler began to believe the worst stereotypes about America. In 1941 he told Mussolini, "I could not for anything in the world live in a country like the United States, where concepts of life are inspired by the most grasping materialism and which does not love any of the loftiest expressions of the human spirit such as music."[5] Just a few months later, at the same time that he grudgingly praised America's industrial superiority, he also condemned the United States as a "degenerate and corrupt state," adding, "I have the deepest revulsion and hate against Americanism. Every European state is closer to us. In its entire spiritual attitude it is a half judaized and negrified society. How could one expect such a state to endure if 80 percent of its taxed income is squandered, a land built entirely on the dollar?"[6]

From what sources did Hitler derive these split images of America? From the very moment America was settled by Europeans, two quite different perceptions of America developed: that of the real land experienced by its settlers, and that of the symbol it represented in the minds of foreigners who never set foot in America. The symbol of America, as it filtered down to the level of ordinary Europeans, was the construction of intellectuals—scientists, novelists, journalists, and philosophers. Much of what they said about a country they had never seen was a mixture of fantasy, wishful thinking, psychological projection, and ethnocentric prejudices. We all know the positive images that spoke of a "New World" as rich as it was enchanting, a world of unlimited opportunities for land-starved and oppressed peasants of Europe. To millions of Europeans, America was the dream the Old World—one steeped in sin and trouble—hoped for. The New World was going to be better; its resources and its open spaces beckoned the failures and adventurers of the Old World to another chance, offering them a refuge from their own past.

Hitler's image of America was not substantially different from what most Germans thought of America. On the one hand, America appeared as a vast and immensely wealthy country offering unlimited opportunities to land-starved and poor Europeans who were still suffering oppression under the rule of their royal masters. America was the land of freedom and a haven for hardworking common people. This benign image of America, however, coexisted with the degeneracy theory of the eighteenth century. Following the Civil War, European intellectuals provided increasingly negative accounts of America. Two broad developments contributed to this change: rapid industrialization, which gave rise to a national obsession with the acquisition of material wealth, especially among the nouveaux riches; and America's ongoing ethnic and racial conflicts. Many Europeans accused America of becoming a nation of soulless materialists, chasing the dollar and concealing its spiritual emptiness by worshipping size: enormous skyscrapers, mansions, tunnels, suspension bridges, luxury liners, and so on. Paradoxically, images of a land of conspicuous consumers and millionaires, lacking any spiritual depth, often represented precisely the qualities many Europeans themselves desired even as they roundly condemned them in the allegedly harried, dollar-chasing Yankee. Despite having fought a civil war over race and the way of life based on it, Americans continued to be deeply divided on racial issues. The rise of biological-racial ideologies, which rested on pseudoscientific and Social Darwinian doctrines, encouraged conflicting views about America's racial dilemma. America's ruling elite, and that included the Roosevelts, saw themselves on the one hand as advancing the progress of civilization through democracy and liberal reform; but on the other hand they also believed that superior civilization derived from English, Dutch, and northern European racial stocks.[7] Theodore Roosevelt, for example, believed that both England and America owed their success to the Germanic stock, and in *The*

Winning of the West, a colorful account of how the West was won according to Roosevelt, he celebrated the spread of the Anglo-Saxon races over "the world's waste space" as the most striking feature of human history.[8] The same sentiments can be found in Owen Wister's novels, especially the widely acclaimed *Virginian* (1902). Wister's cowboys are latter-day medieval heroes who give the Anglo-Saxon race a last chance to regain its virility on the western frontier. Wister was a Philadelphia patrician and a Harvard graduate. Theodore Roosevelt was a New York patrician and also a Harvard graduate. Both men, and others from similar social backgrounds, thought in terms of racial stocks, superior and inferior blood, and American exceptionalism. Such racially conscious elites were alarmed by the influx of "inferior breeds" from Eastern Europe and from Latin countries. They supported strong anti-immigration laws that discriminated against such groups particularly if they came from non-European civilizations. Pervasive fears periodically surfaced in such circles that the huge influx of East Europeans, especially Jews, was creating a mongrel nation in which the creative and dominant Teutonic racial stock would be diluted by inferior blood.

Hitler's perception of America encompassed all of these prejudicial strains that had entered into the thinking of Americans themselves. The Roosevelts had absorbed the typical prejudices of their class; they saw themselves as the crème de la crème by virtue of their older bloodline. In bolstering their class biases they found support in a variety of intellectual sources: neo-Darwinism, muckraking social criticism, and romanticized versions of American history. Their sense of class exceptionalism, however, was not as strong as it appeared to be, for the Roosevelts, whether they came from the Oyster Bay (Theodore Roosevelt) or the Hyde Park (FDR) branch of the family, saw themselves displaced by the new and more aggressive class of entrepreneurs, the financial nouveaux riches, such as the Morgans, Goulds, Vanderbilts, Rockefellers, Fricks, and Carnegies. Possessing an older pedigree and a more modest form of wealth, they could understate and therefore accentuate their social superiority over more recent parvenus. They could also act as tribunes of the people, playing populists to the masses, which sometimes infuriated their own class, who despised them as class traitors.

Europeans did not distinguish between different types of rich Americans; they lumped them all into the same class. They envied rich and powerful Americans while publicly condemning them as vulgar and uncultured—a stereotypical reaction of the powerless. A whole mesh of contradictory attitudes of envy, resentment, and admiration produced the stereotypical image of America as a nation that had become too big for its britches, too wealthy and certainly too powerful for its own good. German critics of America, influenced by neoromantic and *völkisch* ideologies, saw America as an artificial creation rather than an organic growth. America, they said, had been mechanically produced through revolution and a written document conceived by abstract minds. As such, it lacked inner life and spiritual depth. As long as America was ruled by its superior Anglo-Saxon elite, it might avoid degenerating into a mongrel nation without any higher spiritual ideals. Voices were raised claiming that America's hour had already passed and that the country was mired in materialism. One of Hitler's countrymen, the Austrian novelist Ferdinand Kürnberger (1821–79) who had written a maudlin novel called *Der Amerika-Müde* (*The Man Weary of America*, 1855), referred to America as lacking any real moral, artistic, or religious life. Even the vaunted political values of freedom and equality were hollow, for Americans had shown themselves to be unworthy of such blessings.

Another aspect of Amerika Müde (America weariness) was inspired by neoromantic and conservative traditionalists who associated America with the unfettered pursuit of modernity. This view consisted of a set of ideas and attitudes held by reactionaries who yearned for the restoration of the preindustrial way of life. They believed that venerable ancient traditions were being lost under the impact of rapid industrialization and its consequences: urbanism, the activation of the masses, the demythologizing of ancient customs and beliefs, the creation of new cultural forms of expression for a mass audience, and so forth. Fritz Stern, in examining the intellectual precursors of the Nazi mentality, referred to this antimodernism as the "politics of cultural despair," while Jeffrey Herf termed it as "reactionary modernism."[9] Still others, especially during the Weimar period, called it "Amerikanismus," for it was in America that the "new" seemed to have an automatic claim to authenticity. National Socialism has been seen by some historians as a reactionary movement because it wanted to suspend the ideas of 1789, which were associated with the democratic revolution and the decadent values allegedly stemming from mass democracy: cheap popular culture, decadent lifestyles, fast food, mass media sensationalism, and so forth. This is the sort of American cultural imperialism that was so roundly condemned by Adolf Halfeld in his influential book *Amerika und der Amerikanismus* (1928).[10] Halfeld expressed a deep fear that Amerika would export its popular culture and sap the spiritual nature of the western world, leaving nothing in its wake except the promise of "eternal prosperity" and material comfort.[11]

Hitler was not a reactionary antimodernist. He was a revolutionary modernist of quite a different kind who believed very strongly in "selective modernization" of the sort that called for rapid industrialization and the development of scientific know-how but without the resulting democratic vulgarization that Amerikanismus had allegedly unleashed on the Western world. Hitler's vision of a new Europe involved a highly industrialized and Germanized continent run according to authoritarian and elitist notions. By contrast, America was depicted as an industrial, but not a political or cultural, example of how a real *Volksgemeinschaft* (community of the people) should function. Hitler saw Germany as providing a third way between the liberal-Western model of the Anglo-American world and the Communist Eastern model of the Soviet Union. In the halcyon days of the Nazi seizure of power, a variety of *Blut und Boden* (Blood and Soil) reactionaries undoubtedly tried to graft themselves onto the Nazi movement, but their actual influence remained insignificant. There was little that was genuinely reactionary about the Nazi movement. Rather, the opposite is the case: Nazism, not Communism, was the most dangerous and revolutionary movement of the twentieth century. Moreover, it was Hitler rather than Lenin or Stalin who was the greatest threat to the United States.

Hitler gave voice to a powerful political and social movement that challenged both Western democracy and Soviet-style Communism. It took the combined forces of Russia and the Western democracies—Britain and the United States, neither of which could have done it without the aid of the other—to defeat National Socialism. John Lukacs has pointed out that dismissing Hitler and National Socialism as aberrant elements neglects to explain the potent force that Nazism embodied—and not just for the Germans but for other nations in Europe as well.[12] In this connection, we should remember that in the 1930s Soviet-style Communism had few supporters outside the Soviet Union, and Western-style democracy was in retreat throughout Central Europe. Liberal parliamentary democracy was abandoned by the majority of the population in Italy, Spain, Portugal, Hungary, Yugoslavia, Bulgaria, Greece, Romania, Austria, Germany, Albania, Turkey, Poland, and the Baltic provinces. All of these countries, with minor exceptions, lacked a democratic tradition. This did not mean that they completely rejected democracy; what they rejected was Western parliamentary democracy. Modern populist nationalism, conversely, was regarded as a viable alternative. Hitler's revolutionary significance was that he provided this "third way" by linking populist nationalism with a non-Marxist social welfare program that left most private property untouched. When asked whether he planned to nationalize industry he replied, "Why should I nationalize the industries? I will nationalize the people." Hitler had no intention of socializing capital but intended to enlist it in creating a war industry that served the Nazi state.

So there have been multiple Americas, depending on the vision of the perceiver. This was especially true when that perceiver belonged to an intellectual class of critics who never set foot in America and confused the metaphorical symbol of "Amerika"—almost always negative—with the reality of life as experienced and written about by Americans themselves. A closer examination of the two split images of America—America-the-land-of-the-future and Amerika-the-nightmare-of-tomorrow—reveals that the first was embraced very strongly by ordinary working-class people in Europe, while the latter was persistently touted by Europe's intellectual and political elites.

This point can be illustrated by numbers: Between 1820 and 1920, five and a half million Germans immigrated to the United States, and perhaps as many more would have emigrated if they had had the opportunity. Although a certain number (perhaps ranging between 2 percent and 10 percent) returned, the vast number remained and prospered in America.[13] We can reasonably conclude from this pattern of mass exodus that those who left were disenchanted with their homeland and looked to America as the land of golden opportunity. This was also probably true of all other immigrants who came to America voluntarily. Moreover, there never was a period in American history when Americans left their country in massive numbers. There never was a period when a large number of Americans escaped from America to live, for example, in Communist countries such as the Soviet Union, China, Cuba, or Vietnam. When this author came to America in 1959, he was one of 260,686 new immigrants.[14] While this new wave arrived in the United States, this author can think of only one well-known American who went the other way that year—to the Soviet Union, where he renounced his American citizenship and asked for political asylum. His name was Lee Harvey Oswald.

Why, if vast numbers of ordinary Europeans, Hispanics, and Asians, tried to come to America, did their intellectual elites back home strike increasingly hostile anti-American attitudes? One is tempted, in the first place, to attribute the differences between elite perceptions and those of the general public to economic or social conditions. The elites had a greater stake in society because they were invested in it, while the general population felt that they had nothing to lose by leaving. But in addition to this obvious socioeconomic explanation, public attitudes during the late nineteenth century were strongly shaped by a rising tide of nationalism throughout Europe. In Germany, heightened feelings of nationality led to German unification under Prussian rule; these feelings then served the imperial government as an integrative force by which domestic social tensions could be diffused and rechanneled into overseas aggression. The rise of xenophobic nationalism also brought with it increased anti-Americanism. The German imperial elites, and their mouthpieces in the press, big business, and education, saw themselves as conduits of a new German culture that they hoped to impose on Europe.

By 1900, Germany was not only a new economic colossus but also a cultural force to be reckoned with. Educated circles in Central and Eastern Europe assimilated distinctly German intellectual habits, ranging from philosophical idealism to neoromanticism to historicism. John Lukacs points out that the Germans had the potential to "rejuvenate old Europe, to extend the European age, and the primacy of Europe in the world for centuries to come," but he added that they destroyed that prospect through their obsession with their own primacy in Europe.[15] American students, intellectuals, businessmen, and politicians who traveled or studied in Germany before World War I all noticed this compulsive German sense of primacy and denounced it as one of the least desirable aspects of the German character. Both Theodore Roosevelt and Franklin Roosevelt commented on this overwrought or inflated German nationalism. Even before World War I, American elites' opinion of Germany began to shift from favorable to highly negative. Many American critics believed that the Germans had abandoned social democracy for a Prussianized autocracy and militarism. World War I strengthened the image, and the rise of Nazism confirmed it.

German propaganda during World War I greatly embellished the stereotype of "degenerate Amerika." The imperial government sponsored and encouraged elite opinion makers on all sides of the political spectrum to condemn Anglo-American civilization, as Werner Sombart put it in his wartime book *Händler gegen Helden* (*Merchants against Heroes*), as crassly materialistic, rationalistic, and spiritually empty. By contrast, German civilization was supposedly martial, romantic, idealistic, and heroic. A large number of German intellectuals, including Max Weber, Ernst Troeltsch, Thomas Mann, Friedrich Meinecke, Max Scheler, Friedrich Naumann, Walther Rathenau, and Adolf von Harnack, to name just a few, subscribed to what was called by Johann Plenge, a professor of sociology at the University of Münster, the "Ideas of 1914," a fabric of theories that contrasted two visions of civilization—the Germanic and the Anglo-American. The men of 1914 claimed to speak for a more cultivated, disciplined, and heroic way of life than was to be found in the purely consumer culture of the Anglo-Americans. In opposition to the rootless philosophy of laissez-faire individualism, they proposed a *Volksgemeinschaft*, an organically rooted community of the people without class divisions, a society in which individuals performed their duties for the good of the whole. Their anti-American views would constitute the essential point of departure for right-wing as well as left-wing critiques of America in the interwar period.

The strands of anti-Americanism are complex and varied, some based on cultural nationalism, antimodernism, anti-Semitism, and antidemocracy. In Germany all of them converged in the Nazi period. As the world's major engine of modernization, America caused cultural degeneration wherever its influence made itself felt. Behind the drive toward modernization were its chief agents—the Jews. This is why anti-Americanism usually involves anti-Semitism. The Jews who had taken up residence in the metropolis of Amerika were seen as the real embodiment of the capitalistic Moloch.[16]

The very name of America in such circles suggests everything that is "grotesque, obscene, monstrous, stultifying, stunted, leveling, deadening, deracinating, deforming, rootless, uncultured, and—always in quotation marks—"free." As previously shown, this "metaphysical" America existed almost from the beginning of the nation, and it became entwined with an equally metaphysical opposite: America, the land of freedom and of the future. These opposite images created ambiguous perceptions of America, and those who saw the New World from afar did so with ambivalence. Adolf Hitler, like so many Germans, absorbed both images of America and never resolved them in his own mind. America, the progressive, technological society, coexisted in his mind with Amerika, the land of degeneration.

Hitler's Knowledge of America

The consensus concerning Hitler's image of America still holds that he was abysmally ignorant and badly informed about conditions in America.[17] There is little truth in this judgment. Hitler's view of America was not as uninformed as many of his biographers and historians have written. He read widely, if often indiscriminately. His basic intelligence was definitely above average. He was an autodidact who had immersed himself in a wide variety of geopolitical, military, artistic, and technological sources. His knowledge of geography was excellent and he impressed Arnold Toynbee with his mastery of history. Hitler left school at sixteen and never made it beyond the fourth form of secondary school (*Realschule*). By contrast, Roosevelt received a degree from Harvard, attended Columbia University law school, and passed the New York bar examination. Hitler had to repeat the first grade of *Realschule* in Linz and was dismissed from school for repeated poor performance. He then attended one more year of *Realschule* in Steyr, where he failed several subjects and was only promoted after he retook the examination. Hitler also twice failed his entrance examination to the Academy of Arts in Vienna. Yet Hitler's failures should not blind us to his quick intelligence, stupendous memory, and other abilities. He was, as one of his teachers, Dr. Eduard Hümer, testified at his trial in 1923, definitely talented but lacking in discipline and was "notoriously cantankerous, willful, arrogant, and irascible."[18]

Hitler's reading habits were haphazard. He took from books mostly those elements that could be made to fit his convictions. He was not unwilling to learn new things, but he took shortcuts to knowledge by reading biased pamphlets and newspapers or by listening to eccentric "experts." Hitler did not like bureaucrats, especially those who ran the German Foreign Office. He did not trust them, and he did not read their reports. As he put it, in one of his typical outbursts against diplomats, "What did our diplomats report before the Great War? Nothing! And during the War? Nothing! It's the same with others [bureaucrats]. Public offices must be reformed from the ground up. I received better insights from people like Colin Ross and others who have traveled around."[19] His reference to Colin Ross, the popular German globetrotter and travel guide, is important because it was to people like him rather than government experts that he lent an ear. Apart from inherited stereotypes shared by many Germans, Hitler's information about America was gained from conversations he had with Germans who had traveled to the United States or lived there for an extended period of time. Of Hitler's sources of information about the United States there are at least six that can be documented with some degree of accuracy. The first, which can be traced back to Hitler's childhood, were the western novels written by Karl May (1842–1912). Other information about America came from Ernst ("Putzi") Hanfstaengl, Kurt Lüdecke, Colin Ross, Friedrich Bötticher, and Fritz Wiedemann. The novelist Karl May did not set foot in the New World until he had already written his western stories and enjoyed wide popular acclaim as an "expert" on world affairs. Hanfstaengl was a scion of a well-known Munich family, a Harvard graduate, and an early Hitler follower. Lüdecke, a shadowy "businessman," paid several extended visits to America and hoped to educate the führer on conditions there. Ross was a best-selling journalist who wrote travel books on America, the Western Hemisphere, and the Far East. Bötticher was Hitler's only military attaché who reported from the German embassy in Washington, D.C. Finally, Fritz Wiedemann was Hitler's superior in World War I, his personal adjutant, and later German consul to San Francisco. To what extent was Hitler influenced by their judgment of the United States?

In the spring of 1912, an eccentric young wastrel, down on his luck and living in a Home for the Homeless in Vienna, borrowed a good pair of shoes from an acquaintance in order to attend a much-advertised lecture by Karl May, titled "Upward into the Empire of Noble Humanity—Empor ins Reich der Edelmenschen."[20] When the young man, Adolf Hitler, arrived at the packed auditorium, holding close to three thousand spectators, he was thrilled to see his favorite childhood author, a man who had only recently caused considerable scandal when it was discovered that he had spent jail time for theft and fraud as a young man and, even more scandalous, had never visited any of the countries he described in such detail in his novels and travel accounts. All of this made no difference to young Hitler, who vehemently defended Karl May against charges by his compatriots at the Home for the Homeless that his idol was a fraud. Those who were making such accusations, Hitler said, forgot that May was a great writer. As far as he was concerned, May's accusers were nothing but "hyenas and goons."

Interestingly enough, May's lecture was dedicated to the peace movement associated with the pacifist Bertha von Suttner, to whom he had dedicated his recent book *Peace on Earth,* and who sat in the first row of the Sofiensaal on that evening of March 22, 1912. May was really a utopian progressive who dreamt of an empire of peace and justice that would nourish a higher and nobler type of human being, an *Edelmensch* who would redeem the human race from its bondage to violence, greed, and oppression. He even referred to himself as a spiritual aviator soaring higher and higher into the Promised Land.[21] Those who attended that night thought they would be treated to recitations of May's adventure stories or a travelogue taking them to faraway lands; instead, the famous writer waxed philosophical about noble humans. In the end, it made little difference. May received an enthusiastic reaction from the audience that included Hitler.

The fact is that May, who died just two weeks after this lecture, was already a national, even European, icon, and people saw in his works whatever they wanted to see in them. This explains the remarkable reaction to May's stories by so many well-known people of very different backgrounds and beliefs—Albert Einstein, Albert Schweitzer, Hermann Hesse, Thomas Mann, and many others. As to his effect on perceptions of America, Karl May merely reinforced previously existing images and stereotypes, formed by white Europeans who would have agreed with Theodore Roosevelt's triumphalist account of civilized whites settling the American West and conquering the Indians. If one wanted to make a fine western omelet, a few eggs necessarily had to be broken. The red Indian, in the eyes of many whites, was not a man but an animal, and therefore expendable. To others, he was human and therefore worthy of being converted to Christianity and civilized. To still others, he was a noble savage, to be left alone and displayed like a museum piece behind the glass of the reservation or ghetto display case. All these strands contributed to the stereotypes Europeans held regarding America. Karl May was no exception, nor was one of his greatest admirers, Adolf Hitler.

Adolf Hitler was even more caught up in the "May cult" than most young Germans of his time. In 1942 he recalled that as a young boy he had read Karl May with a flashlight under his blanket at night or in the moonlight with a large magnifying glass. A friend of his, Fritz Seidl, allegedly told him that the *Last of the Mohicans* and other Leatherstocking novels were nothing compared to the Karl May stories. So Hitler began to read May, first *The Ride through the Desert* and then *Winnetou* and other American westerns.[22] Hitler claimed that May stimulated his interest in geography and history. In the figure of the Apache chief Winnetou, whom he commended to German soldiers as a role model, he found an early example of heroic leadership. As chancellor Hitler had a special place reserved in his library for the vellum-bound books of Karl May. He even found enough time to reread May, some seventy volumes in all. In 1944, despite the shortage of paper, he ordered 300,000 copies of May's books to be printed and distributed among the troops as exemplary military field literature. The Russians, he told his entourage at führer headquarters, fight like Indians, hiding behind trees and bridges and then jumping out for the kill. Presumably, Old Shatterhand, the hero of May's western novels, the man who could hit a target at 1,500 feet and kill a grizzly bear with his fist, would lead his fellow cowboys against the Russian savages and kill them. What Hitler took away from May was decidedly different from what Schweitzer and Einstein saw in these popular stories. While Einstein and Schweitzer loved the adventure stories and May's emphasis on Christian values, especially peace and goodwill, Hitler embraced the less savory aspects of these stories.

In this respect, it is useful to read May through Hitler's eyes, especially the Winnetou and Shatterhand stories. As previously mentioned, Old Shatterhand is the heroic protagonist in these western novels. He is really a German American named Karl who joins a team hired by the railroads to survey the Arizona territory. The railroad bosses, who are described as greedy and conniving men, willfully violate the rights of the Indians. Led by their chief Winnetou, the Indians captured Karl's surveying team, forcing Karl, or Shatterhand, to prove himself in mortal combat with Winnetou's father. Shatterhand defeats old Winnetou but spares his life. This act of Christian mercy impresses young Winnetou, who suggests to

Karl that they become blood brothers. They actually become more than blood brothers; they become self-appointed justices of the peace, meting out punishment to outlaws and shady businessmen who steal land from the Indians. Winnetou is eventually murdered by greedy Yankees searching for buried Indian treasure.

Karl May saw Winnetou as a noble savage, the neoromantic prototype who, though acting on raw instinct, also possesses a pure heart as yet unspoiled by greedy "civilized" motives. Hitler's perception of May's stories was quite different. He had little use for May's moral message about the brotherhood of man or according intrinsic respect to Indian customs, language, or artifacts. His conception of the *Edelmensch* (noble man) was the vulgarized Nietzschean notion of the blond beast of prey that conquers vast spaces and subjugates or even exterminates inferior races. Hitler conceived of Shatterhand and his white trappers as Germanic Siegfrieds in cowboy hats and boots set against the landscape of the western frontier. As Hitler's concepts of race and space developed after World War I, May's frontier image shifted in Hitler's mind from America to the even vaster space of Russia, where Germany's wild frontier beckoned. The savage Indian now becomes the subhuman Slav, the American frontier the Eurasian land mass extending to the Urals and beyond. Karl May was, despite some of his harsh critics such as Klaus Mann, a gentle mythmaker; Hitler was a brutal mythmaker without a moral conscience.

Specifically, what did Hitler think he could learn from Karl May's cowboys and Indians? In his table talks he insisted that every German officer should carry May's Indian books (Indianerbücher) with him because this was how they would learn to attack the Russians, who fight just like Indians. Officers, he insisted, could learn something about strategic thinking from Karl May; if they did, they would behave more heroically and less cautiously than they did at the present time. Hitler believed that May's heroes were endowed with "muscles of iron and sinews of steel."[23] These heroes, of course, are white Germans, noble and warlike, and their leader Old Shatterhand possesses the kind of qualities a future heroic German leader (führer) ought to have. He should be hard (*hart*) but God-fearing, versatile and creative, and strictly puritanical in his habits. Old Shatterhand does not drink or gamble. In whatever he does he is better than anyone else. His friends as well as his adversaries are constantly amazed by his vast knowledge, which he uses to shame the experts. Moreover, Shatterhand possesses supernatural, paranormal qualities that enable him to foresee future occurrences. He is surrounded by some supernatural aura. His followers know it too, for they obey him instinctively and offer him their lives, and he in return is willing to sacrifice for them. It is important to point out that Karl May's Wild West heroes are of Germanic origin, another reason why Hitler was drawn to these stories.

If Karl May influenced Hitler's image of America, Wilhelm Emil Eber, commonly called "Elk" Eber, probably helped shape his visual image of the American West. Eber was a German painter who had spent some time in the United States, where he became a passionate admirer of Indian culture. In 1929 Eber was initiated into the Sioux tribe, adopting the name of *Hehaka Ska,* the Lakota name for elk. Like Hitler, Eber was a Karl May enthusiast, and he admired the bravery of American Indians. Hitler was impressed by Eber for several reasons. Eber had been an early follower of the Nazi movement, participating in the 1923 coup against the Bavarian government. Hitler prized Eber's artistic talents and the subject matter of his paintings and drawings. Most of Eber's works deal with either Indian or war-related subjects. During World War I, Eber had been a war propagandist (*Kriegsmaler*) who depicted the heroic deeds of German soldiers. Hitler acquired several of these war portraits, one of them called the *Last Hand Grenade,* which depicted a fatigued but determined German soldier who is about to toss his last grenade at the enemy. But Hitler also liked Eber's Indian paintings, especially the most famous of them, called *Custer's Last Battle,* which can now be found in the Karl May museum in Radebeul near Dresden. Eber may have slightly romanticized the Indians, but his technical depiction of them was true to life, as his knowledge of Indian mores and artifacts was extensive. Hitler did not like the Indians as much as Eber did; he thought they were racially inferior to the Germans. What he did like about them was their tribal solidarity, warlike nature, and bravery in battle. In this sense, Eber visually reinforced Hitler's image of the American frontier that he had derived from Karl May.

It was not only Karl May's stories and Eber's paintings that drew Hitler to America. He was also impressed by the industrial capacity of the United States, and on several occasions he even held up American industry as the model Germany should emulate. He attributed America's industrial superiority to the availability of more abundant resources and its modern plant equipment, which allowed U.S. manufacturers to outproduce and undercut European competitors, higher U.S. wages notwithstanding. It would be years, he thought, before Europeans could compete with America. As an example of advanced industrial manufacture, Hitler always mentioned the competitive edge of the American automobile industry. Hitler loved automobiles and enjoyed being driven all over Germany. Henry Ford was one of his great heroes, especially after he learned that the American car tycoon was also anti-Semitic. In 1923 and 1924, Hitler dispatched one of his financial supporters, Kurt Lüdecke, to Italy and the United States in an effort to persuade Mussolini and Henry Ford to provide funds for the struggling Nazi Party. In both cases Lüdecke failed, but Hitler continued to rely on the footloose young businessman for advice on foreign countries, especially the United States. Once, on a long drive from Munich to Berlin in 1932, Hitler asked Lüdecke to talk to him about America. He was delighted to hear that as a boy Lüdecke had also devoured Karl May stories. Hitler asked Lüdecke about Roosevelt, the American financial crisis, the probability of radical change in America, and Prohibition.[24] Lecturing Hitler about the United States from the back seat of his car may not have been very productive, but Hitler allegedly listened very carefully, as he always did when the topic of the United States came up. During this particular trip, Hitler and Lüdecke made several disparaging comments about another of Hitler's corps of America experts, Ernst (Putzi) Hanfstaengl, who, like Lüdecke, had given crucial financial support to the fledgling Nazi Party. Hanfstaengl was a burly giant of a man who had a fondness for good food and music, and a wide circle of friends. His mother came from a well-known New England family, the Sedgwicks. His grandfather had established a flourishing art and photography business in Munich, and his father had set up a branch of the family business on Fifth Avenue in New York. In order to learn the business and eventually take over the American branch, Hanfstaengl was sent to Harvard University, where he made a number of friends, including T. S. Eliot, Walter Lippman, Hendrick von Loon, Hans von Kaltenborn, Robert Benchley, and John Reed. Hanfstaengl also became a close friend of Franklin Roosevelt, then a rising senator from New York. Through Theodore Roosevelt's eldest son, Hanfstaengl received an invitation to the White House in 1908, where he displayed his prowess on the piano. His piano playing actually endeared him to the Harvard football team— he played for them to pep them up before their games. Later, after joining Hitler's entourage, he convinced the führer to apply American entertainment and advertising techniques to politics, especially the practice of using cheerleaders to whip up the enthusiasm of crowds, though in Germany the cheerleaders were not pretty girls in short skirts but handsome young men bellowing through bullhorns.

Hanfstaengl was marooned in America during World War I and did not return to his humiliated and defeated country until 1921, entering the University of Munich to work on his Ph.D. in history. In 1922 he heard Hitler speak and, like Lüdecke, became a dedicated follower. Again like Lüdecke, he gave freely to the party and used his social connections to give Hitler an entrée into business and society circles. Hitler was a frequent guest at the Hanfstaengls, showing particular fondness for Putzi's American wife, Helene. In moments of stress for the führer, Hanfstaengl was at Hitler's beck and call, playing the piano and entertaining him with funny anecdotes. Hanfstaengl knew a great deal about Hitler's private life, including his chief's disturbing personality traits and obsessions. Later he told American intelligence all he knew about Hitler and his inner circle for, like Lüdecke, he would become persona non grata to Hitler and his top henchmen. Hanfstaengl was given to indiscretions; he did not like the direction the movement was taking in the mid-1930s, and he denounced the creeping police terror and the insidious militarism of the regime. Although he served briefly in Hitler's government after the seizure of power in 1933, Hanfstaengl became increasingly disenchanted with the Nazi regime and fled for his life after the Nazis played a cruel hoax on him by telling him that he had been singled out for a secret mission to Spain in which he would be flown to Salamanca to make contact with Franco's forces and help the local German agents establish better relations with the Spanish Fascists. It was a cruel joke, for Goering, who devised the scheme, planned to dump Hanfstaengl by parachute over hostile Communist territory between Madrid and Barcelona. If the prank had succeeded, he would probably have been shot as a spy. The pilot who had been assigned to take Hanfstaengl to Spain revealed the plot to him, and Hanfstaengl managed to persuade the pilot to land the plane on the pretext of engine problems, a ruse that enabled Hanfstaengl to slip away.[25] Putzi fled the country with his son, Egon (he had recently divorced his wife, Helene), not to return until after the defeat of the Nazis.

But the story does not end here. In the papers of Franklin Roosevelt at Hyde Park there are more than four hundred pages of material relating to Ernst "Putzi" Hanfstaengl. This extensive file dates from the summer of 1942 through early 1945; it includes reports that Hanfstaengl sent to President Roosevelt about a variety of subjects pertaining to the Nazi regime. It turns out that after Hanfstaengl's escape, first to Switzerland and then to France and England, Hanfstaengl was interned by the British after the war began. In 1942, however, Franklin Roosevelt interceded with the British and had Hanfstaengl brought to the United States, setting him up in an old-fashioned villa at Bush Hill in Virginia. It was here, under close government surveillance that Hanfstaengl churned out a series of reports under the code name "S-Project," the "S" standing for "Sedgwick," the maiden name of Hanfstaengl's American-born mother.[26]

As for Lüdecke, he too fell out with the Nazis. Having left Germany after Hitler's failed Putsch, he spent some eleven years in the United States pursuing various dubious business ventures and promoting Germany's brand of National Socialism, mostly among German Americans. This proved to be a signal failure, as Lüdecke himself admitted that Americans were not ready to accept a *völkisch* movement along German lines because America was an immigration society whose German element was steadily being assimilated.[27] He also blamed the Jews for exercising inordinate power in America and for imposing their materialistic stamp on American thinking, citing with approval Werner Sombart's infamous anti-Semitic statement that "Americanism is nothing less . . . than the Jewish spirit distilled."[28] Lüdecke married an American librarian, Mildred Coulter, who was working for the *Detroit News*. Hitler's accession to power brought him back to Germany and, he hoped, a place in the rising party, but being by nature an intriguer, he chose the wrong party leaders to intrigue with: Alfred Rosenberg, Ernst Röhm, and Gregor Strasser. He also resumed his infighting with Hanfstaengl, who had accused him of blackmail and extortion. After the Nazi takeover, Lüdecke committed several serious political blunders and was placed in "protective custody," spent time in several concentration camps, and, with Röhm's help, made a sensational getaway that ultimately led him back to the United States. After arriving in New York, he heard news of the murder of Röhm and Gregor Strasser. Four years later, he published his colorful account of his years in the Nazi movement under the title *I Knew Hitler*, dedicating the book to Röhm, Strasser, and many other Nazis who were "betrayed, murdered, and traduced in their graves."

On several occasions Hitler invited the globe-trotting popular au-
thor Colin Ross (1885–1945) for lunch to pick his brain about the United
States. We have documentary evidence, gleaned from the notes taken by
Walther Hewel of the Foreign Office, that Hitler was very impressed by
Ross's views of America. Ross told the führer that he was working on several plans that could bring about better relations with the United States.
This was at the time of the "phony war" (March 1940) when Hitler was
still receptive to proposals about how the United States could be kept out
of the war and how he could counteract British propaganda in America.
Hitler was galvanized by what he heard and ordered the Foreign Office to
give Ross any assistance he required in his important work. He remarked
to Hewel that "Colin Ross is a very clever man, who certainly has many
right ideas."[29]

Who was Colin Ross? Educated, middle-class Germans in the interwar
period turned to two world travelers: the pro-German Swedish explorer
Sven Hedin, whose writings Hitler had carefully read, and the Austrian-
German world traveler Colin Ross. The English name is misleading, for
Ross's first name was probably given to him by his parents because of a
remote Scotsman in the family tree. Ross was by training an engineer,
but he dabbled in many fields, including history, geography, economics,
and philosophy. He received his training from the Technical University
of Berlin and Munich and earned a Ph.D. in philosophy from the University of Heidelberg. In 1902 he paid his first visit to the United States as a
member of a scientific team representing the German Museum of Natural
Science. During this visit he developed a fascination with Chicago, calling
it "the wildest and most wicked city in the world—die tollste und übelste
Stadt in der Welt." He later took his family to the city of Al Capone and
penned some telling stories that captured the ambience of this gangster-
ridden metropolis. That same year Ross went to the Balkans to report for
the *Münchener Illustrierte.* In 1913 he went to Mexico to cover the civil war
that radical Mexican factions were waging against each other, reporting
to his German readers from Pancho Villa's headquarters. During World
War I, Ross served as a war correspondent, and after the German defeat he
embarked on a series of globe-trotting trips that took him—to use the title
of one of his books—*From Chicago to Chang King.*

His visits to America with his family—with kit and caboodle (*mit
Kind und Kegel*), as he called it—stretched over several years and were

recounted in his best-selling travel books, notably *Amerikas Schicksalss-tunde* (1935), *Die Westliche Hemisphäre* (1942), and *Unser Amerika* (1942). In these "Amerika" books, Ross admitted to a love-hate affair with the United States—but more love than hate. "If I were not a German," he confessed, "I would want to be an American."[30] He saw in America a dynamic Western idea, a striving toward humanism, freedom, and progress. The pall of depression that hung over America in the 1930s convinced Ross that America's dynamism had been arrested by two factors: the selfish interest of a small, moneyed elite, and the decline of the Anglo-Saxon ruling class. In his book *Unser Amerika* (*Our America*), Ross propounded the popular right-wing view of German nationalists that the strength of America depended on the creativity of the original Anglo-Saxon, Germanic element in America, and that unchecked immigration had "diluted" the better part of the American people. Such views were not original. In 1916 the respected natural scientist Madison Grant had voiced this fear in a book called *The Passing of the Great Race*, in which he bemoaned the weakening of the genetic pool through intermarriages between the old colonial stock and new immigrants with non-Anglo-Saxon genes. This prejudice was also shared by Hitler, who attributed the entrepreneurial strength of America to the Nordic race and the sound immigration laws the United States had put in place to exclude non-Nordic people. As long as America remained an Anglo-Saxon–Teutonic state, it would continue to be a leader in the Western Hemisphere; but if it pursued multiethnic and multicultural policies, it would disintegrate into a tangle of unassimilated nationalities.

Ross was not a racist or an anti-Semite, though his many remarks about the power and influence of Jews in America led Hitler to believe that he was. Ross's critique of the continuing effects of slavery and the mistreatment of black people was often incisive and unvarnished, as were his colorful descriptions of the excesses of popular culture in America. In his *Schicksalsstunde* there is a prescient chapter called "God or the Devil's Country," in which Ross sketches out the extremes in American culture. In a chapter titled "The Phenomenon Ballyhoo," Ross captures the extremes of the Roaring Twenties—ranging from riotous living and gangsterism to the wonderful generosity and helpfulness (*Hilfsbereitschaft*) of its people.[31] Crass contrasts, he noted, were part of America: for example, Al Capone and Mae West next to Charles Lindbergh and Franklin Roosevelt. One of the keys to the American extremes, according to Ross, was "the phenom-

enon of the ballyhoo," which manifested itself in mass media sensationalism, which, in turn, stemmed from a fondness for turning what is normal
or important into something abnormal or trivial. Americans, he held,
were easily swayed by mass media advertising and were prone to believe
the unbelievable. No people in the world were so obsessed with mouth-
washes, deodorants, facial creams, or patent medicines than Americans.
In his judgment, the phenomenon had reached epidemic proportions. The
same was true of the endless preoccupation with violence and crime and
a disturbing tendency to cheer for outlaws and gangsters. The country,
he said, was ricocheting from one public scandal to another. Today it is
the Lindbergh kidnapping, tomorrow a demented actor, a deadly boxer, a
Florida real estate shyster, or even a New Deal chiseler.

All this, of course, was said just as well, and more humorously, by H.
L. Mencken. Ross's picture of popular culture in America was superfi-
cially true, but what it lacked was cultural perspective. If Americans were
gullible consumers of prepackaged news, so were the Germans, even more
so under state-controlled Nazi news agencies. That Americans lacked civil
courage (*Zivilcourage*) is debatable; that Germans lacked it is indisputable.

In 1935 Ross visited Washington and took a tour of the White House,
accompanied by his well-known American guide. Suddenly, he tells us,
he found himself, along with a throng of journalists, in the Oval Office,
standing right in front of the president's massive desk.[32] A press conference was underway. Ross was astonished at how friendly and informal it
was. The president treated the occasion like a brotherly meeting between
friendly advisers, joking and fielding questions. As the president answered
all sorts of questions, Ross considered this remarkable and smiling man—
the fact, for example, that he was a cripple but that no one paid any attention to that fact. The famous smile, Ross seemed to think, had something
inscrutable about it, a bit like a Confucian sage. It was more of a mask,
concealing a painful awareness that there is much suffering in the world
and that the best way of addressing this fact of life was to soldier on and
keep on smiling. Ross thought that FDR was a pragmatist, whose New
Deal was not a revolution but a series of emergency measures that did not
undermine capitalism but propped it up for the foreseeable future. As to
Roosevelt's foreign policy, Ross became convinced that in the name of
freedom and American national self-interest, America would eventually
intervene in Europe and discard its neutrality. He noticed an increasingly

hostile anti-German mood, which he attributed to the reaction of the Jewish-controlled press to events in Germany.

Hitler was surely impressed when Ross confirmed his own prejudices about Jewish money controlling American public opinion. Writing in 1942, Ross toed the party line when he condemned the uninhibited anti-German hysteria in America as the machination of a few Jewish plutocrats.[33] Roosevelt now became a danger to world peace, a schemer who would, under the cover of protecting the Western Hemisphere, extend American power and influence around the world. The Hyde Park tribune of the people had turned into the "Sun King," an accusation, of course, that many anti-Roosevelt Republicans had been making for years.[34]

Ross warned that the United States would enter the war in order to protect and continue dominating the Western Hemisphere, while at the same time reserving the right to be the world's moral referee. He claimed that another reason Roosevelt would plunge into war was to solve the economic depression that his New Deal policies had failed to address successfully. By the time Ross's last book, *The Western Hemisphere*, appeared in print, Germany was at war with America.

As previously mentioned, Hitler did not like diplomats. Most of them lived well and rarely got out to talk to ordinary people. They moved in closed circles, and the less they knew, the more they talked or wrote stupid reports. Hitler made a few exceptions to his rule that diplomats were of little use. One was his own military attaché in Washington, Lieutenant General Friedrich von Bötticher.[35] He believed that Bötticher was giving him accurate information on what Washington was planning; he also felt that his attaché really understood the American mentality, so he read his reports with great interest. Bötticher was able to look behind the scenes and provide sound judgments about Americans and their views.[36]

Between 1933 and 1941, Bötticher was Germany's only military attaché in the United States.[37] A military attaché was a quaint custom of a bygone age, when diplomatic embassies housed military officers who had specific orders from their governments to "observe, judge, and report on foreign military events and economy, organizations, developments, personalities, material, perhaps even military thought as well."[38] The attaché was to be the soul of discretion and maintain a strictly objective attitude. He was expected to establish close contact with military personnel in the host country and to abstain from any espionage activity. The ideal was to promote peaceful relations with the host country. This was the instruction Bötticher received from his commander in chief, President Paul von Hindenburg, when he left Germany for the United States in March 1933. Although a general in the German army, Bötticher reported to the German ambassador to Washington, Hans Luther, and to his senior political advisor, Dr. Hans Heinrich Dieckhoff, and his later replacement, Hans Thomsen. All of these America experts were competent men who spoke English fluently and had a good understanding of U.S. history. Bötticher was an expert on the American Civil War; he had also written books on Frederick the Great and Alfred von Schlieffen.

Bötticher approached his position in Washington with the utmost seriousness because he knew that the United States had been the single most important factor in the defeat of Germany in 1918. Much nonsense has been written about Bötticher by historians who have mentioned him as a tunnel-visioned Prussian staff officer who got just about everything wrong on the United States. David Brinkley, in his book *Washington Goes to War* (1988), depicted Bötticher as a short, heavy, and bullnecked Prussian officer who appeared in public bedecked in ribbons and medals, wearing, of course, a monocle. This stereotype of the arrogant Prussian officer astride the world in his polished jackboots still seems compelling to those weaned on Hollywood war movies. In Bötticher's case, the reality was otherwise. He was not a Prussian but a descendent of a cosmopolitan family of Baltic and English lineage. His mother came from the English Yorkshire seaport of Hull, while his father hailed from the Kurland (now Latvia). On both sides of the family, his ancestors came from solid commercial backgrounds. In the 1850s his mother, who was then married to a man called Hermann Anton Wippermann, immigrated to Davenport, Iowa, but she returned to Germany after a few years of disappointment and disillusion with the United States. After her first husband died, she married Walter Bötticher, a Dresden physician who had a patent of nobility, hence the aristocratic "von" in the family name. Friedrich Bötticher was born in 1881, grew up in a loving and cosmopolitan home, and learned to speak English at his mother's knee. He received an excellent classical education and superb military training, serving with distinction on the Great General Staff during World War I. While in later years he put on some weight, he was never bullnecked, nor did he ever wear a monocle.

Upon his arrival in Washington, Bötticher tried hard to get along with the German diplomatic staff, for technically speaking he was subordinate to the ambassador and his senior staff (Dieckhoff and Thomsen). He adjusted well to the Washington social scene, and his wife and three children also adapted quickly to American life. While in Washington he became a regular fixture among high-ranking American military men in the War Department, with whom he exchanged ideas and information and made close contacts. In his efforts to gain insight into American military preparedness, Bötticher was assisted by a first-rate technical advisor, Peter Riedel, a daredevil glider pilot who held several world records. The Bötticher-Riedel partnership yielded some very fruitful insights into the strengths and weaknesses of the American military establishment. By invitation of the War Department, they inspected all sorts of plants scattered across the country and pored over U.S. government statistics and reports. Bötticher had daily contact with the highest-ranking officers of the War College and the War Department. He found the company of U.S. officers quite congenial; his U.S. counterparts were openly anti-Semitic, favored restrictive immigration laws, and supported better U.S.-German relations. General Douglas MacArthur was on friendly terms with Bötticher and allegedly told him in 1933 that he agreed with Hitler's policy of seeking military parity with France and Britain.[39]

What Bötticher did not understand was that the relatively small circle of officers he met was not representative of the whole U.S. military establishment. The men he was particularly close to, notably Lieutenant Colonel Truman Smith, were anti-Roosevelt and anti-New Dealers. Some of them were also anglophobic. Bötticher thought he knew them better than he really did. All his U.S. military contacts were of no use when, after the outbreak of war, secret joint military staff meetings were held between British and American military officials to discuss methods of defeating Germany. Bötticher had no inkling that such plans were afoot. On the other hand, he never had any illusions about America's military capacity, making it clear on numerous occasions, "I warn against overestimating the weaknesses and underestimating American efficiency and the American determination to perform."[40]

In February 1939, Bötticher returned to Germany to attend the annual attaché conference, during which he was invited, along with others, for lunch with the führer. As he sat to the right of Hitler, the dictator turned to ask him about President Roosevelt's alleged Jewishness, claiming that he had reliable evidence that the American president was indeed Jewish. He told Bötticher that he might reveal this little tidbit to the rest of the world. Bötticher responded by telling Hitler that such evidence was patently false and that revealing it was politically very unwise. Hitler then abruptly turned away from him and spoke not another word to him during the luncheon.[41] What Hitler really wanted from Bötticher was neither confirmation of Roosevelt's Jewishness nor his attaché's knowledge of American life and culture. What he wanted to know was America's military capacity. This is why Bötticher was so important. What could Bötticher tell Hitler about the time the United States would need to mobilize its forces and gear up its industrial system so that it could seriously challenge the Reich? If war broke out in Europe, when—not how or on what side—would the United States intervene? It was all about timing. Hitler needed to keep the United States out of the war that he knew would happen because he wanted it to happen. In the initial stages of the war, he wanted to keep the United States at arm's length. This could be done through a variety of tactics: scrupulously avoiding hostile encounters with the United States; encouraging American isolationism; diverting America's attention elsewhere, such as the Pacific; discouraging the United States through alliances with other Fascist powers (Italy and Japan); and so forth. In this sense, Bötticher's thinking ran parallel to Hitler's, for both wanted to keep America out of a potential conflict with Germany. The difference between them was that Bötticher did not want war with America at all, whereas Hitler had no qualms about engaging the United States eventually. Hitler fully expected the United States to enter the war against Germany in the long run, but it was the short run that he was concerned about. How long could he keep the United States at bay? If he could keep America out of the European war until Germany had conquered the continent, the United States could no longer defeat Germany. Bötticher's critics may have been right in saying that he sent flawed reports that misjudged the political situation in America. All Hitler wanted from Bötticher were accurate military projections. Bötticher obliged and did so accurately, telling his führer that America could not seriously challenge the Reich for at least two years after the commencement of hostilities in Europe, if then.[42] Bötticher had the figures in black and white. In 1939 American troop strength was less than 200,000, and the country had mobilized less than 10 percent of its industrial capacity. At the time of Pearl Harbor the picture was not much better.

Besides Karl May, Ernst "Putzi" Hanfstaengl, Kurt Lüdecke, Colin Ross, and Friedrich von Bötticher, Hitler also picked up scraps of information about America from party members who had visited the United States and who usually told him what he wanted to hear, namely that the country was decadent, mired in depression, and militarily unprepared. This negative image was the party line, but Hitler was too shrewd to swallow his own propaganda. He was willing to learn from the people he trusted. The problem was that he relied too heavily on unorthodox "experts" of the sort just mentioned, bypassing the professionals, especially those in the Foreign Office, whom he did not trust. His former superior and adjutant of the List regiment in World War I, Fritz Wiedemann, visited the United States in 1937 and returned from his tour with a healthy respect for the United States. In his *Memoirs* he pointed out that, among party members, knowledge of America was abysmal. Hitler shared many misconceptions about America with his party cronies and encouraged the dissemination of negative reports about the United States. When a well-known woman journalist embarked on her visit to America, according to Wiedemann, she remembered her chief editor sending her off by saying, "Don't forget to send us only negative reports." "But suppose the weather is beautiful? Am I not allowed to report this?" "No," said the editor, "even the weather has to be bad."[43] Wiedemann pointed out, however, that the Americans often contributed to the negative stereotype of their country by exporting countless gangster films that gave a wholly misleading impression of the United States. Hitler watched many American gangster films, but he also amused himself with big musical productions from Hollywood. At times Hitler seemed to believe that the majority of Americans lived more like the Okies depicted in *Grapes of Wrath*, a movie he saw on several occasions. *King Kong*, we are told, was his favorite movie. Wiedemann probably had little success in correcting Hitler's misconceptions. When he came back from his visit, whose purpose was not entirely clear, he tried to set Hitler straight on America, just as Lüdecke, Hanfstaengl, and Ross claimed to have done.[44] Knowing that Hitler liked art and architecture, Wiedemann gave him thirty illustrated books about American buildings and bridges of all sorts. Hitler purportedly was very happy to receive them; he perused the books and then remarked that Germany would build even more monumental marvels. After looking at the Golden Gate Bridge, Hitler promised to build an even more colossal one over the Elbe River in Hamburg—a bridge perhaps not as long; the width of the Elbe did not permit it—but much wider so that it could accommodate more traffic running in both directions. He told Wiedemann that he would build huge skyscrapers in Hamburg.

One day, between Christmas and New Year's Day 1938, the führer took Wiedemann aside: "Well, tell me some more about your impressions of America."[45] Wiedemann proceeded to take Hitler on an imaginary tour of the Empire State Building, all the way to the top, describing the panoramic view of New York and its incredible forest of skyscrapers at dusk. After recounting the gradually setting sun and how the surrounding buildings disappeared in the gray haze of twilight, he invited the führer to descend to street level in the elevator and then, amid the traffic noise of the city, experience the magic of witnessing the largest skyscraper in the world light up, from the bottom to the top, like a draping pearl necklace. What had previously appeared as a dark and powerful mountain dissolved into a shimmering filigree of light. Wiedemann told his boss that he hoped he would someday have the opportunity of showing him in person the setting sun from the Empire State Building.[46]

Wiedemann wanted to use Hitler's receptive attitude about America to convince him that Germany should participate in the 1939 World's Exhibition in New York. Hitler declared himself in agreement with the plan as long as the cost was right. Walter Funk, the Reich economic minister, who happened to be staying down the mountain at Berchtesgaden at the time, eagerly supported the project. Coincidentally, Hitler was hosting the actor Emil Jannings, who had starred along with Marlene Dietrich in *The Blue Angel*. The actor and his wife joined Hitler, Wiedemann, and Funk in an informal conversation in which each person told something about America. The drift of the conversation, as Wiedemann remembered it, was positively American friendly (*amerikafreundlich*). The harmony did not last; before long, Hitler was upset that the view of the German pavilion was partially blocked by another building. "It is an outrage (*Unveschämtheit*) to offer us such a spot." Funk's interjection that the contract had already been negotiated left the führer cold: "I don't care, gentlemen," he said, "see to it that you get out of this business."[47] He then stormed out and left his guests sitting there.

What, if anything, should Hitler have learned from his America experts? What he actually learned from them is, of course, another question. Judging from his writings and speeches, Hitler was well aware of the potential threat of U.S. intervention in European affairs, and he said so in several passages in *Mein Kampf*. In his second (unpublished) book, discovered after World War II by the historian Gerhard Weinberg, Hitler referred to the "hegemonic position" of the United States, warning that the United States would shift its expansionist energy from the Western Hemisphere to the entire globe.

His experts all agreed that Germany should do everything possible to avoid a war with the United States. Hanfstaengl claimed that he warned Hitler repeatedly that Germany could not afford to antagonize the United States, and reminded him of what had happened in World War I. In the early 1920s he said to Hitler, "Well now, you have just fought in the war. We very nearly won in 1917 when Russia collapsed. Why, then, did we finally lose it?" "Because the Americans came in," responded Hitler. "If you recognize that we are agreed and that is all you need to know."[48] A decade later Lüdecke said that Hitler was very receptive to the idea of winning the goodwill of the American people. Even when he touched upon the anti-Nazi propaganda in the United States, which branded Hitler as a megalomaniac, Hitler waved him off: "Not credible." "He already wanted to hear no more of that."[49]

The goodwill of the American people was of interest to Hitler because he knew that they were strongly isolationist in the postwar period. It was in Germany's interest to encourage this isolationism, but if this should fail, he wanted enough time to keep America out of the war until all of Eurasia was his. This is why, with the outbreak of war, Bötticher's reports appear to have influenced his war plans.[50] There is evidence that Bötticher's reports about America's military preparedness had a strong bearing on his timetable. What Hitler wanted to know from his military attaché, as previously mentioned, was how soon America could militarily intervene in Europe. The technical information Bötticher supplied was excellent but lacked political context—that is, sound knowledge of how American democracy really functioned. When Hitler said that he liked Bötticher's reports because they demonstrated a real insight into the American mentality, he meant that he liked them because they reflected his own stereotypes of America. Neither Hitler nor Bötticher understood the American mentality, just as they failed to understand the psychology of other nationalities. What both did understand were the military strengths and weaknesses of other nations. Their cultural and political ignorance, combined with a German tendency to overestimate their own superiority, made them less intelligent about the potential of their enemies.

From all the available evidence, it appears that Hitler's image of America was generally positive until the mid-1930s—the time when he became aware of the fact that the United States would oppose his expansion. By the spring of 1938, he realized that Roosevelt might be a determined supporter of the Western democracies. Hitler's pronouncements, both private and public, became more anti-American; yet his view of the world was substantially cast in stone by the late 1920s. As previously argued, Hitler's picture of America (Amerikabild) was and would remain split: positive and negative stereotypes alternated, even though, when America once more tipped the scales of war, he found emotional satisfaction in his abusive rants against "the society that was "half judaized and half negrified."[51] Hanfstaengl was right when he observed that Hitler was really not anti-American; there were many things about America that he admired. He marveled at its size and material wealth, and he was impressed and envious of its industrial power. When visitors touted America's astounding technical achievements, he would always reply defensively and boastfully that he would build bigger highways, better automobiles, taller skyscrapers, and sturdier, more modern housing developments for German workers. In short, Hitler was envious of the United States, an envy that contained as much admiration as it did contempt. Whether Americans were decadent or not was important to him only in connection with their ability or inability to resist German power. One historian, James Compton, claims that Hitler had mental blocks to any realistic attitude toward America.[52] While this may have been true about many aspects of American life and culture, which Hitler, like many Europeans, saw in terms of popular stereotypes, it was decidedly untrue when it came to a fairly realistic understanding of American economic power. As will be seen, Hitler put up with frequent American violations of neutrality and gave repeated orders to his military chiefs not to engage the Americans in a conflict and, when attacked, to make sure that the first shot was fired by the Americans. Even after he declared war on the United States and gave Joseph Goebbels carte blanche to unleash anti-American propaganda on the German public, he did not want this to be so overdone so as to make America, and Americans, look like a negligible power. In the spring of 1942 he ordered the German press to engage in a broad polemic against America that highlighted the enemy's cultural deficiencies. The press, he ordered, should expose America's distasteful worship of film stars, addiction to sensationalism, grotesque female boxing, mud wrestling, and gangsters. It would be entirely false, however, Hitler insisted, to ridicule America's technological progress. The press instead should emphasize that Germany was building better roads and faster automobiles, and that its scientists were making greater strides in discovering synthetic products that would ensure the triumph of German economic power in the world.[53]

The German ambassador to Italy, Ulrich von Hassell, observed that Hitler and the Americans spoke such an entirely different language that an understanding between them was almost impossible.[54] Yet there were all too many Americans who shared Hitler's racial and anti-Semitic views. After all, the United States practiced segregationist, anti-immigration, and anti-Semitic policies. Hitler spoke a language that resonated with more Americans than is commonly admitted by historians. "Lots of people out here [in America]," a telegram to the White House read, "think Hitler is alright. We'd just as soon have him as Roosevelt."[55] Another read, "Many persons who detest the mention even of Hitler's name, are in favor of Hitler's manner of dealing with the Jews."[56] Right-wing critics of Roosevelt, such as Fritz Kuhn, Father Charles Coughlin, and William Dudley Pelley, to name just a few pro-Fascists, ceaselessly inveighed against the Jewish-Bolshevik conspiracy that had allegedly insinuated itself into the highest government circles, including the White House. The Germans also found numerous right-wing fellow travelers and subsidized their anti-Roosevelt and isolationist campaigns.

America's greatest hero of the 1920s, aviator Charles Lindbergh, had considerable influence among isolationists and admired the Nazi military, especially its air force. The "Lone Eagle" was a member of the America First Committee and made prominent radio broadcasts and speeches opposing Roosevelt's anti-Nazi policies. He also accepted the highest decoration given by the Nazis to a foreigner—the Service Cross of the German Eagle with Star, later prompting Roosevelt to tell Henry Morgenthau: "If I should die tomorrow, I want you to know this—I am absolutely convinced that Lindbergh is a Nazi."[57] Lindbergh was not a Nazi, but he was impressed by Germany's technological progress and its growing military power, and he warned the American people to stay out of European conflicts. There were many critics of Roosevelt's internationalism who agreed with Lindbergh's sentiments.

Roosevelt's Image of Germany

Hitler and Roosevelt, coming as they did from entirely different worlds, spoke a different political language, but they understood each other as being implacable enemies. Roosevelt never thought Hitler was a Charlie Chaplin caricature but believed him to be a deadly threat to the United States. He read Hitler's *Mein Kampf* in the original German, something very few statesmen in the prewar period were able to do.[58] He also listened to some of Hitler's speeches during the 1930s. Similarly, Hitler knew that Roosevelt was an extremely popular leader who represented a powerful industrial country whose interests were quite different from those of his own.

Since Franklin Delano Roosevelt and Adolf Hitler came to power in the same year and the same month (January 1933) and died twelve years later, again in the same month (April 1945), it is important to understand what the American president knew about Germany and how this might have affected his decisions during his tenure of office. Unlike Hitler, Franklin Roosevelt was a patrician from a well-known and wealthy New York family. He presided over a democratic and pluralistic America, while the plebeian Adolf Hitler imposed a one-man dictatorship on the German people. Roosevelt revitalized a sagging democratic system by offering the American people a "New Deal," which turned out to be a pragmatic approach to social democracy, while Hitler dismantled the democratic Weimar constitution in favor of a new, racial empire (Reich) that would last "a thousand years." Roosevelt won and Hitler lost. There are several paradoxical twists and turns in this story. Democracy survived in America because Roosevelt was an uncommon man who came from the ranks of one of its older patrician families, a man who was completely secure and comfortable with his pedigree and harbored little resentment against the rivals he competed with on his way to the highest office in the land. By temperament cheerful and optimistic, he overcame the handicap of crippling polio on the very threshold of a promising political career. Despite being paralyzed from the waist down and unable to walk for the rest of his life, confined to a wheelchair or carried about like a Raggedy Andy, he became a better man: more sensitive, caring, and empathetic. Roosevelt had always been a good man, a bit arrogant and supercilious perhaps, a Groton and Harvard man who carved out a place for himself among America's elite. But he had always possessed a good heart. Being a cripple did not deform his character; it strengthened it.

In a democratic age, both Hitler and Roosevelt skillfully connected with the feelings of ordinary people. Franklin Roosevelt was one of the great pioneers in cultivating popular support, a skill that came from his outgoing and charming temperament as well as from his role models, notably Thomas Jefferson, Andrew Jackson, Abraham Lincoln, Theodore Roosevelt (his cousin five times removed), and Woodrow Wilson. It was, in fact, from Teddy Roosevelt, who came from the Oyster Bay branch of the family, that he derived real practical insight into the craft of gaining and maintaining popular support. Theodore also encouraged his interest in history, with emphasis on the dramatic and heroic. There was no doubt in the minds of the Roosevelts that they were tribunes of the people, advancing the progress of democracy at home and abroad. Both saw the United States as the lever that was destined to move the world, for it was in America that civilization would reach its highest point. Their role was to serve as agents of democratic change, using the full range of their skills and social position to bring it about.

Adolf Hitler also assiduously cultivated the common touch. He, too, saw himself as an ordinary man who had been discovered miraculously by millions of Germans looking for a new kaiser. Hitler characterized his dictatorship as a German expression of the democratic spirit. The centerpiece of this claim was the Nazi practice of paying homage to the *Volk* (the people). The word *Volk* in German evokes all sorts of mystical connotations. Borrowing the meaning of the term from the romantics, who had made a cult of the *Volk*, the Nazis took it to mean the unique racial essence of Germandom (Deutschtum), which distinguished it from all other ethnic groups in the world. Each *Volk*, they believed, had acquired a unique character as a result of its relationship to its native soil and climate and its shared historical experiences. The unique worship of the *Volk* and what it symbolized was considered by these *völkisch* superpatriots as a form of religion that commanded Germans "to love the fatherland more passionately than laws and princes, fathers and mothers, wives and children."[59] A person must shed his individuality and give himself heart and soul to the

Volk. Such zealous nationalism had deep roots in German romanticism and in late nineteenth-century racial doctrines, undergirding the fragile national fabric in the imperial period (1870–1918).

This German cult of the people was quite different from the American cult of the people, for it focused on the racial and ethnic characteristics of the German people, rather than on the equal rights enjoyed by the plurality of people who made up the United States. It was the difference between neoromantic nationalism, which celebrated ethnic, racial, and cultural qualities allegedly inhering in specific national groups—Germans, French, Italians, English—and the democratic rights of citizens of different ethnic groups who happened to live in a multiethnic society. In short, it was a clash between the universalist position of the Enlightenment, embodied in the principles of 1776 and 1789—the American and French revolutions, respectively—and the neoromantic appeal to some kind of primeval ethnicity or racial essence, which ranked tribalism higher than universal human rights. This is why the Nazis announced, appropriately on July 14, 1933 (Bastille Day), that the false democratic principles of 1789 had been suspended. Rights were seen to be rooted in each *Volk*, not in the laws of nature, nature's god, or rationality.

What Hitler wanted was a populist state (*völkischer Staat*), to be based, of course, on coercion and terror, but also, and just as importantly, on popular support. Germans were to be forced into compliance with Nazi beliefs and institutions, by terror if necessary, but they were given enough freedom so that many of them supported the regime. Dictatorship was popular. People believed that they were free to do most of the things they had been doing before the Nazi takeover. Many historians have wrongly depicted Nazi Germany as an oppressive prison camp chock-full of sullen and unhappy victims. Looking at the Hitler regime from the outside and with full knowledge of its legacy, it is hard to believe that ordinary Germans who toed the party line—as did most Germans—would give their heart and soul to such a system.

The Nazi regime rested primarily on Adolf Hitler's popularity, which in turn was based on his charisma and his superb skills in using the new technology of mass persuasion. Robert Gellately has correctly labeled Nazi Germany as a modern mass media society that was in the vanguard of modernity.[60] Just because it did not replicate the modernist tendencies of the Western democracies, it was not, as some historians have claimed, a "reactionary modernist" society. Nazi officials were extraordinarily vigilant in monitoring the regime's popularity, sending out thousands of agents to keep a careful watch on just about every popular expression. The reports we have from such surveillance activities clearly indicate that the regime, and particularly Adolf Hitler, was never in any serious danger of being overthrown by popular uprising. Franklin Roosevelt had always hoped that the German people would stage a popular revolution against the Nazi regime; he thought that if the German people really knew the facts they would not support such a cruel establishment.

How good was the president's knowledge of Germany? In general terms, it can be said that Roosevelt was better informed about Germany than Hitler was about the United States. Roosevelt had spent six summers (1891–96) in Bad Nauheim, Germany, where his father, who had a heart condition, took his mineral bath cure and entrusted himself to the doctors of the local cardiac clinic. The Roosevelts always stayed at the hotel Villa Britannia, which catered to well-to-do Anglo-Americans. In 1891 Franklin, then nine years of age, began attending the small German elementary school (Volkschule) at Bad Nauheim, where his knowledge of German, which he had already been taught by his private German governess, improved greatly. He got along well with his schoolmates, noting in his diary, "I go to the public school with a lot of mickies . . . and we have German reading, German dictation, the history of Siegfried, and arithmetic . . . and I like it very much."[61] His German schoolmaster later remembered the young American boy very well, for he wore a blue sailor's suit and quickly impressed him as "an unusually bright young fellow. He had such an engaging manner, and he was always so polite that he soon was one of the most popular children in the school."[62]

Although Franklin enjoyed going to school in Germany during the summer months of 1891–96, he was often rankled by the superior air of German nationalism. On one occasion Franklin caricatured the German kaiser by drawing mustaches on top of his paper. His German teacher punished him by having him write the sentence *"Ich muss brave sein"* (I must be good) three hundred times.[63] Franklin probably sensed the growing regimentation of German life under the Kaiser; he would later often comment on it. The habit of discipline and obedience, which was second nature to many Germans, seemed insufferable to liberally minded Americans. Germany had too many petty rules and arrogant officials; its people were annoyingly provincial and ethnocentric. What made the Roosevelts especially prickly were officious Germans in uniform who overstepped their authority. Even among the children there was much talk about German superiority over all other nationalities. Americans were often described as a barbarian people who cared only about money.

One of Franklin Roosevelt's secretaries, Grace Tully, later wrote that the President's view of Germany was "bound up in his mind with his own trips to Germany,"[64] a judgment that is confirmed by the fact that when he talked about Germany or the Germans he would frequently draw upon his personal, prewar visits to Germany. He took swimming lessons near Bad Nauheim and traveled extensively. In the summer of 1896 he went on a bicycle tour with his tutor, and when they got themselves in trouble with the law—for picking cherries from trees, taking their bicycles into railroad stations, and entering Strassburg, a fortified city, at nightfall on their bicycles—young Roosevelt spoke enough German to talk himself out of jail. He did have to pay a five-mark fine for running over a goose, however.[65] That summer he bicycled from Bad Nauheim to Baden-Baden, Strassburg, Frankfurt, and Wiesbaden. Upon his return, his parents took him to Bayreuth, where he listened raptly to four Wagnerian operas—*Das Rheingold, Die Walküre, Siegfried*, and *Götterdämmerung*. His mother said that he was "most attentive and rapt during the long acts and always sorry to leave, never for a moment bored or tired."[66] The Wagner cult was at its greatest height at the time. Both Roosevelt and Hitler were introduced to it at the age of fourteen.[67]

Roosevelt's later reminiscences of Germany shifted focus with the times. In 1939 he claimed that he was neutral, not really pro-British or pro-French. He said at the time that he did not know Great Britain and France as a boy but he did know Germany. If anything, he added, "I looked upon the Germany that I knew with far more friendliness than I did on Great Britain or France."[68] After returning from Yalta in February 1944, he remarked that he had witnessed the rapid militarization of Germany decades before, giving the impression that even in the pre–World War I era he had recognized that Germany would be the future rival of the United States.[69] What he took away from his personal experience, and later his studies at Harvard, was the recognition that Germany was the most advanced industrial and technological society on the Continent. Writing in the *Harvard Crimson* in 1903 and 1904, he spoke with great admiration of German culture and technical efficiency.[70] There was one major blind spot in his thinking: the misconception that conservative and reactionary Prussian Junkers ruled Germany. He still believed this during the 1930s. Being a liberal Progressive, he was especially influenced as a student by the Harvard historian Silas McVane, who taught English and European history in the liberal Progressive mold. The modern age, according to this view, represented the triumph of liberal democratic ideals and institutions, with the United States leading by example. Nondemocratic societies were seen to be on the losing side of history. Germany was no exception. Already it possessed a strong liberal and democratic element in progressive labor and its advanced liberal intellectuals. These liberal forces, it was hoped, would eventually batter down the reactionary Prussian wall propped up by militarists and big industrialists. Professor McVane taught his students a model of a split Germany, "drawn in two opposite directions by two conflicting tendencies. The one is monarchical, bureaucratic, and militaristic, springing from the Prussian government . . . the other tendency is democratic, springing from the new populations of the great cities and manufacturing districts, but now beginning to extend to the rural sections and to affect even the Conservatives."[71]

When Woodrow Wilson, a Progressive, succeeded in getting his declaration of war from Congress in April 1917, he made it clear that he wanted to make the world safe from the autocratic rulers of the German Empire. His assistant secretary of the navy, Franklin Roosevelt, agreed with this wartime image of a brutal militaristic Germany ruled by Prussian Junkers. Serving in Wilson's government, Roosevelt strengthened this image of a split Germany; he believed that the war was a moral clash between diametrically opposed ideologies and cultural assumptions—Prussian militarism versus democratic freedom. World War I, in his estimation, was a necessary crusade against German aggression, but the Germans had not learned their lesson. On his last visit to Germany in 1919, still in his capacity as assistant secretary of the navy, he was surprised to learn that the Germans did not think that they had really been defeated. On an inspection tour near Koblenz, then under American occupation, he saw the fortress of Ehrenbreitstein, which overlooked the Rhine. He expected to see the Stars and Stripes fluttering from the castle and asked why the American flag was not there. The answer from the American commanding officer was that flying the American flag would upset the German people. Roosevelt was angry, and after returning to Paris he interceded with General Pershing and managed to reverse the matter.[72] Subsequent developments in Germany under Hitler convinced him that the Germans should have been made to recognize that they had lost the war. If they had, World War II might have been avoided.

Adolf Hitler was an extreme believer in the idea that the German army had been stabbed in the back by internal subversives—pacifists, social democrats, Communists, and Jews. For Hitler, the war had never really ended. The humiliating peace treaty had been imposed on his country by trickery and deceit. Roosevelt, conversely, followed popular opinion in America at the time of the armistice in November 1918 and demanded that Germany be forced to surrender unconditionally. He backed the peace treaty and expected the United States to play a leading role in the League of Nations. This did not happen. But Roosevelt never lost his belief in internationalism, viewing America's withdrawal into isolation as a temporary waning of the crusading spirit. However, he did appear to have taken Wilson's failure to heart: if he ever assumed national leadership, he would avoid Wilson's mistake.[73] The Germans, in his view, had not learned their lesson, and the rise of Hitler was a result of this. Yet, as a politician, he had to respect the prevailing mood of isolationists and appeasers, knowing full well that Hitler would take advantage of them.

Roosevelt was right about Hitler; he was also right about the German obsession with continental domination. He disliked the Germans personally, finding them, on average, arrogant, annoyingly militaristic, narrow-minded, and authoritarian. He acknowledged their virtues of hard work, managerial talent, and high cultural achievements. These qualities actually worried him in the late 1930s, because he was not sure that he could mold the great majority of Americans in resisting a wholly militarized people like the Germans or the Japanese. How Roosevelt became increasingly aware of Hitler's intentions, and how Hitler responded to the American challenge to his long-range plans, is the subject of the following chapters.

CHAPTER 2

Hitler Takes Risks and America Legislates Itself into Neutrality: 1933—1937

The Third Reich and the New Deal, 1933–1934

Looking back on the first five years of the Nazi regime, Hitler's propaganda minister, Joseph Goebbels, gave a direct and blunt answer to the often asked question, "Why did the Western powers let Hitler do what he wanted for so long?" On April 5, 1940, he told representatives of the German press,

> Up to now we have succeeded in leaving the enemy in the dark concerning Germany's real goals, just as before 1932 our domestic foes never saw where we were going or that our oath of legalism was just a trick. We wanted to come to power legally, but we did not want to use power legally. . . . They could have suppressed us. They could have arrested a couple of us in 1925 and that would have been that, the end. No, they let us through the danger zone. That's exactly how it was in foreign policy too. . . . In 1933 a French premier ought to have said (and if I had been the French premier I would have said it): "The new Reich Chancellor is the man who wrote *Mein Kampf,* which says this and that. This man cannot be tolerated in our vicinity. Either he disappears or we march!" But they didn't do it. They left us alone and let us slip through the risky zone, and we were able

to sail around all dangerous reefs. And when we were done, and well armed, better than they, and then they started the war.[1]

During the first few years Hitler took a rather cautious approach to foreign policy. He spoke of freedom and international peace while secretly preparing for rearmament and war. Hitler performed this deception so well that many people, inside and outside of Germany, fooled themselves about his real intentions. The new German government tried to establish cordial relations with the United States, and initially Roosevelt also adopted a wait-and-see attitude. On January 30, the day Hitler assumed power, the *New York Times* correspondent in Berlin reported that "Herr Hitler is reported to be in a more docile frame of mind." Just one day later that same *New York Times* reporter opined that "Hitler Puts Aside Aim to be Dictator," a form of wishful thinking that was also widely indulged in by conservative circles in Germany. Roosevelt reserved judgment, undoubtedly hoping that political experience would moderate the German leader. His selection of William E. Dodd, a professor of history at the University of Chicago who had received his Ph.D. from the University of Leipzig in 1900, as ambassador to Germany in 1933 was probably motivated by the president's desire to use the liberal professor as a conduit to the moderate, old-school elements in German society and public life.[2] Dodd was a distinguished professor of history and an old-style liberal who believed that "he could have some influence in moderating the policies of the Nazi regime."[3] A Jeffersonian and a Wilsonian internationalist, he shared with FDR, whom he greatly admired, a faith in the basic decency of human nature and a universal desire on the part of people for democratic freedom. His view of Germany was an illusionary and romantic image of prewar Germany, commonly held by Americans of his generation. Dodd showed considerable sympathy for what Germans had gone through during the war and after, and deplored the humiliation the country had suffered as a result of the Versailles Treaty, political instability, and economic chaos. As he set off for Germany with his wife and two grown children, he was hopeful that he could play an important part in bolstering the forces of moderation, mistakenly believing that the Germans were by "nature more democratic than any other great race in Europe."[4] With blinders such as these, Dodd was in for a shock, and he quickly discovered just how brutal the new Nazi government really was. Instead of exercising his role as an objective diplomat, Dodd allowed himself to become so emotionally involved in what he saw that it undermined his diplomatic effectiveness. He took a visceral dislike to Hitler, confiding to his diary, "I have a sense of horror when I look at the man."[5] Hitler returned the compliment, calling Dodd an old imbecile (*alter Trottel*) whose bad German he could never really understand.[6] Dodd's good-looking daughter, Martha, became so intimately entangled with various Nazis that her father feared that her behavior might lead to a serious diplomatic scandal. Dodd had good reason to be concerned, but not in the way he thought. His daughter later married a Czech, became a Soviet agent, and chose to live behind the Iron Curtain after World War II. Hitler blamed the men of the Foreign Office for missing an opportunity to get to Dodd through his "accessible daughter."[7]

Dodd served for four and a half years (1933–38), witnessing the excesses of the Nazi regime at close range and sending some rather telling accounts of what he saw to Washington. His correspondence with Roosevelt is particularly intriguing, for it reveals that both men, though slightly blinded by their liberal misconceptions of Germany, sensed very early on just what kind of threat Hitler represented to Europe and therefore potentially to the United States. FDR asked Dodd to accomplish three goals as ambassador: to press the Germans for repayment on all private American loans; to help moderate persecution of the Jews; and to influence trade arrangements on certain items in order to facilitate German debt payments to the United States.[8] Dodd failed on all three counts, but this was hardly his fault. No American diplomat could have deflected Hitler from his single-minded goal, to expand German power. At the same time, Dodd was surely the odd man out in Berlin: a moderate academic who hated diplomatic niceties and lavish parties, who had great difficulty in conforming to the Washington bureaucracy, and who took a deep dislike to the people he was supposed to get along with. For this reason, Franklin Ford's judgment of him was surely right: Dodd was "ineffectual as an ambassador less because he failed to achieve his aim of changing the Third Reich by example and persuasion than because that was the aim he set himself."[9] Once Dodd became fully aware of his failure, he became despondent and psychologically incapable of representing his country during the various grave crises into which the Nazis plunged Europe—the Röhm purge, German rearmament, the annexation of Austria, the Czech crises, and the Crystal Night pogrom against the Jews.

During the first two years of Nazi rule, U.S.-German relations were, if not warm, at least diplomatically correct. The State Department did not want to pick a fight with the new German government and hoped that Hitler would not last too long or would moderate his aggressive policies. The German Foreign Office, in turn, scrupulously tried to avoid any hostility with the United States. In April 1933 Roosevelt, concerned over German loan repayments, even invited Hitler to Washington; the führer sent Hjalmar Schacht, president of the Reich Bank, instead.[10] In 1933 parallels were often drawn between the New Deal and National Socialist economic policies. John Cudahy, Roosevelt's ambassador to Poland, stopped in Berlin before assuming his post in Warsaw and reported back to the president that the Nazis were harmless. His sense was that there was a new "patriotic buoyancy and unity in the new Germany." As to the Brownshirts (SA), they merely represented an "outlet for the peculiar social need of a country which loves display and pageantry."[11] He seemed to believe that the brownshirts were a kind of fraternal order, like the Elks in America. On the German side, the *Völkische Beobachter*, the official organ of the Nazi Party, commented positively on Roosevelt's new book *Looking Forward* (1933), translated almost immediately into German, by admitting that many statements in this book could have been written by a National Socialist. The *Beobachter* even claimed that "Roosevelt has a good deal of understanding for National Socialist thought."[12] Between 1933 and 1936, Hitler made no recorded anti-American remarks.[13] In 1934 Roosevelt and Hitler actually exchanged cordial messages. In one of them Hitler praised the American president for the outstanding work he was doing in leading his country toward economic recovery. Hitler congratulated FDR on his "heroic efforts" on behalf of the American people and expressed his agreement with the president's view that the "virtue of duty, readiness for sacrifice, and discipline should dominate the entire people."[14] Roosevelt remarked to Harold Ickes at the time, "What we are doing in this country are some of the things . . . that are being done under Hitler in Germany. But we are doing them in an orderly way."[15]

In reviewing Hitler's first year in office, American magazines drew two exaggerated images of Hitler, focusing on his Charlie Chaplin–like appearance on the one hand and his dictatorial megalomania on the other hand. *Time* magazine showed Hitler in a somewhat more favorable light by covering his generosity toward his former wartime comrade Ignaz

Westenkirchner, who asked for Hitler's help in rescuing him from depression-ridden America. Westenkirchner had immigrated with his family to Reading, Pennsylvania, after the war, but the Depression had left him unemployed, so he asked Hitler for help. Hitler not only sent tickets but also lined up a position for him as superintendent of a Nazi Party building in Munich. *Time* magazine quoted Westenkirchner as saying that Hitler was "a kind man" who deeply cared for the poor, raising them up without permitting the upper classes to be leveled.[16] *Time* followed up the Westenkirchner rescue mission with another "kind Adolf" story several months later. This one involved Anton Karthausen, a German immigrant who was unable to make a living as a dressmaker in Brownsville, Texas. Hitler promptly responded with tickets that enabled the Karthausens to return to Germany. These repatriation efforts were good propaganda for the Germans; they were intended to show that Germans belonged back home and that America was not the land of opportunity it was rumored to be.

References to "kind Adolf" changed drastically in 1934. The bloody Röhm purge of 1934, along with Nazi attacks on the churches and party-sponsored book burnings, soured American public opinion of Germany because it revealed the brutal nature of the Nazi system. General Hugh Johnson, head of the National Recovery Administration, went on record in a public speech confessing that the Nazi blood purge made him "physically and very actively sick." The only comparisons, he said, that came to mind, were the Pancho Villa ravages in Mexico and "among semicivilized people or savages half drunk on sotol and marijuana. But that such a thing should happen in a country of some supposed culture passes comprehension."[17] The German chargé in Washington vigorously protested against such an intemperate outburst but was told that Johnson had merely expressed his personal opinions rather than that of the American government.

Nazi street violence, especially against Jews, caused great concern in the United States. As early as March 1934, the American Federation of Labor and the American Jewish Congress sponsored a mock trial of Hitler under the provocative title "The Case of Civilization against Hitlerism." The event attracted a number of well-known personalities, including the mayor of New York, Fiorello La Guardia. Bainbridge Colby, Woodrow Wilson's last secretary of state, presided over the meeting, which was held at Madison Square Garden and attracted an audience of twenty-two thousand people.[18] By using the phrase "crime against civilization," the sponsors of this mock trial, headed by Rabbi Stephen Wise, wished to avoid a purely partisan attack on Hitler and portrayed the sponsors as representatives of humanity who wanted to defend the civilized values of the Judeo-Christian heritage. The prosecution even made a pretense of judicial objectivity by inviting representatives of the German government. The Germans declined the honor, and vigorously protested to the State Department that the trial was a slander against the new German government and should be stopped. The State Department, while expressing some sympathy for the German complaint, pointed out that the trial was purely private in nature and was an expression of freedom of speech. When the trial convened, the court crier announced, "Hear ye! Hear ye! All those who have business before this court of civilization give your attention and ye shall be heard." The charge was that "the Nazi government in Germany has not only destroyed the foundations of the German Republic, but, under penalty of death, torture, and economic extermination, and by process of progressive strangulation, has reduced and subjugated to abject slavery all sections of its population."[19] At the conclusion of the trial, a vote was taken by the audience, and Hitler was found guilty. Despite protests by Hans Luther, the German ambassador to Washington, the State Department was unable to prevent the trial from taking place. In Berlin, Foreign Minister von Neurath protested to Dodd, who regretted the proposed mock trial but said he could do nothing to prevent it. Although Hitler said nothing publicly, he did curse the Jews in an interview with Dodd, intimating that if the damned Jews in America did not stop their agitation he would "make an end of all Jews in Germany."[20]

German protest through diplomatic channels did no good. German American relations continued to be diplomatically correct, but in the field of public relations there were frequent flare-ups. Congressman Samuel Dickstein of New York, chairman of the House Committee on Immigration and Naturalization, conducted investigations of Nazi agents active in the United States, and large department stores boycotted German goods all over America. The Communist Party in America also stirred up anti-German sentiments and sponsored anti-German demonstrations. On July 26, 1934, Communists boarded the German liner *Bremen*, beat up German sailors, and ripped off the swastika flag, hurling it into the river. A melee ensued that had to be broken up by the New York Police. American public opinion was turning against the Nazi regime, whereas the German public was much more favorable toward the United States.

The anti-Nazi demonstrations and boycotts in America, especially by Jewish organizations, confirmed Hitler's stereotypes about Jews dominating public opinion in the United States. Although the American authorities were generally scrupulous in maintaining a neutral position during these anti-Nazi protests, there were exceptions that raised dark suspicions among the German diplomatic officials. Mayor La Guardia, as previously mentioned, made various insulting remarks about the Nazi regime and participated in anti-German agitation. Judge Louis Brodsky, who presided over the *Bremen* case, delivered a gratuitous injudicious outburst against the Nazi regime and its "brazen display of an emblem that is antithetical to American ideals." The sight of the swastika, he opined, made the ship a pirate ship in the eyes of the rioters, who saw it as an atavistic throwback to the dark ages.[21] The Nazi press had a field day with this and similar anti-German pronouncements in America, with the *Völkische Beobachter* denouncing the *Bremen* decision as "scandalous Jewish justice in New York."[22]

Extremist activities in America were followed almost immediately by similar reactions in Germany; the difference was that the extremists in America were merely a nuisance but in Germany they were in power. After becoming aware of just how unpopular anti-Jewish action in Germany was in the United States and elsewhere, Hitler increasingly looked at the German Jews under his control as hostages to be used as pawns in his relationship with the Western powers. The major stumbling blocks for relations between Germany and the United States, apart from the difference between their political systems, were disarmament and debt payments. Hitler disingenuously told the Western powers that he was perfectly willing not to arm (*aufrüsten*) if they disarmed (*abrüsten*). Although the German negotiator at Geneva, Rudolph Nadolny, was making some progress in gaining concessions from the Western powers, Hitler had no intention of negotiating seriously because he wanted to rearm as rapidly and as massively as he could get away with. Thus, on October 14, 1933, he withdrew from the Disarmament Conference and simultaneously terminated Germany's membership in the League of Nations. In this he had the complete support of the German Foreign Office and of conservative nationalists whose revisionist plans coincided with Hitler's long-range expansionist ideas. In order to soften the foreign impact of this bombshell, Hitler submitted his decision to the German people in a plebiscite. On November 12, the German electorate ratified Hitler's actions by an overwhelming margin of 95.1 percent. There was very little that the Western powers, including the United States, could do about the German rejection of disarmament. Nor could the United States do much about German defaults on debt repayments.

On May 8, 1933, Hjalmar Schacht announced that the German government would stop payments on its foreign debts, which at the time amounted to about 5 billion dollars, of which nearly 2 billion dollars were held by Americans. That drastic step was regarded as necessary because of the Depression, but perhaps more so because the new Nazi government made rearmament its top priority. This meant finding enough money in the budget and experimenting with deficit spending, a step that represented a radical reversal of the conservative and deflationary policies of the Brüning government. As Hitler saw it, the key to his ambitious rearmament program, which at first had to be hidden from the Western powers, was to change the tight money policies of the Reichsbank. Thus, when Hitler asked the president of the Reichsbank, Hans Luther, to open the money spigot, the president told him that he could give him 100 million marks, the legal limit at the time. Hitler could not believe what he heard; he was thinking in terms of billions rather than piddling millions. Clearly, Luther had to go, preferably as far away from the Reichsbank as possible. He sent Luther to Washington, where he served as ambassador from 1933 to 1938. In Luther's place, Hitler picked the wily Hjalmar Horace Greeley Schacht, one of the most important financial experts during the interwar period. Schacht's parents had immigrated to the United States in the 1870s but returned to Germany to take advantage of the new opportunities opened up by the recent German unification. Schacht's middle name, Horace Greeley, was chosen by his father, who greatly admired the well-known American abolitionist, social progressive, and failed presidential candidate, Horace Greeley. Schacht was by all accounts the most brilliant member of the Nazi regime. He had studied medicine, German philosophy, political science, and economics, receiving his Ph.D. in economics from the University of Berlin. When Hitler appointed him president of the Reichsbank and subsequently minister of economics, Schacht had already served his country in a variety of important posts. Initially, the stiff-collared and prickly Schacht, calling himself a National Socialist, supported Hitler and introduced him to prominent members of business and industry. Although he would ultimately break with Hitler over the brutal nature of the regime, he threw all his energy and talent behind the German effort to rearm on a large scale. To do so, Schacht invented an ingenious and surreptitious system called Mefo-Exchange (Mefo-Wechsel) by which the government converted "Mefo" bills, secured by a dummy corporation founded by the government and several private corporations, into a concealed form of money. By 1938 the government had used 12 billion Mefo bills to finance its rearmament program. The secretive nature of this financial scheme was indicative of how the Nazi regime tried to avoid its financial obligations to the Western powers, especially the United States.

Schacht's mission was to find ways and means to renege on reparations payments and to obtain the necessary funds for massive rearmament. The very notion of subordinating most economic activities to rearmament was bound to alarm the democracies, once they got wind of it. It did not take Roosevelt very long to realize that the new German government was pursuing policies—trade discrimination, a managed economy, and autarky—that violated every principle of free enterprise capitalism.[23] Like Woodrow Wilson, Roosevelt was an internationalist who believed in free trade and low tariffs. Nations who traded freely and reduced tariffs were unlikely to go to war. The president's secretary of state, Cordell Hull, was an even more passionate believer in reducing barriers to trade, and he was instrumental in getting Congress to pass the Reciprocal Trade Agreement Pact, which allowed the president to reduce tariff rates by as much as 50 percent, providing that the trade partners did likewise. Hull succeeded in negotiating pacts with twenty-one nations. The Germans rejected the American vision of a free-trade international economic system. Their aim was self-sufficiency (autarky) on the assumption that overdependence on international markets, especially when controlled by hostile powers, could lead to embargos or economic blockades, as in World War I. To make up for Germany's lack of crucial resources (rubber, copper, base metals, minerals, oil), the Nazis invested in research and development of synthetic goods. Two major corporate giants, I. G. Farben and Wintershall, received lucrative government subsidies to develop synthetic substitutes for the armed forces.

These economic measures undoubtedly stimulated business and industry, while at the same time reducing unemployment. They also accelerated the development of an increasingly bloated, overmanaged, and centralized government. Furthermore, the Germans ran serious balance of trade deficits, exacerbated by the fact that they did not strengthen their export markets. Schacht countered Western free-trade agreements, which he denounced as discriminatory to Germany, with his "New Plan" that called for bilateralization of all trade and payment balances, import limitations and planning dependent on national priorities, and encouragement of exports based on barter.[24] Schacht's New Plan also called for government regulation of imports and bilateral trade agreements with southeastern Europe.

The American response to these German economic policies was vocal opposition. Secretary of State Hull was particularly offended by Schacht's deceptive strategy of evading debt payments, calling it a colossal fraud. When Schacht came to America in May 1933, President Roosevelt told Hull to receive Schacht but to pretend to be looking at certain papers, letting him stand there for a few minutes, thus hopefully putting him in his place.[25] What so riled both Roosevelt and Hull was that the Germans were not only defaulting on the interest on their foreign bonds that had been sold in the United States during the 1920s, but also profiting from these defaults and thereby financing their rearmament program. By defaulting to their American creditors, the Germans caused the value of the bonds to drop steeply in the American money market; the Germans then turned around and purchased the bonds at a fraction of their face value. They permitted their exporters to keep part of the dollars from their exports in America if they used them to purchase the bonds at low prices. The exporters could then sell the bonds to the German government for Reichsmarks, thus financing further exports. Hull estimated that 85–90 percent of these bonds were repurchased in America by Germany at a great loss to American investors. "In devilish fashion," Hull noted in his diary, "the Germans tied in nonpayment of bond interest, depreciation of bond prices, redemption of bonds at their low prices, and subsidization of German exports and at the same time they were able to continue their enormous purchases of material that went into armaments."[26] The historian Gerhard Weinberg did not exaggerate when he said that this amounted to forcing the American people to subsidize German rearmament.[27]

German Rearmament and Aggression

The early skirmishes between the United States and the new Hitler regime, mostly over economic policies, subsided by the end of 1934. Hitler knew why. By the mid-1930s the United States gave every indication that it would avoid serious entanglements in the affairs of Europe and in the Far East. This isolationist mood manifested itself in 1934 when Congress passed the Johnson Act, which prohibited loans to nations that had defaulted on their financial obligations and set up the Nye Committee charged with investigating munitions makers who had allegedly dragged the country into World War I. There followed three neutrality acts in succession in 1935, 1936, and 1937. These acts prohibited the exports of arms, ammunition, and implements of war to belligerent countries. In cases of war between two or more foreign states, the president was required to proclaim the existence of such a state of war, at which time the exportations of arms became illegal. Violators, the act specified, would receive a fine of no more than $10,000 or imprisonment of no more than five years, or both. The act also contained provisions restricting travel by American citizens on belligerent ships during war.

When Germany revealed on May 9, 1935, that it had reestablished an air force and also reintroduced conscription, the United States hardly made a peep, choosing to stand on the sidelines. Roosevelt hoped that the allied defenders of Versailles would take more decisive action, but the will to resist Hitler was too feeble. The Western powers were concerned enough, however, to convene a conference on April 11 at Stresa on Lake Maggiore. Mussolini still maintained that he supported an independent Austria, which he saw as a buffer against an expanding Germany. He called for more decisive action against Hitler than empty resolutions by the League of Nations. No real action, however, resulted from the Stresa Conference because the Western powers were too divided in their foreign policy objectives. In June the British negotiated a naval agreement with the Germans that tacitly permitted the Germans to rearm by letting them build up their submarine fleet to be on par with the British, though limiting the German surface fleet to 35 percent of the British. Hitler was pleased with Ribbentrop for negotiating this favorable treaty, but he had no intention of honoring it in the long run because he wanted to build up a large navy that had complete parity with the British navy.[28] London signed the Naval Agreement of 1935 in order to stave off the sort of naval race that had poisoned Anglo-German relations in the late 1890s, but the French and the Italians, who had not been consulted, regarded the British action as a breach of the allied unity that they thought had been achieved at Stresa. Both powers would henceforth pursue a more independent path when it came to their own security concerns. In the same month that the British and the Germans negotiated their naval agreement, the United States Senate could not muster a two-thirds majority that would have enabled the United States to join the World Court at The Hague. The measure failed as a result of a furious public relations campaign that had been waged against the internationalist legislation by the Hearst newspapers, Detroit radio priest Charles Coughlin, and isolationist senators such as William E. Borah, Hiram W. Johnson, and Breckinridge Long. It was a bitter defeat for Roosevelt and showed what a vocal and determined minority could do in blocking a more interventionist foreign policy. In October 1935 Mussolini invaded Ethiopia, and by so doing outraged the civilized world except for Nazi Germany. Anxious appeals by the Ethiopians to the League of Nations produced only meaningless resolutions. When the British asked for an embargo, the French balked. Mussolini got what he wanted, and more: an open invitation of Nazi friendship. Thus began Il Duce's fatal embrace with the German dictator.

Hitler became increasingly convinced by these events that the Western powers would do almost anything to avoid another war. With America in isolation and the Western powers indecisive and vacillating, he took his first major gamble, violating the Versailles treaty by reoccupying the Rhineland on March 7, 1936, justifying this step by saying that he was merely reoccupying German territory. The reaction by the allied powers was epitomized by Lord Lothian's matter-of-fact observation that the Germans were "after all only going into their own back garden."[29] The United States did not take a stand and justified its position by saying that it had not been a party to either the Versailles treaty or the Locarno Agreement of 1925.

In the United States, 1936 was an election year. The Democratic platform echoed the prevailing isolationist sentiment by declaring that, "We shall continue to observe a true neutrality in the disputes of others," and the president, in one of his few foreign policy statements that year, said on August 14, 1936, in Chautauqua, New York, "We shun political commitments which might entangle us in foreign wars; we avoid connection with the political activities of the League of Nations. . . . I hate war. I have passed unnumbered hours, I shall pass unnumbered hours, thinking and planning how war may be kept from this Nation."[30] This "I hate war speech" was typical of Roosevelt's sleight-of-hand approach because, while it roundly condemned war, it did not recommend ostrichlike isolation either, as is evident in the caveat, "We are not isolationists except in so far as we seek to isolate ourselves completely from war. Yet we must remember that so long as war exists on earth there will be some danger that even the Nation which most ardently desires peace may be drawn into war."[31]

At the time when Roosevelt was making these remarks about peace, the Germans were hosting the peaceful Olympic Games in Berlin (August 1–16, 1936). The games were a propaganda triumph for the Nazis. Anti-Jewish activities temporarily ceased all over Germany and the international community was impressed by how successfully the games had been managed by the Nazis. Hitler had by then restored economic prosperity and political confidence, and he was about to embark on three years of remarkable diplomatic triumphs. At the very time when the eyes of the world were focused on the Olympic Games in Berlin, Adolf Hitler composed a top secret memorandum in his aerie at Obersalzberg on economic strategy and rearmament. The document, which was greatly at odds with the Olympic spirit of peace and international goodwill, reflected Hitler's impatience with the slow pace of German rearmament and his insistence that the German economy must be ready for war within four years. Hitler's memorandum bluntly stated, "We are overpopulated and cannot feed ourselves from our own resources. . . . The German armed forces must be operational within four years. The German economy must be fit for war within four years."[32]

While Hitler had war on his mind, Roosevelt thought of peace. In the spring of 1937 he sprang a novel idea on the German ambassador, Hans Luther. Why not establish a new and simple policy for rearmament that specified that no nation should manufacture armaments heavier than a man could carry on his shoulders? If followed, this policy should go a long way in preventing aggression. Luther passed along Roosevelt's brainstorm, and so did Ambassador Davies, who stopped in Berlin before going back to Moscow. Davies later claimed that he saw Schacht, who allegedly told him that the president's plan was "so simple as to be the expression of a genius."[33] It was "absolutely the solution." The ingenious plan, however, fell on stony ground with the führer.

While Hitler was composing his readiness for "war in four years" memorandum at Obersalzberg, the spirit of peace prevailing at the Olympic Games could not gloss over the fact that bloody civil war was breaking out in Spain. The United States promptly announced a policy of strict nonintervention, prohibiting arms shipments to any of the warring factions. The Germans, however, openly aided Franco and his anti-Republican forces, and when the German pocket battleship *Deutschland* was attacked by the Republicans in May 1937, the Germans shelled the Spanish town and harbor of Almeria. German and Italian aid to Franco increased substantially over time. Hitler dispatched various forces to Spain, including the Condor Air Legion, a tank battalion and technical advisors. The Condor Air Legion later distinguished itself by pulverizing the Spanish town of Guernica and its civilian population, thus giving the world a preview of terror bombing from the air.

The Fascist powers were gathering and threatening the Western powers in 1936 and 1937. The groundwork was being set for the Rome-Berlin Axis, and when Franco finally prevailed in 1939, France, one of the few remaining democracies on the continent, found itself encircled by three Fascist powers—Spain, Italy, and Germany. On November 25, 1936, Germany and Japan signed the Anti-Comintern Pact, which was designed to monitor and counter Soviet-backed support to international Communist parties.

In 1937 Japan attacked China, an event that signaled the opening round of World War II. The Japanese had been on the move since 1931 when they invaded Manchuria and set up the puppet state of Manchukuo, a move that was condemned by the League of Nations. Japan promptly left the League and proceeded to exploit Manchuria's resources for the Japanese war economy.

Behind the scenes, Hitler was not idle either in preparing his expansionist agenda. The tone of his public speeches also began to change as he cast off his pretensions for peace in favor of belligerent diatribes. In September 1937 Hitler and Mussolini consolidated their growing friendship, culminating in a spectacular state visit by Il Duce to Germany in late September and Italy's adherence to the Anti-Comintern Pact. The Nazis dazzled Il Duce with an awesome display of military might. The result was the beginning of the "brutal friendship" between the two dictators.

Across the ocean, Roosevelt was carefully monitoring the aggressive words and actions of the Fascist nations. On October 5, 1937, the president gave a speech in Chicago, subsequently termed the "Quarantine speech," in which he condemned the creeping "reign of terror and international lawlessness," evidenced by the bombing of civilian populations, sinking of ships, and wanton acts of violence committed without a declaration of war. He reminded the American people that they were not immune from such international aggression, warning, "Let no one imagine that America will escape, that it may expect mercy, that this Western Hemisphere will not be attacked, and that it will continue tranquilly and peacefully to carry on the ethics and arts of civilization."[34] It has been thought that the president primarily had the Japanese in mind, for he made the speech shortly after the Japanese had attacked China. The German diplomats in Washington, however, wondered whether the president's message was not also aimed at them. Ambassador Dieckhoff, who had replaced Luther, immediately asked for clarification about the aggressors Roosevelt had in mind. Sumner Welles, the American Under-Secretary of State, told him that the gist of the president's speech had been the promotion of peace. If any aggressor had been referred to, it was the Japanese rather than the Germans or Italians. Welles then added a most revealing comment, which must have jumped out at Dieckhoff. It was a prophetic warning that "if a world conflict should break out in which Great Britain becomes involved, the United States will be thrown, either at the beginning of the conflict or soon thereafter, on the British side of the scale."[35] Hitler took Roosevelt's Quarantine speech just as seriously as Dieckhoff did. According to his adjutant Nicolaus von Below, Hitler saw the speech as a turning point in American foreign policy.[36] Hitler was offended by Roosevelt's remark that 90 percent of the world's population was threatened by 10 percent of aggressive nations and that he seemed to think that Germany was one of these aggressive nations. He attributed FDR's sudden interest in foreign policy to his failed economic remedies, as evidenced by the increased unemployment in the U.S. workforce. Hitler suspected that Roosevelt was looking to rearmament as a way out of the recent economic downturn in the U.S. economy— the depression within a depression, as some critics of FDR have called it. Hitler said that FDR needed to get congressional approval for large rearmament appropriations and to get it he would incite the American public against so-called aggressor nations, notably headed by Germany.

Roosevelt's first forceful pronouncement in foreign affairs was prompted by a growing worldwide danger to American interests both in the Pacific and in Europe. He viewed these threats as analogous to an epidemic: "When an epidemic of physical disease starts to spread, the community approves and joins in a quarantine of the patients in order to protect the health of the community against the spread of the disease."[37] How he proposed to quarantine the aggression the president did not explain.

Roosevelt, acutely aware of the gathering storm, was groping for a new policy to replace neutrality. As happened several times in his administration on matters relating to foreign affairs, the president took the easy way out by letting things drift, hoping that events abroad would galvanize the American people to the point of demanding more aggressive measures against the Fascist powers. In his Quarantine speech, the president did not name the international lawbreakers, though it was obvious to his listeners that he had Japan, Germany, and Italy in mind. The Quarantine speech was not Roosevelt's signal to abandon neutrality, as Charles Beard and other revisionists seemed to think, but a shift in his thinking about international aggression. At this point he was starting to realize that the American people needed to be educated about the threat from abroad, a reeducation that would not be easy because isolationist feelings were still very strong. On October 16, 1937, he sent his old headmaster at Groton, Endicott Peabody, a telegram thanking him for his support of the Quarantine speech and confessing, "As you know, I am fighting against a public psychology of long-standing—a psychology which comes very close to saying, 'Peace at any price.'"[38]

This is what Roosevelt wanted to change, but he lacked an active policy to do it. Off the record, Roosevelt called Hitler an international gangster who would have to be stopped sooner or later. But who would stop him? Here Roosevelt's intentions became murky. He was simply not the sort of man who wanted to rush into action without painstaking thought about the risks involved for the American people. Those who argue that he could hardly wait to horn in on the conflicts brewing in Europe or Asia, or perhaps that he even conspired to create incidents to justify intervention, do not understand the president's essential style. The notion of giving aid and comfort short of war to the victims of totalitarianism became Roosevelt's guiding policy until the fall of France. Roosevelt's conception of national self-interest could be measured in geopolitical lines of defensive zones. In the Pacific it was the Philippines, Australia, India, and the oil-rich Dutch Indies. Next came French Indochina and Chiang Kai-shek's China, both of which Roosevelt saw as bulwarks against Japanese expansion.

In Europe, Roosevelt's first line of defense was Britain and France, the democratic allies of World War I. In the back of his mind there was the Soviet Union, an international pariah but an important potential ally against the mounting threat of Nazi Germany. In 1933 the Roosevelt administration formally recognized the Soviet Union and established full diplomatic relations with that Communist country. From the beginning of his presidency to the very end, Roosevelt took a somewhat benign view of the Soviet Union, did not seem overly perturbed by Soviet espionage in America, and courted and propped up the Soviet Union when it seemed on the verge of collapse in 1941.[39] He made no intellectual connection about the equivalence of Nazi Germany and the Soviet Union despite repeated warnings by his diplomats.

In 1937 Roosevelt recognized that events in Europe and Asia were beginning to be dangerous, and that ways and means had to be found to support the democracies, even if that meant chipping away—deceitfully, if necessary—at the wall of neutrality Congress had built since the early 1930s. While the American president talked of peace, the German dictator talked of aggression and war. Hitler's timing was very good. By 1938 Germany had rearmed and was both militarily and psychologically at least as strong as the Western democracies. World War I had changed the traditional great power constellation, leaving a vacuum that Hitler was quick to exploit. Of the five major European powers before the war—Italy, Germany, Austria-Hungary, France, and Britain—only France and Britain had remained great powers. Weakened by revolution and civil war, Russia had fallen into the hands of the Bolsheviks, who were as suspicious of the democracies as they were of the Fascist states. The multiethnic Austro-Hungarian Empire had collapsed, and out of its scattered pieces emerged new national states such as Poland, Czechoslovakia, Hungary, and Yugoslavia. Italy was torn by socioeconomic conflicts and felt cheated of the fruits of victory, and Germany was defeated and humiliated. As to the United States, Americans had shown no inclination to assume the imperialist mantle that would have been necessary to keep the peace in Europe.

If the United States had ratified the Versailles treaty, joined the League of Nations, and linked with the French and the British, Hitler—perhaps—could have been stopped. America's wartime idealism turned out to be little more than an ideological justification for fighting the war; it had little effect in waging peace. This would have required a long-range commitment that Americans were not willing to make in 1919.

Hitler knew this. By themselves, Britain and France would not be able to prevent Germany from regaining great-power status. In fact, the leaders of the Weimar Republic, notably Gustav Stresemann, had already liberated Germany from the most crippling restrictions of the Versailles treaty; they had also, by default, if not complicity, allowed antidemocratic institutions a free pass. Hitler then inherited authoritarian and militaristic institutions: the armed forces, the courts, the civil service, and the school system. Hitler would bend these institutions to his will by Nazifying them. Germany had been the most powerful country on the continent in 1914, and the talents of its people enjoyed worldwide respect and envy. The war did not destroy the German potential for European supremacy, nor did it put a damper on the German obsession with gaining continental hegemony. Hitler merely gave voice to what the majority of Germans believed about themselves and their role in Europe. He believed, as they did, that Germany had never been defeated, had, in fact, been betrayed by allied promises of a just peace, and therefore had little choice but to shake off the shackles of Versailles to recoup its place among the great powers. What Hitler brought to the national atmosphere of self-pity and humiliation was a genius for tapping into that mood and converting it into a political mass movement that thrived on anger and revenge. Hitler also gave that movement an ugly racist and Judeophobic direction. He convinced all too many Germans that the Aryan race, being at the apex of biological and cultural evolution, was destined to dominate the world; and because Germany was the *Urquelle* (primal source) of Aryan strength, it was inevitable that the Germans would conquer Europe from the Atlantic to the Urals.[40] The geography lesson Hitler gave the Germans was to link space and race. A people's greatness did not lie in limiting itself to its own territorial boundaries but in expansion and conquest. This vision was the diametrical opposite of Roosevelt's belief in peaceful coexistence, free markets, and democratic self-government. For Hitler, a nation's greatness depended, in the first place, on producing a healthy racial stock and encouraging its members to reproduce prodigiously. In the second place, it meant weeding out inferior racial types through appropriate eugenic measures: preventive medicine, sterilization of people with hereditary or mental illnesses, hygienic institutes, and strict segregation of inferior breeds such as Jews and gypsies.

Finally, Hitler believed that to limit a growing people like the Germans to a small, limited space was to doom them to permanent vassalage to larger nations such as Russia, the United States, and China. This is why Hitler demanded living space (*Lebensraum*) for the German people in Eastern Europe. The vast spaces of Russia would be for Germany what the Wild West had been for the United States. Germany's excess population would settle these areas and provide the fatherland with a permanent breadbasket, plus oil and other necessary materials for further industrialization. Hitler believed that making a geographically small nation into a world power could only be accomplished through the mobilization of all its resources by an all-powerful government. This task also required instilling warlike and aggressive habits into its people. Hitler wanted to breed a hard, callous, and obedient people who would do the bidding of the government. It was particularly the young that he expected to become as "swift as greyhounds and as hard as Krupp steel." In his vulgarized Nietzschean perception, he wanted young people to delight in war and conquest. The chief educational goal of National Socialism was to teach all Germans the habit of being brutal with a clear conscience.

These views, and how Hitler wanted them translated into policy, were discussed in a secret conference on November 5, 1937, with his military and diplomatic chiefs—Werner von Blomberg, Werner von Fritsch, Erich Raeder, Hermann Goering, and Konstantin von Neurath.[41] Hitler spoke at length, telling his chiefs about his plans to strengthen the German racial community by expanding its territories into Eastern Europe. He indicated that Germany could not solve its economic problems without territorial expansion and conquest. His immediate objective, he said, was the annexation of Austria and the destruction of Czechoslovakia in order to secure Germany's eastern and southern flanks. The minutes of the conference were kept by Colonel Friedrich Hossbach and were later introduced as evidence at Nuremberg of Germany's premeditated decision to wage a "war of aggression" on the world. This claim goes too far. The so-called Hossbach memorandum was more in the nature of a "testing of the waters" with his military chiefs than a blueprint for aggression. In fact, judging by their cautious, if not downright alarmed, responses, Hitler knew that he had to shake up his high command in order to get what he called obedient generals who would do his bidding like "mad dogs."

The Deterioration of German-American Relations

Toward the end of 1937, two apparently unrelated events revealed just how unfriendly relations between Germany and the United States had become. The first event centered on the sale of American helium to Germany. In May, the German Zeppelin airship *Hindenburg* had exploded at Lakehurst, New Jersey, probably as a result of static electricity and the highly flammable hydrogen the Germans had used in fueling the huge dirigible. If the Zeppelin Company had used nonflammable helium, which at the time was the exclusive monopoly of the United States, this disaster might have been avoided. Following the Lakehurst disaster, the Germans halted further construction of their hydrogen-fueled dirigibles and waited for U.S. deliveries of the nonflammable helium. In September 1937 Congress passed the Helium Act, authorizing the Secretary of the Interior to sell helium to foreign countries, with the proviso that the helium would not be put to military use. The Zeppelin Company promptly ordered 17,900,000 cubic feet of helium.

What happened next illustrates how low the relationship between Germany and the United States had sunk by late 1937 to early 1938, for the politics of helium went on for six months. When German tankers arrived in Houston to pick up the helium, a hitch developed. Although the navy had no objection to the transfer of the helium, the secretary of the interior, Harold Ickes, did. Ickes refused to sign the contract for the sale of the helium, arguing that the Nazis should be punished for their aggressive actions. He specifically mentioned the "rape of Austria" as one of the reasons for denying the sale. The State Department deplored Ickes's independent-minded action; in fact, Ambassador Wilson, Dodd's successor in Berlin, warned that the denial of helium to a German company that was simply engaged in overseas passenger transportation was not only discriminatory but also would lead to further deterioration of relations with Germany. The president and his entire cabinet, however, eventually gave in to Ickes, especially after the U.S. solicitor general, Robert H. Jackson, ruled that the president had no authority over the matter and that Ickes's negative vote was enough to block the sale.

Hitler played a minor role in the helium affair. He told Wiedemann that he had never liked Zeppelins, calling them "laughable blood sausages—lächerliche Blutwürste."[42] He said that they served no useful military purpose because they were slow and vulnerable. He was glad, he said, that he had not followed Goebbels's advice to name the LZ.129 Zeppelin that exploded at Lakehurst the *Adolf Hitler*.[43] Having the *Adolf Hitler* explode in America would have been harder to bear than the destruction of the *Hindenburg*. It goes without saying that Hitler suspected sabotage of the airship, as did most Germans in May 1937. According to Wiedemann, Hitler did plan to use some of the helium for military balloons (*Fesselballons*), which would, of course, have served military purposes.[44] Perhaps Harold Ickes was right after all.

The second event that revealed the growing rift between Germany and the United States was not so much an event as it was a sign in the form of a memorandum. In mid-October 1937 the chief of the German Chancellery forwarded a memorandum to the Foreign Office with a note that said, "It is sent to you by his personal order."[45] The author of the memorandum, titled "Roosevelt's America: A Danger," was Baron Bernhard G. Rechenberg, a man who was no stranger to the Foreign Office. Rechenberg had been a director of the Reich's foreign trade office in Hamburg, a post he quit under a financial cloud in 1924. He then went to the United States with his wife and children and made a living as a dairy farmer. He also became a propagandist for the Nazi cause in America, and after Hitler consolidated his dictatorship in 1934, Rechenberg decided to return to Germany. His ten years in America seemed to have left him none the wiser about the United States, for his lengthy memorandum was an overwrought warning that Roosevelt was about to plunge his country into a world catastrophe. Drawing on anti-Semitic and anti-American prejudices, Rechenberg claimed that Roosevelt was a terrible danger on two counts: he was a Jew and a Communist who would bring about "the fulfillment of the Communist Manifesto."[46] If not stopped, Roosevelt would pave the way toward the bolshevization of North America and the eventual globalization of the Communist menace. Members of the Foreign Office were scornful of this document; they denounced it not only as pure fantasy, as Ambassador Dieckhoff labeled it, but also as a complete distortion of American society. The diplomats undoubtedly hoped that Hitler would not take it as seriously as the comments accompanying the memorandum seemed to indicate. Ambassador Dieckhoff in Washington, who had received a copy of Rechenberg's memorandum, wrote to Weizsäcker in Berlin that Germany could ill afford a conflict with the United States—a country that had grown much stronger since World War I, economic problems notwithstanding.

One month after the Rechenberg memorandum made the rounds of various government agencies, Hitler's company commander in World War I and his personal adjutant since 1935, Fritz Wiedemann, went to the United States on an extensive tour that took him from New York to Chicago, San Francisco, and Los Angeles.[47] In New York he had to brave a horde of American reporters and Communist protesters. He also met with members of the German American Bund in Chicago and was not impressed by what he saw. He later advised Hitler not to meet with Kuhn when the German-American Bund leader visited Germany. Wiedemann gained a good impression of the size and strength of the United States, but he could not help but notice the widespread antipathy toward the Nazi regime. When he returned to Germany, he undoubtedly reported to Hitler what he had seen and heard in America. What did Hitler make of all this?

Some historians have found it tempting to let Hitler play the deluded ideologue who, in this case, uncritically accepted Rechenberg's biases because they confirmed his own.[48] Wiedemann's trip to America, however, was not just an innocent vacation but more likely a fact-finding mission that Hitler encouraged Wiedemann to undertake. In his memoirs, Wiedemann conveniently omitted the details about his trip and why he was allowed, or perhaps even urged, to go to the United States. After all, the arrival of the führer's former company commander in America caused tongues to wag, and rightly so. What was the nature of his trip? Ostensibly a private visit, but then why was the führer's personal aide accompanied by embassy officials throughout his trip? And why did he meet with German-American Bundists? It is quite possible that Hitler sent Wiedemann to America to get another point of view of conditions there. When Wiedemann returned and supposedly told Hitler to reach an understanding with the United States, Hitler dismissed him from his post because, as Wiedemann claimed, he could not abide people in his inner circle who disagreed with his politics. What kind of politics? Was it Hitler's views of the United States? If this is so, why did Hitler in the same breath appoint Wiedemann as consul general to San Francisco? Historians have followed John W. Wheeler-Bennett's acerbic judgment

that Wiedemann was another casualty among the moderates who stood
in the way of Hitler's aggressive foreign policy. With some sense of Greek
justice, Wheeler-Bennett said, he "exiled Wiedemann to San Francisco,
where, as consul general he could practice his own theories of amicabil-
ity with the Americans."[49] What Wheeler-Bennett does not mention is
that, after Wiedemann's return from his tour to America, he let everyone
know that he wanted an appointment as consul general to San Francisco.
Hitler, he admitted, had heard of his request and obliged by offering him
the post as a kind of consolation for replacing him as his personal aide.
Perhaps so, but it is my suspicion that Wiedemann's account contains too
many omissions to be completely believed. It could very well be that Hitler sent Wiedemann to the United States not only because his adjutant
wanted to go there but also because he was the right man to tell the führer
what was really going on in America. Bella Fromm, the prominent col-
umnist for the *Vossische Zeitung*, who had a good nose for what was really
going on in Berlin, recorded in her diary that "it is common knowledge
in Berlin that the real purpose of his [Wiedemann's] appointment to San
Francisco is to spread Nazi propaganda in America. Also, from the West
he would be able to direct German and Japanese espionage activities, for
which his previous Japanese contacts adequately fit him."[50] While in San
Francisco, Wiedemann was joined by his mistress, the notorious but fas-
cinating Stephanie von Hohenlohe, whom the FBI described as a German
spy, "worse than ten thousand men," reputedly "immoral, and capable of
resorting to any means, even to bribery, to gain her ends."[51] Hohenlohe
was an international high society matron with a flair for publicity. She was
not a Mata Hari; in fact, her self-interest always trumped her loyalty to
any nation. Although she was one-half Jewish, Hitler was much taken by
her and greatly appreciated her social connections. Her relationship with
Wiedemann was an on-and-off affair, as were so many of her liaisons with
powerful men. The president told the Justice Department to have her deported. She managed to outwit them all.[52]

　　To summarize, Hitler was split about the United States; he wanted to
hear the worst, but his political instincts told him that he could never underestimate the colossus across the ocean. It was best, therefore, to keep a
tab on developments in America. In 1937 the United States was officially
neutral, its military establishment was negligible, and its economy was
worsening. Hitler's most pressing concern was France and Britain, the two

Western powers that could block his immediate designs on Austria and Czechoslovakia. Anyone who opposed him on this issue, especially cautious generals or timid diplomats, had to go. He made this position quite clear in his secret address to his military chiefs in November 1937 and acted on it in the new year. By that time Hitler had slipped through what Goebbels termed the "risky zone"; Roosevelt was beginning to stir behind his neutrality zone.

CHAPTER 3

Hitler's Year: 1938

The Annexation (Anschluss) of Austria

At the height of the Austrian crisis, on March 8, 1938, a famous American visitor came to call on Adolf Hitler at the Reich chancellery—the former president of the United States, Herbert Hoover, who had been chauffeured from Prague to Berlin in a private automobile. Hoover, by profession an engineer, was very impressed by what he saw on his way to Berlin: splendid new highways, new housing developments, and prosperous towns and villages.[1] In his hour-long conversation with Hitler, Hoover praised Germany's economic prosperity and the prevailing mood of hopefulness throughout the nation. Although Hitler did most of the talking, he did not give the appearance of being a fanatic dictator. The conversation between the two statesmen was largely a "courteous exchange of opinion";[2] it centered on housing, employment, investment, and agriculture. Hoover remarked that the American people took a great interest in the new German experiment, which was quite different from the American version (Hoover was alluding to Roosevelt's New Deal). He admitted that democratic rule had imposed a much slower pace on rebuilding America than Germany. This remark about democracy prompted Hitler to say that he had been democratically elected and enjoyed the full support of the German people. Hoover replied that the restrictive measures accepted in Germany would not work in America because of the importance the American people attached to spiritual and intellectual freedom. Hitler then shifted the conversation to the danger of Communism, which Hoover also acknowledged to be a serious problem. Hitler had always had an intuitive sense that the best way of ingratiating himself with men of Hoover's class—the professional and industrial elites—was to appeal to their fear of Communism. The broad middle, or what Germans called *Mittelstand*, regarded Communism as a deadlier threat than Fascism. Most middle-class Germans, in fact, saw National Socialism as an acceptable alternative to the failed democracy that they held responsible for the postwar crisis. Although disenchantment with democracy was not a political problem in America, fear of Communism was, especially at the height of the Depression and among members of big business and believers in free-enterprise capitalism.

Following Hoover's meeting with Hitler, a minor controversy arose over whether the two statesmen had clashed over the nature of democracy versus totalitarianism, but the American ambassador, Hugh Wilson, who had accompanied Hoover on his visit to Hitler, formally corrected the record by advising the State Department that there had been nothing in the nature of a clash in the interview. That afternoon, Wilson hosted a luncheon for Hoover, which was attended by high-ranking German officials and three foreign ambassadors, at the hotel Esplanade. In the evening the Carl Schurz Society gave a dinner in Hoover's honor. Hjalmar Schacht, Germany's "economic wizard" who was credited (wrongly) with pulling Germany out of the Depression, praised Hoover's political career and expressed regret that the president could not complete his great work. The next day, Hoover was feted in grand style by Hermann Goering on his opulent estate. When Hoover finally got back to his Berlin hotel suite, he was visited by prominent members of German finance and industry.

The Germans were courting Hoover because they believed that he represented an important voice in the Republican Party—the isolationist wing that included Robert Taft, Robert La Follette Jr., Hiram Johnson, Burton Wheeler, Arthur Vandenberg, and others. Among these isolationists—or better put, noninterventionists—there was considerable respect for German efficiency and order. Some of these men, notably Charles Lindbergh, had no problem turning a blind eye to the excesses of the Nazi regime as long as it did not threaten the economic interests of the United States. As John Lukacs put it, "before 1938 there were many Americans who were inclined favorably to the new Germany, in spite (or, in some ways, because) of the barrage of news propagated about the brutalities of Hitler's regime, thinking that that kind of propaganda was greatly exaggerated, the product of special interests."[3] Much of this changed after Hitler's actions in 1938, especially his assault on the Jews in November 1938, but even then prominent American isolationists still wanted cordial relations with Germany. Lindbergh, Taft, and other followers of the America First movement continued to oppose Roosevelt's efforts to commit the United States to a more active role in European affairs. They did so even after France had been defeated in 1940, opposing aid to Britain because it was not in the interests of the United States. Hoover had no illusions about Hitler, but he did not believe that it was in the interests of the United States to involve itself in European conflicts. For his part, Hitler judged Hoover to be a political small fry who could be useful in neutralizing American interventionism.[4]

What is particularly noteworthy about Hoover's visit with Hitler is that it took place on the very day that Hitler got word that the Austrian chancellor, Kurt von Schuschnigg, planned to checkmate Hitler in the political game of chess between German and Austria by proposing a plebiscite to the Austrian people, asking them whether they supported the idea of an independent and Christian Austria. As this chapter discusses later, a yes vote on Austrian independence would have thwarted Hitler's plan to annex his native Austria. None of this filtered through to Hoover and his entourage. Hitler, Goering, and other German officials who were privy to what was happening in Austria put on a good show of normality at the time of the Austrian crisis.

The Austrian problem came to a head in early February 1938 when Hitler shook up his military, replacing recalcitrant commanders (Fritsch and Blomberg) with compliant ones (Keitel and Jodl); declared himself in personal command of Germany's armed forces, and replaced the mild-mannered Konstantin von Neurath with the aggressive and unprincipled Joachim von Ribbentrop as foreign minister. The year 1938 was Hitler's most successful year. That year witnessed one Hitlerean-inspired crisis after another: the annexation of Austria in March, the Czech crisis leading to the appeasement of Hitler in the summer and early autumn, and the horrors associated with the pogrom of German Jews in November. Austrians had strongly supported annexation with Germany in 1919, but the Allied powers decided to set aside their advocacy for democratic principles, because annexation of territories would strengthen rather than weaken postwar Germany. Hitler's opening paragraphs in *Mein Kampf* made reference to his Austrian origins and his sincere conviction that "common blood belongs in a common Reich."[5] As in the cases of the Rhineland and the Saar, Hitler appealed to Wilsonian idealism as his ostensible modus operandi, arguing that he strongly believed in national self-determination for those Germans who had been separated from their fatherland by the Versailles treaty and were living as alien residents—marginalized, discriminated against, and disenfranchised—in Poland (Danzig and the Corridor), Czechoslovakia (the Sudetenland), France (the demilitarized Rhineland, the Saar, Alsace-Lorraine), Belgium (Moresnet, Eupen, Malmédy), and Denmark (northern sections of Schleswig). Hitler had the majority of German people behind him in demanding the return of these lost territories. It was particularly galling to the Germans, who were still filled with a powerful sense of mission and national destiny, that some of their eastern territories had been "stolen" by inferior people.[6]

The Saar and the Rhineland had already been reincorporated into the Reich, the former by popular plebiscite as promised at Versailles, and the latter by a bold and uncontested military operation in March 1936. In February 1938 Hitler had a personal meeting with the Austrian chancellor Kurt von Schuschnigg at the Obersalzberg, and he berated the Austrian leader for resisting the Nazification of his country and its eventual incorporation into the Reich. Hitler demanded a series of concessions from Schuschnigg that amounted to an ultimatum.[7] The Austrian government was to lift the ban on the Nazi Party, release all pro-Nazi agitators, and appoint the pro-Nazi Arthur Seyss-Inquart as minister of the interior with full authority to enforce the terms of these demands. Schuschnigg realized that if he signed the document outlining these demands he would sign away the independence of Austria. He temporized by telling the impatient dictator that, under the terms of the Austrian constitution, only the Austrian president had the legal power to ratify such an agreement. He then slipped down the mountain and headed back to Austria.

Schuschnigg realized that the day of reckoning had arrived. He remembered vividly how pro-German Austrians, supported by the Nazis, had assassinated the Austrian chancellor Engelbert Dollfuss in 1934. The reason they had not succeeded in carrying out their coup was that Mussolini, who considered Austria a buffer against a resurgent Reich, had mobilized his troops and threatened to intervene on behalf of Austria if the

Nazis did not desist. That was 1934. In 1938, the diplomatic situation was different: neither Mussolini nor the Western powers were likely to lift a finger for Austria, though Hitler was not entirely sure of their reaction if he chose to move against Austria. He preferred to subvert the independence of Austria without provoking a military confrontation, hoping that harassment and intimidation would do the trick.[8] In the end, Schuschnigg forced his hand by resorting to a desperate and fatal expedient: the plebiscite asking the Austrian people whether they favored an "independent and social Austria, a Christian and united Austria." Hitler could not allow such a plebiscite to be held, for suppose the Austrian people voted for independence rather than German annexation? Hitler threatened Schuschnigg with military intervention if he did not call off the plebiscite. On March 9, the Austrian chancellor called off the plebiscite scheduled for March 13, 1938. The Nazis then engineered a hastily improvised coup in Austria, forcing Schuschnigg to resign. German troops marched into Austria without encountering any serious opposition. On March 14, Hitler entered Vienna, the city of his unhappy youth, in great triumph, to the Viennese shouting, "One People, One Reich, One Leader, and One Victory."[9] The Western powers did nothing, having resigned themselves to the inevitable. Mussolini took the whole thing "in a very friendly manner," as the German ambassador to Italy reported. Hitler thanked him profusely, telling him that he would never forget him for his stance.[10]

In the United States, Roosevelt was not greatly surprised, though the rapidity of Hitler's annexation caught his administration off-balance. Newspaper headlines and editorials claimed that Austria was "murdered" or "raped." Such indignant reactions were generally prompted by the brutal treatment Nazi officials meted out to the Jews, especially in Vienna. American papers generalized what happened to the Austrian Jews to the whole of Austria, claiming that the country had "been made over into a hell of hate, prejudice, vicious cruelty, and sadism."[11] Allied statesmen on both sides of the ocean had been caught napping. At the suggestion of the Under-Secretary of State, Sumner Welles, Roosevelt had planned an international conference to settle the potentially explosive issues in Europe. Scheduled for January 22, 1938, the conference never got beyond the planning stage outlined to Roosevelt in Welles's memorandum, because the British, notably Prime Minister Neville Chamberlain and his intimate adviser Horace Wilson, did not like the plan, calling it "wooly rubbish."[12]

Chamberlain cabled Roosevelt that the American plan would hurt the British efforts to reach a settlement with Germany and Italy. The major reasons why nothing came of the joint effort by the United States and Britain to draw up a program of international conduct that would preserve the peace were the warlike attitudes of the Fascist powers and the discrepancy between rhetoric and action that characterized the divided democracies. The British subtext in the interwar period was that the United States had chosen to sit on a moral high horse, lecturing the world about international peace, disarmament, and free markets, but did so ensconced behind the safety of two oceans and a paper wall of neutrality acts. The British prime minister, Neville Chamberlain, was later blamed by opponents of Hitler for not following up on Roosevelt's proposal to draw up standards of international conduct to preserve the world peace. Instead, Chamberlain and the appeasers decided to deal with Hitler on their own, without the participation of the United States. They were frustrated by American lectures on international conduct, suspecting that these lectures would not be backed up by military commitments.

Hitler also became convinced that he had nothing to fear from the Americans—at least not yet. Historians who have argued that Hitler paid no attention to the United States and ignored the dire warnings of his diplomats in Washington, notably Dieckhoff and Thomsen, miss the point concerning Hitler's intentions and the timing he thought they required. He knew all along that behind Britain stood the United States, and he did not want to go to war with either in the first place. But should Britain enter a European war, when would the United States be able to intervene militarily? Throughout the 1930s Hitler's America "experts," whether foreign office personnel or self-appointed pundits, reported that the people of the United States were still facing economic hardships that made them loath to get involved in the affairs of Europe. But the old-style diplomats—Dieckhoff, Weizsäcker, and Neurath—warned that the United States was potentially a grave danger to Germany. They also agreed that it would take the United States at least two years to rearm massively before it could challenge the Reich. As previously mentioned, Hitler took a jaundiced view of the German Foreign Office, which he saw as one of the last strongholds of the old conservative elites; he called them pin-striped snobs and rarely bothered to read any of their reports, except when they were specifically earmarked by his trustworthy advisors. From time to time, Hitler made reference to specific reports he received from Washington, or from unusual sources he trusted or agreed with. The same was true of Roosevelt, who frequently bypassed regular government channels, dispatching trusted friends or business contacts to foreign capitals to sound out people and find out what was really going on. These informal observers were often no better than the "experts," picking up irrelevant gossip, reporting rumors, or plainly misjudging people and events.

Czechoslovakia and Appeasement at Munich

With Austria in his pocket, Hitler had not only acquired more territory and 7 million more people, but had also gained direct access to the whole of southeastern Europe. From Vienna it was only a stone's throw to Czechoslovakia and the Balkans. His next target, in fact, was the small democratic state of Czechoslovakia, where more than 3.5 million frustrated Germans, called Sudeten Germans, had been living under Czechoslovak control since 1919. Hitler's strategy was to use the Sudeten Germans, most of whom lived in the mountainous territory between Bohemia and Silesia, as a battering ram against the fragile new Republic, just as he would later use the Slovaks to foster irreparable separatism that made the Republic ripe for German picking. Telling his military chiefs in March that he intended to smash the Czech state in the near future, he whipped up such a frenzy of war hysteria that the Western powers, headed chiefly by Great Britain, bullied the Czechs into making concessions but stopped short of creating a Sudeten state within a state. The infuriated führer was ready to strike, though some of his generals, especially Ludwig Beck, were so alarmed by the prospect of another war with the Western powers that they seriously planned to topple the dictator and try him in front of the Volksgericht (People's Court).

This did not happen for three reasons. During the Czech crisis in the summer of 1938, Hitler took another important step to protect himself from possible opposition from the traditionalists in the German army. Ostensibly to clarify the relationship between the elite guard or "defense squad" (*Schutzstaffel* or SS) and the regular *Wehrmacht*, he authorized a top-secret decree on August 17, 1938, that made the two SS *Verfügungstruppen* (Reserve Troops), hitherto subject to the regular army, independent armed forces at the disposal of the führer.[13] Also, at the time of the

Czech crisis, two regiments had grown up around Hitler's personal body guard, the *Leibstandarte SS "Adolf Hitler."* The decree of August 17, 1938, essentially turned these troops into Hitler's private army and police force, whose soldiers were told that they owed personal loyalty and "blind obedience" to the führer. During World War II these *Verfügungstruppen*, renamed the Waffen-SS, were the most feared soldiers of Nazi Germany.

The traditionalists in the army, some of whom would later become resisters, had good reasons to worry, because their control was slipping as the army became increasingly Nazified. At the time of the Czech crisis, they still might have been able to take steps to remove Hitler, but their means of control were being steadily eroded by the wily führer, who never trusted them, and by the weaknesses of the Allies. Whether the SS, including its armed regiments, the police (Gestapo, Kripo, Security Service or SD), and the brown-shirted storm troopers, could have prevented an army coup in 1938 is debatable, for that would have required a concerted and unified opposition. Only a small group of vocal resisters around Colonel General Ludwig Beck and General Erwin von Witzleben, however, were willing to take active steps in the summer of 1938. The rest were fence-sitters. All of them knew that opposition to the Nazi regime would have to be conducted against the will of the German people. Hitler was immensely popular, a second major reason why the military opposition that briefly gathered in the summer of 1938 never got off the ground.

A third and most decisive reason why Hitler was not stopped in 1938 was that the Western powers blinked and agreed to appease Hitler. The Western betrayal of Czechoslovakia is a sordid and tragic story, which justifies W. H. Auden's characterization of the 1930s as a "low and dishonest decade." The British prime minister, Neville Chamberlain, visiting the dictator in his lair at Berchtesgaden on September 15, was so impressed by Herr Hitler's seriousness over the Sudetenland that he made up his mind to pressure the Czechs to give it up. After bringing the Czechs into line, Chamberlain met Hitler again, this time at Bad Godesberg on the Rhine. Hitler told the stunned prime minister that their earlier agreement was no longer of any use because of Czech provocations. Hitler now demanded an immediate Czech withdrawal from the Sudetenland or he would send in his army to expel them. By October 1, he warned Chamberlain, he would occupy the Sudetenland. Chamberlain flew back to London, horrified by the prospect of war, and in his radio address to the British people he called on them to keep calm and work for the defense of their country. There were no Churchill-like exhortations to stand up to Hitler; instead, Chamberlain wondered aloud whether it was fair for a small nation—the reference was obviously to Czechoslovakia—to involve the whole British Empire in a war simply on its account. He answered, "If we are to fight it must be on larger issues than that."[14] The prime minister was hoping for a last-minute miracle that would avert war. This came in the form of a conciliatory message from Hitler, who gave assurances that he did not have designs on all of Czechoslovakia. He hoped that Chamberlain would continue to pursue his negotiations and bring the government in Prague to see reason at the very last hour. Hitler knew his man. Chamberlain then appealed to Mussolini for help in brokering a settlement. Il Duce was only too willing to oblige, partly because Italy was unprepared for war and partly because he did not think that Czechoslovakia was worth another world war.

What came next was the notorious Four-Power Munich Conference (September 28–29) between Germany, Italy, Britain, and France that made *appeasement* a household word.[15] For Hitler, Munich was another personal triumph and a validation of his risk-taking, aggressive foreign policy. Although Hitler received the Sudetenland, he was dissatisfied because, as he later said, he should have pushed the appeasers into making even greater concessions. German troops marched into the designated areas, annexing sixteen thousand square miles of Czech territory, including its richest industrial sites and superb fortifications. President Benes resigned in favor of Dr. Emil Hacha, a more compliant figure who further appeased the Nazis by renouncing the Czech alliance with Russia and surrendering the Teschen district to Poland and the Carpathian Ukraine to Hungary. The end of Czechoslovakia was in sight. Chamberlain and his appeasers may have breathed a sigh of relief, proclaiming peace in our time, but Hitler had clearly triumphed on all fronts: seizing the Sudetenland, excluding Russia from the European alliance system, isolating Poland, and diffusing the gathering resistance against him within the German High Command. General Jodl pointedly declared that the genius of the führer had once more triumphed, which, he said, ought to convert the "incredulous, the weak, and the doubters."[16] But Churchill described the Munich agreement as an act of abject surrender, "a disaster of the first magnitude" that had befallen Great Britain and France. He compared Hitler's method of negotiating to a series of extortions. At Berchtesgaden, Godesberg, and

Munich, he said, "one pound was demanded at the pistol's point. When it was given two pounds were demanded at the pistol's point. Finally the dictator consented to take one pound, seventeen shillings and sixpence and promises of good will for the future." He added prophetically that "you will find that in a period of time which may be measured by years, but may be measured only in months, Czechoslovakia will be engulfed in the Nazi regime."[17]

Throughout this first Czech crisis, Roosevelt's administration stood on the sidelines and watched events unfold without knowing what to do about it. On September 26, Roosevelt had sent a brief message to Hitler, Benes, and the prime ministers of Great Britain and France, but his note did not contain an offer of mediation. With an eye to the isolationists, he chose not to take sides in the dispute. This was good news to Hitler, who had not ignored Roosevelt's movements; in fact, he decided to answer the president's telegram and its "lofty intentions" about finding peaceful solutions for the future good of humanity. He reminded the president that Germany had laid down its arms in 1918 in hopes that peace would be conducted according to Woodrow Wilson's ideals. In creating the new state of Czechoslovakia, Hitler pointed out, the peacemakers willfully ignored the rights of the Sudeten Germans, making a mockery of Wilson's principles of national self-determination. Furthermore, he accused Prague of making every effort to violate the basic rights of the Sudeten Germans. Hitler claimed that 214,000 persecuted Sudeten Germans had fled across the border into Germany. If the president objectively reviewed the history of the Sudeten Germans, he would realize that the German government had been more than patient, and willing to find a peaceful solution to a problem that Germany did not create. The fault, he said, rested with Czechoslovakia rather than Germany.[18] Roosevelt sent a second appeal to Hitler on September 28, but it was not answered. The fact is that the Americans were indecisive and inactive; the spirit of appeasement was as strong on their part as it was among the English and the French. It cannot be overemphasized that they acquiesced in appeasement over the heads of the Czechs, who were not even invited to Munich—an egregious betrayal of the fragile democratic Republic. But then neither Chamberlain nor Édouard Daladier wanted to fight another world war, and certainly not over a territorially flawed state. Roosevelt's diplomats basically felt the same way. Ambassador Wilson, who had replaced Dodd in Berlin, sympathized with the Sudeten Germans and hoped that the Czechs would make concessions rather than jeopardize peace. Ambassador Joseph Kennedy was much more vocal and pro-German, favoring appeasement at almost any price, confessing, "I can't for the life of me understand why anybody would want to go to war to save the Czechs."[19] Roosevelt's ambassador to Prague, Wilbur J. Carr, had just assumed his new post, had never served abroad, and knew next to nothing about the country he was sent to.

Since there was no official or even unofficial U.S. response to appeasement, some historians have concluded that Roosevelt was on the side of the appeasers in the fall of 1938. This is misleading. The president did send a two-word telegram to Chamberlain after he learned that the British prime minister was going to attend the Munich conference: it said, "Good Man."[20] Trying to prevent war was hardly appeasement, but giving Hitler everything he wanted was. It was Chamberlain, not Roosevelt, who appeased Hitler without calling his bluff. Roosevelt had a sinking feeling that the Munich settlement had not really settled anything and that peace through fear was unlikely to endure.[21] If he knew that, why did he remain on the sidelines, limiting himself to sending appeals to the dictator? The president's small-stick approach to international relations was prompted by several causes, such as isolationism, fear of another devastating world war, the president's banking on the British and the French as his first line of defense, domestic blows to the New Deal, and so forth. Some historians have pointed to a kind of "What's the use" attitude on the part of the president in 1938—for it should be remembered that Roosevelt saw himself as a lame duck, wondering what to do after his retirement from the presidency.[22] At the time of the conference at Munich, Roosevelt was still in this indecisive mood, letting things drift until new outrages by Hitler and the Japanese later roused him to renewed efforts, sending ineffective appeals abroad and encouraging more effective military preparedness at home. Like Chamberlain and Daladier, he resigned himself to the dismemberment of Czechoslovakia.

Abandoned and betrayed, the Czechs had little choice but to let go of the Sudetenland. During this first Czech crisis, Hitler gave solemn promises that this would be the last territorial demand he would make; he even swore to God that he would fulfill this promise! He also went on record that he only wanted Germans and not Czechs, giving the false impression that he would not grab the rest of Czechoslovakia.[23] But since it had all been so easy at Munich, with the British and the French "acting like little worms" rather than real men of action, his intention to dismember the whole of Czechoslovakia was greatly strengthened. It was just a matter of timing, and of neutralizing the democracies—Britain, France, and, more remotely, the United States.

Kristallnacht

On November 7, 1938, a secretary in the German embassy in Paris, Ernst vom Rath, was fatally shot by a seventeen-year-old Polish refugee named Herschel Grynszpan, acting in response to the mistreatment of his family and seventeen thousand others by the Nazi government. In March 1938, Poland had passed a law specifying that Polish nationals who had resided outside Poland for a period of five years would be stripped of their citizenship. The law was specifically aimed at about fifty thousand Polish Jews who had been residing in Germany, and whom the Polish government did not want to return to Poland. Grynszpan's parents, who had emigrated from Poland and had lived in Hanover since 1914, automatically became stateless. The German government regarded the Polish law as a provocation designed to dump their Jews permanently in Germany. In response, the Gestapo rounded up some seventeen thousand Polish Jews and transported them to the Polish border, but since the Polish authorities refused to accept them, they were herded into camps where they lived under deplorable conditions. Young Grynszpan wanted to send a message of protest through his desperate deed.

The Nazis were quick to retaliate. On November 9, the day the Nazi leadership celebrated the anniversary of the 1923 beer hall *Putsch* (coup) in Munich, Ernst vom Rath died in Paris. News of his death was conveyed to Hitler while he was eating dinner with his "old fighters" (*alte Kämpfer*) in the Old Town Hall in Munich. The evidence indicates that Hitler authorized a proposal by Goebbels to set in motion "spontaneous demonstrations" against the Jews throughout Germany, slyly suggesting that the storm troopers "should be allowed to have a fling."[24] Hitler then playacted his typical script of fading into the background to immunize himself in case the pogrom should backfire. The result was an orchestrated nationwide pogrom later referred to as Kristallnacht (Crystal Night), after the glass shards from the shattered windows of Jewish businesses that littered the streets of Germany. The actions of party functionaries, storm troopers, and incited mobs produced widespread devastation of property and many injuries and deaths. It is estimated that 267 synagogues were burned to the ground and their contents looted or defiled. More than 7,500 businesses were vandalized, and 91 Jews were killed, while others in despair committed suicide.[25] These crimes were perpetrated openly and blatantly because they were sponsored by the government. The police were helpless because orders had been given that the führer did not want them to interfere except when German lives and property were directly involved—and he did not regard German Jews as Germans.

The American reaction to Kristallnacht was one of outrage. The German ambassador in Washington, Hans Dieckhoff, cabled Berlin and said that the public in America was incensed by the violence in Germany. Close to one thousand editorials condemning the pogrom were published in newspapers all over the United States. The American Legion and the Congress of Industrial Organizations (CIO) denounced the violence in Germany. Dorothy Thompson, the first American reporter expelled from Germany for her critical articles on the Nazi regime, made an emotional plea on behalf of Herschel Grynszpan on a nationwide CBS radio program, asking, "Who is on trial in this case?" She answered, "I say we are all on trial. I say the men in Munich are on trial, who signed a pact without one word of protection for helpless minorities. . . . The Nazi government has announced that if any Jews anywhere in the world protest at anything that is happening further oppressive measures will be taken. They are holding every Jew in Germany as a hostage."[26] Roosevelt told the press that "I myself could scarcely believe that such things could occur in a twentieth-century civilization."[27] He then recalled Ambassador Hugh Wilson from Berlin, a significant diplomatic protest that let the Nazis know that the United States condemned such anti-Jewish violence. Wilson was replaced by a chargé d'affaires, Alexander Kirk. Though diplomatic relations were not discontinued, Roosevelt showed his displeasure with Nazi mistreatments of Jews by downgrading the Berlin position to the chargé level.[28] The Germans retaliated by recalling ambassador Dieckhoff, and it looked as though diplomatic relations between the United States and Germany might be broken altogether. This did not happen, but the two sides were now steadily sliding down the slippery slope to open conflict.

The German pogrom of November 9–10 accelerated the refugee crisis that had festered during the previous four years of harassment against the Jews of Germany. It had begun with a boycott of Jewish businesses on April 1, 1933; was followed by a stream of discriminatory anti-Jewish measures, notably the Nuremberg racial laws; and culminated in the infamous pogrom of November 1938. The Nazi objective had been to make life so miserable for German Jews that they would see no future in Germany and leave the country. After November 1938 this policy of forcing emigration by harassment was greatly accelerated by an additional outrage called Aryanization. The essential intent of Aryanization was to expropriate Jewish property. Until 1938 it was euphemistically called "voluntary Aryanization," allowing Jews to transfer Jewish-owned firms to Aryan buyers at a fraction of their real market value. After Kristallnacht, the Nazis prepared the way for the complete exclusion of the Jews from the German economy. An increasing number of Jews were pauperized, while at the same time being encouraged to emigrate. But what country would take in destitute Jews? What would the United States do about the refugee crisis?

When Roosevelt became president there were severe restrictions on immigration, and throughout the 1930s Congress was in no mood to relax them. The opponents of immigration argued that immigrants would take away jobs that should go to Americans, especially at a time of widespread unemployment during the Great Depression. Most Americans agreed with this argument. Polls taken in 1938 revealed that the public was strongly opposed to increased immigration: between March and December 1938, opposition to relaxing immigration quotas rose from 75 percent to 83 percent.[29] The president was torn by conflicting impulses, alternately toying with plans of actively involving the government in Jewish rescue efforts and letting things drift by doing little, if anything at all. He also received conflicting views from his advisers. Top officials in the State Department were more concerned about Communism than Nazism; they were also anti-Semitic. Some of his ambassadors, notably William Bullitt, sent the president letters in which they expressed anti-Jewish sentiments.[30] The former ambassador to Poland, John Cudahy, played down the Jewish pogrom by stating that "the handling of the Jews by the present German government, which may be shocking and revolting, is from any realistic or logical approach a purely domestic matter and none of our concern. It is not stretching the analogy too far to say that Germany would have just as much warrant to criticize our handling of the Negro minority if a race war between blacks and whites occurred in the United States."[31]

Despite the fact that Roosevelt had attracted a number of Jews to his administration, it was only Henry Morgenthau who strongly urged the president to take decisive action against the Nazis on account of their anti-Jewish policies. In the fall of 1938, the most urgent situation that had to be confronted by Western leaders was the refugee crisis. In October 1938, a month before Kristallnacht, Roosevelt appealed to Neville Chamberlain for help in addressing the refugee problem. Since Chamberlain had negotiated with Hitler before, the president wanted the British prime minister to explain to Hitler that the German policy of racial persecution against the Jews had done more harm in undermining German-American relations that any other German policy. Chamberlain refused to relay this message to Hitler. The prime minister did not trust Roosevelt, and he did not like Jews. He attributed German persecution of the Jews to two motives: "a desire to rob the Jews of their money and a jealousy of their superior cleverness." He added, "No doubt the Jews aren't a lovable people; I don't care about them myself, but that is not sufficient to explain the Pogrom."[32]

It is interesting to note that Roosevelt was the only world leader who went on record in condemning the Nazi violence against the Jews. Yet, beyond allowing about fifteen thousand German and Austrian refugees to remain as long as possible in America on their visitor's permits, Roosevelt did nothing officially to improve the refugee crisis, nor did any other Western nation. In FDR's defense, it must be said that behind the scenes he encouraged and supported efforts to find a solution to the Jewish refugee crisis. When Britain refused to entertain the idea of using Palestine as a homeland for the Jews and, in fact, restricted immigration to Palestine, FDR asked Isaiah Bowman, president of Johns Hopkins University and a renowned geographer, to identify places in the world where Jewish refugees might be settled. Bowman and the State Department studied the issue for two years and failed to come up with a meaningful solution. Sumner Welles suggested the Baja peninsula of Mexico in exchange for settling a long-standing U.S.-Mexican oil controversy.[33] The Nazis at the same time were entertaining a Madagascar solution, but the outbreak of war and the British domination of the sea made that option unworkable. The Jewish tragedy thus continued from bad to worse. As the leader of Zionist movement, Chaim Weizmann, put it, "the world is divided into two groups of nations, those which want to expel Jews and those which do not want to receive them."[34]

Roosevelt and Appeasement

Roosevelt and his diplomats were as passive as the European appeasers in 1938. All of them let Hitler slip into the danger zone and permitted him to dictate his terms. Talk about boycotts, blockades, or economic sanctions on both sides of the ocean remained just that—empty talk. Hitler knew this and drew the obvious conclusion that he could push his territorial demands even more aggressively. In a secret address to the group commanders of the army, Hitler said that "all our actions during 1938 represent only the logical extension of the decisions which began to be realized in 1933."[35] The decisions he referred to were to rearm the nation without the permission of foreign governments; in other words, a deliberate and carefully laid plan to break the shackles of the Versailles treaty. To accomplish this task, the country had to rearm, the Rhineland had to be remilitarized, and Austria and the Sudetenland had to be brought home into the Reich. He knew that circumstances might force delays or temporary accommodations, but the final objective was never in doubt.

Hitler's address illustrates that he knew precisely where he wanted to lead his country and what methods he was willing to use to accomplish his goals. By contrast, the Western powers were indecisive and vacillating. Their broad aim, to be sure, was to avoid war, but they still did not know how far they were willing to go in appeasing the dictator. At Munich they gave Hitler the distinct impression that they would do almost anything to avoid war; he later judged their statesmen to be "small worms . . . I saw them in Munich."[36] That was, unfortunately, an accurate assessment of the mettle shown by these men—Daladier and Chamberlain and their retainers—when Hitler encountered them at Munich. But was this also true of Roosevelt and his men? Is it true, as A. J. P. Taylor opined, that the Americans later condemned the British and the French for doing what they would have done in their place?[37]

This is a clever but misleading judgment. It falsely assumes that Roosevelt was made of the same pusillanimous stuff that Chamberlain and Daladier were made of; that he, too, was as credulous of Hitler's "honorable intentions" as the European appeasers. Already in February 1938

FDR had criticized the British for being passive during the Austrian Anschluss crisis. He also condemned Britain's legal recognition of Italy's conquest of Ethiopia. Secretary of State Hull told the British ambassador that "if any important country like Great Britain suddenly abandons this principle [the nonrecognition of conquered territory] . . . the desperado nations would capitalize it as a virtual ratification of their policy of outright treaty wrecking and the seizure of land by force of arms."[38] Both FDR and Hull felt that the Europeans were making a big mistake in appeasing the dictators; they thought that appeasement weakened the democracies and incited the dictators to further aggression. The president had a very low opinion of Chamberlain, calling him a slippery fellow who could not be trusted because he belonged to those who wanted peace at any price. He also felt obliged to encourage any opposition against Hitler by the Western democracies. Privately, he doubted that the British and the French would form a solid front against the Fascist powers, and the Czech crisis confirmed his suspicion that they would sell out Czechoslovakia, afterward "washing the blood from their Judas Iscariot hands."[39]

FDR was little more than an interested observer as the Czech crisis unfolded and then culminated in appeasement at Munich. Unlike Chamberlain, however, he did not believe that the Munich agreement meant "peace in our time." That year, 1938, had been a bad one for the president: the downturn in the economy—"depression within the depression" that occurred in 1937—was still causing widespread suffering. Congress had turned down his "court-packing scheme," a plan that had caused vocal opposition among the American people, including the charge that the president had dictatorial intentions. Furthermore, isolationism was as powerful as ever, forcing the president to tread very carefully before committing his country to a more interventionist position. Given these obstacles, it should not be surprising that in 1938, Roosevelt felt that it was up to the European democracies to deal with the aggressive Germans and Italians. Deep down, he knew that sooner or later Europe would blow up and then America would have to "pick up the pieces of European civilization and help them to save what remains of the wreck—not a cheerful prospect."[40] History proved that Roosevelt was right; and that A. J. P. Taylor was wrong when he implied that the American president would have acted just like the appeasers if he had been in their place.

Did Hitler Have a Fifth Column in America?

In 1936 one of Franco's generals told Republicans defending Madrid that, besides the four columns outside the capital, he had a fifth one inside waiting to rise and fight for him. The term *fifth columnists*, referring to internal subversives who were plotting to undermine the fighting troops behind the lines or on the home front, came into wide circulation by the late 1930s. German propagandists often planted rumors that their cause was being supported by friendly forces in the midst of their enemies. In subverting the territorial integrity of certain European countries, the Nazis always found willing allies among right-wing sympathizers who helped pave the way for eventual German conquest and occupation. They also relied on German minorities, the *Volksdeutsche* (German ethnics) who lived in various countries of eastern and southeastern Europe. Nazi propagandists had high hopes that Germans in the United States and Latin America could also be enlisted in furthering the cause of the Third Reich. Between 1938 and 1942, rumors were rife in the United States that Nazi fifth columnists were active in America, poised to strike at the heart of the nation's democracy. Mass media stories caused a veritable panic among the general public. Americans were inundated by a flood of newspaper articles, magazine stories, novels, comic books, and films that suggested that Nazi spies were on the loose. The FBI under J. Edgar Hoover kept a careful watch on Nazi activities, which, contrary to widespread belief, were small scale and ineffective. Public fears rose proportionately with Hitler's aggression in Europe, and the panicked atmosphere that was incited or ballyhooed by mass media, especially in the wake of a celebrated espionage trial in 1938 in New York. Between 1933 and 1938, the FBI received an average of 35 reports per year of alleged espionage activities; in 1938 that figure went up to 250, in 1939 it was up to 1,615, and in May 1940 it reached 2,871.[41]

By that time American popular culture, a force never to be underestimated, was fully active in the anti-Nazi campaign. Hollywood had gone on the warpath with a number of chilling spy movies, the most overwrought of which was *Confessions of a Nazi Spy* in 1939. Famous actors lent credibility to public perceptions that there were fifth columnists in America. Hollywood actors who were on the trail of Nazi spies included Robert Young, Errol Flynn, Humphrey Bogart, Dana Andrews, Alan Ladd, Cary Grant, and Ronald Reagan. In dozens of B-movies, such American favorites as

Charlie Chan, Sherlock Holmes, Ellery Queen, the Invisible Man, Roy Rogers, and Tarzan did battle with Nazis. Comic book heroes also came to the aid of Uncle Sam: Batman, the Green Hornet, Spy Smasher, Wonder Woman, Superman, and Captain America. In 1942 alone, Hollywood produced more than seventy films dealing with fifth columnists.[42]

Until 1938 Americans were only vaguely aware of the existence of certain Nazi groups, notably the German-American Bund; they knew little about any of them and did not seem to be overly concerned. Then came a sensational espionage trial that changed everything. This was the Rumrich case, centered in New York City.[43] Guenther Gustav Rumrich, a U.S. citizen of German extraction, was a freelance agent for the German *Abwehr* (Secret Service) who seems to have been motivated to work for the Germans primarily for monetary reasons and the thrills involved in leading a dangerous double life. He had a shadowy background, having gone AWOL twice as an enlisted man in the United States Army. After scrutinizing Rumrich, making sure that he was not a double agent, the Germans used him for a variety of minor projects, each time raising their demands for more significant contributions. Rumrich's astounding incompetence eventually brought down the whole network. For all his boasting, Rumrich managed to obtain little more than a few bits of insignificant information. His biggest project, which he bungled, involved getting blueprints of two new aircraft carriers—the *Yorktown* and the *Lexington*.

The trial that followed Rumrich's arrest in October 1938 caused a sensation in the United States. Rumrich was sentenced to two years in prison while some of his associates got sentences ranging from two to four years. The case also drew J. Edgar Hoover into the limelight. Hoover was outraged that one of his agents, who had arrested Rumrich, had profited from the affair by telling his story to the newspapers. Such public revelations violated the FBI's code that prohibited agents from breaking the agency's oath of secrecy and exposing it to unfavorable publicity. The FBI agent, Leon Turrou, however, resented Hoover's interference in the matter, saying that he was "just sore because he didn't get to write the stuff."[44] Turrou insisted on his First Amendment rights, even ignoring President Roosevelt's stern public rebuke that the publication of these revelations not only jeopardized the impending federal trial against Rumrich but also showed a lack of patriotism and ethics. The *New York Post* agreed to postpone the Turrou articles until after the trial was completed. Following the trial, the articles were published in syndicated form and appeared in newspapers all over the United States. Random House published a book titled *The Nazi Conspiracy in America*, which became a bestseller. Nor was that the end of it. Hollywood took up the Rumrich story, fictionalized part of it, and released it under the provocative title *Confessions of a Nazi Spy*, starring Edward G. Robinson in the role of Turrou. In what one historian has called "wildly irresponsible promotional campaigns,"[45] theater owners tried to alarm the American people that there was a dangerous fifth column in America, that the German-American Bund represented the head of this snake, and that if Americans did not wake up to the Nazi menace the country might fall into Hitler's hands.

The Rumrich case was one of several Nazi espionage incidents that evoked mass hysteria in America, out of proportion to its actual threat. The Nazis definitely gave the Americans a bad case of the jitters, though some people at the time strongly felt that the country needed a wake-up call, even if the threat to the security of the United States was much exaggerated. Hoover was not pleased by all this publicity, for he knew that his agency had the situation well under control. The film *Confessions of a Nazi Spy*, though dedicated to the great job the FBI was doing, did not impress the FBI director, who said that Warner Brothers had indulged in "all kinds of ballyhoo and publicity" and created "a good deal of public hysteria about spies which is a bad thing because the spy situation is not one tenth as bad as the yellow journals present."[46]

What was the reality behind the American fears of Nazi fifth columnists that were triggered by the Rumrich case? What Nazi groups were active in America, and what did Hitler think of their operations? The Nazi cause in America dates back to the mid-1920s when Lüdecke made contact with Nazi sympathizers, most of whom were recruited from groups of recent German immigrants. After Hitler became chancellor he decided to avoid open conflict with the United States and ordered all Nazi cells in America dissolved. This did not mean that Hitler discouraged German Americans from organizing associations based on National Socialist principles. What he discouraged was subversive activities in America by German nationals. In May 1933 the leader of the former Detroit local of the Nazi Party, Heinz Spanknöbel, who had consulted with prominent Nazi leaders, started a new organization called Friends of the New Germany, or Bund der Freunde des neuen Deutschlands. This organization was to become a noisy and grandstanding cheering section for Hitler in America, later referred to simply as the Bund by Americans.[47]

In response to American concerns about German propaganda in the United States, the German government tried to curtail activities that could be construed as subversive. The Nazi organization responsible for all overseas activities involving German nationals was the Auslandsorganisation (Foreign Affairs Committee), headed by Ernst Wilhelm Bohle, a protégé of Rudolf Hess, the führer's deputy. Bohle's organization was an aggressive arm of the party; its chief mission was to promote the cause of National Socialism among German communities abroad. As was the rule in Nazi Germany, the Auslandsorganisation was often at odds with competing organizations; its chief rival was the German Foreign Office, which frequently complained about the high-handed methods used by Bohle's agents. Thus, while the Foreign Office tried to promote better working relations with the United States, Bohle's zealous agents often caused serious friction with foreign governments. There were other Nazi groups laboring in the same vineyard. Hanfstaengl's office, Amt Auslandspresse (Chief Foreign Press Office), tried to encourage better relations with the United States. Another interloper was Rosenberg's Aussenpolitisches Amt (Foreign Political Office), originally intended as a rival to the Foreign Office. Until 1938 there was also Joachim Ribbentrop's Dienststelle Ribbentrop (Service Post Ribbentrop), which comprised about three hundred well-connected individuals who served as agents for Ribbentrop abroad, informing him about important developments in various countries. Although Ribbentrop used this post as a catapult to a higher position in the Foreign Office, he also used the service post's agents to provide him with information that would impress the führer. If these competing forces were not enough to create overlapping functions and organizational confusion, Joseph Goebbels and his propaganda ministry also tried to control propaganda activities outside Germany. Goebbels's intrusion into matters of foreign policy caused an ugly knockdown fight with Ribbentrop that not even Hitler could resolve, so that both men continued to meddle in propaganda activities outside Germany.

Foreign governments in America and elsewhere worked through officially sanctioned groups or organizations to present their political positions. At the same time, they also used front organizations to disseminate propaganda. In the 1930s the German government officially sponsored and funded two major organizations: the German Library of Information and the German Railroads Information Office, both located in New York City. The German Library of Information had been established in 1936 to promote a better understanding of life under National Socialism. Working under the auspices of the German consulate in New York City, it published a wide variety of pamphlets, articles, and books, most of them in English. The director of the German Library of Information, Heinz Beller, coordinated its operations with the Nazi Party's Amt Auslandspresse, headed until 1937 by Hanfstaengl, and the German Tourist Information Bureau. The German Railroads Information Bureau provided attractive information about travel opportunities in Germany, sending out "candy-coated" brochures depicting Germany as a romantic tourist destination. This material was sent throughout America to hundreds of travel agencies.

Besides these overt organizations there were also front organizations that disguised their pro-Nazi stance under cover of innocuous names, charitable causes, scholarly research, or patriotic clubs. As previously mentioned, some 6 million Germans had immigrated to America in the nineteenth century, and they had brought with them German customs and beliefs. Germans had endowed kindergartens and schools, sponsored choral groups, established German newspapers, opened German restaurants, built breweries, and generally disseminated information about German customs throughout America.

World War I had been a great shock to German communities throughout America, and the wave of Germanophobia that swept over America had seriously undermined the generally benign image Americans had formed of German life and culture. Sensational stories of Nazi brutality in American newspapers did not help in restoring prewar perceptions. Quite the contrary, Hitler struck most Americans as a hysterical rabble-rouser; to some he seemed a comic figure that did not have to be taken seriously. Many believed erroneously, even long after the war, that he had once been a "paper hanger" in Vienna, that he was given to uncontrollable rages that made him chew on carpets, that he was a stooge for Gustav Krupp von Bohlen und Holbach and other industrialists, or—in Dorothy Thompson's absurd statement—that he was the "prototype of the little man." In short, many Americans in the 1930s were misinformed about Hitler, but the same was true of the Germans; they too were misinformed, tragically so because they had only one channel of information, Nazi propaganda.

Americans were exposed to a lot more information, except that such information was often misleading and unreliable.

Two Nazi front organizations, exposed by congressional investigators in 1940, were the Transocean News Service and the American Fellowship Forum. The Transocean News Service was the German version of the Associated Press; it was allegedly an objective news-gathering organization but in fact had been coordinated by the Nazis in 1933. Once indicted as a front group, it was ordered to leave the country. The American Fellowship Forum, headed by a former German instructor at Columbia University, Dr. Frederic Auhagen, tried to encourage isolationism in America, disguising itself as a peace-loving forum through its magazine, *Today's Challenge*, which was followed, after its failure, by a more modest newsletter, *Forum's Observer*.

The most prominent Nazi propagandist in America was George Sylvester Viereck, who was well known to American officials because he had been an agent of the kaiser during World War I. Viereck was a convinced Germanophile who seemed to believe that his father had been the kaiser's illegitimate child. He was actually a very gifted poet who saw himself on a mission to preserve and expand German language and culture in the United States. Following World War I, he became convinced that all too many German Americans wanted to disavow their Germanism (Deutschtum) and assimilate as rapidly as possible. These concerns were real enough, because Germans were great assimilators, all the more so after a devastating war that had made the very name Deutschland suspect in America. To recoup the honor of the fatherland, Viereck and like-minded believers founded the German-American Citizens League in 1924, but it failed to make much of an impression, especially among its intended audience of German Americans. Hitler's rise to power in Germany reinvigorated Viereck's desire to reconcile Germans and Americans, but the way he went about it hardly furthered his cause. In 1933, after visiting Germany and consulting with Nazi officials, Viereck became a paid agent of the Nazis who worked closely with the German embassy in Washington.[48] He had passed from propagandist to traitor, but before being caught, tried, and convicted of espionage activities, Viereck used his political connections and German money to try to change the outcome of the 1940 campaign. Working with Thomsen, Viereck hatched a plot to influence the Democratic Convention of 1940 and to manipulate the November election in favor of Roosevelt's opponent. The plot involved using the labor leader John L. Lewis, who had come to despise Roosevelt, as a wedge between the president and his labor constituency. As described in the next chapter, Hermann Goering agreed to provide as much money as necessary to unseat Roosevelt. Goering discussed this plan with Hitler and got his consent to go ahead. In the end, Lewis overestimated his influence with the rank and file of American labor, and all the Nazi machinations made no difference to the outcome in November 1940.

The end result of these competing and uncoordinated efforts was to weaken the cause of National Socialism abroad. In this respect the Nazi Party was quite inferior to the Communist Party and its international web of cells and agents. The Nazi web in America was a feeble one by comparison. It had a führer, but a weak and corrupt one. His name was Fritz Kuhn. In 1936, after yet another change in name, German American citizens who had been vetted by the Friends of the New Germany reestablished the old organization under the new name of the Amerika Deutscher Bund, or German-American Bund, headed by Kuhn, a man who strutted around like Hitler, aping the führer's style and mannerisms. Kuhn was born in Munich in 1896 and served as a lieutenant in the German army. Following the war he joined the Free Corps unit commanded by General Ritter von Epp, one of Hitler's early followers in Bavaria. In 1921 he studied chemical engineering at the University of Munich, but lack of opportunities in the Depression-ridden postwar period compelled him to emigrate, first to Mexico and then to America, where he became a naturalized citizen in 1934. Kuhn was a humorless man with narrow intellectual views that were shaped by the military and nationalistic circles he had known in Germany. He did have excellent organizational talents, but his morality was that of an opportunistic bully with venal predilections.

Kuhn wanted the American branch of the Nazi Party to be a duplicate of its German counterpart. It did not seem to occur to him that the majority of the American people would not accept the idea of a white racial party based on totalitarian principles. Many of his followers were equally oblivious to American public opinion. Bundists made no secret of their German loyalties, though they pretended that their allegiance to their former fatherland was not incompatible with loyalty to their new homeland. Their raucous behavior and unabashed display of Nazi regalia did not endear them to the American public. Every Bundist meeting began with a recitation of the motto "To a free gentile-ruled United States and to our fighting movement of awakened Aryan Americans, a threefold rousing Free America! Free America! Free America!"[49] The Bundists also encouraged young people to join the movement, establishing several youth camps in which they indoctrinated young men and women in Nazi ideology. The most important of these camps were Camp Siegfried on Long Island and Camp Nordland near Andover, New Jersey. In St. Louis, which had a larger German population, the Bundists tried to organize German language courses through the public schools, but when this came to the attention of the public, the project was rejected before it could be put into operation.

The St. Louis incident revealed that whenever the American public got wind of such Nazi activities, the result was outrage, followed by demands to have them investigated and stopped. Kuhn and his Bundists, however, seemed to believe that they could convert enough white Americans to return their country to its Nordic roots. Kuhn set up several newspapers in major cities, the most important being the *Deutscher Weckruf und Beobachter* (the *German Wake-up Call and Observer*) in New York. As membership rose and the Bundists attracted more publicity, Kuhn took on all the trappings of an American führer, surrounding himself with a personal entourage of storm troopers and living beyond his means. His fondest dream was to be accepted by Hitler. In 1936 he visited Germany with a contingent of his personal followers and received a short audience with Hitler, which he milked for all it was worth upon his return to America. Photos showing him with Hitler were supposed to prove that Hitler had recognized him as the genuine American führer. He misread Hitler badly. The dictator was not impressed by Kuhn, and the warnings he received from Wiedemann and the Foreign Office that the Bundists were highly unpopular in America convinced him to disassociate his government from the German-American Bund. Ambassador Dieckhoff in Washington had warned the Foreign Office in Berlin that most Americans looked upon the Bund as a Nazi Trojan horse, despite the fact that total membership in the Bund was probably less than 6,000. Dieckhoff calculated that in Chicago, for example, there were 700,000 people of German descent. Of these 700,000, he added, 40,000 were members of clubs that had a definite German character. Only 450 German Americans in Chicago, however, were active in the German-American Bund and stood up for the Nazi cause. These figures, Dieckhoff believed, spoke for themselves. Given that perhaps 450 out of 700,000 German Americans actively promoted Nazism in the Chicago area, a fairly representative region that had a significant German population, the conclusion had to be drawn that "any attempt to urge or force any pro-German political activity on the German Americans would not lead to unification; on the contrary, it would rather intensify the existing differences."[50]

Dieckhoff's assessment came after another protest from Washington about German subversive activities in America. Already in 1935 the German government had agreed to sever official contact with pro-Nazi organizations in America. If such groups continued to operate, it would be clear that they were homegrown American rather than covertly sponsored German organizations. Fritz Kuhn's aggressive activities sorely tested this informal agreement. Kuhn wanted German financial support and recognition, one of the reasons he went to Germany in 1936.

Hitler appeared to have been somewhat torn because, while on the one hand he supported efforts to disseminate Nazi racial ideas in America, on the other hand he also realized that public opinion in America, undoubtedly influenced by Jews, could turn out to be very harmful to Germany. When Wiedemann went to America in 1937, he met with Bundists in Chicago and listened to their concerns. Several months later, Kuhn went to Germany again to try to persuade the Germans to rescind the ban of March 1938 that prohibited German citizens from joining the Bund and severed all connections with the Bund by German agencies. Kuhn made no headway with German authorities, and when he met Wiedemann to get a personal interview with Hitler, Wiedemann put him off. In his memoirs Wiedemann wrote that he told Hitler not to receive Kuhn.[51] Hitler followed Wiedemann's advice, probably because he had never expected much from the German-American Bund or from any overseas ethnic German activities. Hitler publicly denied that the German government had anything to do with the Bund and promised "to throw any official into the North Sea who sent Nazi propaganda to the United States."

This stance, of course, was misleading. Nazi propaganda was sent in large quantities to German front groups in America, though Hitler's order to leave the Bund to its own devices was largely obeyed. As far as the American public was concerned, however, Bundists were still seen as being in cahoots with the Nazis after the ban. On February 20, 1939, the Bund shocked Americans by holding a monster rally at Madison Square

Garden, ostensibly to honor George Washington, whose birthday fell on that day. The image of thousands of Bundists in uniform, wearing swastika emblems, was an unnerving spectacle. Kuhn, standing in front of a thirty-foot portrait of George Washington, boasted that the Bund would soon have 1 million followers. Fistfights broke out among hecklers and Bundist storm troopers. Mayor LaGuardia's policemen had their hands full keeping order. Although twenty-two thousand people showed up for the rally, which looked like a Nuremberg party rally in miniature, not all of them were actually Bundists.

From the point of view of German-American relations, the Madison Square Garden rally was a public relations disaster. The German consul general reported to his superior in Berlin that the Bundists had managed to perform a disservice to the Reich, recommending that some of Kuhn's followers be encouraged to go back to Germany.[52] As it turned out, the Madison Square rally was the last hurrah of the Bund and of Kuhn personally. New York district attorney Thomas Dewey had Kuhn arrested on May 26, 1939, successfully prosecuting him on embezzlement charges. The Bund was also investigated by the FBI and the Dickstein committee; in the words of one historian, it was harassed out of existence by a number of repressive measures. On December 8, 1941, the Bund was dissolved and its camps were closed.

From the available evidence, it appears that Hitler did not take much of an interest in the activities of ethnic Germans outside Europe. He delegated responsibility for such matters to a variety of competing agencies and party functionaries. Among those competing agencies, two opposing views about what should be done in America emerged by late 1933. One party, which consisted of men like Hess and his protégé Bohle in the Auslandsorganisation, favored the establishment of a unified German bloc that would express its pro-Nazi ideas through an American Nazi Party like the Bund. The other party, led by propaganda chief Joseph Goebbels, preferred a more indirect, even camouflaged, approach that focused on a well-coordinated propaganda campaign aimed at German American organizations.[53] Goebbels believed that an aggressive political approach by a small and disorganized group of ethnic outsiders, lacking support from major American institutions, was not only doomed to failure, but also would discredit the cause of National Socialism and that of Hitler himself. Although we do not have direct evidence, there is every reason to believe that Hitler agreed with Goebbels's assessment, as his subsequent actions confirmed.

In the fall of 1934, Hitler met with Theodore Hoffmann, president of the Steuben Society of America, who told him that the Bund was undermining German-American relations through its un-American activities. Hoffmann reported that German officials, notably Hans Borchers, the consul general for New York, had participated in a Bund-sponsored Germany Day. Hitler responded cautiously by assuring Hoffmann that Germany had no intention of controlling the Bund, and that he thought he had made it clear that German nationals, especially members of the diplomatic corps, were under orders to refrain from involvement in the Bund. He followed this up by sending a memorandum to Rudolf Hess, asking whether Hoffmann's complaints had any validity. Bohle replied to the memorandum by discounting the importance of Hoffmann's complaints, saying that the Steuben Society resented the growing influence of the Bund because it weakened its own standing with German Americans. The Auslandsorganisation, Bohle told Hitler, had no connection to the Bund. This was a lie, but it temporarily delayed Hitler's further inquiries into the matter.

Hitler was not privy to the convoluted struggles that were unfolding in the United States among a host of contending forces. The German diplomatic corps in America, hoping to improve German-American relations, was alarmed by the antics of the Bundists and tried to disassociate itself from their activities. In the meantime, the American public was becoming highly agitated by mass media stories about the presence of Nazi rabble-rousers. Undeterred by these developments, the German government increased its propaganda campaign in the United States on the grounds that the American public needed to be "enlightened" by the truth, namely that the new Germany posed no threat to the interests of the United States. This campaign of enlightenment was a dismal failure, due in large part to the antics of Kuhn. When Kuhn went to Berlin in August 1936, Hitler made a great mistake in receiving him. As previously mentioned, Kuhn twisted the brief meeting he had with Hitler into a seal of approval for his leadership over German Americans. The meeting, however, was merely a friendly exchange of pleasantries. Hitler promised nothing, giving Kuhn a pat on the back and telling him to go back to America and "continue the fight."[54] He later admitted to Dieckhoff that he had made a mistake, a regrettable one in light of the fact that it came at the time of the Olympic Games, when he was photographed with all sorts of people. Hitler never intended the Bund to represent the interests of Germany abroad; in fact, he did not want them to speak for the Nazi Party either, as Kuhn subsequently realized. When the Bund briefly revitalized itself after interminable party dissensions, Berlin was taken by surprise and hoped that with further neglect and American investigations of its activities the Bund would collapse. Ambassador Dieckhoff wrote to a colleague in November 1937 that "nothing has resulted in so much hostility toward us in the last few months as the stupid and noisy activities of a handful of German-Americans."[55] As previously mentioned, in February 1938, at the time of the Austrian crisis, Kuhn went to Germany again to salvage what he could from the deterioration of his organization. He got the cold shoulder, only talking briefly to Wiedemann, who told him that he could not help him. The führer's decision that German nationals must withdraw from the Bund was final. When Kuhn replied that this was tantamount to the destruction of the Bund, Wiedemann reminded him that the Bund had contributed to the growing rift between Berlin and Washington.

What Wiedemann increasingly suspected was that Hitler placed little hope in sowing the seeds of National Socialism across the ocean. Hitler later admitted that "National Socialist doctrine, as I always proclaimed, is not for export. It was conceived for the German people."[56] Hitler was never a proponent of the missionary idea, as Roosevelt was. Hitler was a conqueror, whose aim was to displace whole races and exploit their resources for the benefit of the Reich. Fifth columnists were useful to the Reich because they could subvert their countries and make them ripe for German conquest. Even when Hitler received support from Fascist groups in other countries, he never included them on a coequal basis in the Greater German Reich; their role was to be subservient helpers, never equal partners. While for a short time he entertained the belief that German Americans were Aryan blood brothers, Hitler quickly persuaded himself that the multiracial nature of American society had degraded the fiber of transplanted Germans. America was a seductive place, deforming racially pure newcomers in a way that no other society in the world was able to do. "Transplant a German to Kiev," he said, "and he remains a perfect German. But transplant him to Miami and you make a degenerate of him—in other words, an American."[57]

CHAPTER 4

Hitler's War against the West: 1939—1941

The Road to War

Adolf Hitler opened the year 1939 with a promise and a threat aimed at the Western democracies and the Jews who supposedly dominated them. On January 30, in a speech to the Reichstag, Hitler complained about self-righteous democratic leaders who stuck their noses into the affairs of sovereign nations and tried to impose their form of government on them. He referred specifically to Churchill, Eden, Cooper, and Ickes, calling them "apostles of war" (*Kriegsapostel*).[1] He pointed to an orchestrated, worldwide attack on the Third Reich, claiming that it was inspired by Jewish leaders. These Jewish opponents of the Third Reich had allegedly laughed at the National Socialist movement and at him from the beginning; they apparently regarded his movement as a joke. But now their "resounding laughter" (*schallendes Gelächter*), he wagered, must be stuck in their craw. Then, wagging his finger, Hitler delivered a public threat to the Jews: "Today I shall be a prophet again. If international finance Jewry should once more plunge the world into a world war, then the result will not be the bolshevization of the world and thus the victory of Jewry, but the destruction of the Jewish race in Europe."[2]

This remark, which has been much quoted, and rightly so, was Hitler's angry reaction to what he perceived to be a hate campaign launched by Jewish leaders in America and Europe. His reference to "laughing" Jews is particularly interesting. Why did Hitler believe that Jews were laughing at him? Was it merely a rhetorical device on his part to inflame his Nazi audience, for what is worse than thinking of your enemies laughing at everything you hold dear? Or was it a personal fear that the Jews might be smart enough to manipulate the Western powers to stop him from achieving his goals? Whatever it was, Hitler had convinced himself that the Jews were secretly mocking him, and he had to shut them up so that they would never laugh again. For all he knew, Roosevelt might be a Jew himself, as he suggested to Bötticher shortly before he delivered his Reichstag speech. Despite his suspicions that the United States was under the control of Jewish financial interests and that Roosevelt himself might be Jewish, Hitler still tried to convince Americans that Germany was not a threat to the freedom and independence of the United States. In his Reichstag speech he said that the anti-German hate campaign in the American press, being instigated by the Jewish-controlled U.S. mass media, was not shared by the public at large. Average Americans, he believed, did not harbor hateful feelings against Germany. They wanted peace and friendship.[3] As he told the members of the Reichstag,

> Our relationship with the North American Union is straining under a campaign of denunciation, which under the pretense that Germany threatens American independence or freedom, seeks in the service of transparent political and financial interests to malign the whole continent against the European states ruled by the people. All of us, however, do not believe that such attempts are identical to the will of the American citizens, who despite the Jewish capitalist press, radio, and film propaganda, cannot help doubting that there is a word of truth in these [anti-German] assertions. Germany wishes to live in peace and friendship with America. We decline to meddle in domestic American affairs and equally expect America to refrain from meddling in German affairs. Germany is a sovereign and great Reich and does not have to submit itself to scrutiny of American politicians.[4]

Roosevelt was not fooled by Hitler's rhetoric. By late December 1938, Roosevelt seems to have made up his mind that something had to be done to stop Hitler. He encouraged efforts to revise the Neutrality Act of 1937, repealing the arms embargo provision and allowing democratic nations to purchase weapons on a cash-and-carry basis. In his January 4, 1939, annual message to Congress, he made reference to the fact that the forces of aggression were loose in the world, hinting that there are "many methods short of war, but stronger and more effective than mere words, of bringing home to aggressor governments the aggregate sentiments of our own people."[5] Some of the methods Roosevelt hinted at were diplomatic. Using trusted diplomatic channels, FDR sent out feelers to anti-German statesmen that the United States would provide support if they opposed Hitler. The activities of several of these diplomats, Joseph Kennedy in London, Anthony Biddle in Warsaw, and William Bullitt in Paris, were carefully monitored by the Foreign Office in Berlin, and for good reason. Kennedy was an isolationist, but he was also a powerful man with many contacts in the business world. Both Biddle and Bullitt were determined opponents of Hitler who thought, just as Roosevelt did, that Hitler had to be stopped. When the Germans occupied Warsaw in October 1939, they found documents in the Ministry of Foreign Affairs. On March 28, 1940, the German Foreign Office released what it hoped would be a bombshell: sixteen Polish documents that purportedly implicated the three American ambassadors—Kennedy, Biddle, and Bullitt—in a Roosevelt conspiracy to draw Germany into a war. Several of these documents were memoranda written by Count Jetzy Potocki, the Polish ambassador to Washington, who informed his government that the United States would support Poland in case of war with Germany. Bullitt had told him in November 1938 that he foresaw the coming of another war, and that the United States, Britain, and France had to rearm massively and quickly to oppose Hitler.[6] Bullitt did not say that the United States would directly provoke war but that it would enter the war if Britain and France were drawn in.

Several questions must be raised about these documents and what they supposedly reveal. The Germans had high hopes that the revelations contained in these documents would so tarnish Roosevelt's presidency that either he would be impeached or he would be unelectable for a third term in the fall of 1940. Goebbels was convinced that the German white paper revealing these documents would actually prevent Roosevelt's reelection in 1940. He told German newspaper editors to be subtle in their campaign, letting the captured documents speak for themselves.[7] Goebbels misread public opinion in America. The majority of the American people simply did not believe a word the German government said, even if it happened to be the truth. The Germans published a selection that would prove their case—namely, that American diplomats were encouraging the Poles to resist German peace efforts. The German white paper was a display of sixteen carefully selected documents that did not prove more than a strong commitment to Poland by the Western democracies. In a note to the American edition (published by Howell and Soskin in 1940), mention was made of other "voluminous dossiers," of which only two more issues were published.[8] The American translation of the book, with a foreword by the isolationist historian C. Hartley Gratton, changed few minds, though voices were raised in Congress about the authenticity of the documents.[9] Assuming that Bullitt, a close friend of FDR, spoke for the president, he said nothing to Potocki that could be construed as conspiratorial. Bullitt was a dapper, flamboyant patrician who spoke his mind freely, perhaps sometimes too freely. He had been in close contact with FDR, and his remarks to Potocki accurately reflect the president's growing conviction that Hitler had to be stopped. It is in this sense that the white paper documents are one of several indicators that Roosevelt was changing course toward an active foreign policy that was bound to lead, at some time, to American intervention in case of war with Germany. The president had to tread very carefully because isolationism was still running strong in the United States. The White House denounced the documents as sheer propaganda, "to be taken not with one or two, but with three grains of salt."[10]

On the day after Hitler's speech to the Reichstag, Roosevelt met with the members of the Senate Military Affairs Committee and gave them a comprehensive view of Hitler's threat not only to Europe but to America as well. He warned the participants that, starting in 1936, the aggressive powers of Japan, Italy, and Germany had begun to coalesce into what could become a deadly force against democracy. The United States had to strengthen its lines of defense against them. In the Pacific, America's first line of defense was to secure key islands in order to prevent the Japanese from dominating the entire Pacific Ocean. In the Atlantic, the key was to strengthen the democracies, chiefly Britain and France, America's two great allies in World War I. Roosevelt believed that Hitler was clearly the deadliest threat because he was a megalomaniac. He called him a "wild man . . . We would call him a 'nut.'"[11] One senator came away from this meeting and leaked a story that FDR had said that America's first line of defense was on the Rhine, which the president probably meant but did not say in those exact words. The leak caused a howl of protest from the isolationists and irked the president to no end. He denounced the leak as a "deliberate lie," adding that "some boob got that off."[12]

On March 14, 1939, Slovakia declared its independence, which left a truncated rump of what used to be the state of Czechoslovakia. Hitler had successfully exploited the separatist tendencies in Czechoslovakia by playing the Slovaks against the Czechs. In a desperate effort to salvage the integrity of the Czechoslovak state, Dr. Hacha and his foreign minister, František Chvalkovski, went to Berlin to prevent the separation of Slovakia. Hitler had no intention of saving Czechoslovakia, forcing Hacha into signing a document that placed the fate of Czechoslovakia into German hands. The document Hacha signed stated that, in order to restore law and order in Czechoslovakia, the Czech people would place themselves under the protection of the German Reich; they would then be "guaranteed an autonomous development of their ethnic life as suited to their character."[13] Hitler was beside himself with excitement over his bloodless triumph, bursting into his secretaries' room, inviting them to kiss him, exclaiming, "Children this is the greatest day of my life. I shall go down in history as the greatest German."[14] If he had died at that time his boast might have turned out to be true.

After Dr. Hacha signed over his country to Hitler, the German army marched into what remained of Czechoslovakia and Hitler established Bohemia and Moravia as a German protectorate, or vassal state. As to Ruthenia, he eventually allowed the Hungarians to take it over. He then had himself chauffeured into Prague to survey his new possession from the Hradschin castle above the Moldau River. Once more, Hitler had outwitted his opponents, and he had done it so rapidly that friends and foes alike could hardly keep up with the tempo he set. At the same time, he had crossed the line of his credibility, even with some of the appeasers. Czechs were not Germans, and swallowing up a foreign state was not national self-determination.

FDR sent an urgent message to Hitler on April 15 asking the German leader whether he would provide a guarantee that he would not attack some thirty-one independent nations listed by him. He sent the same message to Mussolini. On April 28, Hitler marched into the Reichstag and gave his reply to FDR. It was a brilliant demagogic performance. Hitler depicted himself as a humble servant of the people who had risen from an obscure soldier in World War I to a leader of his people. His only desire was to free his people from the humiliating terms of the Versailles treaty. After an hour and a half of justifications of his policies, side-stepping his recent dismemberment of Czechoslovakia, Hitler turned to answer FDR's urgent message. The tone of his speech now shifted to sarcasm. Making reference to Wilson's fourteen points, he trumped them by offering twenty-one points of his own. In the years between 1919 and 1938, he said, fourteen wars and twenty-six bloody interventions had occurred throughout the world. Germany was not involved in any of them. America, conversely, had conducted six military interventions during this period. These interventions, he charged, were conducted in an atmosphere of public hysteria and journalistic sensationalism. The American people, Hitler said, had been led to believe the most outlandish rumors, including the story that aliens from other planets had landed on earth—a clever reference to Orson Welles's notorious radio broadcast in which Martians had allegedly landed on earth, setting off a nationwide panic.[15]

Hitler said that he knew of no nation that felt itself threatened by Germany. As for putting one's trust in the effectiveness of international conferences, Hitler reminded the president that the United States, despite its advocacy of a new League of Nations, had neither joined that organization nor ratified the peace treaty. By leaving the League he had merely followed America's example. The American president, Hitler insinuated, was apparently so naive as to assume that nations could have their differences adjudicated by some international body acting as an impartial court. How does Herr Roosevelt conceive of such a tribunal and by what rules does it operate? Who shall serve as a judge, and to which higher authority is such a judge responsible? As to the president's proposal that nations should openly declare their government's short- and long-term objectives, Hitler reminded Roosevelt that he had been the most forthright spokesman of German intentions. He observed the president's temerity in expecting a German leader to provide him with an accounting of his current policies. He could just as well turn the tables on the president and ask him what foreign policy goals America planned to pursue and on what foundation it prepared to anchor them. He would, of course, never make such unreasonable demands, and he fully expected the president to regard such an imputation as being tactless.[16]

In an attempt to discover what nation could possibly feel threatened by

Germany, Hitler said, he had contacted the countries listed by Roosevelt only to find out that none of them felt threatened. Some of them, like Syria, could not answer because they were currently deprived of their freedom by freedom-loving democracies. That Ireland was on the list was surely a historical error, for Britain, not Germany, was depriving the Irish of their freedom. The same was true of Palestine, which was currently under British occupation.

Hitler said that he appreciated Roosevelt's concern for world peace, but he wondered what motivated such concerns. Perhaps it was the sheer territorial size and immense riches of the United States that allowed its leaders to take on the burdens of the world and somehow feel responsible for the fate of all the peoples of the world. "Herr President Roosevelt," Hitler said, "I am put in the position of a far more modest and smaller space. You have 135 million people living on 9½ million square kilometers. You have a country with incredible wealth, all the natural resources, fertile enough to feed half a billion people and to supply them with all necessities."[17] By comparison, Hitler depicted Germany as a small and densely populated country that had endured enormous losses since 1919; his only task for the last six years had been to lead Germany out of the chaos of the postwar period. This had left him with little time on his hands to worry about the fate of the world.

The most revealing moment of the speech was the dictator's ridicule of President Roosevelt's listing of twenty-one countries that he asked Hitler not to attack. As Hitler read the name of each country, the puppet delegates roared in unison at the ridiculous notion that Germany would attack the likes of Palestine, Iceland, Turkey, Switzerland, Syria, and so on. The American journalist William Shirer noted in his diary that "Hitler was a superb actor today—he drew every last drop of irony."[18] Goebbels was delighted with Hitler's performance, boasting that the führer had flogged Roosevelt and smacked him around the ears. He praised Hitler as a political and rhetorical genius and added dismissively that Roosevelt was a "pygmy of a man by comparison."[19]

What did President Roosevelt think of Hitler's performance? Hitler's speech was broadcast by radio, both in Germany and on the main American stations. FDR realized that his appeal had been rejected. His task was to convince an isolationist-minded America that there was a real threat to the Western Hemisphere. This was not going to be easy. *Newsweek* magazine opined that Hitler's speech was bound to strengthen isolationist sentiment in America, and *Time* magazine ventured the same prediction, saying that it was clearly "Hitler's Inning." The *Nation* magazine seemed to believe that Hitler "managed to sound like a mélange of American isolationist senators."[20]

In a secret speech to his military chiefs on May 23, 1939, Hitler revealed even more of his warlike intentions, now about Poland. "We shall not be drawn into war," he said, "but we cannot get around it. 80 million Germans," he reiterated, "needed living space in order to live."[21] The foundation of world power was measured by territorial acquisitions. It was a matter of political rise or fall. Further progress could not be achieved without shedding blood. Germany's long-range goal was not Danzig; it was expansion in the East. Should there be a confrontation with the West, Germany would conquer territories in the East and use them as future arsenals for survival. Though he favored a quick lightning war against the West, Germany had to prepare itself for the possibility of a ten- to fifteen-year war. England was now the engine driving the war effort against Germany. The only way to defeat her was to deliver a knockout blow to her naval forces, making it possible to starve the island into submission. England's land army could not fight effectively on the continent without French support. The necessary preparation for war must be laid with the utmost secrecy; not even Italy or Japan must be informed.[22]

Just one month after Hitler's speech to his military chiefs, one of the most important military plans of World War II was presented to FDR. Later called Rainbow 5, it was a broadly conceived plan that outlined American strategy in case of war with Germany and Japan. Over the next two years, Rainbow 5 would undergo significant reformulations, but the original intent of the plan had not changed since mid-1939: "The broad strategic objective of the Associated Powers will be the defeat of Germany and her Allies."[23] This task would be accomplished by destroying Axis sea communications, launching sustained air offensives, eliminating Italy in the early stages of the war, supporting neutral powers, building a large land army of 10 million men, and capturing strategic territories from which offensives could be launched (the Azores, Cape Verde, the Marshall and Caroline islands). The plan gave priority to the Atlantic and European theaters of war, while at the same time keeping the Japanese at bay. Once finished, Rainbow 5 called for a large expeditionary force that would invade Europe. Rainbow 5 considered Germany a greater threat to the United States than imperial Japan. In Washington, Bötticher had inklings that such contingency plans were being made, but he discounted the immediate threat they posed to Germany because America was militarily unprepared and would continue to be so for at least two years.[24]

Hitler prepared the attack on Poland without giving much thought to the United States. He was convinced that the United States would remain neutral as long as her vital interests in the Western Hemisphere were not directly threatened and as long as Americans continued to adhere to isolationism and neutrality. He encouraged Goering's efforts to strengthen isolationists in America and even authorized financial assistance to the labor leader John L. Lewis, who opposed FDR in the 1940 presidential campaign. Roosevelt was keenly aware of such isolationist sentiments, as he was of any shift in the public mood, and he pointed out that domestic developments had to be monitored, and that it was necessary "to watch Congress and public opinion like a hawk."[25] Hitler in turn was also aware of public opinion in the United States, and he told the premier of Hungary, Count Paul Telaki, that Roosevelt was fighting for his reelection and that isolation sentiment, expressed in the neutrality acts, would make it extremely unlikely that America would go to war anytime soon.[26] Hitler read the American political atmosphere more shrewdly than historians have given him credit for.

After concluding the Nazi-Soviet Non-Aggression Pact, Hitler was confident that he could proceed with his attack on Poland. He did not believe that the Western powers, having backed down in the face of his aggression before, would lift a finger to assist Poland, especially since he now had an ally in the Soviet Union.[27] FDR, even at this late stage of the final crisis, believed that peace was better than war and sent two urgent messages to the dictator on August 24 and 26; but just as Hitler had not seriously accepted Roosevelt's earlier appeals, he also chose to disregard this final one. He ordered Weizsäcker to inform the American chargé in Berlin, Alexander C. Kirk, to acknowledge receipt of the president's messages, which he said had been forwarded to the German foreign minister. The president had sent similar appeals for peace to the Italian king, Victor Emmanuel, and President Ignacy Mocicki of Poland. He suggested an immediate settlement of the German-Polish conflict by offering himself as a mediator if both sides agreed to respect each other's territorial integrity. No one expected that these appeals would succeed; in fact, Ambassador

Kennedy in London described FDR's messages as "a complete flop in London," and Adolf Berle, U.S. assistant secretary of state, said that these messages "will have about the same effect as a valentine sent to somebody's mother-in-law out of season." Robert Dallek has pointed out that Roosevelt sent these messages primarily for their domestic effect, trying to go on the record that, despite America's neutrality, the people should know that the real aggressor in the coming conflict was Germany rather than Poland. "The bill should be clearly put on Germany."[28]

Blitzkrieg, Sitzkrieg, and the Fall of France

At three o'clock in the morning on September 3, 1939, President Roosevelt was roused from his sleep by a telephone call from Ambassador Bullitt in Paris telling him that Hitler had invaded Poland. That morning Roosevelt gave a press conference, and when a reporter asked him whether the United States could stay out of the European war, he replied, "I not only hope so, but I believe we can."[29] Two days later, Britain and France declared war on Germany. On September 4, FDR told the American people in a fireside chat that "this nation will remain a neutral nation, but I cannot ask that every American remain neutral in thought as well," and that sentiment included the president himself.[30]

Hitler's attack on Poland forced Britain and France to declare war on Germany. Hitler banked on the defensive mentality of his Western foes; he was certain that they would not strike unless struck first by his forces. Events proved him right. While the *Wehrmacht* was slashing its way through the Polish defenses, all was quiet on the Rhine, where the Germans had inadequate forces to repel a combined British and French attack. He told General Halder that he would fight a "sham war . . . in the West,"[31] later referred to in American newspapers as the "phony war," or *Sitzkrieg* by German soldiers. Hitler also gave orders to the navy to stop all attacks on passenger ships.[32] This came after the September 4 sinking of the British passenger ship *Athenia* by a German submarine. Hitler gave this order to prevent a repeat of the sort of anti-German feelings that had swept over America in April 1915 when a German submarine had sunk the passenger ship *Lusitania*, killing everyone aboard, including 128 Americans.

Roosevelt had already decided that he would do everything possible to support the democracies by either working around the neutrality laws or eliminating them. The neutrality laws contained prohibitions against the export of arms, ammunitions, or implements of war to two or more belligerents, and included discretionary travel restrictions and bans on long-term loans to belligerents. In 1938 public support for a mandatory arms embargo was substantial. A Gallup poll revealed that 73 percent of the American people supported the ban. Following Hitler's attack on Poland, however, public support dwindled, with 62 percent favoring repeal of the embargo.[33] Hitler expected that the Western powers would accept his decisive victory in Poland and refrain from interfering in his postwar reorganization of the Eastern territories. What point was there for the Western powers to interfere in the reorganization of Eastern Europe? Hitler was telling Britain and France that their vital interests were unaffected by the conquest of Poland. He blamed the Poles for dragging the British and the French into the war. Neither Roosevelt nor Churchill, who had just been appointed first lord of the Admiralty, saw it this way. Bypassing regular diplomatic channels, the two men began corresponding with each other as early as September 1939. Their correspondence shows clearly that they were of one mind when it came to Hitler's threat to the Western world.

After the Polish war was over, Hitler portrayed himself as an apostle of peace, approaching the Western powers with a new "sensible peace offer;" but just in case such an offer were rejected, he gave orders to prepare for an attack on the West. Even while the Polish campaign was being fought, diplomatic contacts were under way to prevent a wider war and to bring the current conflict to a peaceful conclusion. Two important American visitors to Germany offered themselves as unofficial mediators to end the war. They were William Rhodes Davis, a wealthy businessman and generous donor to the Democratic Party, and James D. Mooney, a General Motors executive.[34] Davis had cleared his unofficial visit to Rome and Berlin with Roosevelt. For Davis and Mooney, there were significant economic interests involved in these diplomatic maneuvers. Working with Joachim Hertslet, who represented German banking and industrial interests in Mexico, and with Mexican president Lázaro Cárdenas, Davis had arranged the sale of large quantities of Mexican oil to Germany. A war in Europe, Davis feared, would seriously disrupt future sales. Davis had several meetings with Goering, who supposedly told him that if President Roosevelt would undertake mediation talks, Germany would agree to "an adjustment whereby a new Polish State and a new Czechoslovakian independent government would come into being. . . . As for myself and my government[,] I would be glad to attend and in the event of such a conference I would represent Germany. I agree that the conference should be in Washington."[35] As a proviso, Goering stipulated that Germany's conquest of Poland had to be accepted. On October 3, Goering told Davis that he had discussed these proposals with Hitler, who expressed agreement with them. Davis should regard the führer's forthcoming Reichstag speech on October 6 as a direct answer to Roosevelt's peace feelers.

Hitler's speech of October 6 made a vague appeal to European nations to work together on a common solution to peace. He made no reference to the United States at all, only to the nations of the European continent. Now he emphasized that the primary role in this settlement should be played by Germany and Russia. Hitler did leave the door open to the possibility of reconstituting a Polish state, a clever sop to the Western powers, for by the time of his speech the Germans were creating a rump of Polish territories in central Poland that they could use as a bargaining chip with the Western powers. Hitler still counted on the influence of appeasers in Britain and France and hoped that they would put enough pressure on their governments to negotiate with Germany.

What was the American response to Hitler's peace overture? When Davis returned to the United States to report on his recent trip, the president declined to meet with him. Roosevelt's personal secretary, Missy Le Hand, told him the president was too busy with lengthy conferences—an obvious evasion. Davis then wrote a lengthy letter to the president that recounted the events of his recent trip to Berlin. The letter changed nothing. This raises the question of whether Roosevelt was ever serious about mediating the European conflict. Perhaps we can answer this best by saying that he was half-serious, still waiting for Britain and France to take the initiative. If they wanted him to take the lead, he would do so; if not, he would remain in the background. A press release from Hyde Park in late October stated that the president would not act in the current crisis unless Britain and France did so first.

Hitler did not wait long. On October 9 he issued Directive No. 6 (Case Yellow), ordering a lightning attack on France through Holland and Belgium. The quick defeat of France, he believed, would force England to negotiate for peace. When Hitler set the attack against France for November 12, his generals persuaded him with uncharacteristic force that the campaign against the West should be postponed until spring.

In the meantime, there was little enthusiasm for continuing the war on the Allied side. The French fighting spirit was, to say the least, uninspiring, and even the British were lukewarm about taking the offensive, and then only if the Germans struck first. The exception to this half-hearted spirit was Winston Churchill, who had been appointed as first lord of the Admiralty by Prime Minister Chamberlain. As noted earlier, Roosevelt and Churchill began corresponding with each other in September 1939. As their relationship strengthened, the two men exchanged regular messages. During the course of the next five years, Churchill sent 1,161 written messages, while FDR responded with 788.[36] Churchill reinforced FDR's conviction that a German victory would be catastrophic for both Britain and the United States.[37]

Meanwhile, the Nazi-Soviet Non-Aggression Pact had assigned eastern Poland, the Baltic provinces, and Finland to the Russian sphere of interest. On November 30, 1939, Stalin attacked Finland without a declaration of war. He did not want all of Finland but certain southeastern frontier territories close to Leningrad and several islands in the Finnish Gulf. Such strategic outposts, the Russians argued, would secure Russian territories. There was shock and consternation in Western capitals and in the United States about the Finnish war, which the Russians fought with surprising incompetence, reinforcing Hitler's belief that the Red Army had feet of clay. Americans were outraged by this attack on "brave little Finland," a democratic nation that had faithfully paid its debts to the United States. Roosevelt denounced the Russian invasion as a "wanton disregard for the law" and promised financial support to Finland.[38] Congress provided a $30 million loan for civilian needs and granted a moratorium on further debt payments. British and French war planners drew up a plan to assist the Finns by sending an expeditionary army to Finland through Norway and Sweden, hoping that this would not only aid Finland but also cut iron ore supplies that the Germans were receiving from Sweden. A month later, in April 1940, Hitler invaded Denmark and Norway.

Roosevelt dithered in his own peculiar manner, or so it seemed. America was officially neutral and Hitler wanted it to stay that way. When Admiral Raeder called for an all-out submarine war, Hitler turned him down, issuing a directive that stated that "by order of the führer, on no account are operations to be carried out against passenger steamers, even when under escorts."[39] The German press was instructed not to make hostile remarks about Roosevelt or the United States. Goebbels's propaganda ministry gave instructions on September 23 that caution had to be exercised when mentioning America.[40] The Foreign Office also emphasized the importance of keeping America neutral in the present conflict. Weizsäcker sent Ribbentrop a memorandum in which he said that "we have a great interest in preventing the United States from throwing her weight into the scales on the side of our foes."[41]

At the same time (September 1940), the American-sponsored Panama Conference convened in Panama City. Comprising delegates from twenty-one nations of the Western Hemisphere, it issued a joint declaration of neutrality with distinctly unneutral features. One was the creation of a "neutrality zone," a kind of "chastity belt" around the Western Hemisphere within which belligerent nations were not allowed to operate.[42] The lines of this belt ranged from 300 to 1,000 miles out to sea from southern Canada to South America. This scheme was not only unenforceable but also contrary to international law. It invited incidents, because belligerent ships were bound to either stray into such a wide belt or mistakenly sink neutral ships. What was so dangerous about the neutrality zone was that the Americans decided to dispatch "neutrality patrols," or warships, to make sure that belligerents did not violate it. The American navy patrolled the entire area and reported the positions of the vessels it encountered "in plain English." This was a convenient way of alerting British close patrols. Dozens of German ships—steamers, freighters, warships, and even luxury liners (the *Columbus*)—were sunk, scuttled, or captured by the British with American help.[43] On October 9, an unarmed American cargo ship, the *City of Flint*, was stopped by a German cruiser off the British Isles; it was searched and taken over by a German crew. Under diplomatic protests, the American ship was eventually released and returned to the United States. Many similar incidents, each raising more protests on both sides, would continue over the next two years in what has been called the "unneutral war" between Germany and the United States. In November, Congress passed the revised Neutrality Act of 1939, which allowed foreign purchasers to carry back munitions on their own ships—the controversial cash-and-carry provision. The act permitted only sea-controlling democracies to purchase such munitions, thus excluding Germany.

A significant and dramatic event occurred between December 13 and 17, 1939, in South American waters off the coast of Uruguay. The German "pocket battleship" *Admiral Graf Spee* fought a lengthy battle with three British cruisers and, heavily damaged, sought refuge in Montevideo harbor. Invoking strict neutrality restrictions, the Uruguayan government ordered the German vessel to leave after seventy-two hours, obviously not time enough to repair the ship. On Hitler's orders, the captain then scuttled the ship; he later committed suicide in a Buenos Aires hotel room. Following this incident, Roosevelt gave orders to increase the number of American "patrol" vessels, which had been operating since September in waters that extended 200 to 300 miles offshore from eastern Canada southward to the Gulf of Mexico and the Caribbean.[44]

During the first three months of 1940, at the time Hitler was finalizing his plans to strike at the West, Roosevelt encouraged another effort to explore the possibility of negotiating a peaceful settlement to the war in Europe. This involved sending Sumner Welles on a peace mission to Europe, a curious interlude during the phony war that historians usually dismiss in less than a paragraph as a futile undertaking. Welles was an old friend of Roosevelt; he was, like the president, a product of Groton and Harvard. The press described him as an exquisitely dapper and dignified diplomat—unflappable and very reserved in his bearing. His fatal weakness, which would cost him his position, was his reckless indulgence in homosexual affairs, and not always with consenting partners. Welles's mission may have been a failure, but it confirmed for Roosevelt that Hitler could not be budged from his single-minded pursuit of reorganizing Eastern Europe to fit his notion of a Greater German Reich. Hitler had reluctantly agreed to see Welles, but before meeting him, or allowing any German official to talk to him, Hitler dictated what is called in diplomatic practice "talking points" (*Richtlinien*) defining the topics that could be discussed. Hitler took pains to explain to Welles what the German position was, so that there could be no misunderstanding about his intentions. Only Germany and Russia had a legitimate interest in Eastern Europe. The war in the West, he wanted the Americans to know, had been forced on Germany by France and Britain. Hitler's talking points went out to Ribbentrop, Hess, and Goering, the Nazi officials Welles was scheduled to meet besides Hitler. Welles had been given strict instructions by Cordell Hull in January 1940 to act as a good reporter gathering information, not a negotiator authorized by the government to mediate between warring parties.[45] Isolationists in America, as Hull pointed out in his memoirs, had already seized upon Welles's proposed trip as proof that the United States was about to involve itself in European quarrels.

Welles found Ribbentrop detestable, Goering ostentatious, and Hess stupid. Ribbentrop lectured him for two hours with misinformation and deliberate lies, "hissing" when he mentioned the word *England*.[46] Citing the German white papers almost verbatim, the German foreign minister blamed France and Britain for inciting the Polish government to refuse to conclude an agreement with Germany. Now that Poland was conquered, it was up to Germany and Russia to redraw the map of Europe. Germany "wished for nothing more in Europe than the United States had in the western hemisphere through the Monroe Doctrine."[47] Welles's subsequent discussions with Hess and Goering covered the same ground, exactly as Hitler had outlined in his talking points. Hitler's chief translator, Dr. Paul Schmidt, later wrote that Welles essentially listened to the same gramophone record over and over because Ribbentrop, Hess, Goering, and Hitler had rehearsed the same script, with Hess actually taking a copy of the *Richtlinien* out of his desk to make sure he would not deviate from it.[48] When Welles saw Hitler on March 2, he found him to be pleasant if overly formal: "He had in real life none of the ludicrous features so often shown in his photographs. He seemed in excellent physical condition and in good training. He was dignified both in speech and in movement. His voice in conversation was low and well modulated. It had only once during our conversation . . . the raucous stridency which is always heard in his speeches. He spoke with clarity and precision and I was able to follow every word in German, although Dr. Schmidt interpreted—and at times, inaccurately."[49]

I have quoted this sharp observation by Welles at length because it provides a real glimpse into Hitler's underrated skills as a statesman. Hitler did not once bring up the subject of the deterioration of German-American relations, but he wanted to make certain that Welles would return to America with a clear understanding of the German position. Moreover, Hitler wanted Welles to understand that his views were identical to what the German people believed. He told Welles, "I am fully aware that the Allied powers believe that a distinction can be made between National Socialism and the German people. There was never a greater mistake. The German people today are united as one man and I have the support of every German. I can see no hope for the establishment of any lasting peace until the will of England and France to destroy Germany is itself destroyed."[50]

Welles was a capable diplomat, elegant in his bearing and incisive in some of his detailed observations of people and events. He came away with a somber appraisal of the European impasse, reporting that the Germans lived in a hermetically sealed society, holding views of other countries that were not only untrue but fantastically untrue. He felt depressed until he crossed the Swiss frontier. His report to President Roosevelt left no doubt about the futility of his mission.

When Sumner Welles departed Germany for Switzerland and then continued on to France and Britain, another American visitor came to see Hitler and Goering—James D. Mooney, the president of General Motors Overseas. Mooney had received the German Order of Merit of the Eagle in 1938 for his outstanding service to the Reich, and he clearly wanted to go on doing business with Germany.[51] This was his second visit to Berlin since September 1939. Mooney, like Welles, conveyed President Roosevelt's concerns about the European situation. Hitler gave Mooney the same answers he had given Welles: Germany was determined to reorganize Eastern Europe and resist French and British aggression.

On March 28, the Nazis published the German white paper of the selected Polish documents they had found in Warsaw. Roosevelt and Hull denounced the documents as a German forgery.[52] As previously mentioned, some of these documents implicated certain American diplomats, notably William Bullitt, U.S. ambassador to France, because they had made incriminating remarks to Polish diplomats that, in a war between the democracies and the Reich, the United States would place all its resources at the disposal of Germany's enemies. The Germans were disappointed that publication of these documents did not topple the Roosevelt government, as they naively believed that they would. Now, in the spring of 1940, Hitler was counting on his experts in Washington, particularly General Friedrich von Bötticher, to tell him what the American government was capable of doing for Britain and France. Thomsen had already warned Berlin in September that "Roosevelt is determined to go to war against Germany, even in the face of resistance in his own country."[53] Bötticher reported that the American general staff opposed U.S. involvement in a European war, but he added that the United States would intervene if its vital interests in the Western Hemisphere were threatened. At the moment, Bötticher said in October 1939, the United States was not dangerous because of the neutrality laws. Bötticher's reports were not just filed away in the Foreign Office but went to the chief command of the armed forces, General Keitel, who then presented them to Hitler himself.[54] Thus, there is compelling evidence that Bötticher's reports had a bearing on Hitler's war plans or, more accurately, on his timing.

Time was very much on Hitler's mind. In November he had escaped an attempt on his life. Shortly afterward, he told his senior *Wehrmacht* officers that, unlike in World War I, Germany no longer faced a war on two fronts, since Poland had been defeated and could now be secured by a few divisions. Referring to the recent attempt on his life, he said, "I must in all modesty describe my own person: irreplaceable. Neither a military man nor a civilian could replace me."[55] He added that attempts on his life might be repeated. Time was of the essence. In the long run, Germany's opponents had time on their side; but now the time was propitious for Germany. By the spring of 1940, Hitler felt even more certain that the time to strike at the weak democracies had come. Britain and France had shown hesitation and weakness. They could have been a serious threat if they had invaded Germany by crossing the Rhine and striking at the industrial Ruhr in the fall of 1939; instead, they dug in behind their Maginot line and waited for the Germans to attack.

Hitler was ready with a massive force in the spring of 1940. His eastern flank was still secure, especially after the Soviets defeated the Finns and forced them to conclude a peace agreement on March 12. On April 9, 1940, Hitler invaded Denmark and Norway in a brilliantly conceived and executed amphibious operation. The small German force not only surprised the Danes and Norwegians, whose armies were obsolete and unprepared, but also outwitted the British in their race for Norwegian ports. The invasion of Denmark and Norway had important repercussions in America. During World War I the majority of Scandinavian Americans had been pro-German, among them Charles Lindbergh's father, a congressman and a strong opponent of American intervention in World War I. The German attack and subsequent military occupation of Denmark and Norway shifted these isolationist sentiments among Scandinavian Americans.

On the heels of this campaign came Germany's attack on the West on May 10. Hitler set a clever trap for the Allied powers by substantially modifying the Schlieffen plan of World War I, which had called for a quick knock-out blow of France by unleashing eighty-two German divisions through northern Belgium. The German right wing was supposed to wheel through Belgium into France, attack the French army on its left, and take Paris along the way. In a kind of "revolving door" movement it was then supposed to push the enemy against the Swiss frontier. This ambitious plan had failed in September 1914. During the winter of 1939, Hitler approved a much more sophisticated plan called the sickle-cut (*Sichelschnitt*). The plan was designed to fool the Allies into believing that the Germans would once more attack the French on the right. They did, but it was a weak feint that drew the Allied forces forward toward Belgium and Holland. The real attack, bypassing the Maginot line, came on the left in southern Belgium, where Hitler had amassed most of his forces, including his tanks. These mechanized forces advanced rapidly through the thickly wooded Ardennes forest—thought to be impassable to heavy armor—crossed the Meuse River near Sedan and headed straight for the channel ports. The French divisions and the small British Expeditionary Army were trapped as the Germans closed the ring around them and pushed their forces against the sea. In only fourteen days, Hitler's sickle-cut had been executed so swiftly and surgically that it spread panic among the French, causing such serious morale problems among the fighting troops that the French High Command began to think seriously about surrender. What so confused the defense-minded French was not just German tanks slashing through French lines, but the German Luftwaffe completely dominating the air, strafing the retreating French forces at will. Holland and Belgium surrendered quickly in succession on May 14 and May 28, with the surrender of Belgium leaving the British Expeditionary Army of 250,000 trapped against the sea at Dunkirk, facing possible annihilation by General Rundstedt's Panzers. Hitler ordered a halt to his tanks, which made possible "the miracle of Dunkirk," as British vessels of all sorts—naval ships, yachts, tugboats from the Thames, fishing boats, barges, and privately owned boats—lifted about 330,000 British and Allied troops from the beaches at Dunkirk. Hitler later claimed that he wanted to give the British a "sporting chance" and convince them that it was pointless to keep on fighting.[56] A more likely reason for the halt order at Dunkirk was that Hitler agreed with Rundstedt that German armored divisions needed refitting and repair after having covered so much terrain. Hitler's experience in World War I may also have played a role. He did not think that tanks were of much use in a terrain crisscrossed by so many canals.[57] Finally, there was Goering's boast that the Luftwaffe could prevent any large-scale escape of the trapped Anglo-French armies at Dunkirk.

Whatever the reason for Hitler's halt order at Dunkirk, an army was saved to fight another day, but as Churchill, who had become prime minister on May 10, said afterward, "wars are not won by evacuations." He told the British people that "we shall not flag or fail. We shall go on to the end, we shall fight in France, we shall fight in the seas and oceans, we shall fight with growing confidence and growing strength in the air, we shall defend our island. Whatever the cost may be, we shall fight on the beaches, we shall fight on the landing grounds, we shall fight in the fields and in the streets, we shall fight in the hills; we shall never surrender."[58] To his son Randolph, who asked him whether Britain could defeat the Nazis, he said: "Of course . . . we can beat them. I shall drag the United States in."[59] At the time of Dunkirk this was easier said than done. Roosevelt knew the terrible danger Britain was facing, and in a secret discussion with the Canadian prime minister, Mackenzie King, he had already discussed the possibility of sheltering the British navy in American and Canadian ports. Churchill made it quite clear to both leaders that the British navy would not go to the New World under his watch. Writing to the Canadian prime minister, he said, "We must be careful not to let the Americans view too complacently the prospect of a British collapse, out of which they would get the British fleet and the guardianship of the British Empire minus Great Britain."[60] Roosevelt prepared for the worst at the time of the French collapse. He knew that Britain was his last line of defense in the Atlantic, but he was not sure that Britain could survive by herself for long without American military support.

In the summer of 1940 Roosevelt knew that the United States could not fend off the German threat with the navy and army air corps alone. He knew the military facts of life. At the time of the Battle of France, Germany had 3 million men under arms on the western front. The Luftwaffe had 4,020 planes and the German army about 2,445 tanks.[61] If we compare these figures to the strength of the American military, the differences are striking. A report by the War Department in May 1940 showed that the United States had fewer than 150,000 men under arms and lacked sufficient supplies. The air force, then called the army air corps, had 1,350 planes and could manage to increase that number, given 1940 production levels, to 3,000.[62] The United States could not seriously challenge Hitler in 1940 or 1941.

On the diplomatic front, things were not much brighter at the time of Dunkirk and the subsequent collapse of France. The U.S. government had to institute a communications blackout with its diplomatic missions throughout the world when it was discovered that the American "gray code," in which the personal messages between Churchill and Roosevelt had been encrypted, had been compromised. A cipher clerk in the American embassy in London, Tyler Kent, had intercepted the messages and then promptly handed them over to his pro-German contacts. Kent later claimed that he merely wanted to expose FDR's plot to drag America into a world war.[63] Although this episode in the history of World War II is sometimes mentioned by historians, its real importance is usually overlooked—namely, that the Germans were getting top secret information from two Western leaders, one of whom was supposedly "neutral."

For the Germans, Dunkirk was only a short setback because it secured their right wing and enabled them to attack on a broad front from Sedan to Abbéville. On June 10, Italy declared war on France; on June 17, Marshal Henri Philippe Pétain, who had replaced Paul Reynaud as head of the French government, asked the Germans for an armistice. On June 22, Hitler dictated his terms to the French in the same railroad car, and in the same location at Compiègne in which Marshall Ferdinand Foch had forced the German delegation to sign the armistice terms in 1918. It was a supreme moment of triumph for Hitler, who rightly felt that he had avenged the defeat of 1918. Hitler then went sightseeing in Paris and watched the swastika flutter from the Eiffel Tower. His entrance into Berlin was reminiscent of the return of an ancient caesar after a great victory. All of Europe seemed to lie at his feet.

Saving Britain

There were several obstacles to Hitler's complete control of Europe. One was Churchill and the British, who refused to throw in the towel. The second was Roosevelt and America. While German troops were rampaging through Holland, Belgium, Luxembourg, and France, several crucial events unfolded behind the scenes of battle that would shape the course of things to come.

If Roosevelt ever got a wake-up call that spurred him into action, it was the frightening successes of the German *Wehrmacht*. On May 15, Churchill sent an urgent message to FDR saying that American aid was vital if the Allied cause was to be salvaged. "I trust you realize," he told the president, "that the voice and force of the United States may count for nothing if they are withheld too long. You may have a completely subjugated, nazified Europe established with astonishing swiftness, and the weight may be more than we can bear."[64] Churchill asked for fifty old destroyers, the latest types of aircraft, and antiaircraft equipment and ammunition, promising to pay dollars for it as long as Britain could afford it. On May 16, only six days after the German attack on the West, the president appeared before Congress and asked for hefty increases in military appropriations. He received 1.5 billion dollars. In his message to Congress, Roosevelt warned that the United States was no longer an impregnable fortress. With a watchful eye on what was happening to the Dutch and the Belgians, he mentioned the threat posed by new motorized armies, long-range bombers, parachute troops, and fifth columnists. To meet this threat, America had to produce vast amounts of armaments; he even mentioned the need to produce fifty thousand planes a year—a fantastic figure in 1940.

Three weeks later, the president delivered an even more ominous speech at the University of Virginia at Charlottesville. It was a most unneutral commencement speech. Roosevelt told the graduating students—one of them his son Franklin Jr.—that America could no longer afford to be a lone island surrounded by a world dominated by force. America's sympathies, he said, must lie with those nations that were giving their blood to fight those who were only guided by force. Here he had France in mind because it was on the verge of defeat. On the day of the president's speech, France was also betrayed by its Italian neighbor who declared war when it became obvious that France would fall. FDR insisted on inserting the following phrase in his speech: "On the tenth day of June, 1940, the hand that held the dagger has struck it into the back of its neighbor." The president had a palpable sense that what was formerly a distant danger was coming closer and closer to the shores of the United States. If Britain fell to the Nazis, there would be nothing but the Atlantic between America and the German army. In his University of Virginia speech, he admitted that the Nazis had not yet developed long-range bombers that could reach the shores of America, but he left no doubt in the minds of his listeners that such a day was drawing close. A project to develop an America bomber that could operate at a range of 12,428 miles had already begun in Germany in 1937. About the time Roosevelt gave his speech on June 10, 1940, the Germans were already at work on a two-stage missile that could hit targets in the United States. It was called the "America Rocket."[65]

As noted earlier, Roosevelt and Churchill had exchanged letters since September 1939. Now that Hitler was defeating France, their correspondence took on a more urgent tone. Whether Hitler knew anything about this is not known, but he did know that Britain's hope rested on America. On June 13, a week before the French signed the armistice with the Germans, Hitler granted an extraordinary interview to Karl von Wiegand, a veteran reporter from the Hearst papers. He met Wiegand at his headquarters at Bruly-la-Pêche in Belgium. Hitler rarely granted private interviews with foreign reporters, but Wiegand was different. His background was German and he had held pro-German views during World War I. In 1940 Wiegand wrote for the isolationist paper the *New York Journal American*. Present at the interview, which was clearly aimed at American public opinion, was Joachim von Ribbentrop, Hitler's foreign minister. Hitler carefully scrutinized the text of the interview before releasing it to the German press. The interview occurred on the same day that the French president, Paul Reynaud, issued his last plea to Roosevelt for help. Hitler told Wiegand that Germany had no territorial or political interests in the Western Hemisphere. He spoke of the Monroe Doctrine and wholeheartedly agreed with George Washington's position that America should not engage in entangling alliances outside the Western Hemisphere. When asked by Wiegand about the reaction to possible U.S. intervention through the delivery of war materiel to the allies, Hitler responded by saying that such supplies would not alter the outcome of the war. He also denied rumors that Germany had a fifth column in the United States. Germany's enemies, he insisted, would lose the war because they had poor military organizations and feeble-minded politicians, not because they faced a nonexistent fifth column.

Referring to Great Britain, Hitler reaffirmed his claim that he had no intention of destroying the British Empire. He reminded Wiegand that he had offered the British an olive branch, only to have it rejected. British leaders were inciting their people against Germany; they publicly demanded that Germany be permanently divided up and demilitarized. He had never harbored such intentions about the future of Britain. Now that the English were losing one battle after another, their leaders were turning, tears in their eyes, to the United States for help. He predicted that British leaders would end up destroying their empire, and he sincerely hoped that the United States would not rush to their defense. He wanted to reassure the American people that they had nothing to fear from Germany. Europe should be for the Europeans and America for the Americans—a clever appeal to American isolationists.[66] At one point in the interview Hitler called the American isolationists "radical nationalists" who were not pacifists but people opposed to intervention in 1940. In the postwar period (the late 1940s) they transformed themselves into vocal "cold warriors."[67]

Hitler's interview with Wiegand did not make a big splash in the American press because it was overshadowed by the fall of France a week later. Among American isolationists, however, the interview seems to have struck a responsive chord among, for example, Charles Lindbergh and his circle, soon to become the America First Committee. These isolationists took issue with Roosevelt's pro-British foreign policy; they were fearful that America would intervene in a European war that did not threaten the United States.

In the meantime, Hitler prepared to consolidate his control over the territories he had just conquered—Holland, Belgium, and France. But across the channel there was still a defiant Britain. This defiance was on full display on July 3, 1940, in the Mediterranean. On that day a British fleet under Admiral Somerville attacked and destroyed much of the French fleet at Oran in southwestern Algeria to prevent it from falling into German hands. By the terms of the armistice, France had agreed to transfer its warships to German control to prevent them from sailing to Britain or the United States. The French warships were allowed to stay in French ports under German supervision. The British presented the French government at Vichy with several unpalatable demands: turn over the French fleet to the British navy, sail to a British port and allow the fleet to be impounded, immobilize the French fleet in the West Indies, or scuttle the fleet. The German-controlled government at Vichy, headed by Marshal Pétain, refused to accept these terms. Churchill then gave the order to destroy the warships at Oran and nearby Mers-el-Kébir. The pride of the French navy went to the bottom of the sea, and with it 1,297 French sailors. There was great popular outrage in France. Admiral Raeder reported to Hitler that he had had a long discussion with French admiral Darlan, the commander in chief of the French navy, who told him that he had always disliked the British and was now in favor of a rapprochement with Germany.[68] Although German propaganda had a field day with Churchill's "cowardly attack" on the French navy, Hitler was unable to exploit the opportunity of seizing the French fleet at the time of the armistice. The French navy was the third largest navy in the world; its warships might just have enabled Hitler to challenge the British fleet. The significance of Oran illustrates Churchill's determination to continue fighting Hitler, "no matter what the cost."

On July 19, 1940, Hitler gave an important speech to the Reichstag in which he praised the *Wehrmacht* for its victory over the French. At the conclusion of his speech he appealed to the common sense of the English people. Now that the fighting in Europe was over, he saw no reason why the war should continue. He made reference to his previous peace offer following the Polish campaign, which he said had been undermined by Western warmongers like Churchill, Duff Cooper, Eden, and Hore Belisha—men who stood to profit financially from war. He warned them that this would be his last appeal for peace. His message to Britain was the same as before: Europe to the Europeans (dominated, of course, by Germany) and a guarantee that Germany would respect the integrity of the British Empire.

Two days before Hitler gave his victory speech to the Reichstag on July 19, Franklin Roosevelt was renominated by his party at Chicago. Cordell Hull said that FDR's choice to run for an unprecedented third term was "an immediate consequence of Hitler's conquest of France and the specter of Britain alone standing between the conqueror and ourselves."[69] By the president's own calculations, his first line of defense (France) against Hitler was gone. He wanted to warn the American people that they faced a serious crisis and that there might be a Trojan horse in America. He also used the more recent term *fifth columnists*—disloyal citizens who betray their own nation to the enemy. America must be prepared to deal with traitors, spies, and saboteurs. As the president was saying this, German agents were trying to change the outcome of the Democratic Convention. They pumped $160,000 into the anti-Roosevelt campaign by supporting the candidacy of John L. Lewis, the head of the United Mine Workers of America. There is some evidence that Goering actually rained 5 million dollars on this futile scheme, which involved two pro-Nazi American oil millionaires and opponents of the president.[70] The German embassy in Washington, which had received a tiny fraction of this money, donated its anti-Roosevelt campaign funds toward promoting American isolationism. The embassy relied once more on Sylvester Viereck, mistakenly thinking that he had powerful connections in Congress.

Hitler's peace speech on July 19 was meant to be a signal not only to Britain but also to the opponents of FDR in the United States. He knew that the November 1940 election in America was crucial because the re-election of Roosevelt could lead to American intervention. The American people were split between the interventionists, spearheaded on the one hand by the Committee to Defend America by Aiding the Allies, headed by William Allen White, a close friend of the president, and on the other hand the America First Committee, chaired by General Robert E. Wood, chairman of the board of Sears, Roebuck and Company. Around these two committees ranged the various interest groups that supported either isolationism or interventionism. The country seemed to be in a state of uncertainty about the war in Europe.

Throughout the summer of 1940, a heated debate raged in America about the course the country should take now that France had fallen to the Nazis. The Committee to Defend America lobbied for immediate material aid to Britain, particularly after Churchill sent urgent pleas to supply the British with fifty old destroyers. This plan faced opposition from within the military, whose spokesmen reminded the president that the military already faced shortages and therefore should not redirect war material to Britain. Roosevelt had to be very careful before releasing American weapons. He looked for loopholes in the neutrality acts before sending aid. After the fall of France, however, he was committed in principle to do anything short of entering the war to defend Britain. A remark to Grace Tully, his secretary, captures his grim determination to help Britain: "Congress is going to raise hell about this, but even another day's delay may mean the end of civilization. . . . If Britain is to survive, we must act."[71] One immediate step undertaken by the president was to reinstate conscription, a controversial measure because the American people had a traditional dislike of compulsory peacetime service. The Selective Training and Service Act, however, had enough public support, and it was approved by Congress on September 14, 1940, and signed into law two days later by the president. It allowed the government to draft 900,000 men for a period of no more than one year. A significant sop to the isolationists was the provision that the draftees could not serve outside the Western Hemisphere. Henry L. Stimson, who had just become Secretary of War, called the Selective Service Act "one of the two or three most important accomplishments of the American people in the whole period before the outbreak of active war."[72]

A month after the fall of France, the Battle of Britain had begun. Hitler ordered the German High Command to draw up a plan called Operation Sea-Lion (*Seelöwe*), which called for an invasion of England. A precondition for landing was sea and air supremacy, neither of which the Germans enjoyed. An invasion force, however, was hastily assembled while the German Luftwaffe staged massive bombing raids on British airfields and later on major cities. Starting in August 1940, the Germans inflicted heavy damage on British cities, factories, airfields, and harbors, but they did not break British morale. German losses in the Battle of Britain proved prohibitive, as postwar figures revealed. The Royal Air Force (RAF) brought down a total of 1,733 German fighters and bombers by the end of October, as compared with a loss of 915 British fighters.[73] Hitler postponed and eventually scrapped the invasion.

Now Raeder presented Hitler with a victory plan over Britain. The admiral's plan called for an all-out war in the Atlantic and the Mediterranean aimed at disrupting Britain's seafaring routes and starving the island into submission. Raeder tried to impress on Hitler the importance of Gibraltar and the Suez. If Germany could cut Britain off from the Mediterranean route to India, while at the same time putting a stranglehold on the British Isles through U-boats and constant air attacks, England would either be ripe for invasion or sue for peace.[74] Hitler may have briefly entertained such notions, but after his futile diplomatic efforts to enlist the help of Spain, Italy, and Vichy France to deliver a deathblow to the British Empire, he turned his attention eastward. Hitler had always been a continentalist, looking for expansion in Eastern Europe. Unlike Churchill and Roosevelt, who loved the sea and were experts on naval affairs, Hitler had a morbid fear of water. He freely admitted as much, saying, "On land I'm a hero but on the sea I'm a coward."[75] At any rate, he felt that the future of warfare lay on land rather than water. National greatness could only be attained by acquiring contiguous territory. The day of the battleship, Hitler was convinced, was over. Armies rather than navies would make the difference on the continent of Europe.[76] This does not mean that Hitler did not appreciate the influence of sea power on history. He had read Admiral Alfred Mahan's influential book on this subject, but his imperial vision was continental rather than global. As will be seen, he was relying on Japan to keep the United States at arm's length until the Soviet Union was defeated and Germany's living space (*Lebensraum*) was secured. He may have entertained long-range plans of bringing the German navy up to parity with the U.S. Navy, boasting on several occasions that he would build a big fleet of battleships and aircraft carriers unmatched by any great power. This notion was behind the ambitious Z-Plan that Admiral Raeder proposed and Hitler approved in January 1939. Its long-term production targets included a lengthy list of ships of all sorts: 13 battleships, 8 aircraft carriers, 70 destroyers, 249 U-boats, and many other crafts.[77] The dream of investing in big battleships turned into a nightmare after the British, with some help from American naval patrol aircraft, sank Germany's biggest battleship, the *Bismarck*, in May 1941. He told Raeder, shortly before dismissing him, that "heavy ships are utterly worthless"[78] and that from now on he would concentrate exclusively on U-boats.

On July 31, 1940, Hitler held an important military conference at the Berghof. Present were Halder, Brauchitsch, and Raeder, among others. After Raeder reported that the navy would not be ready for an invasion of Britain until mid-September, if then, Hitler expressed skepticism about ending the war by invading Britain. He then revealed what had been on his mind lately: conquering Russia and thus ending Britain's hope of winning the war once and for all. As he put it, "England's hope is Russia and America. If hope of Russia disappears, America disappears too."[79] War with the Soviet Union had been one of the major goals of National Socialism all along. Even before the war against France had been won, Hitler had directed Halder to draw up a military plan to defeat the Soviet Union. What made Hitler think that by fighting Russia, and thus inviting a potential war on two fronts, he could eliminate Britain as a serious threat to the Reich? In Hitler's calculation, Britain could not be defeated by invasion—at least not yet. The way to bring her to heel was to defeat the Russians. Russia was Britain's last hope on the continent; if she were eliminated, only America would remain. Both powers had to be eliminated, one at a time. There was nothing Hitler could do about America in 1940 except delay her entrance into the war; but there was something he could do about Russia. Halder recorded Hitler's train of thought in his war diary: "Decision: In light of these discussions it follows that Russia must be finished off by spring of 1941. The sooner we destroy Russia the better."[80] Having conquered Russia, the Germans would be unbeatable. Even the United States would then be unable to offer hope for Britain, particularly if Japan could be persuaded to challenge America's position in the Pacific.

On September 2, 1940, the United States concluded the destroyer deal with Britain, another example of Roosevelt's skillful political talents. In exchange for giving Britain fifty old but still serviceable destroyers, the United States would receive from Britain the use of strategic military bases scattered over four thousand miles in the Western Hemisphere.[81] These bases were made available to the United States on a ninety-nine-year lease. A Gallup poll showed that a majority of the American people (62 to 38 percent) approved of this exchange of old ships for strategic bases in Newfoundland, Antigua, St. Lucia, Trinidad, Bermuda, Jamaica, and New Guiana. Churchill called it a "decidedly un-neutral act. It would, according to all standards of history, have justified the German Government in declaring war upon them."[82] The Germans complained that it violated the Hague Convention (XIII, article 6), which said that "the supply in any manner directly or indirectly, by a neutral power of warships, ammunitions, or war materiel of any kind whatever, is forbidden."[83] In a note to Senator David Walsh, chairman of the Senate Committee on Naval Affairs, FDR said that the destroyer swap was "the finest thing for the nation that has been done in your lifetime and mine." He added that he did not think that America would get involved in a shooting war "unless Germany wishes to attack us."[84]

Roosevelt's destroyer-for-bases agreement, though supported by 70 percent of the American people, had been made without the advice and consent of Congress. It was concluded by executive decree, a potentially serious violation of the Constitution. The president and his advisers justified it by arguing that congressional deliberations would have been too time-consuming and that by the time the isolationists had made their points, Britain would have been defeated. Moreover, in late June 1940, Congress had ruled that the president could not transfer military equipment to a foreign power unless the chief of naval operations certified that it was not essential to the defense of the United States. This legal obstacle was overcome when the chief of naval operations certified that the United States had a surplus of destroyers and that the swap would result in a net gain for the United States.[85] While the isolationists vigorously protested the destroyer deal, the Committee to Defend America by Aiding the Allies embarked on a publicity campaign to persuade the American people that Britain was the last defense line between Hitler and America. The committee's most effective spokesman on this issue was the World War I hero General John J. Pershing, who gave several effective radio broadcasts on the destroyer deal, telling the American people that "if the destroyers help save the British fleet, they may save us from the danger and hardship of another war."[86]

Hitler had been carefully monitoring Roosevelt's political moves during the summer and fall of 1940. On September 27, Germany, Italy, and Japan concluded the Tripartite Pact in Berlin, which may be seen as Hitler's direct response to the destroyer-for-bases agreement. By the terms of the treaty, the three powers pledged to come to each other's aid if one of the signatories should be attacked by a power that was not involved in the European or Sino-Japanese conflicts. The power being referred to was the United States. Japan had joined the Axis powers for two main reasons: German military might and the danger of possible U.S. intervention in the Pacific. Hitler's swift victories over Holland, Belgium, France, Denmark, and Norway impressed Japanese militarists, practically inciting them to rampage throughout Southeast Asia. When Hitler defeated Holland and France, he cut them off from their colonial possessions in Asia. This included the Dutch East Indies, rich in oil and rubber, and the whole of French Indochina, equally rich in resources the Japanese needed to fuel their military machine. Although Britain was not down-and-out, the empire was extremely vulnerable. What better time for the Japanese to ally themselves with the Germans? The Japanese calculated that the British and the Americans would be tied down in Europe for the foreseeable future, allowing the Japanese to complete their conquests and construct a solid "Greater East Asia Co-Prosperity Sphere" free from British and American domination.

In the United States, 1940 was an important election year; it was also the first time that an American presidential election would play an important role in world affairs. As the elections got underway in September, the fate of Europe as well as Asia hung in the balance. Roosevelt's opponent, Wendell Willkie, a feisty Midwesterner, was a critic of FDR's domestic policies, but he was, like the president, an internationalist who wanted to save Britain from Nazi domination. Hitler knew that the Republicans were by and large more isolationist than the Democrats. By the fall of 1940, Roosevelt had made his intention public: he would do anything short of war to aid the British and stop aggressor nations like Germany, Japan, and Italy.

From Hitler's point of view, any opponent of Roosevelt was a gain for the German side. He counseled caution on the diplomatic front until the American elections had concluded. In October he criticized Mussolini for having invaded Greece before the American presidential election.[87] He also felt that the Japanese should take advantage of American preoccupation with the presidential election by striking at Singapore. On the eve of a presidential election, the United States would have found it impossible to intervene.[88]

The major issue of the American presidential of campaign of 1940 was still isolationism versus intervention. The Democratic platform read, "We will not participate in foreign wars, and we will not send our army, naval and air forces to fight in foreign lands outside the Americas, except in cases of attack."[89] On October 30, while addressing a large audience in Boston, the president appealed to American mothers, saying that "while I am talking to you mothers and fathers I give you one more assurance. I have said this before, but I shall say it again and again: Your boys are not going to be sent into any foreign wars." The juggler Roosevelt added the qualifying statement, "They are going into training to form a force so strong that, by its very existence, it will keep the threat of war far away from our shores. The purpose of our defense is defense."[90] Roosevelt wanted to make sure that he did not give the Republicans an excuse to label him a warmonger. He did not have to worry very much about this because his opponent, Willkie, was not an isolationist; he had been the choice of eastern-seaboard liberal Republicans, most of whom were pro-British. Willkie ran a strong race, but Roosevelt was reelected for an unprecedented third term on November 5, 1940.

On December 8, 1940, Churchill wrote one of the most important letters of his public career. It was addressed to Roosevelt and was in the form of an urgent plea for immediate American aid to Britain. The letter, delivered by seaplane, reached the president while he was relaxing on a cruise aboard the USS *Tuscaloosa* off Antigua. Churchill asked for massive military aid: two thousand aircraft a month, munitions, artillery, vessels, and tanks. The stakes, he pointed out, were very high; they concerned the survival of Britain, and with it the survival of Western civilization. He said that "Hitler has shown himself inclined to avoid the Kaiser's mistake. He does not wish to be drawn into war with the United States until he has gravely undermined the power of Great Britain. His maxim is 'one at a time.'"[91] There was a desperate tone to Churchill's letter. The war was bankrupting the country, because the cash-and-carry arrangement with America was draining Britain of hard currency. Churchill put it as bluntly as he could: "The moment approaches when we shall no longer be able to pay cash for shipping and other supplies."[92] According to Harry Hopkins, the president initially did not seem to be very moved by Churchill's letter, but then one evening he came out with the whole program of how Britain could be bailed out, though he told Hopkins that he was not sure that it could be done legally.[93]

On December 17, Roosevelt revealed the scheme he called "lend-lease" in a press conference. He used a simple analogy to explain it. Suppose your neighbor's house is on fire. If you are a good neighbor, you lend him your garden hose.[94] Once the fire is out, your neighbor either returns the hose or replaces it with a new one. Britain, said Roosevelt, is a good neighbor who needs a hose to put out the Nazi-set fire. In other words, the British could borrow weapons and supplies and put out the fire without questions asked. Critics found the analogy far-fetched and condemned the whole program as illegal and unneutral. Would the British, once having borrowed weapons such as tanks, vessels, rifles, and bullets, return them after they had been used? In a fireside chat several days later, the president rejected charges made by his critics that the lend-lease program violated neutrality by saying that it was simply a way to help democratic friends and thereby safeguard U.S. national security. He then mobilized congressional bipartisan support for HR 1776, which authorized the president to aid any country he deemed vital to the defense of the United States. The bill provoked a firestorm of opposition from the isolationists, who condemned lend-lease as an act of war. The *Chicago Tribune* denounced it as a bill calculated to destroy the American Republic, because it gave the president almost dictatorial powers. Charles Lindbergh said that "we are strong enough in this nation and in this hemisphere to maintain our own way of life regardless of the attitude on the other side. I do not believe we are strong enough to impose our way of life on Europe and Asia."[95] Senator Burton Wheeler predicted that lend-lease would "plow under every fourth American boy."[96]

Yet the president had strong bipartisan support for the bill; Wendell Willkie, too, urged its passage. On December 29 the president delivered his strongest attack on Nazi Germany to date, declaring that the "Nazi masters of Germany have made it clear that they intend not only to dominate all life and thought in their own country, but also to enslave the whole of Europe to dominate the world."[97] Roosevelt then made a point that he would later use as a justification for his policy of "unconditional surrender" by saying that there was no use in negotiating with the Nazis: "The experiences of the past two years has proven beyond doubt that no nation can appease Nazis. No man can tame a tiger into a kitten by stroking it. There can be no appeasement with ruthlessness. There can be no reasoning with an incendiary bomb. We know now that a nation can have peace with the Nazis only at the price of total surrender."[98] America, Roosevelt said a week later, would serve as the "arsenal of democracy." Churchill had his answer to his radio appeal to the American people, in which he had said, "give us the tools and we will finish the job."[99]

Hitler was largely, but not wholly, wrong about America's intentions regarding Britain. American progressivism was not as pure as the driven snow. Behind the noble rhetoric of open markets and a peaceful democratic world was a doctrinaire ideology of American exceptionalism that was no less imperialistic than the one advocated by British supporters of "liberal imperialism" in the late nineteenth century. Hitler helped accelerate the process of the decline of the British Empire that was already under way in the 1930s. When Churchill came begging to the Americans and received the generous lend-lease program, he knew that there was a price to be paid for what he later called "the most unsordid act in the history of any nation."[100] It was the beginning of British dependence on the United States, which only grew more extensively during the course of the war. By 1945 Britain was only a minor power among the two new giants on the block—the United States and the Soviet Union. Britain's preeminent role in the world was coming to an end.

On December 17, Hitler told Jodl, "We must solve all continental European problems in 1941 since the USA will be in a position to intervene from 1942 onwards."[101] FDR's public statements were causing alarm in Berlin. Goebbels confided to his diary that he was afraid that America was sliding into a kind of war psychosis. Would FDR declare war on Germany? Hitler's response was to accelerate plans for the invasion of the Soviet Union. One day after Roosevelt announced his support for lend-lease to Britain, Hitler's adjutant, Major Engels, recorded in his diary that "Directive for Barbarossa (the code name for the invasion of Russia) has been initiated. . . . In my opinion Führer does not know himself how to proceed. Suspicious of his own military leadership, Führer constantly preoccupied by uncertainty over Russian strength, disappointed by the tenacity of the English. . . . Hopes that the English will give in. [He] does not believe that the United States will enter the war."[102] As this rare glimpse into Hitler's mind reveals, he was determined to force a final decision to the conflict with Britain by invading the Soviet Union in 1941. The die had been cast.

CHAPTER 5

The World Will Hold Its Breath: 1941

Hitler's Collision Course with Russia and the United States

In his annual message to Congress on January 6, 1941, President Roosevelt once more stressed the necessity of supplying the victims of aggression with all the materials and weapons they needed to fight predatory nations. Looking to the future, he hoped that the world would be governed by four vital freedoms: freedom of speech and expression, freedom to worship God, freedom from want, and freedom from fear. Hitler's New Year message to the German people had quite a different tone from Roosevelt's. It was a recapitulation of German military triumphs and a prediction of future ones to come. He warned the English that he would not let them escape as easily as he had in June 1940. Their leaders had turned down his peace offer and responded with vicious night attacks on German cities. His warning that he would retaliate ten or one hundred times, for each British attack had been answered with "laughter" (*Gelächter*). He characterized the coming war as a fight against the plutocratic elite of the Western world, whose only goal was greed and profits for the few. Their only God, he said, was money, whereas the goal of National Socialism was the good of the community. The armies of National Socialism were fighting for a nobler ideal; and judging by their resounding military victories, God had been on their side and hopefully would not abandon them in the future.[1]

A week later, Hitler bluntly told his military chiefs that the Gordian knot could only be cut by invading Russia. He repeated his previous reasons: Britain was staying in the war because she hoped that the United States and Russia would intervene. In this case, the German war effort would be severely taxed. He planned to avoid this by eliminating Russia before the United States could intervene. American intervention became more than just a remote possibility.[2] In February, the House passed lend-lease by a vote of 260 to 165; in March, the Senate followed suit by passing it 60 to 31. The initial appropriation was 7 billion dollars; by the end of the war the total had reached 27 billion dollars.[3] When Hitler heard the news, he said that the Americans had finally let the cat out of the bag. Lend-lease, he said, could be regarded as an act of war. Sooner or later, one way or another (*so oder so*) there would be war with the United States. Roosevelt and the Jews wanted war to protect their economic interests in Europe. Hitler added that he wished Germany had long-range bombers that could attack U.S. cities.[4]

On March 27, Hitler told the Japanese foreign minister Matsuoka what he had been saying for the past six months: Britain's hope lay in Russia and America. He tried to give his Japanese visitor the impression that Britain was as good as defeated and that American help, if it got through at all, would come too late.[5] This was why Japan should take immediate advantage of British weakness by attacking Singapore. Hitler hoped that a Japanese attack on the British island base at the tip of the Malaysian peninsula would threaten British sea routes to the Orient and the Dutch East Indies. Singapore guarded India from the east and Australia from the north. All of Britain's Southeast Asian possessions would be threatened, causing her to end the European war. In Hitler's calculations Japanese expansion in Southeast Asia would make the United States think twice before involving itself in the European theater of war. The Russians, he assured Matsuoko, were no threat to Japan because they faced powerful German armies on their western frontier. Matsuoko was evasive, telling Hitler that he could not make any promises on behalf of Japan at the moment; he explained that this was the result of internal divisions in Japan between the military expansionists and certain prominent court circles whose members had been educated in Britain and America and were undermining Japanese traditions.[6] Matsuoko was an ambitious and devious opportunist. He neglected to tell Hitler that he had been educated in the United States himself, receiving a law degree from the University of Oregon. What he said about internal divisions in Japan was true, however, for at the very time

he was discussing aggressive expansion in Berlin, another Japanese diplomat, one-eyed Admiral Nomura, expressed his respect and friendship
for America in his discussions with the president. Since the Americans
had broken the top secret Japanese "Purple" code, they had now become
aware of Japan's internal divisions. After his discussion with Hitler, during which he made more misleading statements, Matsuoka returned to
Tokyo via Moscow. Stalin suggested a Russo-Japanese nonaggression
pact, which the Japanese foreign minister signed after quickly clearing it
with his government.

After the signing of the Russo-Japanese neutrality pact, there occurred
a curious episode at the railroad station where Stalin and his entourage said
farewell to Matsuoka. The dignitaries were in a festive mood, having con-
sumed a great deal of alcohol; they exchanged bear hugs and even kissed
each other. Stalin was overheard to say to Matsuoka: "Now that Japan and
Russia have fixed their problems, Japan can straighten out the Far East;
Russia and Germany will handle Europe. Later together all of them will
deal with America."[7] The Russian dictator then asked to talk to the German ambassador, Friedrich von der Schulenberg, and upon locating him,
put his short arms around the tall shoulders of the German diplomat and
exclaimed, "We must remain friends and [you] must now do everything
to that end!"[8]

Hitler had already convinced himself that Russia was an enemy.[9] As to
the Japanese, he was taken aback by the Russo-Japanese neutrality pact.
In 1942 he said that he would have preferred a Japanese attack on Russia
in Manchuria, coinciding with a German attack on Russia in the west. In
the spring of 1941 he encouraged the Japanese to expand to the south in
the Pacific against the British. He believed that the German army could
take care of the "colossus with clay feet" without Japanese help. The Japanese attack in the south did not help the Germans at all. The alliance with
Japan only provided Hitler with one of several reasons to declare war on
the United States in December 1941. He believed that Germany's naval
weaknesses were being compensated for by Japanese naval strengths. He
would now fight the undeclared naval war with the United States by letting the Japanese defeat the American navy. In the absence of a large German navy, the Japanese could fight the naval war with the United States for
him. Hitler had ordered a study from his naval chiefs about the possibility
of delivering crippling blows on the American fleet by means of U-boats,

which had shown that such undertakings were not feasible.[10] It was therefore best to wait until Germany and Japan were allies. In the meantime, he would build up his own mighty navy, but that probably would not happen until 1946. Hitler later said that he regretted that the Japanese did not enter the war against Russia. If they had, victory would have been achieved by Christmas of 1941.[11]

In the spring of 1941, the German High Command was busy preparing for the attack on the Soviet Union. The timetable for the invasion of Russia had originally been set for May 15, 1941, but it had to be slightly delayed because of two unforeseen events: the Italian defeats in North Africa and a coup in Yugoslavia. In both cases, German troops had to be diverted to theaters of war that played a minor role in Hitler's strategic calculations. In both cases, the British had a hand in probing the vulnerability of Hitler's Greater German Reich at its outer perimeters. The Greeks had been defeating the Italians in Greece, and the British defeated them in North Africa. Thus, in order to prevent a collapse of the whole Mediterranean theater of war, Hitler issued several directives in December 1940 to prop up his Italian ally and keep the British at bay. As a result, Hitler overstretched German resources and sent German troops into southeastern Europe—Yugoslavia, Greece, Rumania, Bulgaria, and Crete—and North Africa (Rommel's Africa Corps). The Russian invasion was delayed by five weeks, until the summer of 1941.

Although Hitler's timetable had to be slightly revised by the campaigns in the Balkans and North Africa, new opportunities were also opened up by the brilliant performance of the German army. The Balkans had been conquered in three weeks, with the British suffering ignominious defeats in Greece and on the island of Crete, which was taken by German airborne divisions. There was a revolt in Iraq against the British. Rommel had thrown the British back to the western frontier of Egypt. Hitler could have chosen to invade the Middle East, take Suez, and accomplish what Napoleon had failed to do—break the back of British imperial power in the West; but his imperial vision was still focused on the defeat of Russia. Stalin wanted to trust Hitler, ignoring the massive German troop buildup on the demarcation zone in Poland. Moreover, Stalin kept on sending vast freight trains loaded with raw materials for the German war economy. The German ambassador, Count von Schulenburg, told Hitler that Stalin had no warlike intentions. Hitler was not convinced.

What troubled Hitler was the certainty of involving Germany in a two-front war if he decided to attack the Soviet Union. For years he had lectured his military commanders that Germany should do everything possible to avoid a repeat of World War I. With this in mind, he had sent out peace feelers to the British even as the Battle of France was still raging, and contrary to conventional historical opinion, he continued to encourage secret peace overtures to Britain for the next eight months. Hitler knew that his deputy, Rudolf Hess, had contacts with influential anti-Churchill leaders in Britain. He hoped that by exploiting these contacts he could possibly bring about a shift in Britain's rigid anti-German position. What Hitler and Hess did not know was that these British contacts were none other than British intelligence answering directly to Churchill and the nation's elite leadership at Whitehall.[12] In contrast to Hitler, who may have toyed with the idea of peace with Britain before attacking Russia, the British leadership did not want peace with Hitler. They wanted to drag out the war, because they knew that if they did the Germans would lose. Their hope was that both Russia and the United States would be drawn into the war. Hess had met the Duke of Hamilton during the Olympic Games and thought that he was a friend of the new Germany. In the fall of 1940, Hess began corresponding with Hamilton, not realizing that he was actually talking to British intelligence.[13]

On May 10, 1941, Hess took inspiration from Neville Chamberlain's 1938 flight to seek "peace in our time" by secretly flying solo to Scotland on a "peace mission." Decades of speculation have failed to provide conclusive explanations as to why Hess undertook this hazardous mission. The official Nazi position was that Hess had gone mad, and Hitler put on a command performance, playing the distraught leader who had been betrayed by one of his closest followers.[14] The complete truth of this mysterious flight by the deputy führer will never be fully known, but the event is open to speculation. One conjecture is that Hitler probably encouraged Hess to contact British leaders who might be receptive to an Anglo-German peace agreement. Hess may have interpreted Hitler's suggestion literally, thinking that he had to do something spectacular—which he certainly did by flying to Scotland at night and bailing out over the Duke of Hamilton's country estate. It is safe to assume that the British broke Hess and acquired information, which confirmed what they had learned from other sources, that Germany was about to invade the Soviet Union. They did not know whether Hess was mentally stable and acting on behalf of Hitler. At any rate, at this point in the war the British did not want a peace proposal, no matter who offered it. The official British version of Hess's flight was similar to the German one, though for different reasons: Hess was mentally unbalanced, and his peace proposal was meaningless because the Germans themselves had disavowed it. The real British side of this story has not been fully exposed, because the files on the matter are still closed; if all the details were to come to light, it might reveal some inconvenient truths.[15] This brings us to a third supposition that can be supported by some evidence. One important consequence of Hess's flight was that it heightened Stalin's suspicions of the British. The Soviet dictator suspected that the British were seeking a rapprochement with Germany. One of their agents in London received information from Kim Philby, who worked for the Russian NKVD and later defected to the Soviet Union, that Hess had brought a peace offer from Hitler and that he was empowered by Hitler to initiate negotiations with the British.[16] In her postwar book *Prisoner of Peace* (1955), Hess's wife also claimed that her husband had undertaken his peace mission with Hitler's full knowledge. There are other sources—none of them conclusive—that also assert that Hess flew to Britain to negotiate a settlement as a prelude to the invasion of Russia. Whatever the real truth, Stalin suspected a Western plot; he believed—not without good reason—that the British were scheming to detach the Germans from their alliance with the Russians. The deal Hess was proposing to the British, the Russians claimed, was to grant the Germans a free hand in Eastern Europe in return for allowing the British complete control over their imperial possessions, including hegemony in the Mediterranean.

President Roosevelt, anxious to learn more about the Hess flight, sent Churchill a message asking him what the interrogation of Hess had revealed. He said that Hess's flight had captured the imagination of the public in America and that "the story should be kept alive for just as many days or even weeks as possible."[17] Churchill's reply to FDR's query about Hess did not add much to what the president already knew. This was deliberate on Churchill's part. The prime minister skirted the question of whether Hess had come in an official capacity, but he did tell FDR that the Germans did not want to negotiate with the present British government. Hess also denied rumors that the Germans planned to attack Russia. Churchill did want to let FDR know that Hess had made disparaging remarks about the

United States and the degree of assistance the US would be able to furnish Britain. In addition, Hess did not think much of American aircraft design and production. Churchill said that if Hess really believed that there was a "peace movement" in Britain it would be "an encouraging sign of ineptitude of German Intelligence Service."[18] He promised to have Hess treated well but indicated that, as he was part of a criminal regime, his fate would ultimately have to be determined by the "Allied Government."

FDR did not believe that Churchill's cable told the whole story about the Hess affair, but he chose not to pursue the matter. He had already made it abundantly clear that America stood solidly behind England. Just how close America had drawn to Britain was not quite clear to General Bötticher, who was monitoring American developments in Washington. During the first three months of 1941, top secret staff meetings between American and British general staff officers were underway. The product of these talks was summed up in a joint report called ABC-1, which recommended that if the United States entered the war its first objective would be to defeat Hitler. ABC-1 was an outgrowth of the previous Rainbow plans of the War Department that dealt with potential conflicts with foreign powers, chiefly Germany and Japan. As previously mentioned, Rainbow 5 envisioned a world war and recommended "getting Hitler first," because he represented the greatest threat to the security of the United States. The plan had not been finalized because the military and civilian planning officers had not coordinated their efforts. The military planners called for an army of nearly 9 million—a total of 215 divisions—before a successful expedition could be sent abroad. Bötticher apparently had no idea about these plans. Like most of the Americans he lived among, he heard about these war plans only after the *Chicago Tribune* revealed the details, publishing the leaked secret documents on December 4, 1941.

In addition to lend-lease and secret staff meetings, Anglo-American cooperation also involved the sharing of intelligence. In February 1941 American Army Intelligence gave the British code breakers at Bletchley Park a complex machine called "Purple" that could decipher the Japanese diplomatic messages, code-named "Magic." The British later reciprocated by sharing their decryption of the German Enigma machine, allowing the Allied Powers to read some of the most secret German military messages. There is still some doubt whether secret military information sharing was a two-way street before December 7, 1941.[19] Some historians have even accused Churchill of withholding secret military information about the impending attack on Pearl Harbor, but no credible evidence of this has been produced.[20]

Several American historians have argued that the United States drifted aimlessly during much of 1941, maintaining that this was due largely to Roosevelt's deep-seated aversion to war.[21] Judging from the president's actions in 1941, the opposite is probably the case. Roosevelt's actions against both Germany and Japan were positively provocative, including the previously mentioned programs of cash and carry, lend-lease, neutrality zones, restoring conscription, increased defense appropriations, and secret war plans. In March 1941 Roosevelt informed the British that they could have their ships repaired in American docks, and that same month the president ordered the seizure of all Axis vessels in American ports. On April 10, Roosevelt extended the security zone all the way to the eastern coast of Greenland, negotiating the use of military bases on the island with a Danish official who did not have approval from his home government. If we add the various economic sanctions the president imposed on Japan, it is hard to escape the conclusion that Roosevelt was preparing the nation for war.

Hitler wanted to avoid confrontation with America as long as possible, taking all sorts of precautions to avoid a collision. His orders to Admiral Raeder to restrain his U-boats have already been mentioned. He went so far as to order Admiral Canaris, chief of the Abwehr, not to engage in any sabotage activities in the United States. J. Edgar Hoover knew this but failed to inform the president of this fact.[22] Once the Lend-Lease Act was passed by Congress in March 1941, both Hitler and Roosevelt realized that the shooting war would come next, because lend-leasing arms required escorting non-American merchant ships with U.S. warships. On May 23, Hitler told John Cudahy, the former American ambassador to Belgium, that American escort of British vessels was an act of war, but reiterated his previous assurances that Germany had no intention of attacking the Western Hemisphere. He laughed when Cudahy told him that many Americans feared the likelihood of a German invasion, telling his American visitor that "the idea of Germany invading the Western Hemisphere was about as fantastic as an invasion of the moon. . . . He assured me that Germany had too many problems in Europe ever to give any thought to an American invasion."[23] Cudahy seemed impressed by Hitler's sincerity, but then we have to remember that this was the same man who had compared the Brownshirts to a fraternal order in 1933. Cudahy subsequently wrote a misleading fluff piece about his interview with Hitler for *Life* magazine. Hitler's willingness to meet Cudahy indicates that he was still trying to influence public opinion in America, but just one week later Roosevelt gave him another rebuff. In a fireside chat to the American people, he proclaimed an "unlimited national emergency" because the Nazis were steadily encroaching on the Western Hemisphere. He mentioned Hitler by name, something he had avoided before. The Nazi world, he said, does not recognize any God except Hitler. On June 14 the United States government froze all assets of the Axis powers in America. Roosevelt also gave orders to close down all German propaganda agencies in America—the Library of Information, the German Railway and Tourist Agencies, and the Transocean News Service. All German consulates, except the German embassy in Washington, were also closed.

What was left of Hitler's fifth column in America was reduced to ineffective propaganda efforts to prop up the isolationists.[24] Thomsen funneled money to congressmen and to various committees battling interventionism in the summer and fall of 1941. Sylvester Viereck was particularly active in trying to influence a number of congressmen and senators with whom he had developed close connections. In September 1941, however, a grand jury began an investigation into foreign propaganda that would lead to the conviction of Viereck and other pro-Nazi agents. Hitler had lost the propaganda war in the United States. Noninterventionists and critics of the administration, however, continued to accuse the president of not doing enough about fifth columnists that were allegedly loose in America. The House Select Committee on Un-American Activities (HUAC), under the direction of Martin Dies, constantly inflated the threat from fifth columnists, criticizing both the president and the FBI for failing to offer the nation enough protection from subversives of all kinds: Nazis, Communists, Fascists, and Japanese. In the end, Hoover gained control of the national intelligence apparatus, and FDR reminded Dies that law enforcement resided in the executive branch. Nazi spy activities had been brought under complete control by 1942. The figures speak for themselves: during the summer and autumn of 1941, the FBI exposed three German spy rings, effectively dismantling German spy operations.[25] In 1945 the FBI reported that no verified acts of sabotage had been committed, an exaggerated boast considering what we now know about Communist subversion, but true enough when it came to bungled German operations. The only German espionage coup was the theft of the Norden bomb sight, and that one did not bring significant benefits to the Luftwaffe because it was not installed in German bombers until after the Battle of Britain. As previously noted, Hitler never had much hope of converting American public opinion; he only wanted to delay American entrance into the war long enough for him to conquer Russia. Although he encouraged propaganda efforts to strengthen isolationism in America, even supporting Goering's scheme to influence the election of 1940, he held out little hope for a Nazified America.

For President Roosevelt, it was useful to magnify the Nazi threat, for he wanted very much to convert the American people to an interventionist course. This is why his public statements became increasingly alarmist. Hitler was painted as an implacable enemy both at home and abroad. The president claimed that Hitler wanted to destroy America through "an inside-job," sowing the seeds of suspicion, distrust, and subversion.[26] He labeled his isolationist critics not only Nazi sympathizers but also agents of Hitler. In the president's judgment, Lindbergh was a Nazi, and he told Morgenthau: "If I should die tomorrow, I want you to know this. I am absolutely convinced that Lindbergh is a Nazi."[27] The president's heightened sense of the existence of subversives was in part the result of a steady stream of rumors he was fed by various sources. He had made it a point for a long time to avoid scaring the American people needlessly, but now in the spring and summer of 1941 he believed everything had changed, and with historical hindsight, it had.

Hitler was a menace, and he was about to unleash his fury against the Russians. The world, he said, would "hold its breath." The world did. On June 22, 1941, he sent the following message to the German people via his mouthpiece Joseph Goebbels: "German People! National Socialists! Weighed down with heavy cares, condemned to months of silence, the hour has come when I finally speak freely. . . . German People! At this moment a march is taking place that in extent and scope is the greatest the world has ever seen. . . . I have decided to place the fate of the German Reich and its people into the hands of our soldiers. May God help us all in this battle."[28]

It was a fait accompli: Hitler had invaded Russia without a declaration of war and with an army six times the size of Napoleon's Grand

Armée of 1812. Before unleashing it, he had told his generals that Operation Barbarossa, named after its medieval namesake, Emperor Frederick "Red-beard" Barbarossa, was not just a conventional military but a biological-racial war. He told his senior commanders not to worry about the Geneva or Hague conventions because the coming campaign was a struggle of ideologies and racial differences. The war with Russia had to be "conducted with unprecedented, merciless, and unrelenting harshness."[29] He regarded the Russians as subhuman and the Soviet territory as a "bolshevized wasteland" to be conquered, ethnically cleansed, and resettled by German pioneers. He told Jodl, "We have only to kick in the door and the whole rotten structure will come crashing down."[30] The rewards would be enormous because great riches would flow into the fatherland from the resources of the Ukraine. All of Russia would eventually become the Reich's granary (Kornkammer); it would be Germany's new frontier, where proud Aryan colonists would reenact in the east what the American pioneers had achieved in the American West. There would naturally be obstacles, just as there had been in the American West, in the form of unfamiliar terrain and natives. As a Karl May enthusiast, however, Hitler predicted that these natives would fall like ripe wheat to the Nazi scythe. With Russia in his pocket, no single American would ever be able to land in Europe. Germany and its allies would then control the same amount of territory as the United States; in fact, in population size, 500 million Europeans would dwarf the mere 230 million Americans. The half-civilized continent of North America would therefore play a purely subordinate role in the world. The future would once more be in Europe, not in the New World.[31]

Hitler defended his attack on the Soviet Union as a preventive war, claiming that Stalin was about to attack Germany. He also justified the invasion of Russia as a crusade against "Jewish Bolshevism." There is some evidence to suggest that Hitler probably did not believe that Stalin's actions were motivated by Bolshevism but by Russian nationalism.[32] Rainer Zitelmann has argued that Hitler's equation of Western capitalism with Soviet Communism was largely propagandistic, as was his claim that both of these systems could be reduced to a worldwide Jewish conspiracy. Zitelmann argued that in 1941 Hitler's major concern was to increase the industrial capacity of the German Reich so that it could wage a possible war of attrition against the Anglo-Americans. He quotes Hitler as saying that "in order to prevail in the fight for survival with America, Europe requires the wheat, meat, lumber, coal, iron, and oil of Russia."[33] There is no doubt that in the spring of 1941 space and resources were uppermost in Hitler's calculations, but so was his Jewish obsession, which he was about to link in the most horrible way to his paranoid fear that capitalism and communism were Jewish inventions. The need for Russian resources did not make an ounce of difference to Hitler's hatred of the Jews.

These were the stakes Hitler was pursuing in the summer of 1941, and they were not as demented as historians have made them out to be. If German military triumphs in Scandinavia, Poland, France, and the Balkans were any indication, the collapse of Russia within three months was not an entirely unreasonable expectation. Russian armies had performed poorly in Finland; they were inadequately equipped and badly led. Stalin's brutal purges of the army, which involved the dismissal and execution of more than thirty-four thousand officers in the immediate prewar period, had left its mark.[34] Hitler held the initial advantage as a result of his sneak attack, which caught the Russian army completely by surprise and led to spectacular early successes. What Hitler had not counted on was the resilience of the Russian soldiers, the strength of the Communist system, and the adverse conditions of Russian terrain and climate. Most important, banking on an early victory, possibly well before Christmas 1941, Hitler had not foreseen the emergence of what he later called the "unnatural alliance" between Russia, the United States, and Britain.

Roosevelt acted quickly in the wake of the German invasion of Russia, assuring Stalin that the United States would provide maximum support to Russia. To prove that he meant business, he sent his most trusted advisor, Harry Hopkins, to Moscow at the end of July with the reassuring message, "I ask you to treat Mr. Hopkins with the identical confidence you would feel if you were talking directly to me."[35] The talks centered on supplying the Russians with American aid in the hope that this would avert a collapse of the Red Army. Hopkins returned with a glowing account of Stalin's courageous leadership. "Uncle Joe," as FDR would later call the brutal dictator, was being promoted by New Dealers as a social progressive. In a press conference, the president described the Soviet Union in a favorable light, drawing attention to the Russian constitution of 1936 that guaranteed freedom of conscience and religion. The president's ambassador to the Soviet Union, Joseph Davies, a wealthy businessman and personal friend of FDR, assumed his post with high expectations of Russian politics. His optimistic view of Russia made him oblivious to the brutalities that were happening all around him. Davies attended the notorious show trial of Stalin's enemies and judged the proceedings just and fair. He also trusted the integrity of Walter Duranty, the *New York Times* reporter in Russia, who uncritically swallowed Soviet propaganda and wrote the most absurd articles. He even adamantly denied that Stalin had anything to do with the enforced famine in the Ukraine (1932–33), the North Caucasus, and the Lower Volga area that killed more than 5 million people. For his "sterling reportage," Duranty received the Pulitzer Prize for "dispassionate, interpretive reporting of the news from Russia."[36] As to Davies, he wrote a widely acclaimed book, titled *Mission to Moscow* (1941), in which he said, among other things, that the Soviets wanted "to promote the brotherhood of man and to improve the lot of the common people. They wish to create a society in which men live as equals, governed by ethical ideas. They are devoted to peace."[37] One could argue that these illusions about Russia were necessary to maintain Allied unity against Hitler. Perhaps this was the price to be paid for allying oneself with the devil to drive out Beelzebub. As Churchill so memorably put it, "If Hitler invaded Hell I would make at least a favourable reference to the Devil in the House of Commons."[38]

On either side of the ocean, Roosevelt and Hitler now became acutely aware of the importance of favorable timing. Hitler was haunted by it throughout the war, but especially so in the spring and summer of 1941. Facing certain defeat in 1945, he rued the fact that time had not been on his side, saying, "The tragedy for us Germans is that we never have enough time. Circumstances always conspire to force us to hurry, and if at this point time is lacking it is primarily because we lack space."[39] Time and space were, in fact, Hitler's two arch enemies. His attack on Russia, he later confessed, had been motivated by his concern that he would have to wage a long war of attrition with Britain and her likely ally, the United States. He needed the space of Russia because, in a long war, time would have been on the side of Germany's enemies: "Time—and it's always Time, you notice—would have been increasingly against us."[40] What Hitler would not admit to himself was that he had chosen poor strategies at the wrong time—the summer of 1941—and in the wrong place—Russia. He had also, like Napoleon, followed his appetite for conquest without digesting the territories he had already conquered. In late 1941 he bragged about wanting to enjoy the taste of continental hegemony to the fullest (*auskosten*) before thinking about world politics.[41] But in 1941 he had not gained complete continental control and, suffering his first major reversal on the Moscow front, he was unlikely to gain complete control over Eastern Europe in the foreseeable future.

Throughout 1941 Hitler tried to buy enough time to keep the United States out of the war until he had defeated Russia. As early as September 1939, the German Naval High Command had received instructions from Hitler that the navy should avoid circumstances that could lead to incidents with the United States. Admiral Raeder later said that "everyone knew that it was important to postpone the entry of America into the war as long as possible, even if it was not possible to avoid it entirely."[42] On several occasions Hitler reminded his naval chiefs that they should avoid "incidents" with the Americans.[43]

In 1941, Hitler, Churchill, Stalin, and Roosevelt knew that the European war would expand into a world war and that timing was everything. For Hitler, it was buying time to keep America at bay; for Roosevelt, it was buying enough time to rearm quickly and massively; for Churchill, it was holding out long enough for reinforcements from America to arrive; and for Stalin, it was holding out and waiting for a second front. Roosevelt spoke for the American side in the spring of 1941 when he said, "But, now, now, the time element is of supreme importance. Every plane, every other instrument we can spare now, we will send overseas because that is the common sense of strategy. . . . Here in Washington, we are thinking in terms of speed and speed now. And I hope that that watchword—'speed and speed now'—will find its way into every home in the Nation."[44]

The president sprang into action on another front—the Atlantic. In late June he ordered the marines to Iceland, which enabled the United States to safeguard its supply routes across the Atlantic. Iceland was an independent republic, formerly under the control of Denmark. The island was of great strategic importance because it provided control of the North Atlantic sea-lanes and the naval exits into the Atlantic from Europe. To anticipate a German invasion, the British had already established a garrison on the island, which was relieved by U.S. forces. Now that the United States had added one more outpost to its imperium, the security zone necessarily had to be extended to embrace Iceland. Public opinion in America strongly supported this further breach of the neutrality laws, as a Gallup poll revealed in July 1941. Bötticher reported from Washington that the American navy was stretched too far and could not carry on a war in both the Atlantic and the Pacific. He added that the same was true of the U.S. Army and Air Force. This fact would greatly benefit the Japanese, because U.S. naval forces would have to withdraw from the Pacific in order to report for convoy duty in the Atlantic. Iceland was also very much on Hitler's mind when he received Hiroshi Ōshima, the Japanese ambassador to Germany, on July 14, 1941.

Hitler was in fine fettle at his military headquarters at Rastenburg in East Prussia when he met Ōshima. He acknowledged Ōshima's accolades about the spectacular successes of the German army and the "death-defying courage" of its soldiers. Hitler was in an expansive mood, trying to entice Ōshima with promises of joint German-Japanese conquests to come. He gave the Japanese ambassador the impression that the war against Russia was as good as won, and then urged his Japanese ally to strike while the iron was hot. He also indulged himself in bashing the Americans, belittling the fighting spirit of American soldiers. He could attest from his own experiences in World War I that American soldiers took heavy losses at the hands of already weakened German troops. Today the German army was much stronger than it had been in World War I. Hitler said that he would not mind if the Americans landed in Europe; if they did, they would be destroyed completely. To be a good soldier one had to have more than dollars. Yet Hitler added that he was "on his guard."[45] Once the eastern campaign had ended, it would be necessary to redirect the energy of German armament production from the army to the navy and especially the air force.[46] He then came to the heart of his comments to Ōshima: Russia was the common enemy of Germany and Japan. Germany was threatened by Russia in the west and the United States in the east. Conversely, Japan was threatened by Russia in the west and the United States in the east. It followed that the Axis partners had to eliminate both Russia and the United States. Hitler was not specific about how this was to be accomplished, other than saying that Russia had to be defeated first. He did not pressure Ōshima to enter the war against Russia at this time because he was convinced that Germany was about to accomplish this feat within the next six weeks. In the meantime, he wanted the Japanese to move south in the Pacific, tying down both the British and the Americans. He did bring up a cautious reminder: "If we can keep the United States out of the war at all, we will only be able to do so by destroying Russia and only if Japan and Germany act simultaneously and unequivocally."[47] He then suggested to Ōshima that Germany and Japan should conclude a military pact against the United States, labeling the United States as their countries' chief enemy. Ōshima listened politely but gave no firm assurances. Hitler, however, seemed to be already looking beyond Russia, because on the same day that he received Ōshima he ordered that the chief weight of armament production be shifted from the army to the navy and the air force. Once Russia had been defeated, the United States and Britain would have to be neutralized, and that would require victory at sea. Hitler's offer to Ōshima of a military pact may have been the result of America's recent occupation of Iceland.

In August, that special Anglo-American relationship Hitler referred to during his talks with Ōshima was sealed when Roosevelt met Churchill at Placentia Bay, Newfoundland. This historic meeting of two gentlemen who had been brought up at the end of the bourgeois age and who firmly subscribed to the Christian values of Western civilization was a memorable occasion. It was more symbolic than substantive, but the sense of common purpose was palpable the day FDR and Churchill sat on the quarterdeck of the *Prince of Wales* beneath the ship's big guns and attended religious services, singing "Onward Christian Soldiers." Just a few months later the Japanese sank the *Prince of Wales,* with most of her men who were present at Placentia Bay, off the coast of Kuantan in Malaya. The result of Placentia Bay was the Atlantic Charter, which listed eight lofty goals: the idea of national self-determination; the right of people to choose their own form of government; equal access to raw material in the world; economic reforms leading to social justice; freedom from fear and want; freedom of the seas; and the abolition of force; and perpetual peace through the establishment of a global security system—the goals of the future United Nations.

Nazi propaganda wrote off the Placentia Bay meeting as hollow Anglo-Saxon phrase-mongering, reminiscent of Woodrow Wilson's airy internationalism during World War I. This dismissive judgment shows that the Nazis had no grand strategy of any humane value whatsoever, for what they offered Europe was little more than brutal German subjugation. Hitler was not a missionary crusader with a message of universal liberty and equality. Among the many people Hitler conquered, there was little support or admiration for the German cause, as there had been—at least initially—for the Napoleonic conquests that were conducted under the banner of liberty, equality, and fraternity. Goebbels began to realize the weaknesses of the German cause as the European war gave way to world war. By mid-1942 German propaganda focused on the mortal peril of Communism to the Christian West, exhorting subject nations to join the German crusade against Bolshevism.[48] This campaign found some support, especially among Catholics, because the Vatican had always regarded the Communists as a greater threat than the Nazis. But as Nazi brutalities became more widely known, people all over Europe realized how hollow German propaganda was. Many Germans also became increasingly aware of the anti-Christian tendencies in Nazi theory and practice. At the time of the invasion of Russia, for example, the Nazis launched another attack on the church, confiscating monastic property and curtailing religious instruction and publication of religious material. In Bavaria, the most Catholic state in Germany, the party tried—unsuccessfully—to remove all crucifixes from public schoolrooms.[49]

Churchill left Placentia Bay in good spirits, hoping—quite mistakenly—that the United States was now prepared to enter the war. Roosevelt judged that the timing for this was not quite right.[50] Congress had only narrowly approved additional appropriations for lend-lease and isolationism was still too strong to risk war. Woodrow Wilson had been far less cautious in World War I than Roosevelt was during much of 1941. As in World War I, American shipping was, if not intentionally, certainly unintentionally attacked in 1941. U-boats torpedoed a number of American vessels, notably the destroyers *Greer, Kearny, Salinas,* and *Reuben James.* After each attack—and it was not always clear who attacked first—the president let loose all sorts of rhetorical fireworks, but he did not go to Congress to ask for a declaration of war. Perhaps he knew that Congress was not about to give it to him unless a compelling incident made war unavoidable. Churchill later claimed that FDR had said he would wage war but not declare it. He would wait for an "incident."[51] Former ambassador Bullitt also remembered the president saying, "we must await an incident," confident that the Germans would shortly provide him with one.[52]

The president's cautious response to German provocations was partly strategic and partly propagandistic. America was still militarily unprepared. Moreover, FDR had told the American people too many times that it was not necessary to go to war unless deliberately provoked. Did this mean that he wanted the Germans or the Japanese to deliver the first blow in the form of a military attack or a declaration of war? So far, FDR was in the boxing ring but mostly sparring. On October 9, he sent Congress a message asking for a revision of the Neutrality Act, allowing him to arm merchant ships. Hardly a week later, a German U-boat torpedoed the American destroyer *Kearny* south of Iceland. The ship was not sunk, but eleven Americans lost their lives. Ten days later the president delivered his most aggressive speech to date in the Grand Ballroom of the Mayflower Hotel in New York. He said that all of America had been attacked by the Nazis in the recent unprovoked torpedoing of the *Kearny*. He told his audience, "The shooting has started. And history has recorded who fired the first shot. In the long run, however, all that matters is who fired the last shot."[53] He also mentioned that he had in his possession a captured map that showed how the Germans planned to divide up Latin America into five vassal states. The map showed that the Germans also planned to control the Panama Canal. Another secret document in his possession indicated that the Nazis planned to abolish all religions and replace them with an international Nazi church. Both documents were fabrications by British intelligence, though it is not entirely clear whether the president was aware of this.[54] Whatever the case, FDR used these documents to arouse public alarm and thereby promote the cause of intervention. It had become obvious to him that methods short of war were no longer adequate. Already in his Labor Day address to the American people he had warned, "We are engaged on a grim and perilous task. Forces of insane violence have been let loose by Hitler upon this earth. We must do our full part in conquering them. . . . We shall do everything in our power to crush Hitler and his Nazi forces."[55] To Hitler this sounded like a declaration of war. As the Germans were slashing their way toward Moscow, "methods short of war" would not stop them. Harry Hopkins summed up the administration's feelings when he said, "I . . . don't believe we can ever lick Hitler with a lend-lease program."[56]

On October 2, after switching his military strategies repeatedly, Hitler finally decided to go for broke, directing Field Marshal Fedor von Bock to take Moscow.[57] The reason Hitler finally approved a decisive blow against Moscow may have been to show the Japanese that they had to commit themselves militarily on the German side. A German victory in Russia would remove the threat to Japan's forces in China, and it would also give the Japanese the green light to expand southward in the Pacific. In a message to his troops, Hitler exhorted them to eradicate their Bolshevik enemies, describing the Russian soldiers as "beasts." "Now that you have seen this workers paradise with your own eyes," he said, "you have witnessed the reign of poverty that is unimaginable for us Germans. This is the result of nearly twenty-five years of Jewish domination; of bolshevism that in its deepest sense is only comparable in general form to capitalism. The carriers in both cases, however, are the Jews and nothing but Jews."[58] If he should fail in Russia it would be the fault of the Jews. He would then exterminate them all. Inspired by this hateful mentality, Hitler's extermination task forces—the *Einsatzgruppen*—had entered Russia with what they thought was a free hand to murder at will. They had followed behind the regular army groups and committed mass atrocities in the rear areas. In a speech of November 8, commemorating the 1923 beerhall coup, Hitler described the Jews as incendiaries who set fires all over the world. The Soviet Union was doing the bidding of the Jews; the same was true of Roosevelt's America. Stalin was a puppet on the Soviet stage, controlled behind the curtain by the Jews. It was also in this speech that Hitler mentioned Roosevelt's use of fake German documents. The president's accusation that Germany planned to destroy the world's religions was ridiculous. Hitler said that he was now fifty-two years old and had no patience with such childish nonsense. He pointed out that in Germany religion was state supported to the tune of 900 million marks a year, while in America churches did not receive a penny from the state. If this was the best that Roosevelt's brain trust could come up with, he could only pity him: "I can only tell Herr Roosevelt: I don't have any experts. My own head (Kopf) is sufficient. I don't need the support of a brain trust (Gehirntrust). If there are important developments anywhere, they will be initiated in my brain and not the brain of experts. . . . I am not a grammar school boy who draws maps out of a school atlas. South America is as far away as the moon as far as I am concerned."[59]

Following the rainy season in October, the eastern front was blanketed by heavy snowfall. Hitler had counted on quick blitzkrieg victories lasting no more than six to eight weeks. When his soldiers invaded Russia in June, he did not anticipate a long winter campaign, and made sure that his troops were well-equipped to fight in bitter winter conditions. Hitler and his generals had seriously miscalculated; they discovered that the Soviet house was not as rotten as they had assumed. In the first four weeks of the Russian campaign, the Germans suffered 100,000 casualties, losing 1,700 tanks and assault weapons and 950 planes.[60] By August, they had lost 189,000 men, still far less than the staggering Russian casualties, but cause for grave concern to the German High Command. The three major army groups that had invaded Russia in June had not delivered final knockout blows to any of the targets they had been directed to attack: Leningrad in the north, Moscow in the center, or the Ukraine in the south. What would happen if Russia were not conquered in 1941? What would the United States do? The answer to these questions came during the first twelve days of December.

Twelve Days in December

Four historic world events took place during the first twelve days of December: the Russian counterattack on the Moscow front (December 4–5) that saved the Russian capital; the Japanese attack on Pearl Harbor (December 7); Hitler's declaration of war on the United States (December 11); and Hitler's final directive ordering the annihilation of European Jewry (December 12). During the night of December 4–5, 1941, the Russians mounted a heavy counterattack against exposed German troops outside Moscow. Although the vanguard of the German offensive had reached the suburbs of Moscow, "seeing the towers of the Kremlin reflecting the setting sun," the whole German advance had already been weakened by the onset of a severe winter, by furious Russian rearguard actions, and by faulty intelligence. We now know that Stalin had secret information that the Japanese were planning to attack the United States;[61] and acting on this information, he transferred thirty-four Siberian divisions (250,000 men) to the Moscow front, thereby staving off almost inevitable defeat. The Germans were caught completely by surprise, and widespread alarm spread through the ranks of Army Group Center, evoking historical recollections of Napoleon's retreat, which had turned into a rout, in 1812. The front held in the end, but the German hope for a quick victory had faded. The myth of German military invincibility had been laid to rest. As Russian military historian Boris Nevzorov put it, "if they [the Germans] had taken Moscow, the war would have ended with a German victory."[62]

As Hitler contemplated this disaster in the making from his Wolf's

Lair (Wolfsschanze) in Rastenburg on December 7, 1941, a press officer gave the führer a message announcing that the Japanese had attacked the American fleet at Pearl Harbor. Hitler's initial reaction was one of jubilation, telling Walter Hewel, his liaison officer at headquarters, "We cannot lose the war at all. We have an ally who has not been defeated in three thousand years."[63] This was a case of wishful thinking, and a dreadful miscalculation. Until 1940, Hitler's timing had been superb. After the fall of France, however, his timing was definitely off; he began to fumble the ball against the British, convincing himself that Britain's only hope was Russia, when in fact, it was the United States. Once he had made the fatal decision to attack the Soviet Union, he was in a race against time that involved both Russia and the United States. By his time schedule—and there was a certain logic that supported it—he planned to win the war against Russia before Christmas 1941. It was crucial for Hitler to keep the United States out of the war during the six months following the invasion of Russia, from June 22 until the end of the year. The invasion of Russia had been planned out since the fall of 1940, but the Balkan and the North African campaigns had delayed Operation Barbarossa, originally scheduled for the spring of 1941, and when it was launched as a blitzkrieg operation, it did not meet its Christmas deadline. The secretive Japanese then forced Hitler's hand against the United States, though strictly speaking Hitler had no formal treaty obligations to follow Japan into a war with the United States.

As previously mentioned, Japan had concluded a neutrality pact with Russia in April 1941 and gave every appearance of respecting it. Hitler could have procrastinated on his commitment to Japan, demanding that the Japanese attack Russia in return for his declaration of war on America.[64] This he did not do. In fact, Ribbentrop assured ambassador Ōshima on November 28 that Germany would come to the aid of Japan in case of war with the United States. On December 4, 1941, Ribbentrop received Hitler's approval for what amounted to a more ironclad Tripartite Pact that specified that if war broke out between any one of the partners of the alliance and the United States, the other two powers would automatically follow their partner into a war with the United States. Ian Kershaw has argued that it followed from Ribbentrop's assurance to Japan that even before Pearl Harbor Germany had effectively committed itself to support Japan in a war with the United States.[65] The Germans, however, had no knowledge on December 4 that the Japanese fleet was already on its way to

Pearl Harbor, and no pact had been signed by the three powers. Hitler did not like surprises by his partners, and he treated pledges or treaty obligations as temporary expedients to be broken if they no longer served national interests. Hitler did not declare war on the United States because he wanted to come to the aid of Japan. The very best he could expect of Japan was that it would keep the United States tied down in the Pacific, which would give him some additional time to mop up the Russian operation. His real reason for declaring war on the United States must be sought, not in military, but in ideological considerations.

Why, then, did Hitler promptly declare war on the United States on December 11, 1941? Shortly after the war, the U.S. State Department sent a special delegation of experts to Germany to interrogate Nazi leaders about Hitler's conduct of the war, and on the question of Hitler's declaration of war on the United States the commission drew a complete blank. No one, it seemed, had a real clue about this baffling issue.[66] In order to answer this question, it may be useful to examine Hitler's public explanation in his Reichstag address of December 11 and then highlight the subtext of his justifications. It will be shown that Hitler's declaration of war on the United States was entirely consistent with his underlying beliefs about the real enemy behind the Russian and American war effort.

Starting his speech with various rationalizations about the conduct of the war, which, of course, had not been his fault, Hitler stated that providence did not intend to spare the German people from the ordeal of war. He was only glad that he had been singled out to lead this historical battle that would determine the shape of Germany, Europe, and the world for the next five hundred, perhaps even one thousand years.[67] The purpose of the Russian campaign had been to fight a preventative war, because the Soviets had planned to destroy all of Europe. He claimed that he did not want war and had, in fact, done everything possible to avoid one; but in order to prevent the bolshevik hordes from flooding the Danubian lands like Attila the Hun, he had sprung to the defense of Western civilization—a curious claim in view of the fact that he admired Attila the Hun and Genghis Khan and had commended their brutal tactics to his generals in August 1939. Then came a flood of statistics aimed at showing that the Russians were practically defeated.

And now he came to the New World, which, he said, was represented by a man who gave fireside chats to his people while German soldiers trudged through ice and snow in Russia. It was the man in the White House who was the chief culprit of the war.[68] It was Roosevelt, as the captured Polish documents showed, who had egged on the Poles in stonewalling meaning-ful negotiations with Germany. Asking rhetorically why Roosevelt would unleash such intense hatred on Germany, a country that had never harmed the United States, Hitler reverted to a stock-in-trade anti-American for-mula that reduced U.S. motivations to the plutocratic interest of finance capitalism. Behind Wilson and now Roosevelt had always stood power-ful business interests that had profited from war. This was true in 1917 just as it was true in 1939. Before letting the real shoe drop—namely, that those financial interests were Jewish—Hitler asked the assembled del-egates of the Reichstag to indulge him in a little comparison between the American president, who came from a very rich (*steinreiche*) family, and his own humble self, who came from a poor family and had to make his way in the world through unremitting work and perseverance. Roosevelt had earned his spurs as a privileged member of the American elite, who made a fortune out of the suffering of other people. Hitler said that by con-trast he fought for four years as an ordinary soldier on the western front, took orders rather than gave them, and returned to civilian life as poor as he had been before the war. Unlike Roosevelt, whose political road was paved with money and privilege, his own rise to prominence had been hard but satisfying because it was guided by a single-minded determination to redeem the honor of Germany and revenge the injustice inflicted on her. The contrast between him and Roosevelt, Hitler suggested, was striking: "Two life paths! When Roosevelt made his way to the top of the United States, he was the chosen candidate of a capitalistic party that had hired him as its servant. And when I became Chancellor of the German Reich, I was the leader of a popular movement (Volksbewegung) that I had created myself."[69]

Hitler then dropped the other shoe: behind Roosevelt stood the Jews, whose real interests were always financial and international but never na-tionalistic or aimed at the good of any nation. It was "the Jew in all of his satanic malice who gravitated around this man" (Roosevelt) and encour-aged him to incite war with Germany. Hitler went on to draw the logical corollary: the Jew who stands behind Roosevelt is the same Jew who had created the abomination called the Soviet Union.

We know what force stands behind Roosevelt. It is the kind of eternal Jew who has recognized that his time has come to do to us what we see and experience with a shudder in Soviet Russia. We have now come to know this Jewish paradise on earth. Millions of German soldiers have been able to gain personal insight into a country in which this international Jew destroyed and annihilated people and property. The president of the United States may not personally comprehend this. In that case it says a lot about his stupidity.[70]

There followed a lengthy and not entirely inaccurate bill of particulars of the many U.S. violations of its own neutrality laws. What is more important, however, is the question of just how serious Hitler really was about linking the United States and the Soviet Union and claiming that both were actually run by the Jews. It is my contention that these remarks went far beyond propagandistic exaggeration; they provide insight not only into Hitler's intense hatred of Jews but also into his paranoia that his enemies, though apparently different because of different forms of government, were actually controlled, directly or indirectly, by conniving Jews. His speeches, proclamations, and monologues at führer headquarters and the many remarks he made to a host of people abound with derogatory, vile, and murderous statements about Jews. Hitler acted on his convictions, and by the time of his declaration of war on the United States, the genocide against the Jews was already underway in the killing fields of Russia. The methods of annihilation were still not fully coordinated, but the murderous *Einsatzgruppen,* or Special SS task forces, were rounding up Jews behind the fighting front and shooting them in cold blood. Thus, when Hitler gave his speech on December 11, hundreds of thousands of Russian Jews had already been killed—men, women, and children. What was still lacking was greater coordination of the annihilation project and more efficient methods of killing masses of people in greater seclusion and secrecy. Hence the construction of death camps in 1942 (Auschwitz, Sobibor, Majdanek, Belzec, Treblinka, Chelmno), gas chambers, the activation of additional killing forces (the infamous police battalions), the broad involvement of governmental agencies, and the complicity of foreign governments. Finally, what the holocaust leadership was still waiting for was a führer order authorizing the "final solution to the Jewish question," a euphemistic phrase the Nazis used to describe the actual biological annihilation of the Jewish race in Europe. As will be recalled, Hitler had prophesied that he would eliminate the Jews in case of war in his speech to the Reichstag on January 30, 1939; he repeated that threat almost verbatim in his speech to the Reichstag on January 30, 1941. Many other well-documented remarks he made, both private and public, attest to his growing conviction that he was waging not only a conventional military but also a biological-racial war; and if he could not win the former, he would certainly win the latter, because he had most of the Jews of Europe under his control. It is my contention that Hitler sensed that the entrance of the United States into the war would cost him his ultimate victory, perhaps even guarantee his defeat. Accordingly, during the first twelve days of December, Hitler crossed the line separating a brutal dictator from a mass murderer. He gave a personal order to Heinrich Himmler, head of the SS, to carry out the physical annihilation of the Jews in gas chambers similar to those that had already been used in the euthanasia program to eliminate mentally ill men, women, and children.

There exists indirect evidence that Hitler may have announced the order to annihilate the Jews during the first two weeks of December 1941, possibly on December 12. The announcement, according to the German historian Christian Gerlach, came in a secret conference with about fifty high-ranking party officials during the afternoon of December 12, 1941.[71] Christian Gerlach was right to single out this conference as a real turning point in the decision making that would lead to the gas chambers, but he went too far in claiming that Hitler's speech was in the nature of an oral führer order to annihilate the Jews. Hitler's speech should not be seen as constituting a definitive and unequivocal order to commit criminal wrongdoing. Hitler always wanted to leave the door open for "plausible deniability" in matters dealing with the mass murder of Jews. He did not want either the German people or the rest of the world to connect his name to mass murder. To his closest henchmen in crime, however, he was far more forthcoming. After all, they had to know that the order to annihilate the Jews had been personally issued by the führer, for they would not have otherwise set in motion the machinery of destruction that led to the death camps. Even then, only three or four trustworthy paladins heard him issue such orders: Heinrich Himmler, Reinhard Heydrich, Martin Bormann, and Joseph Goebbels. Other Nazi leaders, including the high-ranking party functionaries who attended the December 12 conference, probably only heard him say it "in so many words," but he could have twisted these words to blunt the full extent of their murderous intentions if circumstances had forced him to do so. Hitler was one of the most cunning and crafty dissemblers in history;[72] he was, in fact, so devious that no one will ever find the "smoking gun" that catches him in the act of extermination of the Jews once and for all. The closest admission of culpability can be found in his last will and testament in which he justified his treatment of Jews as an act of reprisal for the deaths of millions of German soldiers on the battlefields and the hundreds of thousands of women and children who were firebombed in gruesome air raids. He claimed that the massacres committed by the Allies against innocent Germans justified forcing the guilty Jew to "atone" for his guilt (*für seine Schuld zu büßen*) in starting the war, though their destruction was admittedly accomplished *by more humane means*.[73] Even then, just before meeting his maker, Hitler insinuated that the means used to kill the Jews—putting them to sleep by gas—was more humane than what the Allies had done to German women and children.

In order to bring some clarity and common approaches to the Jewish annihilation project, the Nazis called a conference of high-ranking government ministers and higher SS police officers to coordinate governmental agencies and identify the roles they were expected to play in the coming liquidation of the Jews. Originally scheduled for December 9, the conference was twice postponed because of Pearl Harbor and Hitler's declaration of war on the United States. When it did convene at Wannsee on January 20, 1942, certain key events had already taken place in the direction of the final solution. On December 7, 1941, the day that lived in infamy, seven hundred Jews arrived at Chelmno (Kulmhof), a small town about 70 kilometers west of Lodz; they thought that they would be evacuated to the east to work, a deception the Nazis used to instill a false sense of security in their Jewish victims. Instead, on December 8, they were gassed in tightly sealed vans through exhaust fumes that were channeled back into the interior of the van.[74] Two Jewish prisoners managed to escape, and one of them provided detailed information about the Chelmno camp and its liquidations to the Warsaw Ghetto, and from there it was passed on to the Polish government in exile in London.

The gassing of Jews on December 8 opened the final phase of the Jewish destruction project, for it would become the preferred method of killing Jews. By the summer of 1942 the mobile gas vans had been replaced by stationary gas chambers in the annihilation camps. What undoubtedly pushed Hitler into making his dreadful decision to translate the unthinkable into practice were the events unfolding between December 4 and December 11—the Russian counteroffensive, the Japanese attack on Pearl Harbor, and the declaration of war on the United States. The hypothetical situation he had referred to in his January 30, 1939, Reichstag speech—namely, that in the event that the world were plunged into another world war, the Jews would be annihilated—had now come true. The European war had become a world war because the Jews had plunged everyone into it. It followed that the Jews had to be annihilated. Hitler believed that behind Roosevelt stood the Jews. Goebbels minced no words in his diary on December 13: "the führer has made a clean sweep on the Jewish question [reinen Tisch gemacht]. He made a prophecy for the Jews that if they brought about another World War, he would annihilate them. That was not an empty phrase. World War has arrived; the Jewish extermination is the necessary consequence."[75] The German historian Christian Gerlach argued that the dictator justified his decision on four grounds. First, the Jews had allegedly incited hatred against Germany in both wars. Second, the declaration of war against the United States provided him with another excuse for annihilating the Jews since they had insinuated themselves into the Roosevelt administration. Third, the Jews were now worthless as hostages to prevent the Americans from entering the war. Ever since American Jews had organized anti-German protests and boycotts, Hitler had intended to use the Jews under his control as hostages, as bargaining chips with Roosevelt and his alleged Jewish henchmen.[76] With the United States now in a world war, there was no reason for Hitler to continue holding Western European Jews as "hostages." Rather, it was now possible for Germany to exterminate its Jewish enemies, to divert American power to the Pacific, and to bring down the Soviet Union in 1942.

Finally, being at war with the major powers of the world created a kind of siege mentality in Hitler and the top Nazi leadership.[77] Mortal enemies in the shape of saboteurs and partisans were seen to be ubiquitous. Jews were now regarded as even deadlier enemies; it was best, therefore, to annihilate them all. A small, but perhaps not insignificant, element in this siege mentality (*Festungsmentalität*) was generated by shrill Nazi propaganda that the Jews had managed to persuade the Allied powers that the German people had to be exterminated. In mid-1941 Goebbels became aware of a book, published in early 1941 in the United States, entitled *Germany Must Perish*. Its author was Theodore N. Kaufman, owner of a Newark, New Jersey, theater ticket agency and one-man founder and sole member of the "American Federation of Peace." Kaufman, who was Jewish, self-published the book—or perhaps more accurately, pamphlet—under the imprint of the Argyl Press, of which he was the sole owner.[78] Kaufman's main thesis was that the Nazis "were merely the mirror reflecting centuries-old inbred lust of the German nation for conquest and mass murder."[79] As a solution to the German problem, a kind of "modest proposal," á la Jonathan Swift, Kaufman recommended the sterilization of all German males, the extinction of the German language, forced labor battalions, and permanent political partition. Goebbels regarded the book as a godsend for German propaganda, writing in his diary on August 3 that he intended to publish selections of Kaufman's screed with appropriate commentaries. He was as good as his word. On October 22, he wrote in his diary that the German version of the Kaufman book had already "sold in the millions of copies." He added that the book "has been extraordinarily useful to us domestically. It is impossible to imagine a better illustration of the desires and goals of the other side. The book could not have been more helpful to us if it had been written by a member of the Propaganda Ministry."[80]

After discussing it with Hitler, Goebbels made sure that the contents of Kaufman's book were widely discussed among the German people.[81] Both in the press and on the radio, the Germans were told that the "Kaufman Plan" represented the official policy of the United States. A representative of the German Foreign Office announced that they had learned that President Roosevelt dictated individual chapters of the book himself. The *Völkische Beobachter*, the chief organ of the Nazi Party, ran a frightening headline that read, "Roosevelt Demands the Sterilization of the German People."[82] Inciting such fears in the public was Goebbels's forte. In making use of Kaufman's screed, which had been widely dismissed in America, Nazi propaganda planned to unleash a "rage among the people" (*Volkswut*). In the short run, this failed, but what it did in the long run was to plant a seed of real dread in the public mind that defeat would spell extermination. The Nazi leadership hoped that this public dread of annihilation would instill a fanatical resolve in the German people, urging them on to final victory.

The beginning of the end took place on the eastern front. And it was here that the plan for extermination of the Jews came to a head in December 1941. At that time Hitler justified the mass shooting of Jews by saying that they were committing sabotage in the rear of the advancing German army. This was the meaning behind Hitler's remark to Himmler, recorded in the latter's appointment calendar as regards "the Jewish question. To be exterminated as partisans—Judenfrage/als Partisanen auszurottten."[83] This was not the first or the last time that Hitler referred to Jews as enemy combatants and saboteurs, and he used this characterization as an excuse for exterminating them all. In his obsession with the Jews, he went even further, referring to them as malignant cells, ferment of decomposition, harmful bacilli, and so forth. Such pathogens, he believed, called for the most radical measures. It was a matter of public hygiene, as Hitler explained on several occasions, even claiming that he was a political-biologist pioneer: "I feel like the Robert Koch of politics. He discovered the tuberculosis bacillus and opened up new paths for medical science. I discovered the Jew as the bacillus and ferment of social decomposition."[84] This delusion justified the notion that even children had to be exterminated, because they too were deadly bacilli and, if allowed to live, would become even deadlier enemies against future German generations.

On December 12, Hitler delivered a speech to leading members of the party and announced that the Jews had to be annihilated. No minutes of the speech have survived, nor has a written führer order ever been discovered. Those who attended the secret address, however, came away with a firm conviction that Hitler had authorized the extermination of the Jews. One of them was Hans Frank, the governor of Poland. On December 16, Frank gave a speech to his subordinates in Cracow, telling them what he had learned on his recent trip to Berlin and the führer's words to his Reich and Gauleiters. Frank said, "As a Veteran National Socialist I have to say this: if the Jews in Europe should survive the war, then the war would be only a partial success. As far as the Jews are concerned, I would therefore be guided by the basic expectation that they are going to disappear. They have to be gotten rid of. At present I am involved in discussions aimed at having them moved away to the east. In January there is going to be an important meeting in Berlin to discuss this question [i.e., the Wannsee conference]. . . . Here are 3.5 million Jews that we can't shoot, we can't poison. But there are some things which we can do, and one way or another these measures will successfully lead to liquidation."[85] Those Ho-

locaust perpetrators who testified after the war all agreed that the order
to annihilate the Jews ultimately originated with Adolf Hitler, not with
Himmler, Heydrich, or Goering. As Eberhard Jäckel has pointed out, it
is hard to imagine that an "act of such scope and with such far-reaching
consequences should have been initiated by subordinate agencies."[86]

What did Roosevelt and other Allied leaders know about the holocaust,
and when did they learn about it? Walter Laqueur wrote that "the final
solution was an open secret from the beginning."[87] Information about the
genocidal activities of the *Einsatzgruppen* was relayed by eyewitnesses to the
Polish underground and from there to the Vatican and the Allied powers.
The cover of wartime conditions allowed the Nazis to hide their criminal
activities behind the fighting front, making it difficult to obtain accurate
information. A crime of this magnitude, however, could not be hidden for
very long. Intelligence sources left little doubt that the Nazis were committing massive atrocities, but these atrocity stories were discounted because
similar reports during World War I had afterward turned out to be inaccurate. Revisionists in the West and elsewhere in the world, as Laqueur
pointed out, did not realize that the Germany of the kaiser and the Germany
of Hitler were quite different.[88] Franklin Roosevelt himself did not perceive
the sharp line that separated civilized imperial Germany from uncivilized
Nazi Germany. Roosevelt had been influenced by World War I propaganda
that depicted the Germans as brutal Huns. The rise of Hitler confirmed his
prejudices that Nazi Germany was a logical outcome of the Second Reich.
Yet in 1938, at the time of Kristallnacht, Roosevelt could still say in aston-
ishment that he could not believe that such orgies of anti-Jewish violence
could happen in a modern, civilized society. He knew Germany well enough
to wonder how a strong Christian nation could revert to barbaric tribalism.

What did Roosevelt know about the developing Holocaust? British intelligence had broken the German Enigma machine, which enabled them
to read the most secret Nazi radio signals by the fall of 1940. On August 24,
1941, Churchill broadcast to the British people and alerted them to what
they were up against, pointing an accusing finger at mass executions in
Russia that reminded him of the Mongol invasion of the sixteenth century;
it was, as he put it, a "methodical, merciless butchery" on the scale of the
Mongol horror.[89] He did not mention the Jews, for that would have revealed
to the Nazis that British intelligence was reading the most secret German
military messages. Churchill believed that the crime was so unique that it

still did not even have a name. British intelligence shared these secret messages with the Americans, and therefore we can be sure that Roosevelt was informed about the general nature of these Nazi crimes.

FDR had pieces of the genocide puzzle but not the whole puzzle. When Felix Frankfurter confided in him his fear that the Jews were being systematically exterminated, the president told him not to worry too much. His information was that the deported Jews were simply set to work on the eastern frontier to build fortifications.[90] Within his administration it was only Henry Morgenthau, his treasury secretary, who kept appealing to his conscience about Nazi mistreatment of Jews. The State Department was in the hands of hidebound conservatives, some of whom were social anti-Semites. The military was not much better, especially in the highest circles, where anti-Semitism was strongly entrenched. As previously mentioned, General Bötticher felt quite at home in the social atmosphere of the War Department and the War College. Roosevelt was a cosmopolitan who welcomed individuals from all backgrounds into government service. Some of his closest advisors, cabinet members, and court appointees were Jewish, including Samuel Rosenman, Herbert Lehman, Henry Morgenthau, Louis Brandeis, Felix Frankfurter, Herbert Feis, Abe Fortas, Benjamin Cohen, David Lilienthal, and many others who had flocked to the New Deal experiment. In fact, Roosevelt had so many Jewish supporters and advisors that he was regularly attacked by Jew-baiters as a dupe of the Jewish conspiracy.[91]

The available evidence suggests that Roosevelt knew about the "final solution," but he did not know much, if anything, about it in detail. Nor did he really know what to do about it other than win the war. In the meantime and under Morgenthau's urging, he did take baby steps to alleviate Jewish suffering by tweaking immigration quotas, taking in more refugees, withdrawing the American ambassador from Berlin in protest against the November 1938 pogrom, and repeatedly warning the Germans of "fearful retribution" if they continued mistreating Jews.[92] Roosevelt did not "abandon" the Jews; he did not enable the Germans to do what they did, and thus was not complicit in the tragedy that led to the Holocaust.

Hitler's Prospects and Premonitions

Japan's attack on Pearl Harbor and Hitler's declaration of war on the United States meant the end of the European war and the beginning of a prolonged world war. Hitler had thrown all caution to the wind. If he had ever followed what Churchill surmised—that he would take on his enemies "one at a time"—he now took on all of them at the same time. When he added the Soviet Union to his list of enemies in the summer of 1941, Britain still had not been defeated. It had been a whole year since France had fallen, but this did not spell the end of the war in the west. Hitler believed that the war in the west could be ended by a war in the east. The timing was crucial. Russia had to be defeated by the end of 1941, before the United States could become a military threat to his continental ambitions. Initially, Hitler believed that the Russians could be defeated in three months. His generals, despite what some of them said afterward, agreed with Hitler's optimistic predictions about the eastern campaign. The American military establishment also believed that the German army could defeat the Russians within three months. The British were even more pessimistic about Russian prospects for withstanding a German attack, giving them no more than six to eight weeks before succumbing to the German juggernaut.[93]

Contrary to conventional historical opinion, Hitler was well aware of the danger looming across the Atlantic from America. He did not underestimate the industrial potential of the United States. What he underestimated was its military potential. He did not think much of the U.S. military and grossly caricatured the fighting capacity of its troops. He had been warned on this score. Dieckhoff, for example, warned him in January 1941 that it would be a matter of grave consequences if the United States entered the war against Germany. He pointed out that the United States had great potential to change the course of the war against Germany. It was therefore in Germany's interest to keep the United States out of the war.[94] Thomsen and Bötticher said the same thing. Historians have generally described Bötticher as a blithering idiot, but this assessment is unfair. The German military attaché accurately reported American military weaknesses in 1941. The enormous spurt of industrial expansion between 1942 and 1945 could not have been predicted by anyone except those blessed with historical hindsight. In 1940 the United States Army was listed as twentieth in a world military ranking, one place behind the Dutch.[95]

Hitler had great confidence in his military forces, and for good reason. With Germany having defeated all the Continental powers in short blitzkrieg wars, why would the war against Russia be any different? As shown earlier in this chapter, Hitler justified the war against Russia not only on ideological grounds—the acquisition of living space—but also on the basis of geopolitical considerations: the Soviet Union was Britain's last potential ally. Russia was also the Far Eastern sword of both Britain and the United States pointed at Japan. Germany and Japan had no time to waste. Both powers had to complete their expansionist aims: Germany in Eastern Europe and Japan in the South Pacific. In 1941 Hitler believed that U.S. intervention was highly likely but that it would come too late to make a difference in the outcome of the war. Given his aggressive temperament, it must have been very hard for him to put up with President Roosevelt's provocations during the period historians refer to as the undeclared war between Germany and the United States (1940–41). Having invaded Russia, Hitler was particularly cautious in keeping the United States at bay; but when he defeated Russia, as he expected to do in three months, Hitler was fully prepared to face the United States because he knew that she was the last hope of Great Britain. This is when Hitler once more gave greater attention to naval affairs, encouraging Admiral Raeder to dust off the Z-Plan that he had authorized in 1939.[96] In the meantime, the Japanese could keep the Anglo-American navies at bay. In December 1941 Hitler admitted that he did not know how to defeat the Americans; he said that he was thinking about it.[97]

Hitler was facing serious problems in December 1941; he could no longer win the war, but this did not mean that he had to lose it. But did Hitler think the war could no longer be won? There is some evidence that he had a premonition that the war was no longer winnable at about the time he reluctantly permitted von Bock to resume his drive toward Moscow in November. According to Halder, he was overheard telling a group of generals that "the recognition that neither force is capable of annihilating the other will lead to a compromise peace."[98] Jodl later wrote from his prison cell at Nuremberg that "today one often hears it said that his [Hitler's] military advisers should have made it clear to him that the war was lost. What a naïve thought! Earlier than any other person in the world, Hitler sensed that the war was lost."[99]

Jodl did not have the nerve to tell Hitler what he thought, but there were some who did. One was his outspoken minister of armaments, Fritz Todt, who arranged a conference in November on armament production. During the course of this meeting, which included Hitler, Jodl, Keitel,

Brauchitsch, and Leeb, the head of German tank production, Walter
Rohland, informed Hitler that the Soviets were producing a much greater
number of quality tanks than the Germans. Rohland also mentioned the
danger of U.S. industrial capacity; he warned that if the United States
turned its industrial might against Germany, the war would be lost. Todt
then startled everyone by stating bluntly that the war could no longer be
won militarily, which prompted Hitler to ask, "How, then, should I end
this war?"[100] Todt replied that a political solution was in order, but Hitler
brushed this suggestion aside by saying that he could not quite envision a
political solution to the war.

By late November, then, Hitler had a strong premonition that the war
could no longer be won. His sense of foreboding was probably strongly
reinforced by an unexpected event that occurred on December 2. On that
day, Hitler paid a visit to his military leaders of Army Group South at
Mariupol to discuss the military problems that had developed at Rostov.
He had originally planned to return to his headquarters at Rastenburg,
but bad weather forced him to stay over at Poltava, the place where Charles
XII of Sweden had suffered a devastating defeat by Peter the Great, which
ended his dream of conquering Russia. Hitler and his entourage had to stay
overnight in an"old tumbledown bug-ridden castle."[101] Worse, Hitler was
cut off from the outside world, including his own headquarters and, according to his servant Heinz Linge, suffered excrutiatingly at the thought
of what might be happening behind his back at headquarters and in Berlin.[102] Ribbentrop was desperately trying to get in touch with him because
the Japanese wanted the Germans to sign a new mutual assistance pact.
At Poltava, Hitler experienced real panic, and it was not just because he
was afraid of a military coup by his generals but because Poltava undoubtedly served as a historical reminder that previous would-be conquerors of
Russia—Charles XII and Napoleon—had come a cropper in the vast and
inhospitable spaces of Russia.

Just two days after this unscheduled stay over at Poltava came a major
setback to the previously victory-flushed Germany army on the Moscow
front. Hitler then knew—without admitting it to his inner circle—that the
military war could no longer be won. "From this moment," in John Lukacs's judgment, "Hitler had but one overriding concern: to prolong the
war, and to impress his opponents with the unbeatable toughness of Germany, so that their unnatural Coalition would sooner or later fall apart, so

that the Russians or, preferably, the Anglo-Americans, would feel compelled to negotiate with him. His will had started the Last European War. His will could no longer end it."[103]

The war Hitler thought he could still win, however, was the biological-racial war against the Jews. This would explain the events leading to Hitler's secret instructions to Himmler to mobilize the instruments of mass destruction culminating in the Wannsee conference and the construction of the death camps in Poland. The rush to more and more radical measures was now underway. The road to the gas chambers was less than six months away after December 1941. Direct confrontation with the United States would not occur until German soldiers first encountered the Americans in North Africa in February 1943. By that time, the Allied forces had adopted a policy of "unconditional surrender," pledging to maintain a common front against Hitler.

At this point in the war historical accounts of Hitler and the United States have always shifted from diplomatic relations between the two countries—now, of course, formally severed—to military events. This is as it should be, but it has also obscured important policies that were made on both sides behind the scenes of battle. One was the politics of unconditional surrender on the part of the United States, and the other was Hitler's strategy to keep on fighting until the "unnatural alliance" between the Western powers and the Soviet Union had collapsed. The full story behind Hitler's efforts to split this unnatural alliance has not been adequately told, a shortcoming that the following chapters will address.

CHAPTER 6

The Tide of War Shifts in Favor of Hitler's Opponents

The Propaganda War: German and American Style

In mid-January 1942 the German navy launched a surprise operation, code-named Paukenschlag (Drumbeat), on American shipping off U.S. coastal waters, extending from Maine to the Gulf of Mexico. In the years prior to 1942, Hitler's naval chiefs had been straining at the bit to retaliate against American warships, which had shadowed German vessels and reported their location to the British. As mentioned earlier, there had been frequent clashes between German U-boats and American "neutrality patrols," but Hitler had given strict orders to the German navy again on June 21, 1941 (one day before the invasion of Russia), to refrain from provoking the Americans. Now that the two nations were at war, Hitler called for all-out attacks on American shipping. On January 14, a U-boat torpedoed the tanker *Norness* sixty miles off Long Island's Montauk Point. It was the first of thirty-five tankers and freighters that German U-boats would sink in U.S. coastal waters over the next three weeks. By June 1942, German U-boats had sent 397 ships to the bottom of the ocean.[1] Given the weak U.S. coastal defenses, these attacks were like a shooting gallery for the Germans. Sometimes they occurred close to the U.S. shoreline, in plain sight of American spectators, who gasped when they saw ships being blown out of the water and looked on in horror as bodies of dead sailors

washed ashore. Hitler wondered how a country could be so militarily unprepared, but he attributed it to FDR's mental condition: "Roosevelt is
mentally ill . . . he declared war and allows himself not only to be thrown
out of East Asia but also lets his commercial ships sail up and down the
American coast as in peace time and go off with a big bang. . . . The way
he carries on makes the whole country hysterical. How else would it be
possible that as a result of a live radio play alleging that Martians landed
in Chicago a panic breaks out among rational people? This Mr. Roosevelt
has also not counted on our U-boats. . . . Our U-boat weapon is one of the
most decisive weapons in this war."[2]

These bold U-boat attacks on the United States did not last, but they
strengthened Hitler's conviction that, given such weak defenses, which left
American coastal territory largely unprotected, it would be years before
the Americans could seriously think about challenging him on the European continent. There were three crucial factors that Hitler had to keep in
mind about the United States at the beginning of 1942: the time at which
the United States could make a difference in the war, the true nature of its
armament potential, and the quality of its fighting forces. As to the first
factor, Hitler had a strong feeling that time was no longer on his side. Bötticher had reckoned that it would be about two years before the United
States could fully mobilize its industrial capacities in order to pose a serious threat to Germany. But knowing what we do about Hitler's praise
of American industry, he must have been greatly concerned about how
little time it might take to transform its consumer economy into a wartime economy. We have conflicting evidence from his own words to his
military and party leaders about American industrial strength. Just two
months before declaring war on the United States, a discussion at the führer's headquarters touched on U.S. armament capacity. It was prompted
by statistics reported in an American publication that listed how many
artillery pieces, tanks, airplanes, warships, and so forth the United States
had produced and could produce for the years 1940, 1941, and 1942. Hitler commented how pathetically low those figures were, adding that even
the Americans did not know, for example, how good their tanks were, because they had not been tested under real military conditions.[3] Hitler also
mentioned an American newsreel, which had reached him by way of Latin
America, that showed pictures of a military maneuver by a fully motorized
American division that he could only describe as laughable.[4] One month

later (October 24), Hitler returned to this topic of U.S. armament capacity by citing "an otherwise anti-German magazine" that had attacked the U.S. aircraft industry for producing airplanes for the British that were proving themselves inferior to those of the Luftwaffe. The so-called "flying fortresses" the Americans were producing could only drop their bombs from great altitudes and simply could not challenge superior German fighter planes. Hitler then expressed the view, which he would stubbornly cling to throughout the war, that Americans were capable of outproducing Germany but that their military machines were cheap mass-produced brands from the same model type.[5] Hitler felt that the Germans were producing better tanks, and that quality would trump quantity. He was probably right about quality but was wrong about quantity. As an American general later admitted, "we never did develop a top tank during the war. We did all right because we made so many of them. That offset some of their weaknesses but we never had a tank that equaled the German tank."[6] By the end of the war, the United States had produced 88,400 tanks, 300,000 military aircraft, and 5,800 ships. In the end, quantity overcame quality. The same was true of manpower, despite Hitler's conviction that the American soldier could not measure up to his German counterpart. For example, on January 5, 1942, Hitler said that he did not believe that the American could fight like a hero.[7]

Yet despite these disparaging remarks, Hitler still recognized the danger America posed to Germany. In March 1942, for example, he dictated various guidelines to Heinz Lorenz, representative of the German News Agency (DNB) at führer headquarters, regarding polemics directed against the United States.[8] He told Lorenz that recent polemics against the United States had relied on "ineffective arguments." What Germany should find objectionable about the United States, Hitler insisted, was first and foremost its complete lack of culture. Hitler wanted the German press to highlight the unpleasant elements of American society: its worship of movie stars, intrusive sensationalism, grotesque spectacles such as female boxing or mud wrestling, the glamorization of criminals, and so forth. In light of these facts, he said, Germany refused Herr Roosevelt the right to preside as a judge over the fate of Germany. It would be entirely wrong, however, to ridicule America for its striving to develop a technological civilization. German propaganda should emphasize that even in this area Germany has proven itself more successful. Elsewhere Hitler acknowledged America's great industrial achievements, especially in coal and iron production. As mentioned earlier, he had great admiration for Henry Ford and claimed to have read many books on "Fordism."[9] His negative comments on American culture can also be misleading, for Hitler watched and liked numerous American films, including Walt Disney productions. Again, in March 1942, while on the one hand criticizing the American "cult of the girl," he spoke with great admiration of the American dancer Miriam Verne, whose "gracious and elegant stage dance was a pure aesthetic pleasure."[10] Although Germany was at war with the United States, he regretted that he could not find a way to get her a permit to travel to Germany. She would be a perfect choice to perform in the Berlin Metropolitan Theater and in the Reich chancellery. He also praised the lissome and long-limbed Marion Daniels, who had performed at La Scala and in Munich's Gärtnerplatz Theater. The Americans, Hitler admitted, had far better dancers than the Germans.[11]

Hitler's thoughts and feelings about America, then, continued to be split between grudging respect for its wealth and power and condescending judgments of its lack of high cultural achievements. Now that he was at war with this strange country, Hitler's remarks about America became increasingly negative, making it difficult to separate propaganda from private conviction. The propaganda war that Goebbels unleashed with Hitler's approval consisted of accusations that Anglo-American plutocracy was in league with Bolshevism and that the link between them was the Jew. Just how much both Hitler and Goebbels really believed their own propaganda has been much debated and cannot be settled here. What can be demonstrated is the way in which the Nazis actually waged their propaganda campaign against their enemies, especially against the United States. We do know what Hitler and Goebbels wanted the German people to know about America. Likewise, we do know what Roosevelt and his government wanted the American people to know about Germany. Judging from the way the two nations conducted their propaganda, there is little doubt that the American effort was more effective and closer to reality. Though impressive in its grandiose scope and technological know-how, Nazi propaganda was ultimately the victim of its own unrealistic inflation.

How did the German leadership view the United States and how did American war leaders see Germany? Perceptions shape policies, and stereotypical perceptions can result in ineffective or even disastrous policies.

Starting in early 1942, the German propaganda war against the United States consisted mostly in belittling American culture and maligning their leaders. President Franklin Roosevelt was depicted as a madman. Interestingly enough, Hitler never called FDR a cripple, though Colin Ross undoubtedly told him about the president's physical handicap.[12] Hitler usually called FDR a madman or Churchill's *Spießgeselle* (accomplice). Behind the scenes, Americans were said to be manipulated by mercenary Jews who had run the country into the ground by causing the Great Depression.[13] America was allegedly a gangster's paradise, violent and lawless. Despite the misleading façade created by Hollywood motion pictures, which showed Americans living in mansions and being waited on hand and foot by butlers, gardeners, and nannies, the majority of them lived like the characters depicted in John Steinbeck's novel *The Grapes of Wrath*. In August 1942 one of the topics of conversation at Hitler's table was the low state of American culture depicted in a recent book that Martin Bormann had given Hitler. The book in question was *Juan in America,* an amusing satire of American mores by the Scottish novelist Eric Linklater.[14] Bormann and Hitler seemed to think that Linklater's satire of crazy Americans actually depicted real life in the United States. Linklater had spent several years in America collecting material for his book, and when it was published it was hailed in both Britain and the United States as a deliciously wicked satire of American cultural excesses. Linklater's outrageous portrayals of zany Americans were not meant to be malicious but were a parody of a country that enjoyed celebrating the outlandish and bizarre as a welcome relief from hard work. Life sometimes imitates art, and Linklater's book can also be read as a gentle reproach to a country that sometimes crosses the limits considered endurable by people who prize reason, sanity, and common sense. The Nazis, however, quickly jumped on the book as a godsend for their propaganda campaign against the United States. Goebbels made sure that copies were widely disseminated, even to the troops at the front. Hitler probably read the book after Bormann gave him a copy in late July 1942. On August 1, Hitler specifically referred to the book during dinner time, saying that the Americans were "as dumb as chickens" (*dumm wie die Hühner*).[15] He prophesied that one day the Americans would be unpleasantly surprised to see their whole house of cards come crashing down. In Hitler's judgment, the Americans had too much of everything and would therefore be ill-prepared to withstand real adversities. He conceded that they currently enjoyed a more affluent standard of living, but that was also misleading:

It is difficult to talk to an American. He says: "Look what a worker gets over here!" Yes, but let's look at the darker side. A factory worker earns eighty dollars. Those who don't work in a plant (Betrieb) get nothing. They have thirteen million unemployed. I saw pictures of shelters made out of gasoline canisters and the like for the unemployed, not all that different from the pictures showing those miserable hell-holes in Bolshevik industrial cities. Granted, our living standard is lower. But the German Reich has 270 opera halls, a balanced cultural life that is unknown over there. They have suits, food, automobiles and a poorly constructed house with the refrigerator in the living quarter. To impress us with these things is like judging the cultures of the sixteenth century by its contemporary toilet. . . . Basically Americans live like pigs in a tiled sty.[16]

During the course of one of his military conferences in March 1943, Hitler delivered another interesting anti-American observation:

HITLER: They [the Americans] will never become Rome. America will never be the Rome of the future. Rome was a peasant's state.
HEWEL: But the Americans have good human material somewhere.
JODL: That's only an outward appearance.
HITLER: Not as much as one might imagine. They live in a few regions where the Europeans are dominating. But on no account do they have the large . . . centers. The farmers are impoverished. I saw photographs. Never before have I seen such pitiful and stunted farmers—nothing but uprooted beings wandering around.[17]

There is obviously something naive about judging a nation's very diverse farming community by pictures showing impoverished farmers in Appalachia. Yet Hitler's image of America came largely from coffee-table books, novels, newsreels, and motion pictures. He marveled at the gigantic size of American skyscrapers but sensed that there was something artificial about them; they seemed like Potemkin contraptions concealing an inner core of human misery and degradation. Hitler believed that America's financial elite, which was predominantly Jewish, had constructed temples on top of a seething underclass of slaves—a cinematic cliché that had taken root among certain German intellectuals as a result of motion pictures such as Fritz Lang's *Metropolis*, which contrasted a glittering urban façade—the upper city—and the enslaved workers that tended a monstrous urban dystopia in the lower city. According to Fritz Lang, he got the idea of *Metropolis* when he saw nocturnal New York with its skyscrapers illuminated by thousands of glittering lights.[18] Hitler was much taken by such motion pictures; in fact, he loved watching films on a regular basis. There is nothing surprising about this, because he had a visual mind with a fine, artistic eye for his surroundings. Hitler was a visual thinker who saw things in pictorial images or impressions. This is how he formed some of his most grandiose ideas. As already mentioned, Karl May's novels evoked for him images of a wild and untamed land where conquest and heroism were still possible. He spent hours on end thumbing through art magazines and the heraldry department of the Munich State Library to find the right symbols for the Nazi Party. Nazi propaganda thrived on pictorial persuasion as much as it did on the spoken word. In *Mein Kampf* Hitler stressed the importance of giving wings to a few slogans by letting them glide on pictorial images. He seized on such images himself and rarely corrected them. His prime symbol of the United States was and would remain the split image of America/Amerika. He was really fighting the first and shadowboxing with the second.

Hitler's propaganda minister, Joseph Goebbels, saw America in much the same light. In a key article titled "Cross Examination of Mr. Roosevelt" (Kreuzverhör mit Mr. Roosevelt), he carried on a mock cross-examination of FDR, accusing him of putting the American people in needless fear of Germany.[19] Reading it today, one is tempted to chuckle, for it was written just a week before Pearl Harbor and Hitler's declaration of war on the United States. Goebbels's ostensible argument centered on FDR's claim that he had in his possession certain documents that revealed that Germany wanted to conquer Latin America and divide it into five German vassal states, a point mentioned in the preceding chapter. Goebbels wanted to prove that FDR was looking for a subterfuge to persuade the American people that they should go to war with Germany. The subtext of the article, however, was Goebbels's belief—and Hitler's too—that FDR was a mere stooge for Jewish financial interests in the United States. By hook or by crook Roosevelt was determined to get America involved in a real shooting war with Germany, but he was not doing it for the noble reasons he was spoon-feeding the American people. Even if Britain fell, the United States hoped to acquire Britain's colonial empire.

Goebbels was convinced that FDR could no longer change the course of the war and reverse Britain's military fortunes. Germany was too deeply entrenched on the Continent to be dislodged by a weak Britain and a militarily unprepared United States. Hitler felt the same way; he also agreed with his propaganda minister's grudging admission that Germany was not capable of attacking America. Both Goebbels and Hitler expressed contempt for America, but they freely admitted that as yet they knew of no way that America could be defeated.[20] The reverse was true as well, as Goebbels put it, "even U.S. trees do not grow into heaven,"[21] meaning that American industrial resources were insufficient to challenge the expanding Greater German Reich. The United States had the additional problem of getting its supplies across the U-boat-infested Atlantic Ocean. When Goebbels said, "We are sitting tight in our part of the world,"[22] he was expressing his führer's conviction.

The question then arises whether both Hitler and Goebbels believed in their own confident rhetoric about Germany's prospects. Did they think that the United States was incapable of landing a large enough army on the European continent? In 1942 Hitler did not believe that the Americans, who were losing 1,027 ships during the first year of war, could mount a cross-channel invasion in the near future. In the meantime, he tried to convince the German public that the war in the East would be won before the first American set foot on European soil. Subconsciously—and he admitted this to a few close military men like Jodl—he knew that Russia could not be conquered completely. In that event, the war on the eastern front would turn into a stalemate, which at the right moment—following a decisive German victory on the battlefield—could be ended in some kind of compromise peace. Hitler hoped that this could be accomplished before the Americans made a significant difference in the war. Here, again, everything depended on timing. Deep down Hitler had a sense that time was running out for the Reich. In the meantime, German propaganda was to focus on America's decadence and its inability to pose a real military threat to Germany. This tactic would change after the United States landed forces in North Africa; suddenly America could not be ignored anymore. The Americans were coming closer; before long they might land on the Continent itself. At this point Goebbels intensified his anti-American propaganda, warning the German people that the Americans would bring the Jewish plague back into Europe, infecting everything with its plutocratic disease. Few Germans were frightened by such anti-American propaganda. The German public feared American power, but it did not fear Americans. Stories about decadent Americans fell on stony ground. Most German attempts to instill hatred of Americans failed, as was later demonstrated during the American occupation.[23]

On the American side, it was more difficult to stir up hatred against the Germans than against the Japanese. In the general atmosphere of shock and anger following the attack on Pearl Harbor, many Americans did not understand the full gravity of Hitler's declaration of war, which came so shortly after the attack. There was a difference in perception between the president and the American people regarding which enemy—Germany or Japan—was more dangerous to the United States. Since the fall of France in June 1940, Roosevelt had come to the conclusion that Nazi Germany was by far the greater threat because it appeared to be capable of conquering the whole continent from the Atlantic to the Urals. If that had happened, it could have directly challenged the Western Hemisphere, both economically and militarily. It could have wiped out the last vestiges of democracy, threatened the United States' trade routes, and linked with the Japanese in driving the United States out of the Pacific. Many Americans saw things differently. They believed that Hitler could not, or would not, threaten the territorial integrity of the United States, so that if strict isolationism had been maintained, the United States could have avoided war with both Germany and Japan. In the long run, the isolationist argument contended, both Germany and Japan would have moderated their aggressive policies, Communism would have been eliminated, the threat of nuclear war avoided, and the anti-Jewish persecutions greatly lessened.

Such isolationist arguments were not shared by Roosevelt, who asked himself how he could persuade the American people that Hitler, who had not attacked the United States, was more dangerous than the Japanese who had. After Pearl Harbor the full wrath of the American people descended on Japan and everything Japanese. The unfortunate recipients of this hatred were those of Japanese ancestry in America. The consequences of that public rage are well known: suspension of civil liberties followed by the internment of nearly 120,000 Japanese Americans in concentration camps in the western United States. The U.S. government spearheaded and maintained a violent anti-Japanese propaganda campaign throughout the rest of the war. One interesting consequence of this anti-Japanese campaign was the underestimation of Japanese power and the overestimation of German strength.[24] This was the other side of American racism, for it involved the false belief that blond and blue-eyed Germans had to be better soldiers, especially pilots, than the "little yellow men" of Japan. When General Douglas McArthur heard about the attack on Pearl Harbor, he said that the Japanese planes must have been piloted by the Germans.[25]

By comparison, anti-German propaganda was less intense, and actions taken against German Americans were milder than those directed against Japanese Americans. Roosevelt wanted to educate Americans about the threat that Hitler posed for America. How far did he intend to promote not just an anti-Hitler but also an anti-German campaign? There were a number of German haters in his administration—Ickes, Morgenthau, and Hopkins—who called for a government-sponsored hate campaign against everything German. This issue surfaced at a cabinet meeting on April 11, 1942, when both Ickes and Morgenthau tried to persuade FDR that government information policy needed to be drastically revised so that the country could segue into a strong "hate German" direction. Morgenthau argued with great passion that "our people ought to be taught to hate Germany," adding "if we do not hate the Germans we will end by hating each other."[26] When Claude Wickard, the secretary of agriculture, asked for clarification about who should be hated—Hitler or the Germans—Ickes shot back by saying that there was no difference between the German rulers and their people. This symbiosis between German rulers and the people they ruled had operated since Caesar's time. In fact, according to Ickes, "the goose-step was a perfect expression of the German character."[27]

Such anti-German attitudes were also beginning to gain support outside government circles. In a nationwide broadcast on NBC/Blue America's Town Hall Meeting of the Air, General Henry J. Riley told his listeners that the United States could only win the war if the American people had been taught to hate the Germans. The German author Emil Ludwig, who had fled from Nazi Germany, pointed out in a widely read article that there was no real distinction between Nazis and Germans. Ludwig also testified as an expert on the German problem in front of the House Foreign Affairs Committee on March 26, 1943.[28] Ludwig told the committee that Americans had misjudged the Germans in World War I. At that time they thought that they could make a distinction between Prussian militarists and democratically minded Germans. In 1917 Germans were militarists; now they were Nazis militarists. Yet opinion polls in 1941 and 1942 revealed that the American people were opposed to a public hate campaign against Germany. Several months after Pearl Harbor, 62 percent of respondents to a public opinion poll stated that the United States should focus on Japan, while only 21 percent supported immediate concentration of men and materiel on Germany.[29] Most Americans still thought that in the long run Hitler was the more dangerous foe, but they overwhelmingly favored getting Hirohito first. The strong measures taken against Japanese Americans, particularly on the West Coast, were popular with the American people. Roosevelt did not take the same harsh steps against German Americans, nor did he follow Morgenthau's advice to launch a public hate campaign against Germany. He followed this course of action for several reasons: an instinctive aversion to inciting hate, deference to public opinion, and attention to the objections of Cordell Hull's State Department.

This did not stop a vigorous campaign of anti-Nazi propaganda by government agencies, notably by the Office of War Information (OWI), by the mass media, and by Hollywood.[30] The academic community also jumped into the fray, with professors writing ridiculous books that distorted German history into a two-thousand-year prologue to Nazi Germany. According to these books, Prussian rulers had all been Potsdam führers, and German philosophers and poets had long preached virulent racism, militarism, and nationalism. What the academy did on a scholarly level the motion picture industry did on the popular level. More than 150 motion pictures were produced in which Germans were depicted in a negative way—as cunning, brutal, arrogant, racist, sadistic, militaristic, guttural, and so forth.[31]

FDR may not have incited hatred against Germany, but he did little to stop it. Between 1943 and 1945, his attitude toward Germany shifted more and more in the direction of the German hater Henry Morgenthau. The secretary of the treasury, who was a neighbor of the Roosevelts at Hyde Park, wanted the Germans punished indefinitely because brutal aggression was part of their historical gene pool.[32] FDR shared this historical perception of German aggression, which had reached its most malignant expression under Nazi rule. By 1943 Roosevelt was convinced that the majority of the German people had been Nazified; they were therefore guilty as a group. The announcement in early 1943 that the Allies would accept only unconditional surrender was a reflection of such beliefs on Roosevelt's part. The German bloodstream had been poisoned; the only solution was conquest, punishment, and perhaps reeducation, though the possibility of regenerating such a brutal people seemed impossible at the time. In short, FDR felt that there could be no negotiation with the Germans, and that included any putative opposition to Hitler.

How far FDR was willing to pursue unabashed vengeance against Germany became apparent with the announcement of the Morgenthau plan in 1944. By its terms, Germany was to be destroyed as a national entity, militarily occupied, and reduced to a pastoral society. As will be seen, the president recoiled from its inhumane consequences, but probably only because there was widespread opposition from the State Department, the War Department, the press, and public opinion. The president had not liked Germans even in better times. As shown in Chapter 2, he had known Germany as early as 1890 and found the country intolerably authoritarian and militaristic. The Nazi experience only confirmed his stereotype of "Prussian militarism," which he identified as quintessentially German. For him, and for many liberally minded Americans, there was a direct causal connection between Prussian militarism and Nazism; the only thing that was different between the two was that Nazism was far worse than Prussian autocracy.[33] His historical view of the German problem allowed for no nuance or correction of misleading stereotypes. George Kennan was startled to encounter such simplistic perceptions when he had a discussion with FDR: "I was shocked to realize in talking with President Roosevelt later in the war that he was one of the many people who could not easily distinguish World War II from World War I and still pictured the Prussian *Junkertum* as [the] mainstay of Hitler's power just as it had been, or had been reputed to be, the mainstay of the Kaiser. Actually, Hitler found his main support on the lower middle class and to some extent in the nouveau riche. The older Prussian aristocracy was divided, but from its ranks came some of the most enlightened and courageous of all the internal opposition Hitler was ever to face."[34]

Although FDR's knowledge of German society may have left a lot to be desired, his understanding of Hitler was better. It was certainly better than Hitler's knowledge of Roosevelt. Some of this was not entirely Hitler's fault. German intelligence never undertook a serious analysis of the American president that could have aided Hitler in gaining a better understanding of his adversary's intentions or his strength of character. By contrast, the U.S. Office of Strategic Services (OSS) undertook a very ambitious study of Hitler's mind and his possible behavior under extreme pressure. The report came up with some shrewd insights, including the prediction that Hitler would commit suicide rather than shoulder full responsibility for his actions.[35] There is no evidence that Hitler was ever fully briefed about Roosevelt by the Abwehr or any of his intelligence agencies. Hitler picked up bits and pieces of information from unorthodox sources, some of them quite misleading.

FDR's sources were much better. German exiles provided a wealth of information. The most useful may well have been the reports sent to the president by Putzi Hanfstaengl. As will be recalled, Hanfstaengl had escaped Germany in 1937, was interned by the British, and then handed over to the Americans to participate in a top-secret project called the S-Project—the S standing for Sedgwick, the name of Putzi's American mother.[36] Hiding out in an old-fashioned villa at Bush Hill, twenty miles out of Washington in Virginia, Hanfstaengl monitored German broadcasts and sent the president periodic and very colorful reports about the goings-on in Nazi Germany. We know that FDR looked forward to Putzi's reports, calling them "my Hitler bedtime stories,"[37] because he enjoyed reading them before turning in for the night. Hanfstaengl was kept at Bush Hill under very light "house arrest," courtesy of the U.S. government. How light it was is evident from the fact that one of his guards was Staff Sergeant Egon Hanfstaengl, Putzi's son, who had joined the U.S. Army.

Exactly what the president learned from Hanfstaengl's reports is not known, but these reports, peppered as they are with insider knowledge of Hitler and his private entourage, provided useful information about the nature of Hitler's world. Included in Hanfstaengl's papers is a particularly shrewd psychological profile of Hitler. It consists of sixty-eight typed pages in which Hanfstaengl assessed Hitler's volatile character and personality. FDR valued these reports because they gave him a kind of pipeline to Hitler's mentality. Whether he fully trusted the soundness of this pipeline, knowing that it was slanted by Hanfstaengl, who was fighting his own war against the Nazi leadership, will probably remain a mystery. The fact is that FDR supported this highly secret project for two full years, a program that bypassed regular American intelligence channels and was even financed out of personal White House funds.[38] The British had warned the president about Hanfstaengl. Yet Roosevelt protected him nonetheless, at least until Churchill himself intervened in the matter at Quebec in August 1944 and succeeded in terminating the project.

During the first six months of the war between Germany and the United States, the two sides fired propaganda broadsides at each other. FDR chose the moral high ground of Wilsonian idealism, while Hitler unleashed more personal attacks on U.S. leaders. On January 1, 1942, the United States joined with twenty-five other nations in signing the Declaration of the United Nations, which pledged to "employ its full resources, military and economic, against members of the Tripartite Pact and not to make a separate armistice or peace with the enemies."[39] The declaration, along with the Atlantic Charter, provided the moral basis on which the Allied powers, calling themselves the "United Nations," would wage war against the Axis powers (Germany, Italy, and Japan).

Nazi propaganda offered no real moral counterpart to Allied proclamations that the war was a moral crusade against Axis militarism and its enslavement of the European continent. Goebbels was certainly aware that the German cause was difficult to defend from a humanitarian position. The Nazis therefore looked for a more positive appeal that could transcend German national self-interest. Goebbels and Hitler thought they had found the answer in anti-Communism. They claimed that Germany was waging a war against Bolshevism; its aim was to save Western civilization from the specter of Soviet Bolshevism. This was a clever ploy that resonated with right-wing groups in many countries, because the fear of Communism, though much exaggerated in hindsight, turned out to be a strong persuader. One of the pope's main concerns was the danger that Communism posed to Western Europe—though he found out during the 1930s that the Nazis were not much better in their treatment of the Christian Church than the Communists. Yet fear of Communism, especially among the middle classes, was widespread, and the Nazis exploited it with some success. The message that Goebbels and his propaganda agencies disseminated was that Germany would take the lead in saving Europe from atheistic Communism. Goebbels charged that Churchill and Roosevelt had become willing helpers of Communism, and that behind the two Allied leaders stood the Jews, who pulled the strings. After Germany engaged both Russia and the United States, Nazi propaganda prominently highlighted the Jewish connection between the two enemy powers. Hitler stressed this connection in late January 1942, on the occasion of the ninth anniversary of his appointment to the chancellorship. He also repeated the threat he had made against the Jews in 1939 when he promised that the Jews would be annihilated if the nations of the world were plunged into another war. Germany, he reminded the nation, was now at war with world Jewry. He would ruthlessly apply the Jewish law that demanded an eye for an eye and a tooth for a tooth.[40]

The God of War Turns Away from Germany
and Goes Over to the Other Side

In the beginning of 1942, German prospects for victory still seemed promising. U-boats were sinking Allied ships at an alarming rate. Rommel was rampaging through North Africa and appeared to be on his way to Cairo, which would have threatened Britain's hold in the Mediterranean as well as its tenuous lifeline to the whole of the Middle East, the Suez, and the waterways to India. Although the Battle of Moscow had been lost, the German front did not collapse but held. By the spring of 1942, Hitler prepared for the resumption of his offensive on the Eastern front. The Continent was still firmly under his control. Yet all was not well with the German war effort, the way it was fought, and the resources on which it was based. On January 20, Hitler had a lengthy discussion with Goebbels about the "crisis of nerves" (*Nervenkrise*) that had been spreading through the ranks of the German army leadership in Russia. The bitter winter and the heavy casualties, combined with the tenacious manner in which the Russians fought back against previously victory-flushed German troops, was beginning to spread a pall of fear in the eastern army (*Ostheer*). The Germans had overstretched their supply lines along a fifteen-hundred-mile front that extended from Leningrad in the north to the Black Sea in the south. Supply lines broke down, gasoline was in short supply, winter clothes were lacking, and casualties were frightfully high.

The German war economy was also showing serious problems that ranged from shortages in raw material, war finances, and manpower to supplying troops stationed at huge distances from the Reich.[41] The head of the army's manpower and armaments, General Friedrich Fromm, told the new Reich armament minister, Albert Speer, in April 1942 that Germany's only hope lay in developing a new weapon that could annihilate whole cities.[42] Fromm said that he knew a group of scientists who were on the track of such a weapon. Speer followed this up with a visit to the Kaiser Wilhelm Institute, where he met a number of scientists including Nobel laureates such as Otto Hahn and Werner Heisenberg, who claimed that certain elemental particles of matter might be able to provide the energy to produce a superbomb. The army command turned a cold shoulder to the project because it would require unlimited resources and finances that Germany did not possess at that time. The Germans postponed plans for a crash nuclear program; they envisioned it as a postwar project, not as a means of winning the war.[43] About the time the Germans put their nuclear research on the back burner, the Anglo-Americans were going ahead full steam with the Manhattan project. This immense project, which at its peak, from 1942 to 1945, employed approximately 130,000 people, clearly demonstrates the great disparity of available resources on the two sides. Speer suspected that the Americans, who were blessed with unlimited resources and the most brilliant Central European scientists, were probably already at work on such a project.[44] He reported to Hitler what he had learned from the scientists. To his surprise, he found out that Hitler had already received information about nuclear research from, of all people, his personal photographer, Heinrich Hoffmann, who was on friendly terms with Post Office Minister Otto Ohnesorge. The German Post Office was responsible not only for the transportation and delivery of mail but also for broadcasting and other technical means of communication. Ohnesorge was very interested in nuclear research and supported an independent research group under the direction of Manfred von Ardenne, a brilliant young inventor who was conducting experiments on electromagnetic mass separators for isotopes. Von Ardenne believed that he could separate small quantities of Uranium 235 that eventually could be used in sufficient mass to produce a nuclear bomb.[45] The Germans were groping their way at a snail's pace to solving the nuclear puzzle, but lack of coordination of the various scientific efforts combined with inadequate resources and finances rendered the project essentially stillborn. Bureaucratic immobility was one of the fatal weaknesses on the German side; it was the product of Hitler's inconsistent management style of encouraging intramural competition among Nazi administrators, which caused fierce rivalries and undermined teamwork. Speer later wrote that the possibility of building an atom bomb "quite obviously strained his [Hitler's] intellectual capacity. He was unable to grasp the revolutionary nature of nuclear physics. In the twenty-two hundred recorded points of my conferences with Hitler, nuclear fission comes up only once, and then is mentioned with extreme brevity."[46] Speer added that Hitler would not have hesitated for a moment to use nuclear bombs if he had been in possession of such weapons.

On the other side of the ocean, Roosevelt immediately acted on the urgent letter he had received from Albert Einstein informing him that the Germans were on the verge of a breakthrough in nuclear research that might possibly lead to the development of an atomic bomb. Considering what FDR knew about Hitler and the Germans, he passed on this information to his trusted adviser, Edwin "Pa" Watson, with a note that said, "this requires action."[47] FDR considered the Germans more than capable of the highest scientific accomplishments; and he must have realized that in the hands of Hitler, atomic weapons would most certainly be used on nations that opposed the dictator. FDR would steadily support the Manhattan project because, like his military chiefs, he believed that the United States was in a race with Germany to develop the bomb. There was no doubt in his mind that the United States would eventually develop such a weapon and drop it on Hitler's Germany. Like Hitler, if he had had the bomb, FDR would not have hesitated to use it.

The growing weaknesses in the German war effort were just beginning to surface in 1942, but there was a lull before the storm broke out in the fall of that year. In both Europe and the Pacific, the Axis powers still maintained their forward momentum. The Japanese followed up their surprise attack on Pearl Harbor by taking one bastion of Western power after another. They captured advance American outposts at Guam, Wake Island, and the Philippines; they seized the British port of Hong Kong and took over British Malaya with its critical supplies of rubber and tin. The Japanese also thrust deep into the jungles of Burma and managed to cut the famous Burma Road, which had been used by the Americans to supply Chiang Kai-shek with the resources he needed to fight the Japanese in China. Like the Germans, the Japanese used blitzkrieg tactics tailored to their own military needs. Their aim was to capture countries rich in the resources needed to fuel the Japanese war industry, which would have been unable to function for long if it had been forced to draw on the meager resources of the Japanese islands. By May 1942 the Japanese had established a firm foothold in the oil-rich Dutch East Indies, then pushed southward by invading the turtle-shaped island of New Guinea, north of Australia. When they landed on the Solomon Islands, they threatened Australia itself. On May 6 the island fortress of Corregidor in Manila harbor, which had held out in the Philippines, finally fell to the Japanese. All of the Philippines were now in Japanese hands. But just one day later came the first Japanese setback, at the naval battle of the Coral Sea (May 7–9). One month later, the Japanese suffered a devastating defeat at Midway Island, which cost them four vital aircraft carriers. These two battles, Coral Sea and Midway, turned the tide in the Pacific. They made it possible for the Allies to take the islands of Tulagi and Guadalcanal in the Solomons, inaugurating the U.S. strategy of "island hopping" toward Japan. The Japanese had overstretched their supply lines and had to face the unpalatable prospect of a lengthy war of attrition against the combined forces of Britain and the United States.

The tide of war also shifted in favor of the Allies in Europe. The Axis powers did not effectively coordinate war strategy or articulate war aims persuasively. One of the few things they agreed on was their respective zones of naval and air operations, which divided Eurasia into two parts along the 70th meridian east. They agreed on disrupting Allied commercial trade routes, but they were never able to establish permanent organizations to work out common strategies, let alone mount significant joint military operations. By contrast, the Allied powers established the Combined Chiefs of Staff (CCS), comprising three British and three American commanders, as well as the Combined Munitions Assignment Board for the allocation of supplies among the Allies. The Allied powers also held ten major conferences, seven of which were attended by Roosevelt and Churchill, while Stalin attended three of them. There were frequent meetings between Allied foreign ministers and high-ranking military officials.

In the absence of a centralized and unified command structure, the Axis powers ended up fighting their own wars. Hitler controlled all aspects of German command and strategies himself. There was no Joint Chiefs of Staff coordinating the war effort and overseeing operations by the army, navy, and air forces. Command decisions were made by Hitler through "führer directives," written instructions that were passed on to the appropriate institution. If there was a formal German machinery for waging war, it was the High Command of the Armed Forces (Oberkommando der Wehrmacht OKW), whose nominal head was the servile Field Marshal Wilhelm Keitel, nicknamed Lakeitel, for lackey. It was through this body, controlled by Hitler as commander in chief, that führer orders went out to the various branches of the services. As the war continued, the weakness in the German command structure became a liability. Hitler had succeeded in one sense: he had spun a huge spider web that allowed him to control all branches of the armed forces with a degree of personal power that was equaled only by Stalin. Ironically, he used that power poorly and inefficiently, committing strategic mistakes that would cost him his victory in the end.

Hitler did not launch a major operation in 1942 until the summer because the eastern army had to be brought up to strength after the Battle of Moscow. One German historian has argued that in September 1942 Hitler gave up his blitzkrieg strategy in favor of a holding action on the eastern front.[48] His attack on the Kursk salient in the summer of 1943 proves otherwise. It is true that Hitler had to do some serious thinking in 1942 about long-range strategy, for he was now at war with the three greatest powers in the world—the Soviet Union, the United States, and the British Empire. He had gone for broke against Russia and failed. Should he regroup and launch one more hammer blow against Russia in hopes of either final victory or a negotiated peace? Hitler decided to go for another decisive blow. In June 1942 he launched another grandly conceived attack on the southern industrial heart of Russia, whose center, Stalingrad, was named after the Soviet leader himself.

The German disaster at Stalingrad is by now well known and does not have to be treated in detail here; but what is significant about this bloodiest battle in history, which stretched from the summer of 1942 to February 1943, was its devastating impact on the German army as well as its psychological shock to German morale.[49] After Stalingrad the public mood turned increasingly pessimistic. Ordinary Germans developed a sinking feeling that the war could no longer be won after the country's best soldiers of the sixth army had been killed or taken into Russian captivity. The gods of war, as Jodl rightly said, had gone over to the other side. While the Battle of Stalingrad was raging, German and Italian forces were suffering heavy losses in North Africa between November 1942 and May 1943. Rommel's Afrika Korps was defeated at El Alamein on November 2, 1942, and retreated headlong toward Tunisia. At the same time powerful Anglo-American forces landed in Morocco and Algeria on November 8. The German and Italian forces were now caught in a vise between Anglo-American forces moving in on them from the west and Montgomery's troops pursuing the German force from the east. When it was all over in May 1943, the Axis troops had been driven out of North Africa. What came next was the invasion of Sicily and southern Italy, which resulted in the fall of Mussolini. The Germans were also losing the war on the high seas and in the air by the middle of 1943.

In hindsight, we know that the outcome of the war was predictable in late 1943, but contemporaries were not at all sure how it would come out in the end. Roosevelt, for example, perceived only a glimmer of hope for a speedy conclusion to the war in 1942–43. America was fighting a two-front war against determined enemies whose troops were combat-ready, superbly trained, and exquisitely indoctrinated with the warrior spirit of their respective martial cultures. Their passion for combat, combined with a singular dedication to professionalism, worried the president. When American soldiers were encountering Rommel's soldiers for the first time in the desert in North Africa, Roosevelt told Sir John Dill, chief of the Imperial General Staff, that the trouble with the British was that they believed they could beat the Germans if they had an equal number of men and tanks. He rejected this optimistic assumption, saying that "the Germans are better trained, better generaled." According to Daisy Suckley, to whom he recounted this conversation with Dill, FDR told Dill, "You can never discipline an Englishman or an American as you can a German."[50] FDR was clearly worried about a head-on assault on Hitler's fortress in Europe, and he wondered whether American troops were up to the task. For propaganda purposes as well as to string the Russians along, he had encouraged reports that America would land an invasion force in Europe by November 1942, but Winston Churchill and his own good sense quickly dispelled such wishful thinking. When Molotov visited Washington in late May 1942, FDR told him to inform Stalin that the United States was preparing a second front that year, knowing full well that this was impossible.[51] What was possible, Roosevelt thought, was to keep the Russians closely tied to the Anglo-Americans, thus presenting a common front against Hitler. When these promises of a second front turned out to be just empty words, Stalin began to suspect bad faith on the part of the Anglo-Americans.

Stalin suspected that the Anglo-Americans planned to hold their forces in abeyance until the Russians and the Germans had bludgeoned each other to the point of exhaustion so that neither of them could withstand the Western plutocracy after they invaded the European continent. Both Stalin and Hitler were acutely aware of the fact that Britain and the United States were not continental European powers because they had never established a long-term presence on the Continent. Stalin realized that the Germans were here to stay in Central Europe, while the British and the Americans were not. In 1939 Stalin had made it clear that Russia would not "pull the chestnuts out of the fire" for France and Britain.[52] He then heard rumors that Churchill allegedly remarked that the two totalitarian giants should be allowed to bleed each other to death before the Western powers would send their young men into the breach. Stalin had additional suspicions relating to Russia's western boundaries. The Soviet leader insisted on regaining the western frontier lines he had wrung from Hitler in September 1939. He also distrusted the Polish government in exile in London, which demanded a strong Polish buffer, to include Poland's prewar borders and the formation of an East European Federation that could discourage future Russian aggression. Stalin also had a dark secret he did not want to share with the Western powers, and that was the mass murder of thousands of Polish officers by the Soviet Commissariat of Internal Affairs (NKVD) in the Katyn forest near Smolensk. In April 1943 the Germans reported the news of these atrocities, which caused a furor on the diplomatic front. The Russians succeeded in blaming the Nazis for having done it, and the Western powers washed their hands of the whole affair.[53]

Stalin had already shown that he could strike an alliance with Hitler if it was to the advantage of the Soviet Union. Although Hitler had betrayed him in 1941, Stalin was by no means averse to a possible rapprochement with Germany during the two years following Hitler's attack on Russia. There is evidence that Stalin sent out several signals to the Germans between 1942 and 1944 suggesting a compromise peace. The Americans had originally promised to extend lend-lease to Russia, which they did, and to mount an invasion of Europe in November 1942, which they did not. Instead of invading Europe they invaded North Africa. Stalin was not impressed by this operation, because it amounted to little more than scuffling at the periphery of Fascist Europe. He wanted unlimited supplies from America and a second front as soon as possible. The year 1942 passed, and so did 1943. There was still no second front. Although Churchill tried to reassure Stalin of Anglo-American support and military reinforcement in a meeting he had with Stalin in Moscow in August 1942, Stalin continued to be suspicious of the Western powers.

Did Hitler know of these developing disagreements among the Allies, and, if he did, what did he do about it? Hitler received regular intelligence reports about what was going on in the Allied camp, and from these he concluded that, sooner or later, the "unnatural alliance" would fall apart. In May 1942 he told the Indian nationalist Subhas Chandra Bose that England, America, and Russia did not play an honest game with one another.[54] He said that America hoped to inherit the British Empire and that Russia wanted to inherit the American legacy. Before Stalingrad, Hitler was not in any mood to negotiate with the Russians, and he rejected all suggestions to conclude a separate peace. After Stalingrad, however, a window of opportunity began to open for both sides. Stalin now felt far more secure than he had before the Battle of Stalingrad. If earlier he could expect little more than unconditional surrender, he could now operate on a foundation of strength, because it was becoming increasingly clear that neither side would score a knock-out blow. The evidence suggests that, even after Stalingrad, Stalin was not convinced that Russia could defeat Germany by herself but only through a combined Russian and Anglo-American partnership. But this partnership, though promising, might not last. It was best, therefore, to be flexible and explore the possibility of a separate peace with Germany.

On the German side, two camps formed around Hitler on the question of a separate peace as early as 1942.[55] One group, consisting of Goebbels, Ribbentrop, and Rosenberg, believed that an accommodation with the Russians would be preferable to one with the Western, noncontinental powers. The other group, including Himmler, Schellenberg, and Karl Wolff, as well as Admiral Canaris of the Abwehr, favored a separate peace with the West and a continuation of the war with the Bolsheviks. In November 1942 Ribbentrop asked Hitler for permission to make contact with Stalin through Madame Alexandra Kollontay, the Soviet ambassador in Stockholm. Hitler did not take kindly to that suggestion, particularly to

Ribbentrop's advice that Germany might have to give up most of its conquered territories in the east.[56] Just a few weeks later, Ciano visited Hitler
at the Wolf's Lair and delivered a message from Mussolini asking Hitler to
make peace with the Soviet Union. Hitler dismissed the proposal and then
launched into a verbal attack on Italy's weak military performance on the
eastern front. Since the situation at Stalingrad was deteriorating from day
to day, Hitler felt that he would be dealing with the Russians from a position of weakness. He told Ciano that the ideal negotiated peace with Russia
would be like the one at Brest-Litovsk in 1918, but that was not possible
under current circumstances. If he agreed to an armistice, the Russians
would simply take advantage of the ensuing pause in fighting and regroup,
so that in six months he would face a more powerful Red Army.[57]

After the disaster at Stalingrad, Hitler took a less rigid line. Unlike
Churchill and Roosevelt, whom he despised, Hitler respected and even
admired Stalin. He could also read the military balance sheet, for after
Stalingrad, German and Russian forces were about even, a situation that
would last until the summer of 1943.[58] Hitler believed that from a purely
military standpoint Russia was by far the greater threat because its leadership and its soldiers were tougher and more resilient. Stalin held similar
views of the Nazi leadership, the fighting quality of the *Wehrmacht*, and
the superiority of German science. Moreover, he believed that no matter
what happened to Hitler and his regime, the German nation would survive
to play an important role in the future of Europe. As late as March 1945,
when the Russians were on the verge of defeating Germany, Stalin made
an interesting remark to a visiting Czech delegation:

> Now we are beating the Germans and many think the Germans
> will never be able to threaten us again. This is not so. I hate the
> Germans. But that must not cloud one's judgment of the Germans.
> The Germans are a great people, very good technicians and orga-
> nizers. Good, naturally brave soldiers. It is impossible to get rid
> of the Germans, they will remain. We are fighting the Germans
> and will do so until the end. But we must bear in mind that our al-
> lies will try to save the Germans and come to an arrangement with
> them. We will be merciless. . . . But our allies will treat them with
> kid gloves. Thus we Slavs must be prepared for the Germans to rise
> again against us.[59]

Determining what Stalin's game was requires some understanding of his statesmanship, which has not been sufficiently appreciated. Stalin was as much a Russian nationalist as he was a Communist, perhaps more the former than the latter. Both Stalin and Hitler proved that they could think beyond ideology when they became partners in 1939. After Stalingrad, Stalin was less receptive to a compromise peace with Hitler. Conversely, he was not opposed to a deal with a different German government, as the earlier quote indicates. Stalin's attempt to establish a Free German Committee in 1943, consisting of German Communists and defectors, lends credence to this argument. We have evidence to show that the Russians extended several peace feelers between 1942 and 1944. Historians have acknowledged that there were indeed discussions between the Germans and Soviet representatives, but they argue that these meetings were between low-level representatives.[60] Stalin did not discourage such contacts, it is believed, because he wanted to blackmail the Western powers into opening a second front and supplying Russia with massive materiel. In other words, Stalin was never really serious about negotiating with the Germans; he just wanted the Allies to think he was so they would give him what he wanted. Maybe so, but Stalin was also a double-dealer who played games with both sides if it suited his purposes. He certainly succeeded in manipulating Roosevelt.[61] In October 1942 he played on FDR's fear that Russia felt like a poor relation by asking for much greater monthly supplies of quality planes, trucks, aluminum, and explosives and considerably greater supplies of foodstuffs. FDR immediately made this increase a high priority and informed Stalin that the items he wanted had been made available for shipment to Russia.[62]

Roosevelt convinced himself not only that Stalin was an indispensable partner in the United Nations alliance but also that he could work with Stalin in shaping a democratic postwar world. Churchill tried to disabuse him of this illusion, but FDR increasingly viewed Churchill as a man trying to defend and maintain British imperialism. He told the Catholic archbishop of New York in 1942 that the people of Europe (not just Eastern Europe) would simply have to "endure Russian domination in the hope that—in ten or twenty years—the European influence would bring the Russians to become less barbarous."[63] In order to lock the Russians firmly into the Western alliance, FDR was willing to do whatever Stalin wanted—send massive supplies, make accommodations concerning Russian territorial

designs in Eastern Europe, and provide a second front; but just in case
Stalin still had doubts, Roosevelt wanted the Soviet leader to know that the
Western powers would never negotiate with Hitler. This was the purpose
behind the dramatic announcement at Casablanca that the Germans must
surrender unconditionally without the possibility of negotiation.

Unconditional Surrender: Casablanca

On January 14, 1943, Churchill and Roosevelt met at Casablanca in
French Morocco to discuss Allied strategy. Stalin did not attend because
he claimed to be too involved in the Battle of Stalingrad, which was wind-
ing down at the time. The primary purpose of the conference was to plot
military rather than diplomatic strategy—at least this is how it seemed
on the surface, because the two Western leaders did not bring with them
any diplomatic advisers:[64] Neither Cordell Hull nor Anthony Eden had
accompanied their superiors to Casablanca. Their CCS were much in evidence, notably General Eisenhower and General Sir Harold Alexander.
Also present were Generals Charles De Gaulle and Henri Giraud, who
represented separate factions of the Free French forces. There were six
items on the agenda: reaffirming the priorities of theaters of war—Europe
or the Pacific, dealing with the U-boat menace, finding a solution to the
problem of who should lead the French, determining future operations in
the Mediterranean, maintaining the bombing offensive against Germany,
and opening up a second front. The participants did not reach specific answers on these points, but they did reach a general agreement that first
priority should be given to the European theater of war, reaffirming what
had already been decided upon in 1941.

Robert Sherwood, the liberal playwright and presidential speech
writer who investigated the question of how Roosevelt came by the phrase
"unconditional surrender," stated that the term did not just flash through
FDR's mind at a press conference he gave at Casablanca toward the end of
the conference. FDR remembered that General Grant had used the phrase
during the Civil War and that in the North Ulysses S. Grant was referred
to as "Unconditional Surrender." When he left for Casablanca, FDR carried with him notes of a meeting he had had with the Joint Chiefs of Staff
during which the phrase was suggested as a "formula of placing the objective of the war in terms of an unconditional surrender by Germany, Italy,

and Japan."[65] Sherwood said that the ghost of Woodrow Wilson was at Roosevelt's elbow at Casablanca, for what troubled the president was Wilson's failure to teach the Germans a lesson that they would never forget, namely that they had been soundly beaten.[66] As FDR put it, "practically all Germans deny the fact that they surrendered in the last war, but this time they are going to know it. And so are the Japs."[67]

Both Roosevelt and Hitler, for different reasons, swore that the year 1918 would not repeat itself. For both leaders, 1918 was the seminal teaching year.[68] Hitler had used 1918 as a point of departure in his political career. Again and again he referred to the betrayal of Germany by the Allied powers, who had seduced gullible and traitorous Germans politicians into laying down their arms in return for empty democratic promises. In Hitler's view, which was shared by most Germans in the interwar period, Germany had never lost the war; instead the fatherland had been betrayed by traitors at home—Jews, pacifists, Communists—who had undermined the home front, and by cunning Western statesmen who dangled democratic phrases in front of the German people about national self-determination, free trade, reduction of armaments, a world organization to keep the peace, and so forth. In addition, Hitler saw 1919 as a year of shame—the year disloyal German politicians had capitulated to the Allied powers by signing the Versailles "Diktat." Capitulation or unconditional surrender would never happen again under his watch.[69] When Hitler's propaganda chief, Joseph Goebbels, proclaimed in his notorious *Sportspalast* speech of February 18, 1943, that Germany would wage "total war," he was echoing his führer. In that speech Goebbels also stated that the term *unconditional surrender* did not exist in the vocabulary of National Socialism. *"Kapitulieren werden wir nie"* (we will never capitulate) became one of the defiant slogans of German propaganda. Apparently the Nazi leadership thought that if the phrase was repeated often enough it would strengthen the will of the German people to resist. Hitler, it must be remembered, was a fierce believer in will power; he saw himself waging not only a war of arms but a gigantic battle of will with his enemies. He was convinced that victory belonged to the true believer, and that National Socialism was the most potent political faith in the world. If that faith was supported by unshakable will, it would overcome the most insurmountable obstacles.

Did Hitler really believe this? There is every indication that he did, with one important qualification: this belief did not blind him to reality, as so many popular accounts have asserted. Hitler was a fanatic, but not the sort who was moved by blind fury, which is inherently emotional. His fanaticism was based on a kind of perverted spirituality and a form of hatred capable of razor-sharp calculation. I have already quoted Jodl's remark that earlier than anyone else, Hitler knew that the war was lost. In January, at the time of the Casablanca Conference, Nicolaus von Below, Hitler's Luftwaffe adjutant, noted in his memoirs that he had "the impression that Hitler knew that a war against both the Russians and the Americans—a war on two fronts—could no longer be won."[70] Having lectured his military staff for years about the fatal error of the kaiser in having waged a two-front war, Hitler now had difficulty defending the steps he had taken that led to a repeat of 1914. How, then, did he defend them? Ribbentrop tells us that Hitler thought he could escape from the threat of a two-front war by a preemptive war against Russia,[71] a view also shared by Keitel, Jodl, and Halder. Even after the war, General Halder, no friend of Hitler, wrote that Hitler's belief that Russia was preparing an attack on Germany was well-founded and that reliable documents had since shown that he was right. He was not.[72] Stalin had no intention of invading Germany, as Ambassador von Schulenburg tried to tell Hitler in his lucid reports from Moscow.[73]

Yet by invading Russia and declaring war on the United States, Hitler prepared the way for the two-front war that he had tried to avoid. Once at war with both the Soviet Union and the Anglo-Americans, Hitler had two and a half years to prevent Germany from being encircled by a two-front war as it had been in World War I. After failing to take Moscow in 1941, he was beginning to doubt that he could win the war as he had originally conceived it. Russia was not defeated by Christmas 1941. Hitler was also wrong in believing that he could keep America out of the war while fighting a quick lightning war against Russia. Britain continued to fight and gave every reason to indicate that she would fight to the end.

Why did Hitler continue fighting after he realized that the war could no longer be won? There are three plausible explanations for this. First, Hitler still believed that one of his enemies would drop out of the war after suffering prohibitive losses. He hoped that if it ever came to a real and bloody trial of strength between German and American soldiers, the Americans might withdraw from the war. Second, he believed that he could still win the war against the Jews of Europe, most of whom (11 million) were now either under his direct control or could be handed over to his SS murderers by satellite nations. Third, he had not given up his ambitious project of establishing a Greater German Reich (Grossdeutsches Reich), now perhaps no longer extending to the Ural Mountains, but at least to be defended inch by inch against the Russians in the east and the Anglo-Americans in the west. He wanted to accomplish this by sheer force of will, believing that spiritual energy could overcome almost any material force.

Hitler's iron-willed resolve, however, was matched by leaders on the Allied side. Stalin said, "If the Germans want to have a war of extermination, they will get it."[74] Stalin was prepared to punish the Germans with the same ferocity as Hitler's troops were unleashing on the Russian people. Stalin, however, always made a distinction between Germans and Nazis, knowing full well that he would have to deal with the German people once the war was over. On the other side of the ocean, FDR took the position, especially after 1941, that there was no difference between Nazis and Germans. For that reason there could be no negotiated peace as there had been in 1918. The Nazis were to be prevented at all costs from finding an escape hatch; they must surrender unconditionally and accept the consequences: military occupation and Allied tribunals meting out punishment for Nazi leaders. The German people, he said, "are not going to be enslaved—because the United Nations do not traffic in human slavery. But it will be necessary for them to earn their way back into the fellowship of peace-loving and law-abiding nations."[75] FDR still thought that at the heart of the Nazi evil was Prussian militarism; in his view, the Hitler regime was simply a continuation, albeit in more brutal form, of the kaiser's Germany. He was much mistaken about this, because the war, especially on the eastern front, produced quite a different military regime than that of the *Kaiserreich*. This is not the place to describe the radicalization of the *Wehrmacht*, which has been written about in detail by historians in recent years. By 1942, Hitler finally got around to giving the German army the kind of makeover Röhm had been pleading for in 1933–34—creating a revolutionary army without the shackles of outworn Prussian traditions of honor, duty, piety, and fear of God.

All sides had barricaded themselves, at least publicly, behind rigid positions that made a negotiated end to the war difficult (but not impossible). The two sides were quite willing to fight a war of annihilation, reminiscent of the wars of religion of the sixteenth and seventeenth centuries. Back then, it had been a conflict between competing religious views of redemption; now it was a conflict between competing ideologies. Was Hitler capable of rising above his ideological rigidity and acting like the brilliant politician and shrewd statesman he had once been? Or would his ideology overshadow his statesmanship? Was this duality the ultimate cause of his downfall? Flashes of his old skills surfaced even during the last years of the war, but by then he had dug his own hole, from which only a miracle could have extracted him.

The principle of unconditional surrender entailed rigidity in theory and brutality in practice. The Germans applied the same formula to their enemies. On May 28, 1940, for example, they told the king of Belgium that he had to accept unconditional surrender (*bedingunslose Kapitulation*) or his country would face greater destruction. In June 1940, Keitel, speaking on behalf of the führer, told the French armistice negotiators to accept German terms "unconditionally."[76] By 1942 it was well known that the Germans treated their conquered people with unprecedented harshness, particularly the Czechs, Poles, and Russians. Even the British were told in late 1939 that their island would be cleared out and turned into a green meadow.[77] But were the Allies right in responding to the Axis powers with the same unbending rigidity?

Some critics have charged that the Casablanca formula of unconditional surrender deprived the German people, especially the opponents of Hitler, of any hope that they might bring down the Nazi regime. Casablanca played into the hands of Nazi fanatics like Goebbels, who used it as a propaganda tool to frighten the German people and incite them to fight to the end. Weizsäcker believed that Casablanca prolonged the war by at least two years because it gave Hitler a further excuse to keep on fighting rather than negotiating.[78] By taking such a rigid position, the Allied powers foreclosed the possibility of engaging in any meaningful diplomacy with the Axis side.[79] This only reinforced Nazi fanaticism and its suicidal impulse to drag millions of people into the abyss. Liddell-Hart strongly made this point when he said, "All to whom I talked dwelt on the effect of the Allies' unconditional surrender policy in prolonging the war. They [the German officers] told me but for this they and their troops . . . would have been ready to surrender sooner, separately or collectively. 'Black-listening' to the Allies' radio service was widespread. But Allied propaganda never said anything positive about the peace conditions in the way of encouraging them to give up the struggle. Its silence on the subject was so marked that it tended to confirm what Nazi propaganda told them as to the dire fate in store for them if they surrendered."[80] Pope Pius XII also considered the unconditional surrender formula a grave error, telling Myron Taylor, the U.S. representative to the Vatican, that it was incompatible with Christian doctrine.[81] Churchill originally seconded FDR's proclamation at Casablanca, saying, "Perfect! And I can just see Goebbels and the rest of 'em'll squeal!"[82] FDR thought it would really please the Russians: "Uncle Joe might have made it up himself."

Churchill would eventually change his mind, but by then he had to play second fiddle to Stalin. Interestingly, Stalin did not think much of this policy of unconditional surrender because the Russian army would be the first to bear the brunt of the fanatical German resistance that the policy inspired.[83] In theory he gave lip service to unconditional surrender; in practice he ignored it. Russian propaganda tried to drive a wedge between the German people and the Nazi leadership, not to strengthen the bonds between them. Just a month after Casablanca he said, "Occasionally the foreign press engages in prattle to the effect that the Red Army's aim is to exterminate the German people and destroy the German state. This is, of course, a stupid lie and a senseless slander against the Red Army. . . . It would be ridiculous to identify Hitler's clique with the German people and the German state. History shows that Hitlers come and go, but the German people and the German state remain."[84] Does this mean that Stalin was therefore more amenable to some arrangement with Hitler? If the diplomatic maneuvers behind the scenes of battle and even formal diplomatic contacts between 1942 and 1945 are any indication, there is reason to believe that Hitler and Stalin were exploring tentative steps to come to some arrangement. This is certainly what Churchill and Roosevelt were gravely concerned about during the whole duration of the war. The Anglo-American war leaders were so worried about the possibility of a Russo-German rapprochement that they were willing to make concessions to Stalin relating to spheres of interest in Eastern Europe. In 1942 Churchill had flown to Moscow to find out whether Stalin was still in the Western camp and what was needed to keep him there. Churchill had good reason to suspect that, still facing the possibility of military defeat, Stalin might bolt the alliance and rejoin his former Nazi partner, assuming, of course, that Hitler wanted him back. The Anglo-Americans clearly based their "unconditional surrender" announcement on fears of a Russian-German settlement not unlike that concluded at Brest-Litovsk in 1918. Churchill and Roosevelt knew all too well that they were dealing with the same Soviet regime that had opted out of World War I. For this reason, Roosevelt was willing to go much further in making Stalin the key figure in the alliance, because he believed that a Soviet defeat would mean that Hitler would either win the war or become so solidly entrenched on the Continent that an Anglo-American invasion would probably fail.

The diplomatic maneuvers that occurred between 1942 and 1945 must be seen within the context of the military situation at any given point during these two and a half years. As is usual during wartime, the situation on the battlefield was closely related to what was happening in the diplomatic camp on both sides. As long as Germany appeared to be winning the war in the east, Hitler saw no reason to negotiate; but that would change after the Battle of Moscow when it dawned on him that the eastern war might turn into a quagmire with neither side capable of delivering a knock-out blow. From the Battle of Moscow in December 1941 until the successful landing of the Allies at Normandy, a window of opportunity existed that might have led to a negotiated settlement. Despite the demand for unconditional surrender, the Germans also sent out peace feelers to the Anglo-Americans during these years.

While not officially encouraging such peace feelers, Hitler did not always discourage them either. He knew about most of them, encouraging some but always insisting that negotiation had to be made on the basis of strength, which meant a decisive military victory that would compel the other side to negotiate with him. When no major victory materialized, Hitler tried one final, desperate strategy: holding out (*aushalten*) and dragging the Allies into such a meat grinder that one of them would drop out. The threads that connect these complicated maneuvers on Hitler's part have not been adequately traced. Too much has been made of the stereotype of the demented dictator who withdraws into his fantasy world, loses touch with what is going on at home and abroad, and discourages all efforts to find a diplomatic way out of his dilemma. I argue, on the contrary, that Hitler was well informed and pondered a variety of options, but in the end was defeated by his own miscalculations and by grandiose dreams of empire that were incompatible with the limitations of Germany's resources, manpower, and even the talents of its extraordinary people.

CHAPTER 7

Prospects for a Separate Peace in 1943

Rumors of Peace with Moscow

In the spring and summer of 1943, Allied intelligence services picked up rumors, many of them surfacing in the capitals of neutral countries such as Turkey, Spain, Portugal, Switzerland, and Sweden, that the Germans were conducting secret negotiations with the Russians to end the war in Eastern Europe. This sent shock waves through the diplomatic ranks of the Anglo-American camp. Roosevelt and Churchill were gravely concerned about the possibility of a Nazi-Soviet rapprochement. Stalin's demands increased in proportion to his battlefield successes, raising dark suspicions among anti-Communists in the Western alliance that the Soviet dictator, like his counterpart in Berlin, had his eye on the conquest of Europe. Churchill had flown to Moscow in 1942 to find out whether Stalin was still firmly committed to the anti-Hitler alliance. Churchill had to submit himself to what Roy Jenkins called a "hard cop and friendly cop" treatment by Stalin, a procedure Churchill found quite disconcerting.[1] Churchill withstood Stalin's treatment with remarkable tenacity and patience; he noted that Stalin's "face crumpled up into a frown"[2] when he had to tell him that the Allies could not land troops in France in the near future. Although Stalin was "glum and unconvinced" by Churchill's arguments, asking impatiently why the English were so afraid of the Germans, he eventually saw logic in the Western plan of mounting Operation Torch (the invasion of North Africa). Churchill left Moscow with some confidence that Stalin was still committed to the alliance; but despite his later disclaimers, he was deeply worried about the possibility that Stalin might reach some accommodation with Hitler, which would have allowed the Germans to direct their forces against Britain and the United States.

While Churchill had his doubts about the "sullen, sinister Bolshevik State"[3] that he had once tried so hard to strangle at its birth, Roosevelt wanted to convince himself that the Russians were building a new society based on common sharing and comradeship. He told Frances Perkins that the Russian people were thinking, first and foremost, about the common good rather than their own self-interests, as Americans were wont to do. Unlike the Russians, he said, "we take care of ourselves, and think about the welfare of society afterward."[4] George Kennan was alarmed by FDR's naiveté about Stalin, and so was the president's longtime friend William Bullitt. In a lengthy letter Bullitt sent to Roosevelt (Kennan considered it a major historical document),[5] Bullitt warned the president that Stalin should be given "the old technique of the donkey, carrot, and club."[6] He pointed out that Stalin wanted nothing less than all of Eastern Europe, and he drew a chilling picture of Russian imperialism that presaged the coming of the Cold War. As Bullitt put it, "We have to demonstrate to Stalin—and mean it—that while we genuinely want to cooperate with the Soviet Union, we will not permit our war to prevent Nazi domination of Europe to be turned into a war to establish Soviet domination in Europe."[7] FDR was not to be deterred from his pro-Russian agenda, regardless of the evidence. Perhaps one of the most compelling illustrations of Roosevelt's approach of giving the Russians the benefit of the doubt occurred when he received news reports about the Katyn massacres.

FDR was not convinced that the Russians had murdered the five thousand Polish officers, and he told his friend and envoy George Earle, who had shown him some of the gruesome pictures of the Katyn site, "George, this is entirely German propaganda and a German plot. I am absolutely convinced that the Russians did not do this."[8] When he got word in March 1944 that George Earle was about to make public what he knew about the Soviet terror machine to the American people, he became alarmed. The feisty former governor felt slighted by Roosevelt, who had become impatient with his personal envoy's loose lifestyle and not always accurate reporting.[9] But Earle proved remarkably prescient about Russia. When he received a brush-off from the president's secretary, who told him that

Roosevelt was too busy to see him, Earle sent a letter to FDR's daughter, Anna, telling her that, unless he heard from the president, he would tell members of Congress and the American people the truth about Russia: "I shall point out why Russia today is a far greater menace than Germany ever was. . . . I shall show how Russia twenty-five years after its Revolution is exactly the same Red Terror it was then, after its 15 million people in concentration camps, of its treatment of the Jews and of Labor. I shall show how Stalin deliberately started the war with his pact of friendship with Hitler so that the capitalist nations would destroy each other."[10]

Roosevelt replied immediately and angrily, saying that he was alarmed by Earle's rash proposal to expose the Soviets because it would shed an unfavorable light on a wartime partner. Publication of a report that implicated an ally would cause irreparable harm to the war effort, especially since it came from an envoy of the United States government. Roosevelt needed the Russians to win the war against Germany, which he thought was more important than making a fuss about alleged atrocities committed by the Russians at Katyn. For this reason, FDR admonished Earle, "You say that you will publish unless you are told before March 28 that I do not wish you to do so. I not only do not wish it but I specifically forbid you to publish any unfavorable opinion about an ally [Russia] that you may have acquired while in office or in the service of the United States Navy."[11] FDR closed by saying that he had no time to see Earle, thanked him for his services, and hoped that one day circumstances would permit the reestablishment of their good relationship.

Since the Anglo-Americans were deeply worried about a German-Soviet peace agreement and were trying their best to keep Stalin tied to the West, what evidence do we have of the existence of peace feelers by the two totalitarian regimes, and how serious were they? Two sources of information are compelling. The first comes from Professor Wolfgang Leonhard, who worked for Rudolf Herrnstadt, the chief editor of the Moscow-based German-language newspaper *Freies Deutschland*. In late August 1943, Leonhard noticed that the National Committee, Stalin's sponsored committee of German communists in exile, was being referred to as the core of the future German government. He also learned that the Soviets planned to announce the creation of a union of captured German officers; the date for this event was to be September 1, 1943—the beginning of the fourth year of World War II. Without explanation, the German staff of *Freies*

Deutschland was informed that the founding of the Union of German Officers would be rescheduled. Then in the early part of September, Leonhard received an advance copy of an article from Herrnstadt bearing the title "Armistice: The Commandment of the Hour."[12] Leonhard was stunned because no one up to this time had ever mentioned the possibility of an armistice on the eastern front. It was clear to him that the article must have come from the highest Soviet source, for it was essentially a peace feeler to the Germans. But just about the time this leading article was scheduled to go into print, Herrnstadt submitted an altered version of the article in which all references to an armistice had been removed. What accounted for this change? In his postwar recollections, Leonhard came across a book by Dr. Peter Kleist, *Zwischen Hitler und Stalin* (Between Hitler and Stalin), that made all the pieces fall into place. In that book, Kleist described Stalin's peace feelers to the Germans between 1942 and 1944. Thus, what had happened in the editorial offices of *Freies Deutschland* was connected to the secret contacts between the Russians and the Germans in Stockholm in the summer of 1943. Leonhard found Kleist's account "entirely credible—durchaus glaubwürdig."[13] This brings up the second, and even more important, source relating to German-Soviet peace feelers.

On December 14, 1942, Edgar Clauss, a Baltic-German businessman residing in Sweden, told the German diplomat Dr. Peter Kleist that the Russians wanted a separate peace with Germany. Clauss had dabbled in intelligence work for both the Russians and the Germans in the interwar period. In the 1930s he worked for the Soviet secret services; in 1939, following the Nazi-Soviet Non-Aggression Pact, he made contact with the German military attaché in Kaunas, Lithuania, who referred him to Canaris's Abwehr. In 1941 he ended up in Stockholm, where he cultivated contacts in the Soviet embassy. The Soviet ambassador in Stockholm at the time was Madam Alexandra Kollontay, the grand dame of Bolshevism and one of the original members of Lenin's inner circle. Although Kollontay was getting on in years and was in failing health, she had an excellent staff of diplomatic military attachés and party apparatchiks who enjoyed access to Stalin, Molotov, and Beria.

Much of our knowledge of German-Soviet peace feelers comes from Peter Kleist, who worked for both Ribbentrop's Foreign Office and Alfred Rosenberg's Eastern Ministry (*Ostministerium*) between 1941 and

1945. In 1950 Kleist published the previously mentioned book *Zwischen Hitler und Stalin*, in which he revealed his role in the tentative peace contacts between Germany and Russia.[14] Kleist was able to make contacts with a number of people who were receptive to the idea of a negotiated settlement of the war. Through a German acquaintance in Stockholm, Kleist was referred to Edgar Clauss as a possible middleman who could help initiate a dialogue between the Germans and the Russians. Kleist was astonished when Clauss told him that if Germany accepted the 1939 border line that had been agreed upon by both Germany and Russia, he could "guarantee peace in eight days."[15] When Kleist returned to Germany, he reported the result of his unusual encounters with Clauss to two diplomats—Adam von Trott zu Solz and Count Schulenburg, both of whom were determined opponents of Hitler and were later implicated in the July 20, 1944, plot on the dictator's life and executed. Kleist was silent on the question of whether the information he reported to these two diplomats reached Ribbentrop.

On June 18, 1943, Kleist made contact again with Clauss in Stockholm. By that time, Ribbentrop, Admiral Canaris, and most likely Hitler himself were well informed about Edgar Clauss and his contacts on the Soviet side. Hitler had told Ribbentrop in late 1942 that he had no intention of dealing with Stalin, and certainly not by surrendering most of the conquered eastern territories, as Ribbentrop had suggested to him as a possible concession Germany might have to make in order to obtain peace. Hitler was clearly hoping for a decisive turn in the war before he would negotiate with either the East or the West. By the summer of 1943, the situation on the eastern front had seriously deteriorated as a result of the Battle of Stalingrad. It was against this background that Kleist's second encounter with Clauss took place. Clauss told Kleist that he could arrange a private meeting with Andrei Alexandrov, the head of the Soviet Commissariat for Central Europe, who would shortly return to Stockholm from a visit to London. When Kleist asked why the Russians were willing to talk after having gained the initiative at Stalingrad, Clauss replied that the Russians did not want to fight a minute longer than they had to, and certainly not to promote the interests of the Anglo-Americans. Russia would eventually win the war, but victory would be Pyrrhic because the country's industrial capacity would be so weakened that it could not complete with the combined industrial systems of Britain and the United States.[16] Clauss also told Kleist that if he talked to Alexandrov he could be assured that the Soviet representative was speaking on behalf of the Kremlin.

In his memoirs, Ribbentrop claimed that during the spring and summer of 1943 he advised Hitler on several occasions that perhaps the time had come to negotiate with Stalin. Hitler told him that Stalin was "undeniably a historic personality of very great stature," but that he (Hitler) must first be able to achieve a decisive military success, adding, "Then we could see."[17] For his part, Ribbentrop wanted to see Kleist to find out more about Clauss and the Soviet peace feelers. Kleist went to führer headquarters, where Ribbentrop was staying at the time, and had a four-hour conversation with Ribbentrop. During the course of this meeting Ribbentrop admitted that Clauss had connections with the Soviet embassy in Stockholm and that he had passed on reliable information in the past. Ribbentrop also agreed with Kleist that Alexandrov was an important contact man. Ribbentrop then reported all this to Hitler, who allowed the resumption of talks, but only for the purpose of gathering information.[18]

On the occasion of the meeting with Ribbentrop at führer headquarters, Kleist also had the opportunity to report to Hitler himself. This came about when Kleist saw Walther Hewel, Ribbentrop's liaison to Hitler, and unburdened himself about the brutal treatment of the eastern population, which he believed undermined the German war effort. He gave Hewel a memorandum on the eastern situation that apparently convinced Hewel to pass the document on to Hitler, who at first was disinclined to read it because he hated such reports from "aristocratic excellencies with arteriosclerosis" in the Foreign Office (*verkalkten, adeligen Exzellenzen*). The meeting gives us one of the few genuine glimpses into Hitler's world at this time of great crisis for Germany. The first thing Hitler said to Kleist in his bunker room at the Wolfschanze in Rastenburg, East Prussia, was, "You have given me a very unfriendly picture of conditions in the occupied eastern territories."[19] Hitler nevertheless gave Kleist a chance to say his piece about the harsh treatment of the conquered people in the eastern areas and what could be done to alleviate their widespread suffering. If Germany won the support of the population in these areas, Kleist told Hitler, the people would side with the Germans instead of turning against them. As it stood, the local population was caught between two equally harsh masters.

During his report Kleist claimed that he had a chance to observe Hitler's curiously split facial features. He found the façade impenetrable because Hitler could change his features to present whatever impression he wanted in order to suit his purpose. Kleist also wondered about the source of the apparently hypnotic expression in Hitler's eyes but could not find a satisfactory explanation. Hitler interrupted his discourse and said, carefully choosing his words, "I cannot change course now. Given the current military situation, each change in my position would be misunderstood as a concession, causing a break in the dam. One does not change horses in the middle of a stream. Once the military situation has stabilized and the initiative is once more in our hands, then we might talk about a change of course or the application of new methods."[20] Hitler then lifted his head and spoke in a more animated voice:

These are all illusions. It is your good right but also your disadvantage to think only about the moment, the current pressing situation. I have the duty to think about tomorrow and the next day, and I cannot forget the future in favor of momentary successes. The German people are going to be a people of 120 million in a hundred years. I need empty space for the people. I cannot promise the eastern peoples sovereign rights and establish for them in place of the Soviet Union a much more solidly framed national structure. Politics is not made by illusions but hard facts. For me the problem of space (Raumproblem) is the decisive element in the east.[21]

That ended the interview.

What stands out in this encounter between the thirty-nine-year-old "eastern expert" (Ostexperte) and the middle-aged dictator was the increasing difficulty of breaking down the wall of isolation, mental as well as physical, with which Hitler had chosen to surround himself. That Hitler chose this isolated form of control was the paradoxical result of wielding absolute power. On April 26, 1942, Hitler had demanded and received omnipotent powers from his impotent Reichstag. The rubber-stamped Reichstag passed a Vollmachtsgesetz (total power law) that made Hitler sole leader of the nation, commander in chief of the armed forces, chief government leader (Regierungschef), chief possessor (Oberster Inhaber) of executive power, supreme judge, and leader of the party. These powers put the capstone on his nine-year dictatorship. Yet the irony was that the way he chose to run the country and conduct the war resulted in an increasingly leaderless state.

By 1943 Hitler had largely removed himself from domestic affairs in order to run the war. He spent most of his time at various military headquarters, where he was surrounded by trusted paladins who formed a wall around him. Hitler had always been uninterested in the actual day-to-day details of government business, which he assigned to subordinates. These paladins—Goebbels, Himmler, Bormann, Sauckel, Speer, and Goering—took advantage of his loose management style to build up their own empires. Hitler enjoyed the spectacle of feuding subordinates because it allowed him to have the final word when conflicts had to be resolved. The problem with this exercise of power was its inherent inefficiency. In an atmosphere of constantly clashing personalities and petty self-interest, the nation's business was poorly conducted. Hitler may have seen himself as a spider, but his net was not as far-reaching as he thought; isolating himself from the routine of government and the nation's home front (Hitler never visited any bombed-out city) was bound to undermine his effectiveness as a leader. Goebbels recognized this danger as early as 1942 and made repeated references to Hitler's insulated life in his diary. General Warlimont spoke of a chaos of leadership within the leader state (*Führerstaat*).[22] Historians have long been fascinated by Hitler's withdrawal into a small circle of military henchmen and trusted party followers and have wondered why the Nazi system lasted as long as it did. The answer to this intriguing question, which does not have to be treated here in detail, surely lies in Hitler's amazing power of persuasion and in his popularity with the majority of the German people. Then, too, there was the talent and sense of duty, loyalty, and obedience embodied in the German people. Roosevelt, Churchill, and Stalin praised—and never underestimated—the organizational and scientific talents of the German people.

In tracing the various peace initiatives between 1942 and 1945, it is necessary to understand the nature of the so-called leader state, a state whose leader chose to divest himself of leading anything directly except the war effort, which he tried to micromanage with a vengeance. As to the activities of various government agencies, Hitler expressed interest only if they either promoted or stymied the war effort. Throughout the war he generally ignored the Foreign Office, though Ribbentrop continued to stay close to führer headquarters, hoping that Hitler would give him an important diplomatic assignment. In 1941 Ribbentrop heard through the grapevine that Hitler had said that the Foreign Office served no useful purpose during wartime.[23] Hitler still paid no heed to diplomatic dispatches and was as suspicious as ever of diplomats of the old guard, as Kleist had discovered. There was something else Kleist noticed after his meeting with Hitler: he learned that Hewel, who had arranged the meeting, had had a serious run-in with Martin Bormann, Hitler's éminence grise and the man who was building the wall to insulate the dictator from negative reports. Bormann informed Hewel that from now on he would strictly forbid unknown people to see the führer unless he had first approved the visitor. Such people could disturb the mental tranquility of Hitler's genius through uncontrollable talk.[24] How successful was Bormann in insulating his genius? Apparently only insofar as Hitler found it convenient to avoid dealing directly with people or issues that he judged to be incidental to his task at hand—the winning of the war, or at least not losing it. The evidence suggests that Hitler was painfully aware of the difficulties he had to face after his attack on Russia and his declaration of war on the United States. He wanted to break their unnatural alliance, and in attempting to do so he allowed various subordinates to gather information about the willingness of his enemies—Eastern or Western—to explore tentative conditions that would have to be met before formal negotiations could be pursued. Hitler himself did not initiate peace feelers, but neither did he discourage subordinates from doing so. He let Ribbentrop pursue the secret talks that were being conducted in Stockholm, though he repeatedly emphasized that he needed a decisive battlefield victory, a signal to the world (*ein Fanal*), before he would seriously talk with either Russia or the Anglo-Americans.

On July 5, 1943, Hitler launched Operation Citadel, another blow to the Red Army that he hoped might break the stalemate on the eastern front. The ostensible reason for the attack was the elimination of the Kursk salient—the bulge that extended into the 1,200–mile German line and threatened to separate the fronts of Manstein and Kluge. Hitler told his reluctant generals that the German offensive, which would involve the greatest tank battle in history, was necessary for political reasons, though he freely admitted that whenever he thought about it his stomach turned. General Guderian took Hitler aside after a military conference and asked, "Why do you want to attack this year at all?" Keitel answered in Hitler's place, "We have to attack for political reasons." Guderian thought the whole plan was folly, and he tried to make his point with a rather pointless remark: "No one even knows where Kursk is."[25] It hardly mattered whether the salient was Kursk or Verdun; it was still a dangerous salient.

What Guderian should have asked Hitler was what he meant by "political reasons." Hitler clearly needed a victory after two serious setbacks on the eastern front—the Battle of Moscow and the defeat at Stalingrad—in order to bolster the home front. So much is obvious, but there is another, often neglected, factor: Hitler knew that splits had developed on the Allied side. Just one month before the Battle of Kursk (June 4), Roosevelt informed Stalin that the second front could not be undertaken before the spring of 1944. Stalin was furious.[26] In May he thought he had made a big concession to the Allies by dissolving the Communist International, though his real reason was not to please the Allies but to strengthen the national rather than the international element in Communism.[27] This move was in line with Stalin's own shift to Russian nationalism during the war. He also pledged to cooperate with the Eastern Orthodox Church, and he went on record saying that the Soviet Union supported a free Europe (whatever that meant). Furthermore, Stalin registered his displeasure with Anglo-American procrastination by withdrawing his pro-Western ambassadors in London (Maisky) and Washington (Litvinov). Robert Sherwood spoke of "an atmosphere alarmingly reminiscent of that which had preceded the Molotov-Ribbentrop Pact of August 1939, and the fears of a separate Russo-German Armistice revived. The Roosevelt-Stalin meeting was postponed indefinitely. It was fortunate that Hitler did not know how bad the relations were between the Allies at the moment, how close they were to the disruption that was his only hope of survival."[28] But Hitler did know about the differences that had developed in the Allied camp, because his intelligence sources had told him so. His problem was not a lack of intelligence, either on his own part or on the part of those who served him, but the use he made of it. As David Kahn has observed, his use of intelligence ceased at the borders of his strategy—that is, it was not allowed to question the grandiosity of his unrealistic war aims.[29]

Hitler did not achieve a decisive victory at Kursk; on the contrary, the Russians were waiting for him because their intelligence network knew all about the impending attack. Even today, the sheer enormity of the battle is difficult to grasp, but figures give us some insight. The two sides committed a total of 6,000 tanks, 4,000 aircraft, and 2 million men. The Russians withstood the best that the Germans could unleash during twelve days of furious fighting. By then, only small dents had been made in the Russian defenses; the decisive breakthrough that would send "a beacon for the whole world" was not achieved. The most dramatic moment of the battle came on July 12 when the badly mauled Fourth Panzer Army engaged the Soviet Eighth Army in a grueling eight-hour battle involving as many as 3,000 tanks on the move at the same time. Hitler had stripped every army on the eastern front of tanks and armored equipment, further depleting Germany's shrinking military resources.

After Kursk, it became difficult to believe in a decisive military victory on the eastern front. Hitler was now no longer quite as averse to a negotiated peace as he had been. Up to the time of Kursk, he had clung to the notion that he could achieve a military breakthrough on the eastern front strong enough to force Stalin to rethink his alliance with the Anglo-American powers. This possibility had by now been largely eliminated, though Stalin had left the door to negotiations slightly ajar. Throughout the summer of 1943 informal contacts continued in Sweden. Ribbentrop sent his assistant Rudolf Likus to Stockholm to test the waters. Kleist once more approached Clauss to find out whether the Russians were still amenable to some understanding. Clauss agreed to see what he could do; but Hitler now faced two more dangerous threats: the impending collapse of Fascist Italy, and the possibility of an Allied invasion of the west in the near future, perhaps within a year.

In late July 1943, German engineers working for the Post Ministry (*Deutsche Reichspost*) broke into a transatlantic telephone circuit connecting Churchill and Roosevelt. They were able to intercept the very voices of the British prime minister and the American president as they flashed in scrambled form across the Atlantic. Within a short period of time, the Germans decrypted the messages and sent the results directly to Hitler. The first dispatches revealed that Italy was about to change sides after the fall of Mussolini and join the Allies. This information allowed Hitler to move with lightning speed and dispatch sufficient forces to Italy to prevent a complete collapse of the "soft underbelly." Most of these forces (twenty-four divisions) were transfers from the eastern front.

Although Hitler's espionage coup provided significant information about military planning on the Allied side, it did not yield specific or detailed facts that might have altered the course of the war.[30] The same was true of another intelligence breakthrough for the Germans that occurred

at the same time. In July 1943, a Nazi agent, code-named Cicero, was employed as a manservant to the British ambassador in Ankara, Turkey. His
real name was Elyeza Bazna, and he was an Albanian who lived in Turkey
and worked for the SD (Security Service) of the SS. He wormed his way
into the confidence of the ambassador and managed to photograph a series
of secret documents from the ambassador's private safe. Through Cicero's
reports, along with the information Ambassador Papen relayed to Berlin,
Hitler learned about Allied efforts to persuade Turkey to enter the war on
their side.[31] He also learned enough about Allied invasion plans to be able
to walk into a military situation conference, carrying Cicero documents,
and announce, "I have studied most of these files now. There's no doubt
that the attack in the West will come in the spring; it is beyond all doubt."[32]
The documents did not reveal where the attack would be launched—Hitler
at first thought it might be Norway, with diversionary attacks in the Bay of
Biscay or the Balkans—but he was now sure that a major invasion by the
Anglo-Americans was imminent. He told his generals that "if they attack
in the West, (then) this attack will decide the war."[33] The moment of reckoning with what until then had been a distant foe was drawing near; the
Americans were at the gates. It is important at this point to stress Hitler's
expectations of the Americans and what the invasion would mean to the
outcome of the war.

　　In the fall of 1943, Hitler was receiving enough intelligence information
about the second front that he decided to transfer sufficient military forces
from the east to the west. The fall of Mussolini had been a catalyst for this
decision, and the Allied landings at Salerno and Anzio confirmed Hitler's
suspicions that the Allies were playing their big cards. Having fought the
Russians to a bloody stalemate for the past two years, Hitler believed that he
could continue holding the line on the eastern front by fighting shield and
sword (*Schild und Schwert*) battles, holding what had already been won and
strengthening the weakest points in the two-thousand-mile line stretching
from Leningrad in the north to Mariupol on the Sea of Azov. Starting in
1943 Hitler's major generals on the eastern front were all experts in defensive warfare—Manstein, Model, Schörner. If things really became bloody
on the western front—assuming of course, that the Allies would gain a real
foothold on the Continent—would the Americans fight like the Russians?
Hitler doubted it. In the meantime, he thought it best to "be on guard like
a spider in its web,"[34] a metaphor he would continue to use to the very end.

The spider may have been on his guard, but he was quite unsure where the greater danger resided. On September 10, 1943, Goebbels had a talk with Hitler in which he brought up the topic of getting out of a two-front war. He reported that "in general the Führer is of the opinion that we would rather do business with the English than with the Soviets. The Führer believes that sooner or later the English would see reason."[35] The time was not quite ripe, Hitler said, for exploiting the divisions in the enemy camp. About two weeks later (September 23) Goebbels brought up the same theme, except that this time Hitler said that he would prefer to negotiate with Stalin. Goebbels replied that Germany had to come to terms with one side or another (*mit der einen oder der anderen Seite ins klare kommen müssen*); he added that Germany had never won a two-front war, and it was therefore imperative for Germany to disengage itself somehow.[36] Then, a full month later (October 26), Goebbels had another lengthy discussion with Hitler about the situation on the eastern front and the possibility of concluding a separate peace with Stalin. This time Hitler indicated that peace negotiations could be based on the border lines agreed upon by Germany and Russia after the defeat of Poland in September 1939. Following a truce with the Russians, Hitler told Goebbels, he would then turn his attention to the British. Any settlement with Russia would be purely temporary. Sooner or later, Russia would have to be attacked again, though this would probably have to be faced by his successor. It is curious that Goebbels made no reference to the United States in this entry, which gives the impression that the British represented the major threat to Germany in the west. Does this indicate that Hitler was underestimating the importance of the United States, as one historian has argued?[37] This conclusion is highly unlikely because it is based only on one of Goebbels's diary entries. When Hitler said he would turn his attention to Britain, he obviously also meant the United States, for he had said often enough that behind Britain stood the United States.

What Goebbels's diary entries reveal are the thoughts and reactions of the two major Nazi leaders who could not really see a way out of the hole they had dug for themselves. At this point—the fall of 1943—they were hoping that the unnatural alliance would break up. In the meantime, they were willing to be opportunistic. As Hitler told Goebbels, in politics it is all a question of personality rather than principle. If Hitler meant this, and there is every reason to believe that he did, the personality he would rather deal with was Stalin and not Roosevelt or Churchill. On the other hand, if the Western leaders should develop second thoughts about their alliance with the Soviet Union, he would entertain a rapprochement with the West. Many Germans, not just Hitler, had trouble understanding why the Anglo-Americans would prefer the Russians to the Germans as allies. Communism was incompatible with capitalism while National Socialism was not. Hitler had pledged repeatedly that private property would remain untouched, and so would big business—provided, of course, that it followed the political guidelines of the state. Oblivious to the fact that the liberal West found the Nazi racial state and its machinery of terror a greater nightmare than the Soviet system, Hitler assumed that sooner or later the Anglo-Americans would rather deal with him than the Bolsheviks. He was mistaken, for both Roosevelt and Churchill had made the alliance with Russia the cornerstone of their foreign policy. As they saw it, either all of Europe was going to be ruled by Germany or the eastern half was going to be ruled by Russia. The Allied leaders totally rejected a Nazified Europe, but they did not mind that one-half of it might be ruled by Russia. Even if the Russians dominated Eastern Europe, which they were likely to do, their control of these diverse countries would not last indefinitely.

German Peace Feelers to the West

In 1943 the Western powers received a number of important peace feelers from key officials within the German government. Two of these deserve closer attention. One came from Admiral Canaris and the Abwehr and the other from a most unlikely source—Himmler's SS. The shadowy figure of Admiral Canaris, the notorious German spymaster, continues to fascinate historians, novelists, and filmmakers. Canaris was a conservative monarchist, more at home in the culture of the *Kaiserreich* than he was in that of the Third Reich. Initially attracted by the dynamic force of National Socialism, his enthusiasm for Hitler gradually gave way to determined opposition. For years he played a double game of pretending to support the Nazi regime while secretly encouraging active opposition to it. He harbored some of the major resistance fighters who wanted to eliminate Hitler, including Hans Oster, Hans von Dohnanyi, Dietrich Boenhoffer, Hans Bernd Gisevius, and many others. Stauffenberg, the man who tried to assassinate Hitler, was not one of them because Canaris considered him too politically immature and dangerously receptive to socialism.[38] This was one of the admiral's bêtes noirs, for he despised the Communists, whom he had previously hounded out of German armaments factories.

In 1943 Canaris decided to make contact with the Americans through a Dr. Paul Leverkühn, head of the Istanbul section of the Abwehr. Leverkühn had been a negotiator working for the Mixed Claim Commission in Washington after World War I. The commission had been set up by the Allied powers to settle war damages involving private business interests on both sides. While residing in Washington during the 1920s, Leverkühn had befriended William J. Donovan, who was now head of the OSS (American intelligence). While in Istanbul, Leverkühn worked closely with Franz von Papen, the German ambassador to Turkey, and with a German ex-diplomat, Kurt von Lersner, who offered himself as a contact man with the Americans. Like Leverkühn, Lersner was well acquainted with the United Sates, having served as a diplomat in Washington, where he had befriended the assistant secretary of the navy, Franklin Roosevelt. The key contact man in Istanbul was none other than George Earle, the former governor of Pennsylvania and a friend of Roosevelt.

What followed was a remarkable meeting between the head of the German Secret Service and FDR's unofficial observer in Turkey. Canaris startled the American by proposing an alternative to the unconditional surrender formula proclaimed at Casablanca. Canaris proposed an armistice in the west and a continuation of the war against the Soviets.[39] Earle was noncommittal but promised to inform Roosevelt of the admiral's proposal. Roosevelt rejected Canaris's offer, holding firm to his unconditional surrender principle. When Canaris tried to renew his contact with Earle, the American declined the offer. Meanwhile, Lersner continued to press for further talks with the Americans. In May 1943 he revealed information about a plan by the German resistance. He told Earle that certain high-ranking German officers were creating a special resistance command within Army Group Center on the eastern front; its objective was to capture führer headquarters, arrest Hitler, and turn him over to the Western powers. In planning this ambitious scheme, Canaris actually sent one of the chief resisters, Count von Moltke, to Istanbul to work out the details with Western contacts. Moltke let it be known that the German resistance was willing to send a general staff official to London to provide the British with important military information that would enable them to breach the western front. The eastern front, however, was to be maintained and the Casablanca formula to be rescinded. The boldness of this plan interested Donovan, the head of the OSS, and he relayed it to Roosevelt.[40]

Canaris was playing with fire, for his actions clearly bordered on treason. When Hitler later complained that he was surrounded by traitors, he was not exaggerating. Many Nazi officials were acting independently, and some of them were conspiring to bring down the regime. In 1943 the German military could see the handwriting on the wall and thought seriously about saving what remained of its authority by turning either to the east or the west. On the whole, most high-ranking officers preferred the west, but there were still former Russophiles with vivid memories of Russo-German cooperation going back to the days of Rapallo that predisposed them toward Moscow. Moreover, Stalin was counting on such officers in 1943 when he formed the League of German Officers, consisting of prisoners of war (POWs) who had declared their opposition to the Nazi regime. One of them was Field Marshal Friedrich von Paulus, who had surrendered to the Soviets at Stalingrad and joined the league in 1944. Admiral Canaris, however, was adamantly opposed to such groups; he had long favored a modus vivendi with the Western powers.

The question was how long the admiral could keep up his dangerous game without being exposed by the Gestapo. Knowing that his enemies in the SS were breathing down his neck, he relied on unofficial middlemen in different countries whose connections to the Abwehr could be disavowed if it became necessary to do so. The admiral had such contacts all over Europe, the most promising residing in Stockholm, Bern, Lisbon, Madrid, and Istanbul. It was in Spain that his contacts arranged the most promising, if not spectacular, meeting with the Allied side. It was a meeting with Allied intelligence officers that was made possible by Franco's secret service, which owed a debt of gratitude to Canaris for services rendered in the past. In the summer of 1943, Canaris met his two counterparts on the Allied side: Sir Stewart Menzies of the British Secret Intelligence Service (SIS) and William J. Donovan of the OSS. This unusual meeting, unique in the annals of military history, if Heinz Höhne is to be believed, took place in Santander on the northern coast of Spain.[41] Canaris outlined his proposal at length: armistice in the west, continuation of the war in the east. But when the two Allied intelligence chiefs returned to their countries, they got the cold shoulder from their superiors. FDR turned down the proposal, and Menzies had difficulty justifying his secret trip to Spain to his superiors. Roosevelt strictly prohibited further contact with German military or diplomatic agents.

Menzies had been told by his superiors not to meet Canaris for fear of offending the Russians. This was precisely the reason why the Anglo-American leaders turned down all peace feelers, even if they originated with honorable German resistance fighters who wanted to get rid of Hitler. Roosevelt and Churchill felt that the alliance with Russia had to be maintained at all costs. FDR did not trust any Germans, even if they claimed to be opposed to Hitler. In the president's judgment the German opposition to Hitler, if it existed at all, was no better than the Nazi regime it wanted to replace. The well-known American journalist Louis Lochner, who had spent many years in Germany as chief of the Associated Press bureau in Berlin, tried to inform the president of the existence of opposition movements in Germany. He wanted FDR to know that not all Germans were Nazis; he even volunteered to put American intelligence in touch with several German resistance groups. After being put off by the president's appointment secretary, he wrote the president a letter revealing radio codes that would enable the administration to make contact with the German resistance. The only response he got was a terse reply from the White House that his insistence was "most embarrassing," and would he please desist bothering the White House.[42]

We should not automatically assume, however, that Roosevelt had closed all doors to a political settlement, for he would encourage unofficial contacts with the opposition for intelligence purposes. For example, in early October 1943, a gentleman who claimed to be an emissary of President Roosevelt visited Ambassador von Papen in the German embassy in Ankara to discuss the possibility of an early peace. He had brought with him a roll of microfilm that outlined the conditions that the Germans would have to meet prior to negotiations. It included the removal of Hitler and surrender to the Allies. Papen found the man credible; he even saw him one more time at the country home of a friend, but nothing came of this curious peace probe.[43] What neither Roosevelt nor Churchill wanted to happen was any independent action by one of the Allies without full disclosure to the rest. By the fall of 1943, both Roosevelt and Churchill were extremely sensitive to Stalin's suspicions. Stalin had good reasons to be suspicious. German ambitions lay in the east. Hitler had no immediate designs on the British Empire, and he certainly had no idea how he could defeat the United States. The majority of the German people feared the Bolsheviks; by contrast, they did not fear the Anglo-Americans. If it had to come down to choosing between them, the Germans did not mind surrendering to the Americans, as was subsequently proven. As the war began to turn against Germany, a deal with the West looked increasingly attractive; the alternative—which later occurred—was to be savaged by the Russians.

For Hitler, surrender to either side was unthinkable, but for his subordinates the possibility, perhaps even the necessity, of giving in to one side while continuing to fight the other was unavoidable. By the end of 1943, the West looked like the preferred alternative. Canaris had come to this conclusion in 1942, and so had the resistance movement. Both sent peace feelers to the West. But there was another pillar of Nazidom that had begun to shake. Long before the resisters in the armed forces took serious steps to remove Hitler, culminating in Claus von Stauffenberg's attempt to kill him on July 20, 1944, there had already been discussions of the most secret kind and by the most unlikely people within the ranks of the SS—that holiest of holies of the Third Reich—that Hitler was leading Germany down the path of defeat and that a peace deal should be struck with the West. It was old, faithful Heinrich Himmler himself, encouraged by his intelligence chief Walter Schellenberg, who was losing confidence in Hitler's ability to bring the war to a successful conclusion. Just when Schellenberg first developed serious doubts about the way the war was going is difficult to determine, but according to his own account it was even before the Battle of Stalingrad.[44] In August 1942 Schellenberg first broached the topic of a separate peace with Himmler at Zhitomir, Himmler's field headquarters on the eastern front. Himmler told Schellenberg that he was more worried about the United States than the Soviet Union because the Americans had built up a much stronger industrial power. The two men then agreed—if Schellenberg is to be believed—to set in motion tentative plans to approach the enemy through unofficial channels, always making sure that they could claim not to be involved in any wrongdoing.[45]

It was not only Schellenberg who was working on Himmler to initiate peace feelers but also his private masseur, Felix Kersten, whose healing hands had become indispensable to the anxiety-ridden *Reichsführer*. Kersten possessed the ability to manipulate not only Himmler's muscles but also his mind, managing to intercede on behalf of many potential victims of the Nazi regime. Himmler came to believe that Kersten was the only man who could heal him from his gastrointestinal ailments.[46] Kersten was of Baltic-German extraction and held Finnish, later Swedish, citizenship. He studied manual therapy under a famous Chinese healer and then became a therapist to various aristocratic patrons, including Count Ciano, the Duke of Mecklenburg, and his brother Prince Hendrik, who was married to Queen Wilhelmina of the Netherlands. In 1939 Kersten was referred to Himmler by a prominent German industrialist, and from that moment he was enmeshed with the racial fanatic Himmler, who referred to him as his "magic Buddha."

On October 3, 1943, Kersten met Abram Hewitt, an OSS officer in Stockholm working undercover for the U.S. Commercial Company. Hewitt was another longtime friend of President Roosevelt; he was a highly successful businessman as well as a scholar with Harvard and Oxford degrees. The OSS believed that Hewitt was just the man to sound out the opposition and possibly cause dissension within the ranks of the Nazi leadership. Hewitt thought that by gaining access to Kersten for his bad back, he might be able to open a dialogue with Himmler himself. Kersten treated Hewitt and talked more about politics than Hewitt's bad back. The two men worked out a proposal for a negotiated settlement with Germany that they believed Himmler would seriously consider. The Kersten and Hewitt proposal included the evacuation of all German occupied territories, the dissolution of the Nazi Party, restoration of Germany's 1914 frontier lines, reduction of the German military to prevent future wars, control of the German armaments industry by Britain and the United States, and the removal and punishment of Nazi leaders. It is interesting to note that despite these obviously unacceptable terms, Himmler did not want Kersten and Hewitt to break off further discussions. He apparently believed that there was room for compromise and that somehow and in some way he could broker a negotiated peace with the West.

Both Kersten and Schellenberg worked hard on Himmler, the former appealing to his conscience and the latter to his vainglorious and inflated ego, to do something about the impending disaster. While Himmler agreed in theory, he did not know how to take decisive action on his own. He agreed that Germany should negotiate; he even recognized that it must be with the West because a Communist Europe was his worst nightmare.

There is also evidence to suggest that Himmler was beginning to realize that meaningful negotiations could not be undertaken as long as Hitler was in power.[47] But Himmler did not have the strength of character to defy Hitler openly until it was too late. Nor did he have support outside the SS. No one liked Himmler. He had no political standing whatsoever; the only thing that kept him in power was Hitler's confidence in his professed unconditional loyalty. Despite the vast police powers Himmler had built up for himself—SD, Gestapo, Kripo, Waffen SS, concentration camps, SS business enterprises—Himmler was little more than a technician of terror, a shadowy figure that the German people dreaded but could not visualize as their leader. Furthermore, Himmler was at heart an indecisive and weak man, especially if he had to operate on his own and without Hitler's authority to back him up. He tried very hard to be like his führer, but he could never really measure up to him. Like Goering, he had to steel himself for his meetings with Hitler, who cast a spell over him that, despite doubts or misgivings, he could never break.

In the meantime, Himmler's psychosomatic illnesses—no doubt caused by the gruesome treatment he meted out to the Jews and other victims of Nazism—wracked both his body and his mind. But Himmler was also an opportunist, a potential weasel who could turn against Hitler if it suited him. The possibility of almost certain defeat caused him to look for a way out, even if that meant turning against the man who had made him the second most powerful man in Germany. Yet Himmler did not have the courage of his convictions; he twisted and turned almost until the end. Schellenberg badgered him to act, Kersten squeezed concessions out of him, his adjutant Wolff acted on his own, and his astrologer delivered stupid forecasts. Moreover, not only did Himmler's extensive surveillance system alert him to an impending attack on Hitler's life, but suspicions have also been raised that he knew about the military coup that was brewing against Hitler and that he chose to sit on the sidelines to see how it would turn out.[48] This seems likely because he was neither a man of action nor a man of deep convictions. In addition, he was deeply deluded about his own importance in the Nazi hierarchy. He believed that the Western powers would be more inclined to negotiate with him than with Hitler, which explains his actions behind the scenes, first as a negotiator on exchanging Jews for money and then as diplomatic mediator seeking some accommodation with the West in the spring of 1945.

There is evidence that Himmler did not want to break off negotiations with Hewitt. According to Schellenberg, Himmler was becoming increasingly alarmed by reports that Germany's situation was worsening rapidly, and felt that contacts with the West should be kept up. "For God's sake," he told Schellenberg, "don't let your contact with Hewitt be broken off. Could you not let him be told that I am ready to have a conversation with him?"[49] Both Donovan and Hewitt thought that an important opportunity to sow dissension in the ranks of the Nazis had been missed when FDR refused, even for opportunistic reasons, to cultivate Himmler and so drive a wedge between the first and the second most powerful men in the Nazi hierarchy. What Hewitt did not know was that a Himmler-Hitler rift was unlikely in 1944 because Hitler did not know at the time that Himmler had been contacting Western intelligence sources in 1943.

In retrospect, it is clear that FDR was too concerned about keeping the alliance with the Soviet Union intact to engage in secret negotiations with an enemy that could easily undermine it. FDR suspected that Stalin or his subordinates were sending out tentative peace feelers at the very time that Hewitt was making contact with Kersten. Why should the American president jeopardize his standing with Stalin at one of the most crucial moments of the war? All too many peace rumors were surfacing in Europe at the time. Who could tell which of them were genuine and which were not? There was a department at führer headquarters whose function was to plant rumors and disinformation throughout Europe. It was euphemistically named Expert Advisory on Questions of Peace (*Sonderreferat*). It was a highly secret department that few people inside or outside Germany knew anything about.[50] Even today we know very little about this small department and what it hoped to accomplish. Was its purpose now to use every possible diplomatic and propagandistic means to extricate Germany from a war that its members knew could no longer be won? Hitler probably used the *Sonderreferat* primarily for propagandistic purposes, planting rumors through agents in Sweden, Switzerland, Turkey, or Spain.

We do know that the British warned the Americans as early as 1942 of such German disinformation activities. The British government also instructed its diplomatic representatives to reject peace feelers from German military or resistance sources because German counterintelligence agents disguised themselves as resistance fighters. This is why, for example, Adam von Trott zu Solz, who was a Rhodes Scholar and a determined opponent of Hitler, was denounced by the FBI as a Nazi spy. Other German resistance fighters did not fare much better; the general view on the Anglo-American side was that all German resistance fighters were suspect because they were most likely Nazis in disguise. This position was by no means universal, because there were officials in the State Department and in American intelligence who saw things differently. A number of Americans, such as Earle, Hewitt, Donovan, Lochner, Dulles, and others, wanted to find some modus vivendi with the Germans in order to avoid further bloodshed. All of them dreaded the prolonged bloodbath on the western front that would most likely await an American invasion force. Hewitt regretted that nothing had come of his efforts at mediation, saying that "if we could have driven a wedge between Himmler and Hitler, the resulting disorganization might have resulted in the collapse of Germany before it actually occurred."[51] A similar opinion was held by Dr. Calvin Hoover, the director of all OSS operations in Scandinavia, who admitted that Hewitt's visit to Stockholm had really been a kind of charade because no one in the OSS wanted to deal with Himmler. But Hoover added that a coup by Himmler, though probably doomed to failure, would have had a shattering impact on the Nazi Party and the German army, perhaps saving the lives of at least one million people.

Roosevelt and Churchill chose a different approach, pursuing complete military victory over Germany, Italy, and Japan rather than exploring a negotiated settlement. The men at the top believed in total war, while some in lesser positions held out for some kind of negotiated peace to the very end. Total victory meant total defeat of the enemy. Both Roosevelt and Churchill recognized that such a victory required complete unity among the Allies. This is why Roosevelt went to extraordinary lengths in late 1943 to appease Russia, even if that meant that he would have to travel thousands of miles to meet "Uncle Joe."

From Quebec to Tehran

In August 1943 Roosevelt and Churchill met in Quebec to discuss the projected invasion of France and the logistics involved in such a huge, amphibious operation. Churchill suggested that the operation should be led by an American, the assumption at the time being that it would be General Marshall. There was also discussion about the future of Germany. Eden and Hull proposed some form of decentralization that involved dividing Germany into a number of small, independent states. In a secret agreement between Churchill and Roosevelt, the two countries pledged to cooperate in the development of the atomic bomb. They agreed never to use the weapon on each other, to use it against a third party only by mutual consent, and to share atomic secrets with a third party only by mutual agreement. They agreed not to share atomic secrets with the Soviet Union. Little did they know that the Soviet NKVD had already mounted a full-scale intelligence effort to find out about the Manhattan project, setting up their own operation to develop a bomb in 1942.[52] The secret agreement between Roosevelt and Churchill speaks volumes about the Anglo-American ambivalence toward the Soviet Union, a country the Anglo-American leaders needed to win the war but which they never trusted. The bond between the Anglo-Americans and the Soviets was dependent solely on the existence of Hitler and Nazi Germany. It was Hitler who brought them together, and it was his defeat that would drive them apart. American suspicions of Soviet intentions were reflected in a secret document, drafted by a high-level military authority, that Harry Hopkins brought with him to Quebec. The document, titled "Russia's Position," stated quite frankly and correctly that "Russia's postwar position in Europe will be a dominant one. With Germany crushed, there is no power in Europe to oppose her tremendous military forces. The conclusions from the foregoing are obvious. Since Russia is the decisive factor in the war, she must be given every assistance, and every effort must be made to obtain her friendship. Likewise, since without question she will dominate Europe on the defeat of the Axis, it is even more essential to develop and maintain the most friendly relations with Russia."[53]

Before the Quebec Conference ended, a message arrived from Stalin inviting the British and the American foreign ministers to a Tripartite Foreign Minister's Conference in Moscow, which convened on October 18, 1943. The agenda included the opening of a second front, the division of the Italian Navy, bringing Turkey into the war against Germany, the future of Poland, and the possibility of a Russian declaration of war against Japan. Few of the items on this ambitious agenda were acted upon at that time but had to wait until the three Allied leaders would meet personally at the end of November in Tehran. One notable outcome of this conference, however, was the establishment of a European Advisory Commission whose function it was to work out the postwar occupation policies for Germany.

It is clear from what transpired at Tehran that Roosevelt had made up his mind to curry favor with Stalin. This put him in an awkward position with Churchill and the British, who got the distinct impression that they would from now on be a distant third in the alliance. Roosevelt made things worse by alternately baiting and ignoring Churchill, a tactic he believed would be well received by Stalin. The Soviet leader, for example, was pleased to hear the American president condemn European imperialism. Roosevelt did not have to be too explicit about the European imperialists he had in mind. Stalin got the message. Stalin was particularly surprised to hear FDR say that Indian society was ripe to be reformed from the bottom up—a remark that took the translator's (Chip Bohlen) breath away.[54] A few days before, FDR had told Churchill, "Winston, you have 400 years of acquisitive instinct in your blood and you just don't understand how a country might not want to acquire land somewhere if they can get it. A new period has opened in the world's history . . . and you will have to adjust yourself to it."[55] Churchill had come to Tehran to push his own plan, which was to postpone Operation Overlord (the invasion of Normandy) and concentrate instead on the Mediterranean theater. Roosevelt and Stalin overruled him. Stalin had made the second front the test of Allied faithfulness; he did not believe that the Mediterranean strategy would lead to a decisive defeat of Germany. He considered that it was at best another British exercise to chip away at the Nazi empire at the outer perimeters, not to deliver a fatal blow. That fatal blow would require a head-on assault on fortress Europe. In Stalin's eyes the British were vacillators who were endlessly avoiding a real one-on-one fight with the Germans. If it were up to them, they would do combat with the Germans only once the last Russian had bled to death.

During a dinner party on November 29 Stalin baited Churchill about his anti-Bolshevik stance in the past. Why had he been so eager to fight the Bolsheviks but now hesitated to fight the Fascists? How many British divisions were currently fighting the Fascists, and why were the British hesitating to employ the 2 million soldiers in India? Then following some banter about what to do about the Germans, Stalin suggested that 50,000 German officers should be executed. Churchill was outraged: "I will not be a party to any butchery in cold blood," he replied to Stalin. The Soviet leader was not convinced, repeating, "50,000 must be shot." Churchill was now really angry, and it showed in his face: "I would rather be taken out now than so disgrace my country."[56] FDR decided to calm the waters by being flippant: "I have a compromise plan," he said, "not 50,000 but only 49,000 should be shot."[57] Churchill stormed out of the room, with Stalin following him, putting his arm around him and saying that it had all been a joke. Unlike FDR, Churchill knew in his heart that Stalin had not been joking. He told his physician, Lord Moran, that he foresaw the most horrible future for Western civilization and wondered if he would be held responsible for it. Moran noted in his memoirs that Churchill thought that Stalin was just another Hitler and that Britain would be powerless to oppose him. "The PM," Moran observed, "is appalled by his own impotence."[58]

This was not true of FDR, who was in fine fettle. He seemed to think that Churchill was a man of the past—which he was—and Stalin a man of the future, which he was not. If he could just "get to" Stalin, FDR reasoned, he could make him an equal partner in reshaping Europe. If FDR was suspicious of Stalin's past or present dealings with the Nazis, he did not show it at Tehran. Unless the Russian archives tell us otherwise, Stalin was too cunning to leave footprints connecting him directly to the activities of his intelligence network. Stalin did not trust anyone, including FDR. But FDR wanted Stalin to trust him. He also wanted Russia's help in defeating the Japanese. Roosevelt came to Tehran without any fixed agenda about the postwar period, often saying that specifics on this issue could wait until after the war had been won. The important thing now was to maintain Allied unity. Stalin, conversely, did not see it that way; he was already looking beyond the war in order to secure Russian national self-interests. Stalin was a realist who had no interest in establishing an international order based on democratic freedom, as FDR envisioned. He wanted to acquire the territories he considered necessary for Russia's future security, and he was banking on the Red Army to make it possible.

At Tehran, Roosevelt and his advisers failed to see the political implications of the strategic military decisions they were making. In this they probably reflected the attitudes of the American people; they certainly had the support of American intellectuals of the New Deal persuasion who believed that the American and the Russian peoples were much alike in their vigorous pursuit of new, progressive ideas.[59] Thus, at Tehran, Churchill lost out on his major positions: Turkey, the Balkans, the timing and location of the second front, and the Mediterranean strategy. Stalin had the advantage because he came to Tehran knowing what he wanted. In regard to Germany he demanded its occupation by the three Allied powers, insisting that East Prussia be awarded to Russia. He favored stripping Germany of its industrial capacity, using 4 million Germans as slave laborers in the East, and liquidating the German general staff. His main concern was that the Allies would adopt a lenient approach toward the Germans. He did not have to worry about this because FDR was already inclined to listen to anti-German hardliners such as Henry Morgenthau, Harold Ickes, and Harry Hopkins. Roosevelt told Stalin that he favored the partition of Germany, hoping that specific details could be worked out in due time, but preferably after Germany had been totally defeated. In regard to Poland, Stalin was happy to learn that Roosevelt agreed with his proposal that Poland's former eastern borders should be moved closer to the western borders, as far as the Oder River. He tacitly admitted that his concern over Poland was as much related to the 7 million Poles who lived in the United States and how they would vote in the 1944 election as it was to the future of the Polish state. The Big Three agreed tentatively to the so-called Curzon Line of 1919 without informing the Polish government in exile. Roosevelt was equally generous regarding the Baltic States, which he expected to be reoccupied by the Red Army. He gave Stalin the impression that he trusted that the Soviets would permit the people of these provinces a measure of self-determination, again reminding Stalin that Lithuanians, Latvians, and Estonians were politically represented in the United States.[60] These concessions to Stalin by Roosevelt, subsequently solidified by the military successes of the Red Army, would enable the Soviet Union to achieve a goal that had eluded tsarist Russia: the domination of Eastern Europe and the Balkans.

Hitler was well informed about these Allied meetings; he knew about the Quebec Conference, the Moscow meeting of Allied foreign ministers, and the Big Three conference at Tehran.[61] Information obtained from Cicero revealed two interrelated facts: that no Allied invasion would occur in the Balkans and that the second front would be launched as a cross-channel landing in France. Hitler even knew that the cross-channel invasion was code-named Overlord, but that was the extent of what he knew. In Directive No. 51, dated November 3, 1943, Hitler made a startling admission: that, while the bulk of Germany's military strength had been placed on the eastern front, the situation had now changed because a new danger had arisen—an Anglo-American landing in the west. He stated that everything indicated that the enemy would "launch an offensive against the Western front of Europe, at the latest, in the spring, perhaps even earlier."[62] He added that he could no longer take responsibility for further weakening the West in favor of other theaters of war. He then outlined the specific responsibilities that had to be assumed by the army, air force, navy, and security forces. Hitler was expecting the Americans, and he thought he was ready for them.

CHAPTER 8

Hitler and the "Unnatural Alliance": 1944—1945

Expecting the Americans

In his January 1, 1944, New Year's address to the German people, Hitler claimed that Germany had successfully weathered the severe setbacks of the preceding year. He mentioned the Allied landings in North Africa, the fall of Mussolini, and the devastating bombing attacks on major German cities such as Berlin, Hamburg, Cologne, and Kassel. He promised to win the war and rebuild Germany's battered cities, to make them more beautiful than they had been before.[1] The hour of revenge would come. The German leadership, he said, was prepared to prosecute the war to its ultimate conclusion and with the "utmost fanaticism." He praised the productivity of German industry, boasting that in both quantity and quality it equaled that of his enemies. The same was true of manpower, which could now be increased because Germany had gained control of the European labor market, allowing the use of cheap conscript workers. He predicted that any invasion attempt would fail as miserably as the British-Canadian raid on the German-controlled French port of Dieppe in August 1942.

This address was for public consumption. What did Hitler really think in early 1944? Judging from what he said during his situation conferences (*Lagebesprechungen*) and what he confided to Goebbels and others, he was greatly preoccupied with the impending Allied invasion, which he expected sometime during the spring or early summer of 1944. He repeatedly asked his generals and admirals how Germany could prevent amphibious landings and where they were likely to occur. "Where will they land?" he asked, adding imploringly, "where are the clairvoyants?"[2] Hitler expected a feint landing, followed by a main attack elsewhere. Would the feint be at the Pas de Calais or in Normandy? Timing was of the essence, because once the real attack had been identified, tanks could be brought in quickly to defeat the enemy on or near the beaches. Hitler thought that if the Anglo-Americans could be pinned down on the beaches for at least six to eight hours, German tanks could be sent into the breach to hurl the enemy back into the sea. It would be a repeat of Dieppe. Hitler hoped that the German air force would possess new jetfighters by the time of the invasion: "The important thing is that he [the enemy] gets bombs on his head the moment he lands."[3] He admitted that he had serious concerns about the western theater of war, but he tried to dispel unwelcome doubts with reassuring arguments. One was that the Allies, especially the Americans, were poorly trained and inexperienced. In North Africa, he said, the Americans had been greeted by traitorous (to Vichy) French generals; in Sicily they had enjoyed the aid of unprincipled creatures of the Marshal Badoglio kind. This time the Americans would be greeted by a determined German *Wehrmacht*. Hitler also banked on the system of fortifications the Germans had been building on the coastline, extending from Holland to Cherbourg. Nazi propaganda had inflated these coastal defenses into a "new Westwall" or the "Atlantic Wall."[4] In reality, what Hitler called a "gigantic bastion" was a linear coastal defense that consisted largely of thinly manned bunkers and fortifications. If he could somehow gain more time he might strengthen this Westwall into an impregnable "Fortress Europe." He boasted to General Guderian, "Believe me, I am the greatest builder of fortresses in history. I have constructed the Westwall; I have built the Atlantic wall. I have poured untold tons of cement, I know what building fortresses means."[5] In 1944 Hitler's Westwall was not manned in any depth at any given point, nor was it equipped with up-to-date weapons. His hope that the projected rocket weapons could be used to repel any invasion force had been dashed by his military experts as premature.

Hitler also assuaged possible doubts by predicting that the "unnatural alliance" would fall apart. On January 4 he told his generals that there were so many differences on the enemy side that sooner or later their coalition would split.[6] Two weeks later the official Soviet party newspaper, *Pravda*, claimed that the British were negotiating a separate peace with Germany.[7] This was probably Soviet disinformation, perhaps even disseminated by Stalin himself, who was trying to light another fire under the Anglo-Americans to compel them to launch the second front. Yet Hitler probably read it as another sign of serious Allied differences. Just how serious these Allied disagreements were would be an ongoing guessing game on the German side. On March 3, 1944, Hitler had a lengthy discussion with Goebbels on the military situation, including the impending invasion in the west. He took the position that a wait-and-see approach was called for because both the British and the Americans were going through an extraordinary political crisis over the Bolshevik question. According to Hitler, Stalin was holding a gun on Churchill and Roosevelt. Since Churchill's Britain was in closer geographic proximity to Russia, the Communist threat was much greater for Churchill than for Roosevelt. Goebbels reported Hitler as saying that he hoped to hold the line in the east, repel the Anglo-American invasion in the west, and then transfer forty divisions from west to east for another, hopefully decisive attack on the Russians.[8]

With hindsight we know that these views were based on flawed assumptions about the military potential of the impending invasion force. In 1943 German military prospects were not as hopeless as they appear to us today. Hitler was still holding the line on the eastern front. The Red Army had not breached the 1,500–mile German front; it had only knocked holes in it. In Italy, the Germans had established an excellent defensive line and put a halt to additional Allied advances. France was ruthlessly controlled by Nazi occupation forces, and frantic efforts were under way to fortify the coastline. In the Balkans the Germans had taken control of previously held Italian territories. The Allied bombing offensive had been temporarily checked, and Hitler placed great confidence in new German weapons such as the ME 262 jet fighter planes and rockets (the V-1 and V-2). Most important, the German home front was secure. Most of the German people trusted their führer and remained loyal to him until the bitter end.

During the six months preceding D-Day, Hitler periodically speculated about political events in the United States.[9] He knew that 1944 was an important election year for Roosevelt. He believed that FDR could not survive the election if the Anglo-Americans failed to invade the Continent. In this he was probably right. Failure to invade would have meant the continuation of the war for the foreseeable future. It might even have led to the defeat of the Soviet Union by the Germans. The fate of Europe was undoubtedly in the balance. Hitler knew this.

What he did not understand was that Roosevelt was more popular than he thought, and he (along with most Americans) also did not know that Roosevelt was a very sick man who was not likely to survive a fourth term in office. Despite his developing coronary heart disease, Roosevelt was still a very determined man when it came to the conduct of the war. The American president's views of Germany and Germans had hardened noticeably by 1944. FDR refused to budge from the rigid Casablanca formula of unconditional surrender. On January 14, 1944, after a discussion with Molotov, Cordell Hull approached the president and asked him whether the Allied policy of unconditional surrender should not be defined in a more flexible form than it had been at Casablanca. FDR did not think that this was a good idea, and remarked that anyone who wanted to know more about the specifics of unconditional surrender could read about Lee's surrender to Grant in 1865. Individual Allied powers could handle the surrender terms as military circumstances dictated.[10] The president still refused to respond to any peace feelers by anyone on the German side. In March, Franz von Papen sent a message to Earle, by way of Lersner, suggesting possible peace talks. Earle told the *Philadelphia Inquirer* after the war that he had relayed the message to Roosevelt, who promptly rejected it. Earle was told that all peace contacts had to go through the supreme military commander in Europe (Eisenhower) before they could be seriously entertained by Washington. Papen saw this as an obvious put-down by the president. Eisenhower was in Britain and was hardly in a position to make independent political decisions.[11]

On May 18, 1944, Roosevelt wrote to Churchill, "What I want to impress on the people of Germany and their sympathizers is the inevitability of their defeat . . . they must know in their hearts that they will be totally defeated."[12] The question was how this could be made public in a way that would not only reach the Germans but also achieve its desired effect. The result was a draft document by the president that was intended to serve as an appeal to the German people. It was drafted three days before D-Day, and it said, among other things, "Your leaders have one remaining hope. It is that they can get a compromise peace if you can be made to resist long enough. The Allied leaders—Churchill, Stalin and I—have said again and again that we will accept from Germany nothing less than unconditional surrender. I say it again. The leaders of the German Army must surrender unconditionally . . . we promise you nothing . . . we do not seek the destruction of the German people."[13] Such an announcement, if it had been made known to the Germans, would have been received with mixed feelings, except for the bland but uninspiring statement that the Allied powers did not seek the destruction of the German people.

On June 4, 1944, two days before the Allies launched Operation Overlord, Rome was liberated by Anglo-American forces. No serious physical damage was inflicted on the city by either side. There is evidence that Hitler had instructed Field Marshal Albert Kesselring to get in touch with American generals to arrange joint measures to leave Rome intact. Hitler did not suggest such measures out of humanitarian reasons, though his passion for architecture may have been a minor factor in his decision to save the eternal city. The real reason was to score propaganda points and to open a channel of communication with the Americans and the British.[14] His use of military means to drive a wedge into the Allied coalition was one of the few options left to Hitler during the last two years of the war.

D-Day and the Collapse of the *Westheer*

In 1942 Hitler had mocked the British for promising a second front and said that no matter where on the European continent Churchill planned to land troops, he would be lucky to remain on land for more than nine hours.[15] The failed British-Canadian raid on Dieppe seemed to confirm this boast. But what Hitler did not take into account, despite General Bötticher's warnings, was that the Americans would be able to supply the needed materiel and manpower to stage a major invasion after two years of active engagement in the war. Such was the case in the spring of 1944; by that time, southern England had turned into a huge encampment of men and arms, giving rise to a frequently heard quip that the whole of the island might sink into the sea under such a massive weight. Besides hundreds of ammunition depots and parking lots for tanks and vehicles, the country teemed with troops of different nationalities: twenty American divisions, fourteen British divisions, three Canadian divisions, and one each of the Free French and the Poles. Additionally, the country was host to hundreds of thousands of special forces and logistical personnel.

On June 6, 1944, the Allies disgorged this massive force in thousands of ships and hurled it onto the beaches of Normandy in one of the most brilliantly conceived and executed operations in history. The Germans were largely taken by surprise. Many hours and even days after the landings had taken place on a sixty-mile arc between Cherbourg and Le Havre, the Germans were still wondering whether it was *an* invasion or *the* invasion. This is because the Allies had played a superb guessing game, using clever counterintelligence operations to deceive the Germans about the precise landing locations. Hitler's intelligence services failed badly; the führer himself was asleep when the landings occurred. His chief of operations, General Jodl, who had been informed about the landings, told urgent callers that there was no reason to awaken the führer until the situation in France had become more predictable. When Hitler was informed about the Allied landings at 10 o'clock in the morning on June 6, his reaction was remarkably optimistic. He said that "the news could not be better! As long as they were in England we could not catch them. Now we finally have them where we can beat them."[16] He felt confident that the invaders could be thrown back into the sea; but still being unsure whether Normandy was the only place where the Allies planned to land, he hesitated to free up the tank divisions he held in reserve under camouflage in the forests northwest and south of Paris. Although he finally permitted four Panzer divisions to be moved to Normandy, they arrived on the battlefield too late to deliver a decisive blow to the enemy. At the time of the landings on June 6, only one Panzer division was within reach of the beaches at Normandy.

The German coastal defenses were badly outnumbered, and reinforcements were difficult to deploy because the Allies enjoyed total air superiority. When von Below pointed this out to Hitler, he was told that the invasion force could be beaten back despite the enemy air superiority.[17] Hitler was banking on increased aircraft production and on the use of the new V-1 and V-2 rockets, which had just become operational. The V-1s— the V stands for *Vergeltungswaffe,* or reprisal weapon—were launched against London from their bases on the French coast in June, causing as much fear as they did damage. It is estimated that nearly eight thousand were launched against Britain before their launch sites were destroyed by Allied troops. The V-2, the first supersonic rocket, was a much larger missile, forty-six feet long and weighing more than thirteen tons. It could reach 3,500 miles per hour and deliver 1 ton of explosives over a distance of

225 miles. Hitler expected too much from these "miracle weapons" (*Wunderwaffen*). They came too late in the action, and their launch facilities in France were quickly put out of commission.

On the first day of Operation Overlord, the Allies had taken their designated beaches—two American (Omaha and Utah) and three British-Canadian (Gold, Juno, and Sword). The objective for the first day, which was largely met, was to establish at least a ten-mile beachhead on a line running from Saint-Mére-Église by way of Carentan and Bayeux all the way east to Caen. The invading forces had been supported by lethal bombardment from hundreds of offshore battleships and by more than two thousand bombers. Some five thousand vessels had appeared through the thinning mist at daybreak on June 6. Dozens of these vessels brought floating piers, tanks, and small artificial harbors with them, allowing the Allies to construct launching sites from which they could supply the invading forces until French, Belgian, and Dutch ports could be captured. By the end of the month the invaders had landed 1 million men, 17,532 vehicles, and 566,648 tons of materiel.

A deadly race now began as both sides built up their forces—the Anglo Americans trying to break out and the Germans trying to close the ring around them and throw them back into the sea. Although the Allies had initially landed only eight divisions against the fifty-eight German divisions in the area, the German defense was seriously hampered by Allied naval and air superiority, by French sabotage activities, and by the massive materiel that was poured into Normandy to supply the Allied armies. The Germans fought valiantly, causing consternation among the Allied High Command. On June 12, Churchill personally flew to Normandy to consult with Field Marshal Montgomery, who commanded the Allied armies. Montgomery's British and Canadian forces were unable, despite several major attempts, to break through the German defenses west of Caen. While Montgomery was trying to breach the German forces in his sector, the Americans performed superbly in their sector, managing to thrust through the Cotentin Peninsula and eventually capture the port of Cherbourg. Behind the scenes there was intense bickering among the Western powers, some of it due to the imperious attitude of Montgomery and some of it the result of Churchill's stubborn pursuit of his Mediterranean strategy. Churchill wanted to cancel Operation Anvil, the Allied plan to stage a second landing in southern France, and replace it with an attack on the

Balkans by way of Trieste and Ljubljana. Rome had fallen to the Allies on June 4, an event almost overlooked in America at the time, and Churchill believed that the time was right to shift part of the western operation to the Balkans. Behind this strategy was Churchill's desire to prevent the Russians from overrunning the Balkans. The Americans wanted nothing to do with this scheme. Churchill was so enraged that he threatened to resign, but thought better of it after recognizing that Roosevelt and Stalin were on the same page and would overrule the British whether he was prime minister or not.

If there were serious differences among the Allies, these paled in comparison to the spreading chaos and confusion in the German High Command. Unlike the Allies, who had established a unified command structure, the German side had no such structure. Field Marshal von Rundstedt, the supreme German commander of the west, was given control of two army groups, but he had no direct control of either naval or air force, whose western commanders took their orders from Dönitz and Goering, respectively. There was a veritable chaos of command, with each of the three services fighting its own war.[18] And looming ominously in the background was a meddling führer who took inappropriate actions at inopportune times. When the Battle of Normandy was over, Hitler sacked Rundstedt; drove his successor, Hans von Kluge, to commit suicide; fired General Schweppenburg; forced Field Marshal Rommel to commit suicide for his complicity in the July 20 plot on the führer's life; and drove General Dollmann, commander of the Seventh Army, to commit suicide for the loss of Cherbourg.

The deep crisis in the German High Command came to a head when Hitler personally traveled to battle headquarters near Margival north of Soissons on June 17. General Hans Speidel, who has left an account of his meeting with Hitler and his commanders, described Hitler as pale and sleepless, nervously playing with his spectacles and the various colored pencils he held between his fingers. He repeatedly criticized Rundstedt and Rommel for not defeating the Allied forces. Rommel countered Hitler's accusations by giving a brutally frank analysis of what he thought was a losing battle. Hitler cut him off repeatedly with promises of stemming the tide with the new rocket weapons, which he predicted would rain death and destruction on the Anglo-Americans. Curiously enough, Hitler's meeting with his commanders had to be resumed in one of the main air-raid shelters of the Margival command post because a defective V-1 rocket reversed course and ended up exploding near the führer's bunker. Rommel predicted the collapse of the Normandy front and told Hitler to draw the necessary political conclusion. Hitler was furious and cut off the discussion by pointedly telling Rommel, "Don't concern yourself with the continuation of the war but with your invasion front."[19]

Five days after this meeting, with Hitler and his generals still in France (June 22), Stalin launched a major offensive against Army Group Center. It was the third anniversary of Hitler's attack on the Soviet Union. The Russians attacked with more than 2 million men, supported by 5,000 tanks and 5,300 planes. In sheer size and scope, this massive offensive was as spectacular as the one in Normandy, though Western historians have usually underreported and underestimated its military significance for political reasons. Within the span of just two weeks the Russians had knocked a huge hole in the German front and destroyed the operational effectiveness of Army Group Center. The Germans lost another 350,000 men, of whom 57,600 were triumphantly paraded through the streets of Moscow. Russian forces then poured through this huge hole in the German line and proceeded to reconquer the Ukraine and the Crimea, driving the Finns out of the war and drawing within striking range of Warsaw.

While the Battle of Normandy was raging, the Republicans held their convention in Chicago and nominated Thomas E. Dewey, governor of New York, a dapper, intelligent, but uninspiring politician. His running mate was Ohio senator John W. Bricker, known for his isolationist views. The Republican platform, however, strongly endorsed the prosecution of the war and the establishment of an international organization to keep the peace. Hitler did not think that there was much difference between the two American parties, but he expressed a preference for Dewey over Roosevelt, calling Dewey "a clean person. And that's something in this country of corruption."[20] FDR had a visceral dislike of Dewey; he also did not think that Dewey was the man who could take America successfully through the rest of the war, let alone help shape the postwar world. Robert Sherwood has argued that if Willkie had won the Republican nomination, Roosevelt would not have run for a fourth term.[21] But Willkie was edged out by Dewey and died of a heart attack in October 1944. In July, FDR was renominated at Chicago on the first ballot, running for an unprecedented fourth term and raising fears among his opponents that he would turn out to be a "lifer" in the White House. A photograph taken shortly after his acceptance speech showed the president looking "haggard, glassy eyed, and querulous."[22] The Republican opponents of the president widely circulated this photograph in their campaign literature with an eye to alerting the American people that the president was a sick man and therefore unfit to run the country at a time when American troops were actively engaged in far-flung theaters of war. The picture did not lie. After having lunch with the president shortly following the convention, FDR's running mate, Harry Truman, confided to his administrative assistant, "You know, I am concerned about the President's health. I had no idea he was in such a feeble condition. In pouring cream in his tea, he got more cream in the saucer than he did in the cup. His hands are shaking, and he talks with considerable difficulty. . . . It doesn't seem to be any mental lapse of any kind, but physically he's just going to pieces. I'm very much concerned about him."[23] There was much more for Truman to be concerned about that he did not know, but should have been told by Roosevelt. FDR deliberately chose not to tell Truman anything pertaining to military, diplomatic, or administrative affairs, including developments relating to the atomic bomb.[24]

What Roosevelt had done well, however, was to place the conduct of the war into the hands of competent generals. At the time of the Republican and Democratic Conventions—June to July 1944—the American forces in Normandy were fighting their way steadily out of their bridgeheads, "relentlessly carting behind them more materiel and soldiers," as Goebbels recorded in his diary on June 22.[25] Goebbels predicted that the decisive turn in the war would occur in the West. Barely one month after this entry, the Allies managed to consolidate a front that stretched from the Dives estuary on the west to the West Coast of Cotentin at Lessay through Saint-Lô. According to von Below, Hitler recognized the danger to the German armies that were trying to hold the line in Normandy. Moreover, Hitler was waiting for a second landing in the Pas de Calais.[26]

To add to Hitler's woes, the crisis in the German High Command was also coming to a head. On July 15, Rommel sent him a telegram warning again of the imminent collapse of the Normandy front and urging him to recognize the political consequences. After sending his report, he told Speidel, "I gave him his last chance. If he does not recognize the consequences, we will act."[27] Rommel had been in touch with the anti-Nazi conspiracy that had reached a critical point in July 1944, and while Rommel himself did not act (he was seriously injured in an air attack), Colonel Claus von Stauffenberg did. On July 20, 1944, Stauffenberg, carrying a British time bomb in his attaché case, walked into a large wooden building at führer headquarters at Rastenburg in East Prussia where Hitler had scheduled an important conference. Stauffenberg placed the attaché case under the large conference table and as close to Hitler as he could manage. He then excused himself on the grounds that he had to make an important telephone call. One of the military commanders, leaning over the table, felt the attaché case and moved it under the table so that it leaned on the upright support some distance away from Hitler, an act that would save Hitler's life. At 12:42 PM, a huge explosion rocked the building, shattering the conference table, collapsing the roof, and sending glass in all directions. Watching the explosion from some distance away, Stauffenberg convinced himself that Hitler had been killed. He then bluffed his way through three control points and took off by plane to Berlin to orchestrate Operation Valkyrie, the military coup to overthrow the Nazi regime.[28]

As is well known, Hitler survived the plot on his life and wreaked terrible vengeance on his opponents and all those even remotely connected to the conspiracy. The important point here is to note the American response to what was after all the most serious act of opposition against Hitler during the Third Reich. On the American side, the response was one of skepticism and indifference.[29] This stands in stark contrast to the Russian reaction, which was one of praise for the resisters for trying to get rid of Hitler and his clique. Radio Moscow broadcast a tribute to the German Resistance by the captured German general Walther von Seydlitz, who had been appointed by the Russians as president of the League of German Officers, a group of German defectors. Seydlitz told the German people, "The die is cast. Courageous men rose against Hitler. They have thus given the signal for the salvation of Germany. . . . Generals, officers, soldiers! Cease fire at once and turn your arms against Hitler. Do not fail these courageous men!"[30] As far as the Americans were concerned, the German resistance consisted of a clique of reactionaries and dyed-in-the-wool militarists. Some of this American propaganda, interestingly enough, originated in the German section of the OWI, headed by Gerhart Eisler, a Communist party member who later defected to East Germany. OWI had been actively promoting the proposition that "the German Army and the Nazi Party are one and the same thing." And in its information guide, it instructed officials to look upon splits between army or industrial leaders and the Nazis themselves as "minor conflicts between the old imperialists and the new imperialists."[31]

In official circles in America the subject of the German Resistance was taboo during and immediately following the war. Louis Lochner, the former Associated Press officer in Berlin whom we have encountered before, found this out when he tried to publish a news story while visiting Paris in October 1944 about a large group of anti-Nazi Germans living in the Paris area. He discovered that every week these courageous resisters were sending several of their own people into Germany where they linked up with their contacts, gave and received information, and returned to France to report on their mission. Lochner thought that these activities would make for a good story, but when he sought permission to send the project stateside, SHAEF (Supreme Headquarters Allied Expeditionary Force) censored the piece and refused to transmit the story. The government official in charge of censorship was forthcoming enough to confide to Lochner that there was a personal directive from the president of the United States "in his capacity of commander in chief, forbidding all mention of any German resistance."[32] As Lochner observed in his reminiscences, "stories of the existence of a resistance movement did not fit into the concept of Unconditional Surrender! My belief that President Roosevelt was determined to establish the guilt of the entire German people, and not only of the Nazi regime for bringing on World War II, had already received confirmation in the summer of 1942."[33]

On July 25, five days after the attempt on Hitler's life, the American Seventh Corps (under General J. Lawton Collins) broke through the weak German defenses near Saint-Lô in Operation Cobra and found itself in open country. The whole western front was wavering as the Americans cut off the Germans, who were caught in the Cherbourg peninsula. In early August, General George Patton's tanks were rumbling through open country heading west into Brittany. A weak German counterattack at Mortain, aimed at separating the American lines at Avranches, was mercilessly devastated by Allied aerial bombing. Except for a few fanatic SS units, fighting on without hope of victory, German resistance and morale collapsed all over Normandy. Even Hitler was surprised by the rapid movement of American tanks, one of the few times he expressed a positive opinion about the fighting abilities of the American troops.[34] His propaganda chief also had to admit that the Americans were now exercising the same blitzkrieg tactics that the Germans had used before on the French and the British in 1940.[35] After the breakthrough at Avranches a sizable part of the German army in Normandy was caught in an elongated horse-shoe pocket about forty miles long and fifteen miles wide. The bulk of this force in the Falaise pocket was devastated by artillery and carpet bombing from the air. The carnage was unspeakable: "the roads were choked with wreckage and the swollen bodies of men and horses. Bits of uniform were plastered to shattered tanks and trucks and human remains hung in grotesque shapes on the blackened hedgerows."[36]

The German army had suffered a major defeat comparable to that at Stalingrad. Hitler had sacked Field Marshall von Kluge during the battle, unjustly suspecting him of treason. Kluge committed suicide shortly thereafter and was replaced by Field Marshal Walter Model, who could do little to stop the tide of the Allied advance. A second Allied invasion was mounted in southern France during the pounding of the German forces in the Falaise pocket. Seven French and three American divisions landed almost unopposed on the beaches of the French Riviera on August 15, took Nice and Marseilles, and then pushed up the Rhone Valley. All over southern, southwestern, and central France the Germans were in headlong retreat toward the Reich, harassed by partisans as they fled eastward. The road to Paris lay open, and the honor of taking it was given to Charles de Gaulle's elite armored division under the command of General Philippe Leclerc. Paris fell on August 25. Six days later, Patton's tanks crossed the Meuse, arriving at Metz on the Moselle on September 1. To the west, Montgomery's forces crossed the Seine and swept to the Belgian frontier, liberating Brussels during the first week of September. The British took the port of Antwerp intact but failed to clear the Scheldt estuary, thus preventing supplies from traveling from the North Sea directly to the Port of Antwerp and to the Allied armies. By the end of September the British were advancing into Holland. A daring but poorly planned and executed operation by Montgomery called Market Garden, designed to leapfrog across the Rhine into Germany, failed badly. The Anglo-Americans had gone "a bridge too far," overstretching their supply lines and underestimating the fierce determination of the German *Wehrmacht* in protecting its last frontier line on the Rhine (the Siegfried line).

The noose, however, was tightening around Hitler's shrinking Greater

German Reich. Hitler still did not believe it was the right time to look for a political solution to bring the war to an end. He told his generals that he had proved often enough in his life that he could gain political successes, but now—during heavy military defeats—was not the time to negotiate. Such a political opportunity might arise after Germany had scored military victories. He reminded his generals that he had offered his hand to the British in 1940, only to have it rejected. They wanted their war and they couldn't go back now. He added, however, that "there will come moments in which the tension between the Allies will become so great that the break will happen nevertheless. Coalitions in world history have always been ruined at some point. We must only wait for the moment, no matter how hard it is."[37] In the meantime it was best "to repair the mess somehow," but not by wasting precious time on half-baked schemes, such as going with the British against the Russians or—even more stupidly—playing one side against the other. Hitler thought that all of this was "pretty naïve." The right strategy was to continue fighting until a reasonable opportunity arose and forced one side or the other to negotiate for peace: "Then I will do it. Because everyone can imagine that this war is not comfortable for me. I've been cut off from the outside world for five years now; I haven't visited a theater, listened to a concert, (seen) a film. I live only for the single task of (leading) this battle, because I know that if there is no strong will (behind) it, the war can't be won."[38]

An Ailing Führer and an Ailing President

Hitler's was the voice of an increasingly desperate man whose strategy now was simply to keep on fighting with an iron will until major victories forced at least one of his enemies to sue for peace. In the same address to his generals at the Wolf's Lair on August 31, 1944, Hitler also used the name he would employ to describe the strategy of holding out (durchhalten): he would use Frederick the Great as his role model. As he put it to his generals, "We'll keep fighting this battle at all costs until, like Frederick the Great said, one of our damned enemies gets tired of fighting and until we (get) a peace that will secure life for the German nation for the next 50 (or 100) years and that (doesn't) damage our honor a second time the way it (happened) in 1918."[39] Hitler then made an important statement about his mental and physical condition that would shed light on his future actions.

He admitted that if he had not survived the defeat of 1918, then he would have been relieved from "worries, sleepless nights and a serious nervous disease. It's only (a fraction) of a second then you are freed from all of this (and have) everlasting peace and quiet."[40]

Shortly after this remarkably revealing statement, Hitler became seriously ill. He complained to his personal physician, Dr. Theodor Morell, that he felt a strange pressure on his right eye with accompanying dizziness and throbbing headaches. He also experienced tremors to his legs and hands. Morell noted that Hitler's blood pressure was high, and after administering an electrocardiogram on September 24, Morell discovered that Hitler was suffering from progressive arteriosclerosis. To make matters worse, Hitler experienced stomach cramps that caused him considerable discomfort. His skin turned yellowish, which indicated jaundice.[41] During the last week of October, Hitler was bedridden and in a sour mood. One of his attending physicians, Dr. Giesing, noticed that Hitler was overmedicating himself with little black pills on Morell's prescription. The pills were labeled Dr. Koester's antigas tablets, prescribed against indigestion and flatulence. These black pills contained a combination of strychnine and belladonna, and if a patient took them in excess, as Giesing thought that Hitler did, they could result in strychnine poisoning.[42] When Dr. Giesing had the pills analyzed and passed on the findings to other physicians in Hitler's entourage, Hitler was furious and got rid of Giesing. He retained his favorite, Morell, a quack whose quick fixes, many by injections, gave Hitler the feeling of having received prompt results. During the last three years of his life (1942–45), Dr. Morell gave Hitler a frightening variety of medications, some of them counteracting each other so that their cumulative effects worsened Hitler's physical and mental condition.[43] His eyes would flash alarmingly, his speech would become even more wildly exaggerated than usual, and his moods would alternate between psychic exaltation and extreme testiness.[44]

These and other findings regarding Hitler's medical condition and treatment at the hand of Morell have led some researchers to conclude that by 1944 Hitler was seriously impaired and no longer capable of functioning as a leader. It has even been argued that after Stalingrad, Hitler suffered from chronic amphetamine poisoning, and that such prolonged drug abuse adversely affected his military decisions.[45] There is no evidence for this. Now, it is true that Hitler was a chronic hypochondriac, constantly complaining about a host of indistinct ailments. We have already seen that Hitler was so worried about his health that he adjusted his political plans to accommodate the possibility of being gripped by a serious disease, most likely cancer. His unhealthy way of living during the war did not help. From the summer of 1941 until his death, Hitler spent most of his time at various military headquarters. One of the worst was the Wolf's Lair in East Prussia, located in a heavily wooded, drab, flat, and gloomy location close to the eastern front. Visitors described this outpost of barbed wire, bunkers, and barracks as a "blending of monastery and concentration camp."[46] In this atmosphere of self-enforced isolation, Hitler's physical and mental well-being steadily deteriorated. Those who saw him after some absence were appalled by his physical deterioration. Goering said that in three years of war he aged by fifteen years; and Goebbels, always oversolicitous in his concern for Hitler, recorded his gradual decline in his diary and said, among other things, that "it is a tragic thing that the Führer has become such a recluse and leads so unhealthy a life (that) he doesn't get out into the fresh air. He does not relax. He sits in his bunker, fusses and broods."[47]

Extensive research by medical experts during the last thirty years has shown that Hitler suffered from serious medical conditions, first and foremost coronary heart disease, as revealed by careful comparison of electrocardiograms taken of his heart between 1941 and 1943. Second, Hitler definitely had Parkinson's disease, a diagnosis first made by Professor Max de Crinis, chairman of the Department of Neurology and Psychiatry at the University of Berlin. This initial diagnosis, obtained from newsreels of Hitler's tremors of the left hand and his general motility, has since been confirmed by numerous other researchers.[48] Fritz Redlich has added three other possible illnesses of a potentially serious nature: spina bifida occulta, hypospadia, and giant cell arteritis.[49] The first, a mild form of spina bifida, is a condition in which vertebral arches do not close, but the meninges and spinal cord do not protrude. The condition, however, may cause urethral sphincter dysfunctions resulting in bladder infections and certain congenital defects, in Hitler's case most likely hypospadia and possibly monorchism. This is the contentious "ball and valve" theory that obsessed "psychohistorians" in the 1960s and 1970s—the claim that Hitler had only one testicle and that he had difficulties in urination and bladder retention.[50] Giant cell arteritis is an autoimmune disease that results in chronic inflammation of medium and larger arteries, often associated with headaches and visual symptoms.

All sorts of farfetched theories have been extrapolated from Hitler's medical problems. This is especially true of the psychological judgments that have been derived from his beliefs, attitudes, and behaviors. But Hitler's problem was not one of psychology but of character. His mind can be only partially described by psychology because his essential nature ultimately rested on a spiritual flaw rather than a deformity in his physical makeup. Hitler was a preternatural character whose behavior cannot be reduced to neurological or psychopathological causes. It is my contention that the Hitler or Stalin phenomenon belongs to the realm of what Eric Voegelin calls "pneumopathology," a spiritual condition otherwise known as sickness of the soul.[51] Furthermore, Hitler was only the extreme manifestation of a larger cultural sickness in the Western world. Hitler's physical illnesses or psychological disorders did not interfere with the decisions he made before or during the war; they did not determine his mistakes. Even Fritz Redlich, a level-headed psychiatrist, admits that his illnesses were not life threatening. His errors and his crimes were not caused by illness—with one possible indirect association between illness and error: the fear that he would not live long enough.[52] What emanated from Hitler was hatred, and that force drove him on to the very end—real physical illnesses or psychological distresses notwithstanding.

The man in the White House was suffering from a more life-threatening illness than Hitler was. In 1944 FDR's health deteriorated alarmingly. After his return from Tehran, his strength began to flag; his face thinned and his frame began to shrink. Deep shadows formed under his eyes. By D-Day he was clearly a sick man. Rumors abounded, including that he had been poisoned by the Russians at Tehran, or that he was suffering from a malignant tumor of the digestive tract. We now know that it was not cancer but progressive coronary disease that afflicted Roosevelt.[53] His blood pressure had steadily spiked throughout the 1930s; in 1941 it had risen to 188/105.[54] In the judgment of Dr. Howard A. Bruenn, the cardiologist who was brought in as a consultant on March 28, 1944 (his personal physician, Dr. McIntire, had ignored the danger signals), the president was suffering from "hypertension, hypertensive heart disease, cardiac failure (left ventricular), and . . . acute bronchitis." The president's personal physician, Admiral Ross T. McIntire, lied to the public about FDR's condition, and removed and later probably destroyed the president's records from the safe at Bethesda Naval Hospital. If Dr. McIntire had continued to treat the president, his patient would probably have died in the summer of 1944. It was when Bruenn took over the president's care that FDR learned the extent of his illness. His response was to draw a veil of secrecy around his illness because he did not want the American people to know that his medical situation was so grave.

As with Hitler, the question arises, to what extent did Roosevelt's physical condition affect his performance as a war leader? Given the successful momentum of the war in both Europe and the Pacific, there is no evidence that the president's physical condition altered the course of events on the battlefield. The Allied Military Command structure was not dependent on one man as it was in Germany. Roosevelt never directly interfered in purely military affairs. The situation was different when it came to postwar political planning; here the president's personal direction was crucial, and the question of how his decisions might have been affected by illness cannot be entirely ignored. The grueling trips Roosevelt took to Tehran and later to Yalta sapped his dwindling strength and undoubtedly clouded some of his dealings with Stalin. In September 1944, FDR's decision to sponsor the controversial Morgenthau plan appears, in retrospect, to be a notable example of his failing physical and mental facilities. Since this had a direct bearing on German-American relations during the last phase of the war, it needs to be carefully examined.

The Morgenthau Plan: Reducing Germany
to a Pastoral Country

In August 1944 Henry Morgenthau, FDR's secretary of the treasury, had visited Britain to discuss lend-lease arrangements and British-American financial relations in general. It was on this occasion that Churchill told him that Britain was facing bankruptcy. When he returned and reported to the president, he told him that Churchill had informed him that Britain was broke, a remark that surprised FDR, who quipped, "This is very interesting. I had no idea that England was broke. I will go over there and make a couple of talks and take over the British Empire."[55] Morgenthau also reported that the British were too soft on the question of what should be done with postwar Germany. This triggered a furious anti-German tirade by the president: "We have got to be tough with Germany and I mean the German people, not just the Nazis. You either have to castrate (them) or you have got to treat them . . . so that they can't just go reproducing people who want to continue to way they have in the past."[56] Morgenthau took this outburst as a kind of mandate to produce a punitive plan for the postwar reorganization of Germany.[57] Although FDR encouraged the plan, he never really believed in Morgenthau's proposal to turn 70 million Germans into "shepherds, apple cultivators, and poultry farmers," and at the first major political opposition from both within and outside his administration, he hung Morgenthau out to dry. For well over six months, however, the Morgenthau plan was the subject of some debate in America. It was taken very seriously by the Nazi leadership and helped them convince the Germans that they did not dare surrender.[58]

The Morgenthau plan proposed to de-industrialize, divide, and denazify Germany to prevent it from ever again becoming a military threat to the world. On September 2, Morgenthau showed the president the plan he and his Treasury Department committee on Germany had worked out. FDR liked the plan and told Morgenthau to accompany him to a conference with the British and the Canadians at Quebec during the second week of September. The Morgenthau Memorandum stated that its purpose was "to eliminate the war-making industries in the Ruhr and in the Saar . . . and [convert] Germany into a country primarily agricultural and pastoral in its character."[59] Morgenthau did not much care about the people in the areas he planned to strip of all industrial plants, having told his treasury peers, "the only thing . . . I will have any part of, is the complete shut down of the Ruhr. . . . Just strip it. I don't care what happens to the population. . . . I am for destroying first and we will worry about the population second. . . . Why the hell should I worry about what happens to the people?"[60]

The Morgenthau plan also called for the dismantling of the German Reich and the division of the country into a South German state, a North German state, and several smaller states. Poland and Russia would take East Prussia, while France would receive the Saar and adjacent territories bounded by the Rhine and the Moselle. The Ruhr would have to be stripped of all existing industries, thus driving a stake into the heart of German manufacturing. All schools and universities were to be closed until an effective reeducation plan had been formulated. The country was to be politically decentralized and administered by the military forces of Germany's Continental neighbors. The plan did not provide for reparations, which followed from the obvious recognition that a pastoral country could not make significant financial or material contributions to its former enemies.

When Morgenthau first presented his plan for the postwar reorganization of Germany at Quebec on September 14, Winston Churchill was shocked by its severity and called the proposal "unnatural, unchristian, and unnecessary." He also told his American counterparts that he did not want to be "chained to a dead German," for that would leave Britain alone facing the Russian bear. Churchill muttered that "I am all for disarming Germany, but we ought not to prevent her living decently. There are bonds between the working classes of all countries and the English people will not stand for the policy you are advocating. I agree with Burke. You cannot indict a whole nation."[61] Churchill made these remarks during a state dinner at the Citadel in Quebec, and as conversation heated up, Charles Wilson, Churchill's physician, got a good look at Roosevelt and wondered whether his health was affecting his judgment. With a little prompting by the Americans, who dangled a 6.5 billion dollar aid package to Britain in 1945 if the Morgenthau plan was accepted, Churchill was converted and approved the plan with minor changes on September 16. However, opposition to the plan in the United States quickly gathered once the details became fully known. There was furious opposition to it by the State Department, the War Department, and the press. Some of this opposition was based on interagency rivalry. Why was the Treasury Department spearheading a plan that should more properly have been formulated by the State Department or War Department?

The most determined opponent of the plan was Henry Stimson, the secretary of war, who denounced it on economic, political, military, and humanitarian grounds. Stimson was bothered by Roosevelt's simplistic attitude that "Germany could live happily and peacefully on soup from the soup kitchens."[62] He stated, to the contrary, "My basic objection to the proposed methods of treating Germany which were discussed this morning was that in addition to a system of preventive and educative punishment they would add the dangerous weapon of complete economic oppression. Such methods in my opinion do not prevent war; they tend to breed it."[63] Stimson also felt that the Morgenthau plan made a mockery of the Atlantic Charter, the official Allied moral position of waging war. The charter had proclaimed as one of its postwar objectives "the enjoyment of all States, great or small, victor or vanquished, of access, on equal terms, to the trade and to the raw materials of the world which are needed for their economic prosperity." Though Stimson suspected that FDR had already made up his mind to go with Morgenthau's plan, he decided to send another strongly worded statement to Roosevelt, for if he had not, "I should not keep my self respect." He pitched the argument on a higher level than before:

> The question is not whether we want Germans to suffer for their sins. Many of us would like to see them suffer the tortures they have inflicted on others. The only question is whether over the years a group of seventy million educated, efficient and imaginative people can be kept within bounds of such a low level of subsistence as the Treasury proposals contemplate. I do not believe that is humanly possible. A subordinate question is whether even if you could do this if it is good for the rest of the world either economically or spiritually. Sound thinking teaches us that . . . poverty in one part of the world usually induces poverty in other parts. Enforced poverty is even worse, for it destroys the spirit, not only of the victim but debases the victor. It would be just such a crime as the Germans themselves hoped to perpetrate upon the victims—it would be a crime against civilization itself.[64]

On October 3, Stimson had lunch with the president, who looked "tired and unwell." The Morgenthau plan had by then encountered so much opposition that FDR reversed his support for it but characteristically took no blame himself. Instead, grinning and looking naughty, he told Stimson, "Henry Morgenthau pulled a boner."[65] He really had no intention of turning Germany into an agrarian state; all he wanted was for some of the proceeds from the Ruhr to go to Britain, leaving the rest to the Germans. When Stimson read him the precise provisions of the Morgenthau plan that dealt with converting Germany "into a country primarily agricultural and pastoral in character," Roosevelt "was frankly staggered by this and said he had no idea how he could have initialed this; that he had evidently done it without much thought."[66]

FDR was simply not sure in his own mind how severely Germany should be treated. Giving him the benefit of the doubt, he probably knew that not all Germans were Nazis and should not be tarred with the same brush, but anti-German passions were running high in 1944. Roosevelt was following the conviction of most Americans that the Germans had to know that they were totally defeated; their military leaders had to be forced to acknowledge defeat by signing terms of unconditional surrender. There would be no repeat of the stab-in-the-back mythology as there had been after World War I. FDR wanted to purge militarism from the German bloodstream, even if that meant massive generational retraining. That the Germans could not do this by themselves was obvious to the president; it had to be imposed on the Germans by the occupying forces. There were two problems the president failed to take into account. Would the Russians cooperate fully in the rehabilitation of the Germans, and how could he expect such cooperation from a regime that operated on totalitarian principles? The resolution of such important questions would have required vigorous and far-sighted leadership, which Roosevelt unfortunately was not able to supply in the fall of 1944.

On the German side, Goebbels had a field day with the Morgenthau plan because it played into the fear he had been trying to incite since his discovery of the Kaufman book *Germany Must Perish*. The *Völkische Beobachter* ran an article under the screaming headline "Morgenthau Surpasses Clemenceau: Forty Million Too Many Germans." The byline said that Roosevelt and Churchill had agreed at Quebec to a "Jewish Murder Plan"; it then served up "Details of the Devilish Plan of Destruction" by Morgenthau, the "spokesman of World Judaism."[67] Goebbels tried to convince the German people that the Morgenthau plan was nothing short of a practical guide to the extermination of the German people. The bombing raids, which constituted one of the major experiences of the war for ordinary civilians, were labeled "terror raids" by the regime. Their aim was to annihilate the German people. To bolster confidence in the regime, German propaganda tried to deflect criticism by hailing the awesome power of new miracle weapons and their expected effect on the enemy. Listening to the propaganda broadcasts during the summer of 1944, Germans got the impression that all of southern England was in flames. Germans were told that the new V-2 weapons would decide the war, and when Britain was not brought to its knees as Goebbels had hoped, German propaganda had once more failed to make good on its predictions. Very few Germans were convinced by dire warnings that the Americans would exterminate the German population. Despite the horror pictures Goebbels tried to conjure about the Morgenthau plan, there is no evidence that German propaganda succeeded in convincing either German civilians or military personnel that the Americans were intent upon exterminating the German people.[68] Nazi propaganda, however, continued to harp on the theme that the Russians or Anglo-Americans were planning to annihilate the German people. Such thinking was the logical outcome of the genocidal mentality of the Nazi leadership, for exterminatory tactics were an intimate part of its arsenal. A genocidal group that had been annihilating its own enemies, real or imagined, had every reason to expect to be annihilated. Its paranoid logic was on display in Hitler's proclamation to the German people on January 1, 1945. In this address, his last New Year's order to his soldiers, he tried to motivate his troops to hold out to the utmost because the enemy was determined to annihilate the German people. Once more he reduced the problem to its ultimate common denominator—the Jewish world conspiracy.[69] In Russia, he said, it was Stalin's "personal Jew" (*Hausjude*), Ilya Ehrenburg, who demanded that the German people (*Volk*) should be battered and exterminated; the same goal had been proclaimed in the U.S. postwar plans for Germany by Morgenthau.[70]

The Morgenthau plan could not be implemented because of allied differences over zones of military occupation and transfer of territories. Germany was expected to cede its extensive agricultural areas in the east to Poland, which would have made it difficult, if not impossible, to turn Germany into a pastoral country. Although the Morgenthau plan was not accepted, its anti-German mentality continued to influence postwar planning. Some of the features in the plan pertaining to denazification, political partition, reeducation, punishment of war criminals, fraternization, and so forth were embodied in American occupation documents, notably JCS-1067, the regulatory manual on which the American occupation was based between 1945 and 1947. When FDR wrote the foreword to Morgenthau's book *Germany Is Our Problem* in 1944, he said that the Germans, having sown the wind, were now reaping the whirlwind. True to his word about unconditional surrender, he declared that "we and our Allies are entirely agreed that we shall not bargain with the Nazi conspirators, or leave them a shred of control . . . of the instruments of government."

As a religious man, he had not relinquished hope that in all people—even the Germans—there lives some instinct for truth, some attraction toward justice, and some passion for peace. He did not bring charges against the German race, did not threaten to enslave them, but insisted that they had to "earn their way back into the fellowship of peace-loving and law-abiding nations."[71]

Hitler's Last Gamble

Following the Allied landing in France and stretching through the autumn of 1944, Hitler pursued a twofold path: he planned a counteroffensive against what he thought was the weaker front, held by the Anglo-Americans, and encouraged rumors throughout Europe that Germany was negotiating a separate peace with one of her enemies. Ambassador Ōshima offered himself once more as an intermediary to bring about a Russo-German rapprochement, while Goebbels sent Hitler a lengthy memorandum also trying to persuade him to make peace with Stalin. At the same time, Ribbentrop asked Hitler for permission to send out peace feelers to both sides. Even Himmler was busy behind the scenes trying to make contact with the Anglo-Americans. The *Reichsführer* SS sent a message to Churchill, marked "Special Message from Himmler," that contained suggestions for a possible peace between Germany and the West. We do not know what it said because Churchill, though acknowledging receipt, wrote in a handwritten note he inserted into the daily intelligence file: "Himmler telegram left and destroyed by me."[72] Just how this telegram was transmitted to Churchill is not known; it was probably relayed by the Foreign Ministry to the British by Ramón Serrano Súñer, the Spanish foreign minister. Since Himmler had involved the German Foreign Ministry in this contact with the British, it is possible that Hitler knew about it.

Hitler also read Goebbels's memorandum dated September 20, 1944. Goebbels considered his report so important that he addressed it to Hitler personally and made sure that he received it.[73] Goebbels agreed with Ōshima and the Japanese that peace with the Russians would be the most effective way of bringing the war to an end. The Japanese calculated that in the event of an armistice with Russia, the Germans could redirect their forces from the eastern to the western theater of war, and do so against much weaker enemies—the Americans. Such a plan, of course, meant at least a temporary compromise of German principles of living space, for it would have meant ceding territories to the Russians. Goebbels thought that such a major shift in policy was necessary under the circumstances. The gist of his argument to Hitler was that the time had come to make concessions and lower expectations. By doing so, Germany might be able to split the enemy coalition, which Goebbels believed was already fraying at the edges. Since Germany could not fight East and West simultaneously, it was imperative to come to terms with one side, and that one, Goebbels believed, should be the Soviet Union. As Goebbels put it, "we can neither conclude peace with both sides at the same time nor in the long run successfully wage war against both sides at the same time."[74] It followed that the time had come to change course. Goebbels confessed that his proposal might strike the führer as radical or utopian, but if it came off, he would be hailed as a great practitioner of the political arts of war. Goebbels anxiously waited for Hitler's reply, but none came. Hitler undoubtedly read the memo but chose not to act on it because he still believed that one side or the other would bolt the "unnatural alliance."

In the fall of 1944 there were certainly cracks in that alliance. The Anglo-Americans, especially the British, observed with apprehension Stalin's romp through eastern and southeastern Europe and wondered what this would mean for the future of a democratic postwar Europe. This fear of Soviet expansionism prompted Churchill to seize the diplomatic initiative by flying to Moscow to arrange some agreement with Stalin on future "spheres of interest." Roosevelt regarded Churchill's action as premature and possibly risky. Without American mediation, what would happen if the British and the Russians came to blows over the reorganization of the continent? Admiral Leahy had expressed his concern to Hull on just such a possibility, saying that in case of war between Russia and Britain, the United States would have to defend the British Isles. He thought that, while this task was probably achievable, the United States would not be able to defeat the Russian army on the continent.[75] As is turned out, Churchill's mission to Moscow, which resulted in an agreement on spheres of influence, staved off the possibility of a falling out between Britain and Russia. This episode, however, illustrates that the members of the "unnatural alliance," notably Britain and Russia, were already maneuvering for favorable positions to safeguard their imperial interests. Hitler knew that the stakes they were playing for were momentous, and if he could help it, he planned to put as many obstacles in the way of the Allies as he could manage to dream up. In the fall of 1944, however, Hitler was running out of good cards. Things were coming down to three possible options: wait for Allied disagreements, probably over the spoils of war; continue fighting until one side gave up; or go on the offensive and score a major victory. Always the gambler, Hitler once more staked everything on one final and decisive military victory over one of his adversaries—the notion of striking simultaneously on both fronts being too unrealistic even for Hitler.

His thinking on these matters goes back to early September 1944 but emerges more clearly when we read his remarks to his senior commanders on December 12, 1944, at the Adlerhorst, his Eagle's Nest headquarters on the western front (near Bad Nauheim). The purpose of the speech was to explain why he had chosen, on both strategic and psychological grounds, to attack the overextended and weaker Anglo-Americans, forcing a decisive shift in the fortunes of war. The huge open spaces of Russia, along with the stubborn tenacity of the Russian soldiers, had sucked up one German army after another. He had come to the conclusion that the Russians were better and tougher soldiers than the Anglo-Americans. There was another advantage to an attack in the west: the Germans would be attacking from well-established fortifications along shorter stretches of territory, which required less fuel and materiel. In his impassioned speech, he tried to generate a feeling of optimism and hope, citing a host of reasons why the war could still be won:

> Never in the history of the world has a coalition existed like that of our opponents which has been assembled from such heterogeneous elements with such extremely different and conflicting goals. What we have as opponents are the greatest extremes that can be imagined in this world: ultra-capitalist states on the one side and ultra-Marxist states on the other; on one side a dying empire, Britain, and on the other side a colony seeking an inheritance, the USA. These are states whose aims are diverging even more every day. And the one who recognizes this development, let us say, like a spider sitting in its web, can see how these oppositions develop by the hour. If a few heavy strikes were to succeed here, this artificially maintained united front could collapse at any moment with a huge clap of thunder.[76]

The thunderclap Hitler referred to was a plan (Operation Watch on the Rhine) to spring a massive surprise attack on American and British forces. Sixteen German divisions—eight of them tank units supplied with the latest Tiger models—were to sweep through the Ardennes and the Eifel, attacking the weakest links in the enemy front, and then head for the channel port of Antwerp. Hitler hoped that he could split the American and the British forces and deliver such a devastating blow that they would sue for peace. The consensus of opinion among his generals was that the plan was far too ambitious in light of the fact that the enemy enjoyed complete domination of the air, and that Germany was rapidly depleting its last reserves in both manpower and materiel. Hitler stubbornly ignored these objections. He had told Speer, "A single breakthrough on the western front! You'll see! It will lead to a collapse and panic among the Americans. We'll drive through in the middle and take Antwerp. Then they'll have lost their supply port. And a tremendous pocket will encircle the entire English Army with hundreds of thousands of prisoners. As we used to do in Russia."[77]

The German attack, launched on December 16, took the Americans completely by surprise and temporarily spread panic among the unprepared and undermanned troops. Few Allied commanders expected the Germans to be capable of launching such a major offensive at this stage in the war. One notable exception was General Marshal, who told Stimson that if the German attack succeeded and the Russians chose not to move in the east, the war in the west would have to be shifted from offensive to defensive. American troops would be forced to assume defensive positions on the Rhine. In such a situation it would be left up to the American people whether they wanted to continue the war.[78] Even "Old Blood and Guts" Patton confided to his diary, "We can still lose this war."[79] This is exactly what Hitler wanted to do—make the Americans squirm and force a shift in domestic support of the war. He told a senior commander at the time that it was just a matter of who would hold out longer (*wer es länger aushält*), adding that "he who stands to lose the whole game must hold out longer. We stand to lose the whole game. If the other side says one day: 'we have had enough' nothing is going to happen. If America says: 'enough, finished, we do not give any more of our boys to Europe,' nothing happens. New York remains New York, Chicago remains Chicago, Detroit remains Detroit, and San Francisco remains San Francisco. Nothing is going to change. If we should say today: 'We're sick and tired, we give up' then Germany ceases to exist."[80]

Operation Watch on the Rhine, known to the Allies as the Battle of the Bulge, did not work out the way Hitler imagined it would. Although the German attack took the unprepared American forces by surprise, Hitler's enemies this time were not the same as the French forces had been in 1940. Although the Sixth Panzer Army slashed its way through the Ardennes and approached St. Vith, a major junction from which a mountain road led to the Meuse, the weak American forces were quickly reinforced by the 82nd Airborne Division and slowed down the German advance before it could get close to the Meuse, let alone the approaches to Antwerp, one hundred miles away. One SS unit, the First Panzer Division, apparently wanted to make up for its lack of progress and did so by murdering seventy-two captured American soldiers at Malmédy. It did not take very long for news of this war crime to reach the American public and sharpen opposition to the German conduct of the war. *Time* magazine reported the massacre only four days after it had occurred. Similarly, *Stars and Stripes* ran an editorial under the title "Murder on the West Front," and a *Newsweek* report of the Malmédy murders followed. The American public and the GIs in the field were confronted with the brutality of the Nazi regime and the behavior of SS units, who had indulged in years of barbarization on the eastern front.[81]

In the southern sector of the battle, the Fifth Panzer Army destroyed two American divisions and, protected by dense winter fog that kept Allied planes grounded, approached the road junction of Bastogne but was unable to take the town. The Allied commander, General Anthony McAuliffe, rejected the German demand to surrender, telling the Germans that his answer could be summarized in one word: "Nuts." Although the Germans had opened up a big "bulge" in the Allied front, they were unable to penetrate any farther. Bastogne was quickly reinforced by paratroopers from the 101st Airborne Division. Montgomery rushed forces to the northern sector, and Patton moved several divisions of the Third Army from the south to break the ring around Bastogne. On December 26 the weather cleared and Allied planes pulverized the German forces in the bulge, as well as their choked up supply lines in the rear areas. A secondary thrust by the Germans toward Alsace during the last days of December also petered out. On January 1, 1945, Goering ordered a massive air attack on Allied airfields, which destroyed 180 Allied planes but cost the Germans 277 planes, thereby making it impossible for the Germans to deliver another major air offensive in the war.

In 1939 an American journalist who covered the Polish campaign said that Poland had been crushed like a soft boiled egg by the German forces advancing from the west and the Russian troops attacking from the east.[82] This fate was now being visited on Germany by the Anglo-Americans from the west and the Russians from the east. Which coalition partner would breach the German front line more quickly and take possession of greater chunks of territories? Would the Germans fight with equal tenacity against all the invading armies? One thing was clear after the battle of the Bulge: Hitler's last gamble had failed. After gambling away the military option of inflicting a decisive defeat on the weaker front in the west, his options were now reduced to two possibilities, both unlikely to succeed. He could follow the Friderician strategy of fighting and holding on to every inch of territory, and at the same time send out peace feelers to both sides—the Anglo-Americans and the Russians—and wait for one of them to take the bait. He hoped that such a split in the enemy coalition would occur in 1945.

CHAPTER 9

"This War against America Is a Tragedy"

The Americans Are Coming

During the second week of September 1944, an American task force, commanded by Lieutenant Colonel William B. Lovelady, conquered the first German town, Roetgen, ten miles southeast of Aachen. The soldiers of Combat Command B of the Third Infantry Division did not expect the welcome they got in this small town. All the houses in Roetgen had white sheets hanging from their windows, a sign that the people wanted to surrender. American soldiers were greeted by German civilians who brought them hot coffee and flowers. The Germans told the American GIs that 90 percent of the population was eagerly awaiting the Allied forces. As one local expressed it, "We have waited for your arrival; the war has brought me nothing but a bombed out house in Aachen. We Germans have had enough of this war."[1] The *Times* of London featured the occupation of the first German town under the headline "Germans Welcome the Invaders." Pictures showed relaxed GIs conversing with the townspeople while being served coffee by smiling young women.

Allied leaders thought that there must have been something wrong with this picture. Had they not expressly ordered that there was to be no fraternization between Allied troops and German civilians? Why had German civilians, who had been inundated with propaganda urging them to hate their enemies, surrendered in such a friendly manner? Was Roetgen a fluke? Over the next five months, however, similar scenes were repeated in other German towns, indicating that American stereotypes about Germans being fanatical Nazis were frequently found wanting. The invading American troops discovered that many Germans did not want to follow their führer to destruction; instead, they were eager to save their hides. Obedience to Hitler and the Nazi Party had worn thin after the war came home to roost and defeat appeared inevitable. The Nazi regime was alienating the population with harsh measures designed to prevent the home front from collapsing. Goebbels warned the people that the Americans were brutal gangsters who would murder and pillage at will; they were no better than the Russian *soldadeska*. Many Germans did not believe it, and events would confirm their suspicions that Nazi propaganda was intentionally misleading. A number of SD (German Security Service, a branch of the SS) reports stated that many Germans felt like the man who said, "If the war is lost, then the Americans will come and things will not be any worse than before."[2] In various monthly reports by local authorities to the Bavarian state governor, it was noted that the Americans and the British were expected to be far more lenient as occupiers than the Russians. People who had come in contact with the Anglo-Saxons commented favorably about their "good manners."[3] As early as 1943, one SD report noted, farmers in the western part of the Reich expressed the opinion that the Americans would win the war and that they had no intention of exterminating 80 million Germans.

By late 1944 serious fissures had developed between the Nazi leadership and the population at large over the conduct of the war. News of the activities of the multinational forces converging on Germany from the east and west was spreading like wildfire. By that time people had a good idea of what they could expect from the Russians in the East and the Americans in the West. There was no doubt in their minds that the Americans would be more humane and accommodating than the Russians. Hitler and Goebbels wanted to quash defeatist ideas at all costs. In his New Year proclamation to the German people, Hitler reminded his countrymen that the Americans were on the same page as the Russians; they wanted to tear apart the Reich, transport 15 to 20 million Germans abroad as slave labor, corrupt young Germans, and starve millions.[4] For that reason, the war had to be continued with the utmost fanaticism. The fate of the German Reich was in the balance; it was a matter of "being or not being" (sein oder nicht sein). Capitulation was out of the question. Hitler then launched into a defense of National

Socialism and its innovative accomplishments. The great tasks of the future could only be mastered by nations who followed the example of National Socialism. The bourgeois age, he said, was over, and with it the domination of modern liberalism. Neither liberalism nor Communism was capable of promoting social order and competitive enterprise and preserving a strong degree of high culture. Only National Socialism had shown the ability to fuse these elements and bring together people of different social classes. The survival of National Socialism, Hitler concluded, was therefore the survival of civilization itself. Some of Hitler's high-ranking generals felt the same way. Jodl said, "We will win because we must win, for otherwise world history will have lost its meaning." Model even expressed the conviction that a German victory was "a mathematical certainty," provided that belief in National Socialism remained firm.[5]

In a separate appeal to members of the German *Wehrmacht,* Hitler once more warned of the malevolent intentions of the Jews. Even now, having been responsible for the extermination of 6 million Jews, Hitler still believed that the Jews were strong enough to orchestrate the destruction of the German people. Behind both Roosevelt and Stalin stood the Jews, notably such German-haters as Henry Morgenthau and Ilya Ehrenburg.[6]

From these remarks to his people and his soldiers it is obvious that Hitler was fully informed about Allied intentions. Near the end of the Ardennes offensive, the Germans had come into possession of secret British documents, including maps that showed how the Allied powers proposed to divide Germany into occupation zones. The documents came with a cover letter dated January 1945. A careful study of the papers, however, revealed that Operation Eclipse, as the operation was called, dated back to November 1944. Hitler had known from Allied announcements at Tehran and from other sources that his enemies planned to destroy the Reich and divide it into zones of occupation. The Eclipse documents provided more detailed and chilling information. The documents stated, among other things, that "the only possible answer to the trumpets of total war is total defeat and occupation. . . . It must be made clear that the Germans will not be able to negotiate in our sense of that word."[7] The Reich was to be divided into three zones: a Russian zone, running along the Elbe River; a British zone in the north and northwest; and an American zone in the south. At the Yalta Conference in early February 1945, the Allies ratified the partition of Germany along the lines suggested in the Eclipse papers. It was obvious to Hitler that the Russians would grab eastern and southeastern Europe for the simple reason that the Red Army would be the strongest force in Europe after Germany had been defeated.

Hitler knew what was in store for himself and his country, but he still hoped that the Allied coalition would split. His intelligence sources told him that the Allies were not as solidly united as they wanted the world to believe. Allied bickering over demarcation lines and areas to be conquered, occupied, and administered gave Hitler a ray of hope that the enemy coalition would rupture. He also banked on the German anti-Communist propaganda war, which was being intensified in 1945. The Germans tried to alert Europeans that Western civilization was being imperiled by a virulent type of Asiatic Bolshevism. German propaganda warned that all of eastern and southeastern Europe would fall under the control of the Soviet Union. Goebbels even used the image of an "iron curtain" descending on Europe.[8] Hitler told the German people that this was no time for defeatism but for fanatic resistance. It was a time for harnessing the last reserves (*Auschöpfung aller Kräfte*). Old people were inducted into the People's Army (*Volkssturm*), provisions were made to organize guerilla forces (the *Wehrwolf* troops), young boys were encouraged to go into battle (the last newsreel of Hitler shows him reviewing and decorating young Hitler Youth "soldiers"), mobile execution squads (*fliegende Standgerichte*) were set up to execute traitors or slackers, and so forth. Then came numerous and ineffective "hold out" orders; and when they proved inadequate, the regime resorted to a "scorched earth" approach to stop or exhaust the enemy. This so-called "Nero order" was designed to destroy everything that might be of use to the enemy. Hitler told Speer that the enemy was to find nothing but a desolate wasteland—no buildings, hospitals, utilities, train stations, churches, monuments, factories, and so forth.[9]

Historians have rightly focused on this lust for destruction on Hitler's part, but that has also created the misleading impression that this is all that preoccupied him during the last four months of his life. The reality is that even then Hitler still believed that there was a ray of hope, a possible way of avoiding the consequences of his disastrous decisions.

Last Peace Feelers

During the second week of January, Hitler gave Ribbentrop permission to send out peace feelers to the western side, with the proviso that Ribbentrop should take full responsibility for the effort.[10] Ribbentrop's plan was to play the Anglo-Americans against the Russians and hopefully cause a rupture in the Allied coalition.[11] In cooperation with Fritz Hesse, his assistant and former representative of the German News Bureau (DNB) in London, Ribbentrop formulated a *Sprachregelung* (specific talking points) report that he intended to send out to reliable officials, who would then relay them to neutral intermediaries. He also dispatched another trusted foreign ministry official, Werner von Schmieden, to Switzerland to convey the talking points to Dulles and the Americans. On January 17, he sent Hesse to Stockholm, which was one of the few remaining windows to the West.

It was widely believed in the postwar period that all copies of Ribbentrop's *Sprachregelung* had been lost. In 1953, Fritz Hesse claimed in his book *Das Spiel um Deutschland* (*The Game over Germany*) that he had assisted Ribbentrop in drafting the document, which he said had subsequently been lost.[12] In the book Hesse reconstructed the document from memory. Hesse's claim that all copies of the *Sprachregelung* had been lost turned out to be mistaken, for in 1967 a copy turned up as an enclosure to a letter Ribbentrop had sent to Grand Admiral Dönitz.[13] This text was at variance with some of the points Hesse had made in his book. Hesse's assertion that the German government was willing to accept unconditional surrender to the Western powers, reserving the right to exercise a different approach to the Russians, was not part of the original document; neither was Germany's alleged willingness to dismantle the National Socialist government, to close all concentration camps, to end persecution of Jews and of religious believers, and to hand over war criminals to the Allies to be tried in neutral countries. None of these points were mentioned in the original document, so Hesse's version may have been the result of either his poor memory or his attempt to distort the record for personal or political reasons. Ribbentrop probably never intended to disseminate the document, except among close initiates for the purpose of providing guidelines for discussion with Western representatives. He never expected that it would fall into Allied hands. In 1978 an English translation turned up in Washington and is now deposited in the National Archives. The *Sprachregelung* was found with other material from decoded German and Japanese top secret intelligence messages.[14]

According to the *Sprachregelung* instructions, German officials were to make contact with British and American representatives and alert them to the grave danger of the Red Army, which was gobbling up vast territories and would not stop until all of Europe was under its control. Germany could serve as a wall against Soviet Communism; but its backdoor in the West had to be secured so that forces could be redirected to the eastern front. The Jewish question, according to the original document, was to be considered an internal matter, to be resolved by the Germans. The document explicitly rejected the Allied demand for unconditional surrender; and it says nothing about any willingness to terminate National Socialism or hand over war criminals to the Allies for trial. This was pure invention on Hesse's part. A careful reading of the original document reveals that it was a transparent effort to drive a wedge between the Allies. It offered no concessions at all, contrary to Hesse's claims in his recollections, and its urgent warnings against the spreading tide of Communism came too soon—that is, before the Western powers clearly perceived the threat of Russian expansionism. In early 1945, German warnings about the danger of Communism were largely discounted by the Allies as self-serving and propagandistic.

Hesse's omissions and retroactive alterations of the record, however, do not make his book uninteresting or even useless. The book manages to re-create the desperate atmosphere of the last few months of the Nazi regime quite well. Of particular interest is an episode Hesse mentioned—and which rings true—that sheds light on the Holocaust. In September 1944, Hesse claimed, he received several English illustrated newspapers by way of Portugal (*London Illustrated News, Sphere*) that provided documentation with pictures of what had happened at a recently liberated annihilation camp in Poland (Majdanek).[15] The stories revealed that Jews had been exterminated there in gas chambers. Hesse claimed that he showed the documents to Ribbentrop, who appeared to be deeply shaken and promised Hesse that he would bring this to Hitler's attention. Two weeks later, Hesse was summoned to Ribbentrop's office where he encountered an angry foreign minister, who threw the English newspapers at his feet and screamed that it was an outrage to have been given such material. Ribbentrop allegedly said that the führer had given him his personal word of honor that accusations of such massacres were the most shameless swindle (*unverschämste Schwindel*).[16] Hitler said that there was no truth to these newspaper stories. Ribbentrop said he wanted to hear no more about it.

Hesse subsequently had an opportunity to talk to Hewel at führer head-quarters and was told confidentially that Ribbentrop had indeed shown Hitler the material about Jewish exterminations but had failed to tell Hesse that Hitler had not been at all surprised by the reports, nor had Hitler given Ribbentrop his word of honor that the evidence was false. Hitler had been angered not by the evidence but by the sloppy job that had been done in covering it up, and he ordered that the responsible security officials (SD) be punished appropriately. If Hesse's remarks are correct, they furnish another example of Hitler's personal involvement in the destruction of the Jews.

In January 1945 the Americans did not want to hear about the possibility of Soviet Communism spreading throughout Europe. Ribbentrop seems to have thought that the Americans might accept a German offer by which both sides would form a common front against Bolshevism. This fantasy had also taken hold among certain conservative members of the German army who could not believe that the Americans or the British wanted to hand over the continent to the Communists. A total defeat of Germany, they believed, would open up all of Central Europe to Bolshevik rule, and from there it would quickly spread to the rest of Europe. Hitler did not oppose Ribbentrop's efforts to send out feelers along these lines, but he told him that "nothing will come out of it."[17] He was not surprised when the Western powers turned down Ribbentrop's proposal. Nevertheless Hitler did not discourage further attempts, some of which had already been under way for some time. One of these was by SS general Karl Wolff, Himmler's adjutant, who had made contact with the Americans in Switzerland. Wolff had started talks with the Americans about ending the war, telling Allen Dulles in a secret meeting in Zürich that, if he was patient, "I will hand you Italy on a silver platter."[18] Hitler had not originally sent Wolff to Italy to engage in such machinations; on the contrary, he had sent him there to provide the necessary security operations so that the *Wehrmacht* could hold the line in Italy. But the good-looking and suave SS general was a master of deceit and double-dealing, always following his opportunistic self-interest and already looking ahead, beyond the German defeat. A recent study of Wolff by Jochen von Lang portrays the SS general as a consummate chameleon and sometimes a brazen liar, who practiced his double-dealing with such ingratiating bravura that it is not surprising that even Hitler was taken in by him. For a long time Wolff had been Himmler's majordomo, and the two men were on good terms until the last few years of the war. Wolff had visited Italy in the company of Himmler many times and he knew the country quite well. Hitler sent him there in 1943 to prevent a collapse of the Italian front after Mussolini's fall from power. Before dispatching him to Italy, Hitler told Wolff to write a report on how he proposed to carry out his mission. When Wolff reported to führer headquarters, Hitler told him that there was one additional and crucial task he had to carry out in Italy: "You are responsible for the Duce. A specially selected unit of the SS must never let him out of their sight."[19] He then also gave him a secret order to occupy the Vatican and clear it out completely. The pope could go to Lichtenstein and the other clerics could be accommodated in various monasteries or castles. This assault on the church never took place, partly because Wolff endlessly dawdled in carrying it out and partly because Hitler dropped this radical project for political reasons.

While in Italy, Wolff came to the conclusion that the Vatican could serve as a bridge to the West. He knew that the war was lost; the time had come to wring the best terms out of the impending defeat. He believed that better terms could be obtained from the Anglo-Americans than from the Russians. On this point, Wolff was on the same page as the German ambassador to the Vatican, von Weizsäcker, who became Wolff's contact man with the pope.[20] Pius XII regarded the Anglo-American formula of unconditional surrender as unacceptable because it encouraged fanatical resistance. His main concern was with the spread of Communism, and he saw America as the best bulwark of anti-Communist resistance.

In May 1944 Wolff had a private audience with the Vicar of Christ, an amazing encounter between two men of such opposing convictions. What the Pontifex Maximus of the church and the chief SS commander in Italy talked about is unknown because the Vatican files on the matter are still closed. We may be sure, however, that the two men discussed the possibility of a negotiated peace with the West. Pope Pius XII was not Hitler's pope, as the title of one recent sensationalistic book has claimed. For the pope, the survival of the church was at stake, and had it not been for his diplomatic skills, the Vatican might have been occupied by the Nazis and the pope abducted to Germany. When the two men parted, the pope was overheard to say, "You are doing something difficult, General Wolff,"[21] which invites the conclusion that Wolff had taken it upon himself to pave the way for a negotiated peace with the Christian West, a necessary step if the spread of Communism was to be resisted. The pope's parting remarks could also have meant, as Jochen von Lang speculates, that Wolff was prepared to defy his commander in chief (Hitler) in fulfilling his self-appointed mission. The words "You are doing something difficult" were supposedly said to Martin Luther in 1521 at the Diet of Worms as he began his difficult mission, though that mission led to the split of the Christian Church. Wolff was not made of the same mettle as Martin Luther, as he lacked the courage of spiritual convictions. Nevertheless, Wolff did have a mission in 1945, and that was to disengage the German forces in Italy from the war. The question is why he did so. Was it to save lives, or was it to disengage the divisions in Italy and transfer them to the eastern front to stop the Russians? If it was the former, it would have run counter to Hitler's wishes in 1945. Whatever the reason, Wolff seems to have acted on his own initiative, bypassing both Hitler and Himmler; and when called to account, he cleverly talked his way out of trouble, perhaps even out of accusations of having committed treason.

In early February Wolff flew to Berlin to consult with Hitler, to determine how far he could go in making contact with the Western powers. He tried to persuade the führer, with Ribbentrop present, that concurrent with waging a military conflict there should be diplomatic efforts to extricate Germany from the war.[22] Hitler seemed amenable and did not oppose either Wolff or Ribbentrop on the issue of negotiating with the Allies, because he saw in it a good instrument to sow dissension in the Allied coalition.[23] Both men took Hitler's attitude to mean that they should continue to explore diplomatic approaches. Wolff pressed ahead more successfully than Ribbentrop did, for he had prepared the stage for what would be called by Allen Dulles "Operation Sunrise," a secret plan to negotiate the surrender of the German forces in Italy.[24] Operation Sunrise was initiated by Wolff through Allen Dulles, who brought in the American military command in Italy. The Soviets, who got wind of the operation, had been left out of the loop and now responded with angry accusations of Allied complicity with the German military. Stalin was furious when the Americans refused to involve Soviet representatives in the discussions that were going on between Wolff and the German military and the Americans. On March 29, Stalin wrote to Roosevelt that he suspected that the Germans were using these negotiations for shifting their troops to other sections of the front, primarily to the Soviet front. Stalin complained, "I cannot understand why representatives of the Soviet Command were refused participation in these negotiations. . . . For your information I have to tell you that the Germans have already made use of the negotiations with the Allied command and during this period have succeeded in shifting three divisions from Northern Italy to the Soviet front. . . . This circumstance is irritating the Soviet Command and creates ground for mistrust."[25]

FDR was taken aback by Stalin's anger. It was not until late March that Roosevelt had been informed about these secret negotiations, but when he was apprised of them he immediately wrote to Stalin on March 31 to explain his previous insistence that the American government had to give every assistance to "all officers in the field in command of American Forces who believe there is a possibility of forcing the surrender of enemy troops in the area."[26] In several messages to Stalin in early April, Roosevelt repeated his assurance that there would be no negotiations with the Germans until they had surrendered unconditionally. Roosevelt's position, as Stalin saw it, had deviated from the unconditional surrender formula at Casablanca. He did not seem to grasp the fact that FDR had considerably tweaked that policy to mean that circumstances in the various theaters of war might dictate greater flexibility. Just forty days earlier, at Yalta, Roosevelt had again gone out of his way to accommodate Stalin, snubbing Churchill as badly as he had at Tehran, if not worse. This was the occasion on which he proposed a toast that began, "You see, Winston, there is something here that you are not capable of understanding. You have in your veins the blood of tens of generations of people accustomed to conquering. We are here at Yalta to build up a new world which will know neither injustice nor violence, a world of justice and equality."[27] Stalin pretended to be moved to tears. Roosevelt was never able to suffer the thought of Stalin's suspicions and tried to reassure him of America's good intentions in Italy.

Hitler, conversely, hoped that the unholy trinity would fall apart, and it is noteworthy that he did not stop Wolff's efforts in Italy. He did draw the line when Ribbentrop suggested a harebrained scheme of taking his family to Moscow as hostages while negotiating with Stalin. Hitler turned this down flat with a telling remark: "Ribbentrop, don't do things like Hess."[28] What he did not mind was having Ribbentrop send out peace feelers in the form of diplomatic blackmail. Both the Anglo-Americans and the Russians were to be approached on a one-on-one basis and told, "if you don't make peace with us, we will deal with the other side." Frank Manuel, the renowned Harvard historian, who was then a young American intelligence officer in Europe, summed it up perfectly: "To the very end the Germans had hoped for salvation—a break between Russia and the other Allies. A political victory to right the balance of the military defeat. As the prospects grew dimmer they put out tentacles in both directions. . . . The old German whore was offering herself to the highest bidder again, to any bidder. 'I, Germania, am in the heart of Europe. If you will have me, Russia, I join with you against them. If they will have me, I join with them against you.' It was inconceivable that nobody should want Germania."[29] Except for this last remark, which would have to be modified just five years later during the Cold War, Frank Manuel's observation was remarkably incisive. Hitler's strategy during the last four months of his life seesawed back and forth, trying to incite fear in one side or the other. The Russians had to be alarmed by the possibility that Germany might conclude a separate peace with the Americans, allowing them to transfer their western armies to the east. The Anglo-Americans had to be frightened by the Red bogey man. Hitler tried to convince himself that the British did not want a Communist-controlled government in Germany. It would not be long, he said, before Stalin proclaimed a national German government in Russian exile, just as he had promoted the claims of his Communist-controlled government in Lublin, Poland. In a military conference, held on January 27, 1945, Hitler revealed an interesting tidbit, telling the assembled commanders, including Goering, Jodl, Keitel, and Guderian among others, that he had secretly passed word to the British that the Russians were about to unleash 200,000 German prisoners under the direction of their German Communist leaders and force them to march against Germany. He was referring to the German officers in Russia who had turned against National Socialism and committed themselves to the liberation of Germany. Hitler thought that information of this sort would "have an effect on them (the British) as if we were to stab them right there with a shoemaker's awl."[30] Goering wholeheartedly agreed, saying that the British had entered the war so that"we wouldn't reach the East, but not so that the East would reach the Atlantic," to which Hitler responded, "That's quite clear. Something like that is abnormal. British newspapers are already writing very bitterly. What is the purpose of the war?"[31]

Hitler's Political Testament

On January 30 Hitler delivered his last broadcast to the German people. Listening to the address today (a recording has survived), one is struck by the raspy and desperate sound of his voice, giving the eerie impression of a voice from beyond the grave. There was no admission of wrongdoing for his part in dragging Germany into the war; instead, he now challenged the German people to rise up against the barbarian hordes flooding into the fatherland. He came not to apologize but to make new demands, calling on the German people to fulfill their duties to the utmost and sacrifice life and limb in this battle for Germany's survival. This battle, he said, "will not be won by Asia but by Europe, headed once again by the nation that has represented the primacy of Europe against the East for five hundred years and for the future—our Greater German Reich, the German Nation!"[32]

Hitler's hopes and visions were all still on display, but now they sounded hollow and unconvincing. He knew that the end was in sight. The Russians had drawn within sixty miles of Berlin, and Eisenhower's forces were closing in on Germany's last defensive line—the Rhine. As the Russians advanced, a Red terror descended on the German population, from Königsberg in the north to Breslau in the south. The roads were jammed with German civilians who had left their homes behind and joined the massive exodus from the east to the west. Those unfortunate enough to be left behind, mostly old men, women, and children, were taken by the Russians and tortured, shot, raped, or crushed by tanks. Even Goebbels, who could not be accused of being squeamish, ordered that these horrifying atrocities should not be reported in detail.[33]

Hitler was fully briefed about these disasters, but he kept them at bay and refused to become emotionally involved. Inasmuch as he showed his emotions, they tended to alternate between self-pity and recrimination. Cooped up for the last four months of the war in the dank bunker beneath the chancellery, he brooded and fussed about what might have been. He blamed everybody but himself. "I'm lied to on all sides," he told his secretary on March 16. "I can rely on no one, they all bother me, and the whole business makes me sick. If I had not got my faithful Morell I should be absolutely knocked out. . . . If anything happens to me, Germany will be left without a leader. I have no successor. The first, Hess, is mad; the second, Goering, has lost the sympathy of the people; and the third, Himmler, would be rejected by the party."[34] As to his own role in the impending catastrophe, he said that he only meant the best for his country. He had been pushed into the war by the Western powers, especially by the Jews who had incited them. The two-front war was not his fault either; it was forced on him when he became aware of Stalin's intention to attack Germany. The British, in their stubborn and willful opposition to Germany's geopolitical goals on the continent, were also to blame. By conquering Russia and gaining control over its industrial and agricultural resources, he wanted to show the British that any further resistance was futile. The declaration of war on the United States was a simple formality because Roosevelt had been waging an undeclared war on Germany all along.

Hitler's thoughts on America during the last few months of the war are particularly revealing. The fragments we have, unfortunately, are not entirely reliable. In February Hitler seems to have decided to set the stage for his departure from this life by having his last thoughts on the war recorded for posterity. He left three testaments, and two of them have come down to us in their original version—a general testament containing his judgments about the war and a personal testament spelling out how his personal possessions should be disbursed. It is the third testament that has been the subject of some dispute concerning its authenticity. This is the one that contains his monologues relating to the final stages of the war—the voice of Hitler speaking to history. It allegedly was recorded in February 1944 when Hitler or Bormann decided to transcribe the führer's remarks on the world situation for future generations.[35] This curious exercise, which certainly expressed Hitler's obsession with his legacy, took place in the führer bunker, hence the name *Bunkergespräche*. The conversation served two purposes: his words would be a continuation of the earlier monologues, during the halcyon days of heady victories in 1941–42, but they would also show the führer during the trying times of defeat, portraying him in an even more heroic mold. Hitler and Bormann probably saw these final conversations as a way of preserving the führer cult for future generations.

Starting in early February and concluding in early April (February 4 to April 2), Hitler dictated his thoughts to Bormann, who had them typed out and signed each page for purposes of authentication. When the project was concluded, Bormann gave the manuscript to a trusted official of the Reich government, who deposited the paper in the vault of an Austrian bank in Bad Gastein. The official, Walter Funk, was subsequently arrested, and facing charges of being a war criminal, he urged a friend to retrieve the documents and burn them, thinking that they could incriminate him. The friend, a prominent lawyer, read the documents out of curiosity to see what they contained. As he did so, it became clear to him that they had considerable historical value, so he decided to make a copy and then burn the original. He thought that by doing so he kept his promise to his friend but also fulfilled certain obligations to preserve the historical record. The manuscript then found its way into the hands of a French Swiss attorney, François Genoud, who subsequently had the Hitler-Bormann documents published in Paris under the title *Le Testament Politique de Hitler.* Two years later, an English translation appeared in London, with an introduction by the Oxford historian Hugh Trevor-Roper, who vouched for the authenticity of the documents.

Entry number fourteen of the Hitler-Bormann document, dated February 24, 1945, begins with Hitler saying, "This war against America is a tragedy. It is illogical and devoid of any foundation of reality."[36] This is an important statement about an enemy whom Hitler had not expected to fight in 1939. Assuming that Hitler used these exact words, what did he mean by illogical and unreal? His following comments about America indicate that he did not believe the United States had any sound reason to involve itself in a purely Continental conflict that was outside its own sphere of interest. We recall that Hitler had spoken approvingly of the Monroe Doctrine on several occasions before and during the war. Why, then, would the United States undermine its long-standing national traditions, violate its neutrality laws, and deliberately provoke a war with Germany? Hitler felt that Roosevelt and the Jews who controlled him had been the major culprits inciting hatred against Germany. If it had not been for President Roosevelt and his Jewish supporters, Germany and the United States would have supported each other "without undue strain on either of them."[37] After all, Germany had made a massive contribution to the United States by providing her with the best Nordic blood. This was exactly the argument that Colin Ross, his America expert, had made in his book *Our America (Unser Amerika)*, a book Hitler appears to have read, because his arguments and choice of words are exactly like the ones used by Ross. Ross and Hitler believed that Germany had an important stake in America because of the outstanding contributions of the millions of Germans who had come to America in the last half of the nineteenth century. In his testament, Hitler even claimed that General Steuben, who helped Washington organize his Continental army, was the decisive agent behind the success of the War for Independence.

Hitler next shifted the discussion to economic issues, observing that he and Roosevelt had come to power at the same time, but that Roosevelt and his Jewish advisers "achieved only a very mediocre success"[38] in dealing with the economic crisis of the 1930s. With its immense territorial size and resources, the United States could survive and prosper even if existing in economic isolation; Hitler wished that the German people could one day see "that same dream come true." He reverted to his obsession about living space, saying that a great people like the Germans had need of "broad acres."

Hitler insisted that Germany had never expected anything from the United States except its neutrality, a situation ideally suited for peaceful coexistence. This possibility was deliberately undermined by the Jews, who had set up residence in America and were inciting the American people against Germany. In twenty-five years, Hitler predicted, the American people would wake up to the Jewish danger because it was sucking out their lifeblood. If Germany lost the war, it would be a victory for the Jews, but he said it would also eventually be a victory for them in America as well. Hitler was not sure whether the American people would wake up in time and recognize the terrible danger represented by the Jews. He thought that this would depend on their political maturity. Up to now, everything had been ridiculously easy for the Americans, a fluke of history and geography. Hitler was convinced that, unlike the Germans, the Americans, divided as they were by so many different nationalities, had not yet been "fused by the bonds of a national spirit," adding portentously, "What an easy prey for the Jews!"[39]

Hitler's rant against the Jews in America culminated in the predictable claim that ordinary Americans had been dragged into this war by FDR and the Jews: "Had they possessed even a minimum of political instinct they would have remained in their splendid isolation. . . . By intervening they have once again played into the hands of the Jews."[40] He obviously believed that if a man other than Roosevelt had been president, he might have kept the United States out of the war and employed more effective economic remedies to cure the country of the Depression. Instead, FDR turned out to be just another economic liberal, a believer in an outworn ideology of a bygone era.

Hitler asserted that American affairs were none of Germany's business, except for the "fact that their attitude has direct repercussions on our destiny and on that of Europe." There followed another jarring snap judgment that "the Germans never really felt the imperialist urge," a statement that Hitler tried to rationalize by saying that the Germans had never been colonial imperialists like the British. Presumably he regarded the German need for *Lebensraum* as a racial-biological need rather than an economic one. Hitler was a believer in social Darwinism, but he saw imperialism not just as an expression of a predatory herd instinct, but also as a spiritual force by which one people (*Volk*) fulfilled its historical destiny.

Hitler's final words add little to what he had said before about Germany and the United States. He wanted the affairs of Europe handled by the Europeans. America should stop meddling in the affairs of other continents and stick to its Monroe Doctrine, forbidding Europeans from interfering in the affairs of the New World. U.S. interference in Europe on the side of Russia was tragic; it should never have happened.

When Speer received a copy of Hitler's political testament while still serving his twenty-year sentence in Spandau Prison, he was shocked by Hitler's lofty philosophical speculations because they struck him as completely surreal.[41] Speer wondered what kind of leader could deliver such thoughts while he was sending young boys into battle against Soviet tanks. Speer vividly recalled that during the last months of the war Hitler was still preaching to everyone about the necessity of fighting to the last bullet; yet here he was trying to explain why the war was lost. Speer wondered whether Hitler believed anything he said. As he was reading Hitler's version of events, he also wondered whether Goebbels had not had a hand in shaping the document. The style had the polish and shrewd touch of the propaganda minister, and it is entirely possible that Goebbels had been brought in for this penultimate work of self-justification by Hitler. Speer added, however, that most of the documents were vintage Hitler— the thoughts, grandiose visions, argumentative style, and so forth. Speer claimed that Hitler had a split personality. On the one hand, he could be brutal, unjust, unapproachable, cold, unrestrained, self-pitying and vulgar, but on the other hand, he could be a caring host and an understanding superior, and he was charming, self-controlled, proud, and passionate about everything beautiful and in the grand manner. In Speer's judgment, based on years of personal knowledge and endless—even tortuous—reflection, Hitler was impenetrable and double-faced (*undurchsichtlich und unaufrichtig*). Speer was uncertain whether he had ever caught Hitler in the act of "just being himself."[42]

In Hitler's view of America, a theme I have stressed throughout the book, Speer found the same kind of duality. We have seen examples of it in his monologues at führer headquarters, in his comments to subordinates, and now in his penultimate testament. Hitler not only had been intrigued by America, but also had commended its industrial and organizational methods to all and sundry. He admired American techniques of advertising and had them embodied in Nazi appeals to the German people. At the same time, he envied the power of America and hoped one day to equal it through conquests of living space in the East. He would build a harder, less "decadent" Reich than the one based on outmoded middle-class liberalism. The war accentuated his envy and resentment of America to the point of hatred. The butt of this hatred was Franklin D. Roosevelt, the Jew-lover in the White House. Hermann Giesler, one of Hitler's favorite architects (the other being Speer), records in his memoirs that Hitler felt himself far superior to Roosevelt and Churchill, viewing them as ephemeral representatives of a bygone era—the nineteenth century.[43]

Stalin, on the other hand, he viewed as a revolutionary figure with distinct modern features. During the course of the war, Hitler's admiration for Stalin grew steadily, whereas his contempt for Roosevelt became more pronounced. He blamed the saturation bombings of German cities on Roosevelt's lust for destruction, which, in turn, had been incited by American Jewry. When he heard about the destruction of Dresden, one of the most beautiful architectural cities in Germany, Hitler was devastated and swore retaliation in kind. He had a fantasy of bombing New York and seeing the skyscrapers light up like torches and fall into one another. It gave him an almost erotic pleasure to visualize the conflagration of this city built on Jewish greed. To Hitler, skyscrapers were architectural manifestations of Jewish capitalism. This was the other side of his "Amerika" picture. A nation hollowed out by the Jews, soulless and decadent, would be unable to bear great suffering for very long. Despite the courageous performance by American soldiers, Hitler refused to let go of his prejudice that U.S. soldiers were inferior. About the time of his last monologue, he tried to convince himself that U.S. casualties for the month of January had been 85,000, which was 50 percent of what they had lost in World War I.[44] Hitler was misinformed about the 85,000 figure; it referred to U.S. Air Force units that had been transferred to the infantry. But Hitler's reference to U.S. casualties was not too far off the mark. If this continued, he thought, surely the Americans would bolt the alliance. When Goebbels told him that the Americans were saying that the Allied coalition would collapse, he wholeheartedly agreed, replying, "It could happen that the isolationists say: 'Why should the Americans die for non-American purposes?' In all those countries there's no democracy at all—for example, Romania, Bulgaria, Finland. The Americans could withdraw here and throw themselves against East Asia alone, thereby binding the Russian here at the same time—because they would free us—so that the Russian can't engage himself so much in East Asia."[45]

Roosevelt and Hitler Die and the War in Europe Ends

On March 29, 1945, a tired FDR decided to leave Washington for a period of rest in Warm Springs, Georgia, his "Little White House" near the thermal springs that had attracted him to Georgia in the 1920s. Before leaving, he had an appointment with General Lucius Clay, who had just been appointed to head the military government planned for postwar Germany. The president did all the talking, reminiscing about his experiences as a boy in Germany. He proposed a huge power development in Central Europe similar to the Tennessee Valley Authority. After the meeting was over, James Byrnes, director of war mobilization, asked Clay why he had not said very much. Clay's response was, "No, I didn't. The President didn't ask me any questions, but I am glad that he didn't. Because I was so shocked watching him that I don't think I could have made a sensible reply. We've been talking to a dying man."[46] Though his body and his mind were failing him, FDR was still alert to what was going on. In his last newspaper interview, given to Anne O'Hare McCormick of the *New York Times* on March 29, he openly expressed a concern that had apparently bothered him for the past months: that the Russians could no longer be trusted to stick to the Yalta agreement. He told McCormick that Stalin was dishonest or no longer in control of the government, a belated recognition of Stalin's double-dealing.[47] When the president arrived in Warm Springs he was tired and worn out. Still, he looked forward to attending the opening session of the United Nations in San Francisco, where the Charter of the United Nations was scheduled to be drawn up on April 25. He never got to go to San Francisco or witness the end of the war. On April 12 the president died of a massive cerebral hemorrhage, surrounded by a small staff that included his former mistress, Lucy Rutherford, and her friend Elizabeth Shoumatoff, a society portraitist who had come to paint what would become the last portrait of FDR.[48]

In Berlin the reports of Roosevelt's death were the best news Hitler had received in a long time. Goebbels telephoned Hitler and excitedly told him, "My Führer, I congratulate you! Roosevelt is dead. It is written in the stars that the second half of April will be the turning point for us. This is Friday 13 April. It is the turning point!"[49] Hitler was more cautious, but when Speer came to call that day, Hitler waved a newspaper clipping at him and urged him to read it: "Here, read it! Here! You never wanted to believe. Here it is! Here we have the miracle I always predicted. Who was right? The war isn't lost. Read it! Roosevelt is dead."[50] Only a few days before, Goebbels had read to Hitler certain passages in Thomas Carlyle's biography of Frederick the Great in which the Prussian king, on the verge of defeat in 1762 during the Seven Years' War, was ready to commit suicide, only to be miraculously saved when the Russian empress Elizabeth, who hated Frederick, suddenly died and was succeeded by the pro-Prussian tsar Peter III. The alliance against Prussia fell apart, and the House of Brandenburg was saved. When Goebbels read these passages, Hitler was supposedly so moved that tears filled his eyes. Now FDR was dead; the prophecy seemed fulfilled.

It says something about Hitler's or Goebbels's state of mind, as well as their historical blind spots, that they would think that the events of the eighteenth century were comparable to those of the twentieth. Given the desperate situation in which they found themselves, however, it is not surprising that they reached for every straw they could find. They hoped that history would repeat itself, but reality proved otherwise. Truman, FDR's successor, had no intention of bolting the alliance. Goebbels sadly admitted shortly afterward, "Perhaps fate has again been cruel and made fools of us."[51] Yet Hitler clung to his holdout (durchhalten) strategy almost to the end.

Just one day after FDR's death, Vienna fell to the Russians, and the American forces in the Ruhr, who had trapped Model's entire army group, mopped up the last opposition, taking 325,000 prisoners and pushing on in their drive to the Elbe. Montgomery's forces crossed the Rhine and swept northward to capture German ports and naval bases. At this point nothing stood between Eisenhower's forces and Berlin. Why did the Americans hesitate to take the capital of the Third Reich? Churchill had persistently proposed a direct assault across the Rhine through northern Germany to capture Berlin. Both Roosevelt and Eisenhower, conversely, wanted to direct the American forces to the south and link with the Soviets on the Danube. They mistakenly believed that Hitler wanted to make his last stand in his Alpine fortress, or redoubt, in the mountains of Berchtesgaden. The myth of the existence of a vast underground fortress in the bowels of the Alps had been spread by Himmler's SS. There was no vast series of underground tunnels harboring armaments factories or ample provisions to allow the Nazis to resist the Allies for many years. The myth played a small role in Eisenhower's decision to let the Russians take Berlin. Eisenhower's major reasons for this decision, however, were dictated by military considerations and Allied occupation agreements. In the first place, Eisenhower told Marshall that from a purely military position Berlin was no longer a particularly important objective.[52] In the second place, Eisenhower calculated that the Battle of Berlin would exact an inordinate price that Americans should not have to pay. General Bradley advised Eisenhower that, conservatively, at least 100,000 casualties could be expected; the actual figure was probably well over 300,000 Russian casualties. Finally, Berlin was in the occupation zone that had been assigned to the Russians at Yalta. The Americans decided (shortsightedly, as it would turn out during the Cold War) that Berlin was not worth fighting for; let the Russians have the honor of taking it.

With sure killer instincts, the Russians were now in a hurry to take the capital; two competing commanders—Zhukov and Konev—were racing each other to Berlin in an attempt to form a ring around the city. Following their opening assault on April 16, the Russians hoped to surround the city in five days, but Zhukov's forces encountered unexpected German resistance, as well as self-inflicted blunders arising out of the turmoil of their advancing and shifting fighting units. The city received a brief respite before the final storm.

On April 18, Wolff saw Hitler for the last time. Also present at this meeting were Wolff's deadly rival Kaltenbrunner and his superior Himmler. When Hitler accused Wolff of negotiating with the enemy, Wolff cleverly responded by saying that he had merely followed up on Hitler's permission, given during their meeting on February 6, to seek contact with the Allies. He assumed at the time that he had been given a free hand. His efforts, he said, had led to considerable disagreement among the Allies. Wolff then remarked, "I'm happy to be able to report to my Führer that through Mr. Dulles I have been successful in opening the gates of the White House in Washington and the door to the prime minister in London for talks. I request instructions for the future my Führer."[53] It is important to note that Hitler did not press the issue of Wolff's disloyalty; instead he said to him, "Had your undertaking failed, then I would have had to let you fall like Hess." If Hitler made these remarks, as Wolff later claimed, Hess was following Hitler's orders when he flew to Scotland in 1941.[54] Hitler then told Wolff to continue negotiating and keep stalling with attempts to obtain better conditions for surrender. This extraordinary remark is unlikely, but Hitler's attempt, even at this point, to split the enemy alliance rings true. Just two months before, Hitler had told his Gauleiters that it was his unshakeable conviction that German diplomacy would succeed in driving a wedge between the Allies.[55] Apparently, he still believed this in April 1945. But now time was running out.

On April 20, Hitler turned fifty-six. His birthday was the last occasion on which the major Nazi paladins paid homage to their führer. Behind his back, some of them were already preparing their defection, making plans to get out of the city and head south. Only Hitler's tenacious willpower kept him on his feet at all. Speer described him as a shriveled-up old man who dragged himself through the narrow rooms and corridors of his underground bunker, located 50 meters below the Reich chancellery.[56] His left hand trembled steadily, and he either held it behind his back or grasped it firmly with his right hand. A newsreel that escaped the eye of the censor clearly shows Hitler's trembling hand behind his back—visual evidence of his progressive Parkinson's disease. Even his voice, normally strong in timbre, became quavering and sometimes incoherent.

On April 22, Hitler lost all self-control during his last situation conference. An expected counteroffensive by General Felix Steiner's tanks northwest of Berlin, designed to relieve the city, had failed to materialize.

This was the final straw. Hitler flew into a rage, accusing his elite SS forces of betraying him. He knew at this point that the war was definitely lost and said so to all those who were present.[57] He said that he would hold out to the last and then commit suicide. The next day he made it clear that he could no longer lead: "I am the Fuhrer as long as I can really lead," but circumstances had made this impossible now. He gave permission to those still present in the bunker to leave if they chose to do so.

On April 25 Goebbels persuaded Hitler that if he held out in the capital of the Third Reich he would set a great example to the movement in future times. As he put it, "I can't keep threatening others if I myself run away from the Reich capital in the critical hour. . . . A captain also goes down with his ship."[58] Hitler regained control of himself, except for two further outbursts relating to Himmler's secrets negotiations with the Allies and Goering's presumptuous request to carry on in his place in the south. Hitler was now primarily concerned with orchestrating his final departure from the stage of history. On the same day that Goebbels urged him to stay in Berlin, a remarkable event occurred at Torgau on the Elbe River, a mere sixty miles southwest of Berlin. The American and the Russian forces met, splitting Germany in half. The world learned that Americans and Russians had embraced, broken out the vodka and whiskey and celebrated throughout the night. The next day the Russians launched their final assault on Berlin; their spearheads were already within reach (four miles) of the Reich chancellery. The devastation that followed beggars description: the city became an inferno that would cost the Russians 300,000 casualties, with nearly 80,000 deaths, while the Germans suffered 125,000 deaths in the siege. The pounding of artillery and the bursting of shells came closer and closer to the Reich chancellery. On the day of Zhukov's final assault, the *Führerbunker* received several direct hits by heavy shells. The roof withstood the shelling, but showers of concrete particles fell from it. The bunker inmates almost suffocated when the ventilation drew in sulfurous fumes from the fire that was raging above.

Now Hitler knew that the end was near and that it was time to put his affairs in order. Early in the morning of April 29, Hitler arranged a bizarre wedding ceremony, marrying his mistress, Eva Braun. The couple celebrated that morning with champagne and food. The bride wore a blue dress with white trimmings, chattering away amiably while the gramophone played sentimental music. Afterward, about 2 AM on April 29, 1945,

Hitler sent for his secretary, Traudl Junge, and dictated his last will and testament, which, as previously described, consisted of two parts. The first was a public declaration of his final wishes and the second a private statement about the disbursement of his earthly possessions. In his public testament he declared that everything he had done was out of love for his people. The war, he insisted, had not been his fault but had been forced on him by the machinations of statesmen with international Jewish connections. His hatred of Jews thus held to the end. As already mentioned, it was at this moment that he came as close as he ever did to admitting personal culpability for the destruction of the Jews, stating that "the guilty Jew has to atone for his guilt (*für seine Schuld zu büßen hat*) in the destruction of hundreds of thousands of German women and children in the fire-bombed cities of Germany. He even claimed that Jews had been killed more "humanely."[59] He then named a new government, appointing Admiral Dönitz as president and commander in chief, Joseph Goebbels as Reich chancellor, and Martin Bormann as party chancellor. He made a special point of pronouncing anathema on Goering and Himmler, expelling the two paladins from party and state for their disloyal behavior. Finally, coming to a personal matter, which made Frau Junge look up from her notes, Hitler confirmed his marriage to Eva Braun. He said that she had expressed the desire to die by his side; he added that it was their "wish that our bodies be burned immediately in the place where I have performed the greater part of my daily work during the course of my twelve years['] service to my people."[60] Hitler's statement about the disposal of his body was dictated by his long-standing anxiety that either he might be captured alive or that his body—dead or alive—might be displayed in a Moscow freak show.[61] He did not want to end up like Mussolini, whose body, along with that of his mistress, had been hanged upside down in a public square; their corpses had been taunted, cursed, and spat upon by an angry crowd.

The next day, April 30, Hitler and Eva Braun committed suicide; he shot himself in the right temple and she took cyanide poison. The couple's bodies, wrapped in blankets, were carried upstairs and placed on a stretch of flat sandy ground a few meters from the bunker entrance. The bodies were doused with several cans of gasoline and set afire. The funeral entourage, consisting of Goebbels, Bormann, Hewel, Linge, and others, stood at rigid attention and gave the final Hitler salute. The atmosphere was what Hitler had imagined it would be—a page out of the *Muspilli* poem, evoking the horrors of world conflagration and the twilight of the gods (*Götter-dämmerung*), when the mountains erupt in fire, the heavens are set aflame, and the final judgment of humanity begins to unfold. The bodies burned for several hours, and their remains—despite endless claims—were never discovered because whatever was left of them was pulverized by constant Russian bombing attacks and shelling. All that was found by the Russians was part of a jawbone and two dental bridges; the former was identified from Hitler's dental records as part of his lower jawbone and the latter as belonging to Eva Braun. This was the only physical evidence of the deaths of Hitler and Eva Braun.[62] The German people were told that their "Führer Adolf Hitler fell this afternoon in his command post in the Chancellery while fighting against Bolshevism to his last breath."

The death of Hitler meant the death of the Third Reich, for without him the Nazi regime quickly collapsed. The day after Hitler's suicide Goebbels decided to make his own inglorious exit from history by allowing his wife to kill all of her six children by poison, apparently claiming that they could not enjoy a free life under American or Soviet control. Goebbels and his wife then followed Hitler's example by shooting themselves. On May 7, the German army, represented by Generals Jodl and Keitel, unconditionally surrendered at General Eisenhower's headquarters at Rheims in France. Several days later, the surrender terms were confirmed at an inter-Allied meeting in Berlin. Hitler's dream of a Greater German Reich as mighty as the United States died with him. Germany was divided and militarily occupied, but out of the ashes of defeat the Germans would be compelled to rebuild and reconstruct a different state and a different society. Hitler never suspected that such a revitalized society would turn out to be the most Americanized society in Europe.

CONCLUSION
Hitler and the End of a Greater Reich

In *Mein Kampf* Hitler had said that either Germany would be a world power or there would be no Germany. When he wrote this line in 1925 there were only two major world powers, Britain and the United States, and the latter was in relative isolation. The Soviets had only just consolidated their grip on the Russian people after several terrible years of civil war. They were in no position to extend their power and influence in Europe. During Hitler's years in the political wilderness, between 1924 and 1929, he paid little interest to foreign affairs other than to denounce the Versailles treaty and to brand Weimar politicians as weaklings because they did not stand up to the Western powers. The years leading to his seizure of power saw Hitler concentrating almost exclusively on domestic concerns. But it is important to emphasize again that by that time Hitler had formed a distinct image of the United States. It was very much a split image, as explained in the first chapter of this book. What Hitler knew or thought he knew about America came from second-hand sources, from visitors to America (Ross, Hanfstaengl, Lüdecke, Hedin); from what he read in newspapers, magazines, and favorite books (Karl May); or even from what he saw in films. Since America was going through a steep depression in the 1930s, while at the same time entrenching itself behind neutrality laws, Hitler thought he had little to fear from it.

During his first few years in power, Hitler pursued a very cautious approach to foreign policy, concentrating on the economic crisis that had been triggered by the stock market crash in New York in October 1929 and that had affected Germany more deeply than it had other Western countries. American journalists at the time suggested that the economic measures Hitler was using to overcome the Depression—deficit spending, extensive public works projects, government regulation of the economy— were similar to Roosevelt's New Deal programs. Even Roosevelt said at the time that his administration was doing some of the same things that were being done under Hitler in Germany. At the same time, the brutal methods the Nazis were employing against their domestic enemies, par- ticularly the Jews, mobilized public opinion in America against Hitler. Until the events of Kristallnacht (November 9, 1938) and even beyond, the majority of Americans did not perceive a direct threat from Hitler; they viewed him as a slightly comic Charlie Chaplin–like rabble-rouser. For most Americans, Germany was too far away to represent a clear and present danger. Isolationism was a powerful national tranquilizer in the 1930s.

However, there were moments when the American public took no- tice of overseas conflicts. One was when the Japanese attacked mainland China in 1937, which prompted Roosevelt's first warning to the public in his famous Quarantine speech in Chicago on October 5, 1937. In that speech FDR alerted the American people to a creeping "reign of terror and international lawlessness," without specifically naming the aggressive powers involved. He did not have to do so because the American people knew very well that they were Japan, Italy, and Germany. Exactly a month later, Hitler disclosed his aggressive intentions in foreign policy to his mili- tary chiefs, insisting that "Germany's problems could be solved only by the use of force."[1] The German problem was lack of living space for its growing population. In this secret address, Hitler specifically mentioned annexing Austria and destroying Czechoslovakia, intimating that further expansion eastward was necessary to prepare Germany for an inevitable confrontation with the Western powers—France, Britain, and eventually the United States. Then in 1938 came a year of diplomatic flurry and ag- gression involving the annexation of Austria, the Czech crisis, appease- ment at Munich, and the first major pogrom against the Jews. By the end of 1938, Roosevelt was convinced that Hitler was a menace to world peace and that something had to be done to stop him. What action, let alone national policy, was required to stop Hitler was not clear to Roosevelt in

1938. Three years of tweaking the neutrality laws, banking on France and Britain as the first and second lines of defense, lend-lease, rearmament, and preparing the American people for war followed.

By the late 1930s, Hitler had boldly stepped out of the shadow of Germany's postwar humiliation and moved very rapidly to fulfill his vision of transforming Germany into a world power that could challenge Britain, the United States, and the Soviet Union. As Churchill put it, his immediate goal was to take on his enemies one at a time—first the Western powers (assuming they opposed his eastern expansionism), then the Russians, and finally, if necessary, the United States. Hitler preferred not to fight the British, let alone the United States, provided of course that they would not stand in the way of his continental ambitions. The claim made by some historians that Hitler took no notice of the United States in the 1930s is false. In his calculations about unleashing war in 1939, Hitler had never lost track of the United States and what might be expected from this sleeping giant. This is when General Bötticher's reports began to play a significant role in Hitler's thinking. His military attaché in Washington indicated that the United States would be unable to make a significant military difference to Hitler's war aims for at least two years. By that time, Hitler believed, his great plan of continental conquest would have been completed.[2] Hitler's vision was continental rather than global.

In this connection, several German historians have propounded the thesis that Hitler had a carefully crafted plan that would lead, step-by-step—hence the name "stepping plan," or *Stufenplan*—to world domination.[3] These historians concede that Hitler was shrewd enough to temporize for opportunistic reasons, setting himself a short-range goal (*Nahziel*) and a long-range goal (*Fernziel*) with distinct station breaks (as on a railroad line) in between. But Hitler's final station (*Endstation*), they argue, was world domination. Looking at some of Hitler's decisions and the actual course of events, we can certainly discern logic in the development of his aggressive behavior. Conversely, the imposition of a pre-designed plan ignores the inspirational and often unpredictable manner in which Hitler reacted to specific events over which he had no control. The analogy of a kind of railroad table, or *Stufenplan*, is little more than a heuristic aid to the understanding of complex events; it falls short if taken literally. This book has tried to make the case for a far more subtle, and thus perhaps more dangerous, Hitler than often postulated. Hitler had no master plan, but he did have plans for Germany's future. These plans rested on a fabric of ideas that he developed during a ten-year period in Munich (1919–29), where the Nazi movement began. Among these plans was his determination to restore Germany to her prewar world power position and, depending on circumstances, to establish an even greater share (*Anteil*) of Western (and white) domination of the world. A subsidiary question suggested by this goal, which he shared with many Germans, is whether Hitler was a continentalist or a globalist. Did he want to dominate Europe, or did he aspire to global (world) domination? This book favors the continental position. Hitler's actions were in line with traditional German territorial ambitions; they are as old as the medieval *Drang nach Osten* (Drive toward the East) by the Teutonic knights. What Hitler would have done after defeating the Soviet Union is a matter of speculation. His utopian thoughts, even at the height of his success, can be interpreted to support opposite positions.

It is revealing to contrast Hitler and Roosevelt on this issue of continental and global expansionism. Roosevelt's internationalism, like that of all American Progressives since Woodrow Wilson, was far more global than Hitler's. The idea of actively promoting the American way of life, including its politics, by force if necessary, has been the guiding policy ever since America abandoned its Monroe Doctrine and embarked on its global mission to export truth, justice, and the American way. By contrast, Hitler said that National Socialism was not for export, that it was designed for the German people. Hitler was in many ways an old-fashioned, brutal conqueror, rather than a missionary such as Roosevelt. The American president probably knew that he had nothing to fear from Hitler's ideas; what he worried about was Hitler's armies. For that reason he had to stop Hitler and then provide the world with the right medicine: the more humane and civilized way of life enjoyed by free Americans.

Hitler never really knew what to do about America; he hoped that the United States would stay out of Europe and remain in isolation. When that did not happen, he hoped to achieve his Continental ambitions before America could intervene. As to the British, he did not want to destroy the British Empire and said so on many occasions; but when the British refused to acknowledge his reorganization of the Continent and continued the war in 1940, he realized that Britain had to be neutralized. The way to accomplish this, he thought, was to conquer Russia and make Germany invulnerable on the Continent.

For Hitler these considerations reached a critical point in 1939; the time had come to act on his grand ambitions. In April 1939 Hitler turned fifty years old; it was an important psychological moment in his life. As a result of his growing hypochondria, he persuaded himself that he would not live much longer than ten years, at most. It was therefore crucial for him to complete his life's great work: the establishment of a Greater German Empire.

In 1939 Hitler's visions of the future were evolving with his military conquests. Across the ocean, Roosevelt's view of the world was, in turn, evolving in reaction to the Nazi threat. FDR countered the brutal Nazi vision of the world with a vigorous reassertion of a New Order of the Ages—*Novus Ordo Seclorum*—as it has been written on all dollar bills since 1935. His articulation of the *Pax Americana* gradually evolved throughout his conflict with Hitler, from his Quarantine speech in October 1937, through the unneutral address at the University of Virginia in June 1940, his "four freedoms" message, the Atlantic Charter declaration, the Casablanca declaration, and so forth. Even before Roosevelt found himself in a shooting war with Germany, he had determined that the war with Germany was a moral clash between the humane values of American democracy and the brutal nature of Nazi tyranny. The four freedoms doctrine was his attempt to universalize the doctrines of the Enlightenment on which the American political experience had rested. That the Russians were not necessarily on the same page had to be glossed over, though Roosevelt tried to persuade himself and the American people that Russia, like America, had developed strong democratic tendencies as a result of her frontier experiences. He thought that Stalin was morally grounded, having once been a seminary student. FDR even told Richard Law, a British diplomat, "There are many varieties of Communism, and not all of them are necessarily harmful."[4] That the Russians had been allies with the Germans in 1939, and ruthlessly dismembered Poland, had to be ignored to maintain the illusion of Allied unity. FDR had a firm and abiding faith in democracy, but it was democracy American-style, or what is good for America is good for the world. This was another example of the missionary zeal that had characterized Wilson's intervention in World War I: the moral grounds that the world had to be made safe for democracy. The American liberal worldview brooked no opposition to its moral and political exclusivity, and it denounced all other political positions as being contrary to the tide of history. Hitler never fully understood how powerful this American missionary force really was. He mistakenly associated it with old-fashioned, nineteenth-century imperialism and Jewish-controlled capitalism.

In the late summer of 1940, Hitler decided to accelerate the pace of territorial expansion and racial purification. Though a year passed before he attacked Russia, when he did, he believed that the Russian campaign would be over by Christmas. During that time he gave strict instructions not to provoke the Americans, but he ended up ignoring his own counsel when he declared war on them anyway on December 11. When he finally became entangled with the United States, he was not pondering the moral differences that divided his vision of the world from that of Roosevelt's America. He was thinking about the length of time it would take the United States to make its military weight felt on the continent of Europe. He believed that this would not happen for several years. He was right on this score, but wrong on his prediction that the Soviet Union would collapse in 1942 or 1943—too late for the United States to make a difference.

The European war had turned into a world war in December 1941, and it required not only a different military strategy—blitzkrieg tactics were now passé—but also a total mobilization of economic resources. Economic historians have pointed out that the German economy, though showing remarkable improvement between 1933 and 1939, was lagging behind both Britain and France in industrial output; its per capita income was modest by European standards.[5] Hitler recognized these and other weaknesses in the German economy, but he believed that in the long run the German economy could not be expanded without a concomitant expansion of territory in the East. Germany would then obtain all the raw materials it needed and control its own markets in the Russian area. As Hitler told Ciano, "the new Russia, as far as the Urals, would become our India, but one more favorably situated than that of the British. The new Greater German Reich would comprise 135 million people and rule over an additional 150 million." Germany would therefore no longer be dependent on any outside power. "America too could 'get lost' as far as he was concerned."[6]

When the European war turned into a world war, the nations of the world witnessed not only a war of arms but also a war of three contending ideologies: liberal capitalism, Communism, and National Socialism. In describing the differences between these three conceptions of life, German propaganda tried to draw connections between Communism and capitalism, making the Jew the link between the two. In addition, Goebbels tried to convince the German people that their major enemies were barbarians who lacked any genuine culture. Goebbels stated that if Germany did not succeed in defeating its enemies, "made up of Bolshevism, plutocracy, and lack of culture, the world will be headed for the densest darkness."[7] This misperception stands in the starkest contrast to Winston Churchill's famous remark that "if Hitler wins and we fall, then the whole world, including the United States, including all that we have known and cared for, will sink into the abyss of a New Dark Age made more sinister, and perhaps more protracted, by the lights of perverted science."[8] Both men were convinced that they were right, but they did not succeed equally in persuading their people of that conviction. Goebbels tried to persuade the German people that the Americans would usher in a dark age if Germany lost the war. The German people did not believe this, and there are two very compelling facts that show this conclusively. These facts are based on the actual behavior of many Germans when they came in contact with their Western enemy.[9] In the fall of 1944, as described in Chapter 9, the civilian population in the west engaged in relatively little resistance to the Americans. Goebbels himself was shocked by what he regarded as disgraceful German behavior in the Rhineland, where dozens of towns offered scarcely any resistance to the invaders. He was repulsed by pictures showing Germans hanging white sheets out of their windows. His own hometown of Rheydt in the Rhineland was one of these towns.

It was not just the German civilian population that refused to swallow Nazi propaganda about barbaric Americans. The military also offered relatively weak resistance to the Anglo-Americans in the west in the spring of 1945. It was entirely different in the east, where the *Wehrmacht* kept on fighting with great tenacity and courage, trying—often successfully—to hold back the Red Army, thus enabling civilians to escape westward to the American or British zones. General Koller recounts that Goering told him in April 1945 to draft a proclamation to the *Wehrmacht* and the German people that the battle against the Soviets would continue, but not the battle against the Anglo-Americans in the west.[10] The evidence is overwhelming that anti-Communist and anti-Russian propaganda had found its mark. Even if it had not, military reality would have produced the same result.

The soldiers of the *Ostheer* knew what they had done to the Russians during the past three years; they expected no mercy from vengeance-seeking Russians, and the terror that descended on East Prussia starting in January 1944 confirmed these fears. In their raw brutality the two totalitarian systems were soul mates.

In view of these stark realities, why is it that Hitler did not give up until Russian soldiers were almost literally knocking on the doors of the chancellery? Hitler had no more bargaining chips, having played his last hand in December 1944. A military victory was now out of the question, but hoping against hope he wanted to drag out the war, no matter what gratuitous suffering it would mean to his people, until the cursed coalition fell apart. Only 130 years earlier Napoleon had been in a similar position facing a coalition of highly different powers—Britain, Prussia, Austria, Russia, and most of Europe. This coalition held as long as Napoleon was in power. A congress had already assembled in Vienna, ready and willing to extend the wartime coalition into the postwar period, redraw the map, and ensure the peace of Europe. A similar design existed in 1945. Hitler knew that the United Nations would assemble in April in San Francisco, formulate a charter, and set the stage for another reorganization of Europe. Hitler did not believe that this could work, because the two superpowers that had emerged on the enemy side, the United States and the Soviet Union, would never be able to find common ground. It was inevitable that they would clash. As he put it just a month before his death,

> With the defeat of the Reich and pending the emergence of the Asiatic, the African, and perhaps the South American nationalisms, there will remain in the world only two Great Powers capable of confronting each other—the United States and Soviet Russia. The laws of both history and geography will compel these two Powers to a trial of strength, either military or in the fields of economics and ideology. These same laws make it inevitable that both Powers should become enemies of Europe. And it is equally certain that both these powers will sooner or later find it desirable to seek the support of the sole surviving great nation in Europe, the German people. I say with all the emphasis in my command that the Germans must at all costs avoid playing the role of pawn in either camp.[11]

Having made such a remarkably prescient observation about the political reorganization of the world after his death, one would think that Hitler would at least offer an explanation, or possibly a justification, of his role in the impending catastrophe. None was forthcoming, except for the accusation in his last testament that the Jews had plunged Europe into a world war. This was to be expected from the public Hitler, who had long ago put on the imperious and impervious führer mask, but what about the private Hitler? Is he knowable at all? This is a historiographic and philosophical problem, a question that has often been asked not just about Hitler but about many personalities who have transformed history. In the case of World War II, biographers have frequently come up short in trying to explain the quintessential character of Hitler, Stalin, Churchill, or Roosevelt.

The essential Hitler has defied his biographers and probably always will, but one of the very best characterizations of him was by Winston Churchill, a man who had uncanny insight into the Hitler phenomenon. Earlier than most observers, he saw in Hitler a populist who embodied the extremes of all of Germany's recent shames, humiliations, and hatreds. He said that Hitler was that rare leader who was able to generate "those measureless forces of the spirit which may spell the rescue or doom of mankind."[12] What makes Churchill's judgments about Hitler credible is that they came out of his role as a participant in this frightful drama. Churchill understood what Hitler was, and what he represented, in a way that Roosevelt never did. Churchill understood the power of Hitler's personality, and he recognized that this power rested, in part, on the remarkable resonance of Hitler's ideas with the German people. He also perceived that Hitler's mind was shaped by his (and Germany's) disastrous experience in World War I and in the interwar period. For all these reasons, Churchill knew what he was up against, and this explains his intense personal jousting with his archrival.

As to what the private Hitler believed during his slide into oblivion, this can only be broadly reconstructed from meager and often contradictory sources. Jodl was probably right when he said at Nuremberg that Hitler had known that the war was militarily unwinnable as early as December 1941, if not earlier. Thereafter he followed a Friderician policy of holding out and fighting on until the accursed enemy coalition had collapsed. He believed that the Americans were the weakest of his opponents from a military point of view. At the same time, he believed that they were the strongest economic power, capable of outproducing the Axis powers. From a psychological point of view, he expected that the American home front would collapse if he put the Americans through the same meat grinder as he had the Russians on the eastern front. Hitler even fantasized that Roosevelt might be impeached by the Supreme Court. Hitler's historical understanding of the United States was, to say the least, distorted by wishful thinking, but not entirely so. As previously mentioned, Hitler had a healthy respect for the economic powers of the United States; by 1942 he knew that Germany could not compete economically with the Allied forces, especially when the United States was drawn into the war. By the spring of 1945, the private Hitler, while still telling everyone to fight to the last bullet, was prepared for inevitable defeat. He was even detached enough to speculate about the shape of things to come after the Third Reich had been defeated.

The private Hitler knew that Germany would be divided and occupied by the victorious Allied powers and that an occupation would mean the division of Germany by Russian Bolsheviks and American capitalists. These two emerging superpowers, Hitler felt, would inevitably come to blows. Joseph Goebbels already predicted in February 1945 that an "iron curtain" (he used this term long before Churchill did) would descend on all of Europe, dividing the Continent into a Russian and an American sphere of interest. Goebbels used this iron curtain metaphor in an article he wrote for his favorite magazine, *Das Reich* (February 25, 1945); titled "The Year 2000," it was one of the more bizarre articles he ever wrote, which is saying a lot given his penchant for long-winded lectures to the German people.

Since Goebbels and Hitler were joined at the hip on such matters, it is highly instructive to follow the propaganda minister, now turned prophet, in his prognostications about the future of Germany, Europe, and the world. Goebbels correctly predicted the Cold War between the Soviet Union and the United States and the division of Europe by a Soviet iron curtain. Behind that curtain, all independent nations would be destroyed and their people reduced to proletarian working animals, a development that would be hailed in the Jewish-controlled world's press. In a short "third world war," Britain and the United States would be forced to abandon the Continent to the Russians. The United States, Goebbels said, would withdraw all its troops from Europe and return to isolationism. The Continent would be prostrate "at the feet of the mechanized robots from the steppes."[13] But this horrible scenario could be averted if the German people resolutely held out and broke the unnatural alliance. For public consumption, both Goebbels and Hitler were still urging the German people to fight on, while privately they were fearing the worst. In his article, Goebbels told his readers that by 2000 Germany would no longer be occupied, having risen by then to the intellectual leadership of humanity. World War II would be remembered as a bad dream, but its sacrifices would be memorialized as a blessing to future generations. Just two months later, neither Goebbels nor Hitler was thinking about immediate salvation; they knew that the Germany they wished for was finished, but they still hoped that in some future time—now in the indefinite future—the "seeds of a glorious rebirth" of National Socialism and a true people's community (*Volksgemeinschaft*) would sprout.[14] What would happen in the interim neither Hitler nor Goebbels cared to reveal. Both went to their deaths with their illusions intact. In Hitler's case, this was also true of his split image of the United States. Like so many European critics and detractors of America, he never understood that both his images of the United States were greatly out of focus.

Hitler's image of America was not only split, consisting of two contrary mental representations, but also naive. This fact is important because the image rested on a great many similarly naive judgments that Europeans had made about a continent they had never visited. Some of the material that made up Hitler's mental representation of "Amerika" consisted of questionable sources, which he bent to fit his own ideological frame of reference. But there is no single image of America that fits some objective frame of reference. America is a protean idea. The reason for this is that America is, and presumably will continue to be, an immigration society— Indian, Anglo-Saxon, African, Asian, Hispanic, and so forth—that has never had a single center of gravity for very long. Critics of America usually miss their target because it is forever moving and shifting—it is almost as unpredictable as the movement of subatomic particles. The canvas on which the various immigrant groups and their descendents have painted their tales does not tell a coherent story with a dominant theme like the famous Bayeux tapestry. It is rather like a patchwork quilt made by different artists. The same is true of the evolving democratic republic, which has been subjected to the same pullulating forces. During the course of its 220 years (the U.S. republic began in 1789, when the first Washington administration took office), the American republic has undergone dramatic changes in about fifty-year increments—in

1789, 1839, 1889, 1939, 1989, and 2009. Hitler was born in 1889, the year the American republic was exactly one hundred years old.

Having grown up in the ethnic, linguistic, and religious diversity of the Habsburg Empire, Hitler could have acquired a more empathetic understanding of multiethnic America; instead he absorbed extreme doctrines of German nationalism and racial (Aryan) superiority. He thought America was still dominated by racially superior Nordic Europeans, writing off the rest of the U.S. population as an "international mishmash of peoples."[15] Like Colin Ross, he regarded the sizable German element in America—more Germans had come over to America between 1839 and 1939 than any other immigrant group—as "Our America" (Unser Amerika). This was the superior Amerika, the creative as opposed to the racially inferior one. Since the Nordic European race, according to Hitler, still dominated the United States, the possibility of its intervention in European affairs had to be carefully monitored. Hanfstaengl had warned Hitler in the 1920s that he should never forget that Germany had lost World War I because of U.S. intervention. Hitler did not forget this, but in 1939 he did not think that the United States would intervene. He certainly considered Roosevelt a warmonger who was strongly influenced by American Jews, but he did not think that the United States would intervene militarily in Europe. He obviously hoped that isolationism would trump FDR's internationalism. When that turned out to be wrong, as America waged an undeclared shooting war with Germany on the high seas, Hitler chose to anticipate an American declaration of war by declaring one himself on December 11, 1941.

One misjudgment of American power followed another. Hitler was surprised by the rapid rearmament of the United States, and the way the Americans propped up both the British and the Soviet war effort. But perhaps one of his greatest mistakes was to underestimate the Anglo-American message of democratic freedom—a message that German propaganda treated with disdain and cynicism but that was greeted by millions of Europeans, including substantial numbers of Germans, as their salvation from totalitarian tyranny. In their hour of defeat, the German people sensed that the Anglo-Americans did not come as brutal oppressors and that they were bringing a more humane message to Europe than the Russians, who were just re-importing an especially brutal form of Communism. By that time, it was too late for Hitler to exclaim to his entourage that the war with America was a tragedy or that they had been fighting the wrong enemy.

NOTES

INTRODUCTION

1. Adolf Hitler, *Hitler: Reden und Proklamationen, 1932–1945*, ed. Max Domarus (Wiesbaden: R. Löwit, 1973), 3:1333 (hereafter cited as Domarus, *Reden*).

2. Klaus Hildebrand, "Monokratie oder Polykratie? Hitlers Herrschaft und das Dritte Reich," in *Der Führerstaat: Mythos und Realität*, ed. Gerhard Hirschfeld and Lothar Kettenacker (Stuttgart: Klett, 1981), 75.

3. Domarus, *Reden*, 2:975.

4. Adolf Hitler, *Mein Kampf*, ed. William Langer (New York: Reynal & Hitchcock, 1941), 950.

5. Ibid., 929.

6. Ernst von Weizsäcker, *Erinnerungen* (München: Paul List Verlag, 1950), 199.

7. Joachim Fest, *Hitler*, trans. Richard and Clara Winston (New York: Harcourt Brace Jovanovich, 1973), 5.

CHAPTER 1

1. Adolf Hitler, *Adolf Hitler: Monologe im Führerhauptquartier, 1941–1944*, ed. Werner Jochmann (München: Orbis Verlag 1980), 255–56.

2. Hitler was greatly influenced by racial-biological studies touting the superiority of the white race, and he believed, as many Germans and Americans did at the time, that miscegenation undermined the superior white gene pool. In the mid-1920s,

the Munich publisher Lehmann, who was probably the greatest purveyor of racist literature, sent Hitler the well-known American book by Madison Grant titled *The Passing of the Great Race*, claiming that the Nordic gene pool in America was being diluted by inferior blood. There is good reason to believe that Hitler carefully read this and other books sent to him by Lehmann. Timothy Ryback, *Hitler's Private Library: The Books That Shaped His Life* (London: Bodley Press, 2009), 110

3. Adolf Hitler, *Hitler's Second Book*, trans. Krista Smith and ed. Gerhard Weinberg (New York: Enigma Books, 2003), 118.

4. Ibid.

5. Quoted in James V. Compton, *The Swastika and the Eagle: Hitler, the United States and the Origins of World War II* (Boston: Houghton Mifflin, 1967), 20.

6. Hitler, *Monologe*, 184.

7. Michael S. Bell, "The World View of Franklin D. Roosevelt: France, Germany and the United States' Involvement in World War II" (Diss., University of Maryland, 2004), 39–40.

8. Quoted in Richard Hofstadter, *The American Political Tradition and the Men Who Made It* (New York: Viking, 1948), 212.

9. Fritz Stern, *The Politics of Cultural Despair: A Study in the Rise of the German Ideology* (New York: Doubleday, 1965); and Jeffrey Herf, *Reactionary Modernism: Technology, Culture and Politics in Weimar and the Third Reich* (New York: Cambridge University Press, 1984).

10. Adolf Halfeld, *Amerika und der Amerkanismus* (Jena: Eugen Diederichs, 1928), esp. 17–50

11. In 1941 Halfeld wrote one of the strangest books of political prognostication, titled *USA greift in die Welt* (Hamburg: Verlag Broschek & Co., 1941). In this book, in which he tried to show that Roosevelt was reaching for world power, he completely ignored Hitler's grand territorial ambitions. Besides Halfeld's book, several other prominent anti-Roosevelt (but not anti-America) books were written before and shortly after America's entrance into the war, notably Werner A. Lohe, *Roosevelt-Amerika* (München: Eher Verlag, 1939); and the Swedish explorer Sven Hedin, *Amerika im Kampf der Kontinente* (Leipzig: F. A. Brockhaus, 1942). We know that Hitler frequently met Hedin, highly prized his work, and most likely read his book on America, which Hedin sent him. Hedin knew a great deal about America and lectured there before the war. There is a good Hitler-Hedin section in Ryback, *Hitler's Private Library*, 186–200.

12. John Lukacs, *The Duel: The Eighty-Day Struggle between Churchill and Hitler* (New Haven, Conn.: Yale University Press, 1990), 11–12.

13. David E. Barclay and Elisabeth Glaser-Schmidt, eds., *Transatlantic Images and Perceptions: Germany and America since 1776* (Cambridge: Cambridge University Press, 1997), 82.

14. U.S. Department of Homeland Security, *Yearbook of Immigration Statistics, Annual Immigration into the United States.www.dhs.gov/files/statistics*

15. John Lukacs, *The Last European War: September 1939–December 1942* (New Haven, Conn.: Yale University Press, 2001), 7.

16. See, Dan Diner, "Onkel Sam und Onkel Shylock," in *Feindbild Amerika* (München: Propyläen, 2002), 90–114.

17. On Hitler's view of America, see Gerhard L. Weinberg, "Hitler's Image of the United States," *American Historical Review* 69 (July 1964): 1006–21; Compton, *Swastika and the Eagle;* Robert E. Herzstein, *Roosevelt and Hitler: Prelude to War* (New York: Paragon House, 1989); and Saul Friedländer, *Prelude to Downfall: Hitler and the United States, 1933–1941* (New York: Knopf, 1967). These works are consistent in their assessment of Hitler's bad judgment about the United States. For two different interpretations, readers should consult John Lukacs, *The Hitler of History* (New York: Knopf, 1997); and Rainer Zitelmann, *Hitler: Selbstverständnis eines Revolutionärs* (Stuttgart: Klett 1990).

18. Franz Jetzinger, *Hitler's Youth,* trans. Lawrence Wilson (Westport, Conn.: Greenwood Press, 1976), 68.

19. Hitler, *Monologe,* 254.

20. For details, see the colorful account by Brigitte Hamann, *Hitlers Wien: Lehrjahre eines Diktators* (München: Piper, 1998), 544–48.

21. Ibid., 546–47.

22. Hitler, *Monologe,* 281, 281–82; also Robert G. L. Waite, *The Psychopathic God Adolf Hitler* (New York: Basic Books, 1977), 11, 68.

23. For the connection between Hitler's hero worship and the Karl May novels, see Vappu Tallgren, *Hitler und die Helden: Heroismus und Weltanschauung* (Helsinki: Suomalainen Tiedeakatemia, 1981), 88–95; also Otto Dietrich, *Zwölf Jahre mit Hitler* (München: Isar, 1955), 164; Waite, *Psychopathic God,* 137; Kurt Lüdecke, *I Knew Hitler* (New York: National Book Association, 1938), 451–53; Hitler, *Monologe,* 281–82.

24. Lüdecke, *I Knew Hitler,* 469–71. On Lüdecke's role in the rise of the Nazi Party, see Georg Franz-Willig, *Die Hitlerbewegung: Der Ursprung, 1919–22* (Hamburg: R.v. Decker's Verlag G. Schenck, 1962), 132ff.

25. For Hanfstaengl's side of the story, see *Hitler: The Missing Years* (1957; New York: Arcade Publishing, 1994), 276–86

26. The majority of the papers relating to Hanfstaengl and the "Dr. Sedgwick" case are scattered through Roosevelt's file on Franklin Carter (PSF: Subject File: Carter, John F.). The journalist John Franklin Carter had been charged by FDR to set up a small, private intelligence service in 1942. It was not known outside the circle surrounding the president and was financed through the president's emergency fund. It was Carter, who had met Hanfstaengl in Munich, who oversaw

the Sedgwick case. Other material related to the S-Project can be found in the president's personal file on Adolf Hitler (PPF 5780); the papers of anthropologist Henry Field, who was in immediate charge of Hanfstaengl; the papers of the historian John Toland, who interviewed Hanfstaengl, his wife, and his son Egon in 1970 and 1971; the papers of Sumner Welles in his office correspondence (Carter, John Franklin, 1942) and his personal correspondence (CA–Ce, 1947). Writing under the name Jay Franklin, John Franklin Carter left his own account in *Catoctin Conversation* (New York: Charles Scribner's Sons, 1947). Two recent works on Sedgwick and American covert operations are Christof Mauch, *The Shadow War against Hitler* (New York: Columbia University Press, 2003); and Steven Casey, "Franklin D. Roosevelt, Ernst 'Putzi' Hanfstaengl, and the 'S Project,' June 1942– June 1944," *Journal of Contemporary History* 35 (2000): 339–59.

27. Lüdecke, *I Knew Hitler*, 298.

28. Ibid., 296.

29. U.S. Department of State, *Documents on German Foreign Policy, 1918–1945*, vol. 8 (Washington, D.C.: Government Printing Office, 1954), series D, 910–13 (hereafter cited as *DGFP*); also, Domarus, *Reden*, 3:1482–83.

30. Colin Ross, *Amerikas Schicksalsstunde: Die Vereinigten Staaten Zwischen Demokratie und Diktatur* (Leipzig: F. A. Brockhaus, 1936), 4.

31. Ibid., 31–37.

32. Ibid., 90–94.

33. Colin Ross, *Die Westliche Hemisphäre als Programm und Phantom des amerikanischen Imperialismus* (Leipzig: F. A. Brockhaus, 1942), 211–24.

34. Ibid., 203–11.

35. Hitler, *Monologe*, 254.

36. Hildegard von Kotze, ed., *Heeresadjutant bei Hitler, 1938–1943: Aufzeichnungen des Majors Engel* (Stuttgart: Deutsche Verlags-Anstalt, 1974), 47.

37. For the most sensible and reliable study of Bötticher, see Alfred M. Beck, *Hitler's Ambivalent Attaché: Lt. Gen. Friedrich von Boetticher in America, 1933– 1941* (Washington, D.C.: Potomac Books, 2005).

38. Alfred Vagts, *The Military Attaché* (Princeton, N.J.: Princeton University Press, 1967), ix.

39. Beck, *Hitler's Ambivalent Attaché*, 67.

40. Ibid., 182.

41. Ibid., 129, 267.

42. Ibid., 132, 224.

43. Fritz Wiedemann, *Der Mann der Feldherr werden wollte* (Dortmund: blick + bild Verlag für politische Bildung, 1964), 214–15.

44. Ibid., 221.

45. Ibid.

46. Ibid., 222.

47. Ibid., 224.

48. Hanfstaengl, *Hitler: Missing Years*, 40–41.

49. Lüdecke, *I Knew Hitler*, 510.

50. Beck, *Hitler's Ambivalent Attaché*, 149.

51. Hitler, *Monologe*, 184.

52. Compton, *Swastika and the Eagle*, 7.

53. Adolf Hitler, *Hitlers Tischgespräche im Führerhauptquartier*, ed. Henry Picker (Stuttgart: Goldmann Verlag, 1981), 155.

54. Ulrich von Hassell, *The Von Hassell Diaries, 1938–1944* (London: Hamish, 1948), 106.

55. George McJimsey, ed., *Documentary History of the Franklin D. Roosevelt Presidency*, vol. 12 (Washington, D.C.: Congressional Information Service, 2003), 298.

56. Ibid., 12:582.

57. *Morgenthau Diaries*, May 20, 1940, Franklin D. Roosevelt Presidential Library, Hyde Park, New York, on microfiche.

58. At the presidential library in Hyde Park, New York, there is a copy of *Mein Kampf* that was in FDR's personal library. It is a truncated version in English translation. On the inside cover is personal note in FDR's handwriting that says that this version is quite different from the original German, indicating that the president had read the original German version.

59. Hans Kohn, *The Mind of Germany: The Education of a Nation* (New York: Harper & Row, 1960), 76.

60. Robert Gellately, *Backing Hitler* (New York: Oxford University, 2001), 6.

61. Elliott Roosevelt, ed., *F.D.R., His Personal Letters: The Early Years* (New York: Duell, Sloan and Pearce, 1947), 19–20.

62. Frank Freidel, *Franklin D. Roosevelt*, vol. 1, *The Apprenticeship* (Boston: Little, Brown and Company, 1947), 33–34.

63. Ted Morgan, *FDR: A Biography* (New York: Simon and Schuster, 1985), 43.

64. Grace G. Tully, *F.D.R., My Boss* (New York: Charles Scribner's Sons, 1949), 70.

65. Freidel, *Franklin D. Roosevelt*, 1:34.

66. Ibid.

67. Bell, "World View of Franklin D. Roosevelt," 35.

68. Roosevelt, *Personal Letters: Early Years*, 943.

69. Samuel I. Rosenman, ed., *The Public Papers and Address of Franklin D. Roosevelt, 1944–45* (New York: Random House, 1945), 560. Also Freidel, *Franklin D. Roosevelt*, 1:34.

70. Bell, "World View of Franklin D. Roosevelt," 72.

71. Ibid., 78.

72. Ibid., 227–29; Freidel, *Franklin D. Roosevelt*, 2:13.

73. Morgan, *FDR*, 657.

CHAPTER 2

1. Quoted in Andreas Hillgruber, *Germany and the Two World Wars*, trans. William C. Kirby (Cambridge, Mass.: Harvard University Press, 1981), 56–57.

2. Joachim Remak, "Germany and the United States, 1933–1939" (Diss., Stanford University, 1955), 18.

3. Gordon A. Craig and Felix Gilbert, eds., *The Diplomats, 1919–1939* (New York: Atheneum, 1963), 2:458.

4. William E. Dodd Jr. and Martha Dodd, eds., *Ambassador Dodd's Diary, 1933–1938* (New York: Harcourt, Brace and Company, 1941), 447.

5. Ibid., 126.

6. Hitler, *Monologe*, 118.

7. Ibid.

8. Robert Dallek, *Democrat and Diplomat: The Life of William E. Dodd* (New York: Oxford University Press, 1968), 192.

9. Craig and Gilbert, *Diplomats*, 2:458.

10. Manfred Jonas, *The United States and Germany: A Diplomatic History* (Ithaca, N.Y.: Cornell University Press, 1984), 213.

11. Morgan, *FDR*, 395.

12. *Völkische Beobachter*, June 7, 1933.

13. Detlef Junker, "The Continuity of Ambivalence: German Views of America, 1933–1945," in *Transatlantic Images and Perceptions: Germany and America since 1776*, ed. Barclay and Glaser-Schmidt, 247.

14. Jonas, *United States and Germany*, 212.

15. Harold L. Ickes, *The Secret Diary of Harold Ickes* (New York: Simon and Schuster, 1953); also Morgan, *FDR*, 396.

16. Michael Zalampas, *Adolf Hitler and the Third Reich in American Magazines, 1923* (Bowling Green, Ohio: Bowling Green University Press, 1989), 44–45.

17. *New York Times*, July 13, 1934.

18. Arnold A. Offner, *American Appeasement: United States Foreign Policy and Germany, 1933–1938* (New York: Norton, 1968), 82.

19. Louis Anthes, "Publicly Deliberative Drama: The 1934 Mock Trial of Adolf Hitler for 'Crimes against Civilization,'" *Journal of Legal History* 42 (1998): 392.

20. Dodd and Dodd, *Diary*, 89.

21. *New York Times*, September 7, 1935.

22. *Völkische Beobachter*, September 9, 1935.

23. Jonas, *United States and Germany*, 210.

24. Ibid., 211.

25. Morgan, *FDR*, 395.

26. Cordell Hull, *The Memoirs of Cordell Hull*, vol. 1 (New York: Macmillan, 1948), 239.

27. Gerhard Weinberg, *The Foreign Policy of Hitler's Germany*, vol. 1, *Diplomatic Revolution in Europe, 1933–36* (Chicago: University of Chicago Press, 1970), 139.

28. On matters of the German navy, see Jost Düffler, *Weimar, Hitler und die Marine: Reichspolitik und Flottenbau, 1920–1939* (Düsseldorf: Droste, 1973).

29. Winston Churchill, *The Second World War*, vol. 1 (Boston: Houghton Mifflin, 1948), 196–97.

30. Rosenman, *The Public Papers and Addresses of Franklin D. Roosevelt*, vol. 5 (New York: Random House, 1938), 289.

31. Ibid., 288.

32. For the whole document, see J. Noakes and G. Pridham, eds., *Nazism: A History in Documents and Eyewitness Accounts, 1919–1945*, vol. 1 (New York: Schocken Books, 1990), 283–87.

33. Joseph E. Davies, *Mission to Moscow* (New York: Simon and Schuster, 1941), 153–59.

34. Robert E. A. Divine, *Roosevelt and World War II* (Baltimore: Johns Hopkins Press, 1969), 16–17.

35. Dieckhoff to Foreign Office, in *DGFP*, series D, 1:639–41. Also see Welles memorandum, in U.S. Department of State, *Foreign Relations of the United States* (Washington, D.C.: U. S. Government Printing Office, ongoing), 1:138–39.

36. Nicolaus von Below, *Als Hitlers Adjutant, 1937–1945* (Mainz, 1980), 47.

37. Divine, *Roosevelt and World War II*, 16–17.

38. Roosevelt, *Personal Letters: Early Years*, 716–17.

39. This is the argument Robert Nisbet made in his book *Roosevelt and Stalin: The Failed Courtship* (Washington, D.C.: Regnery Gateway, 1988). But Nisbet overstated his case by painting Roosevelt as a more deluded Wilsonian internationalist than Wilson himself. Nisbet argues that Roosevelt naively believed that British imperialism was a greater threat to democracy than Soviet Communism (107). As will be shown in later chapters, Roosevelt did not "court" the Soviets; he needed them as partners in a war that required their help, for without the Soviets the United States would not have won the war against Hitler.

40. On Hitler's worldview, the following are particularly useful: Friedrich Heer, *Der Glaube des Adolf Hitlers: Anatomie einer politischen Religiosität* (München: Bechtle Verlag, 1968); Eberhard Jäckel, *Hitlers Weltanschauung: Entwurf einer Herrschaft* (Stuttgart: Deutsche Verlags-Anstalt, 1981); Sebastian Haffner, *The Meaning of Hitler*, trans. Ewald Osers (Cambridge, Mass.: Harvard University

Press, 1983); Ian Kershaw, *The "Hitler Myth": Image and Reality in the Third Reich* (New York: Oxford University Press, 1987), and the same author's two-volume biography of Hitler, *Hitler, 1889–1936: Hubris* (New York: Norton, 1999), and *Hitler, 1936–1945: Nemesis* (New York: Norton, 2000); Lukacs, *Hitler of History*; and Zitelmann, *Hitler: Selbstverständnis eines Revolutionärs*.

41. For the specifics of the November 5, 1937, conference, see Domarus, *Reden,* 2:747–56; and Noakes and Pridham, *Nazism,* 2:680–87.

42. Wiedemann, *Feldherr,* 103.

43. Domarus, *Reden,* 2:691.

44. Wiedemann, *Feldherr,* 103.

45. *Akten zur Deutschen Auswärtigen Politik, 1918–1945: Aus dem Archiv des Auswärtigen Amts,* series D, 10 vols. (Baden-Baden/Frankfurt, 1950–70), 1:525.

46. Ibid., 525–26.

47. For Wiedemann's account, *Feldherr,* 215–18.

48. Gerhard L. Weinberg, *The Foreign Policy of Hitler's Germany,* vol. 2, *Starting World War II, 1937–39* (Chicago: University of Chicago Press, 1980), 252–53. It is unlikely that Hitler regarded the Rechenberg memorandum as a "wonderful document." The Foreign Office had received the Rechenberg memorandum from the chief of the Reich chancellery with a note that said that Hitler had read the memorandum with great interest and wanted it passed on to the Foreign Office. This merely suggests that Hitler found the document, written by a former Reich foreign trade official and erstwhile emigrant to America, sufficiently important to be considered by the Foreign Office.

49. J. W. Wheeler-Bennett, *Munich: Prologue to Tragedy* (New York: Viking Press, 1964), 340.

50. Bella Fromm, *Blood and Banquets* (New York: Harper & Brothers, 1942), 270.

51. FDRL, PSF: Safe, Hohenlohe, *Memo of October 28, 1941.*

52. See Martha Schad, *Hitlers Spionin: Das Leben der Stephanie von Hohenlohe* (München: Wilhelm Heyne Verlag, 2002).

CHAPTER 3

1. For Hoover's visit to Germany, see John Lukacs, "Herbert Hoover Meets Adolf Hitler," *American Scholar* (2001): 235–38.

2. Ibid., 236.

3. Ibid., 237.

4. According to Wiedemann (*Feldherr,* 219), Hitler allegedly told Goebbels that he thought Hoover was a small man whose caliber was like that of a district leader

in Germany—*"ein ganz kleiner Mann, er hat ungefähr das Kaliber wie bei uns ein kleiner Kreisleiter."* I find this remark highly suspect, because Hitler knew quite well that Hoover had been president of the United States and that such an office was hardly comparable to that of a small *Kreisleiter* in the Nazi Party.

5. Hitler, *Mein Kampf*, 3.

6. Richard M. Watt, *The Kings Depart: The Tragedy of Germany; Versailles and the German Revolution* (New York: Simon and Schuster, 1968), 422.

7. Kurt von Schuschnigg, *Austrian Requiem*, trans. Franz von Hildebrand (London: Gollancz, 1946), 21.

8. On the Austrian Anschluss, see Gordon Brook-Shepherd, *The Anschluss* (Philadelphia: Lippincott, 1953); Evan Burr Bukey, *Hitler's Austria: Popular Sentiment in the Nazi Era, 1938–1945* (Chapel Hill: University of North Carolina Press, 2000); Alfred D. Low, *The Anschluss Movement, 1918–1938, and the Great Powers* (Boulder, Colo.: East European Monographs, 1985); Bruce F. Pauley, *Hitler and the Forgotten Nazis: A History of Austrian National Socialism* (Chapel Hill: University of North Carolina Press, 1981); and *The Habsburg Legacy, 1867–1938* (New York: Holt, Rinehart and Winston, 1972).

9. Quoted in Bukey, *Hitler's Austria*, 27.

10. International Military Tribunal, *Trial of the Major War Criminals before the International Military Tribunal: Proceedings and Documents*, 31:369, doc. 2949–PS.

11. Zalampas, *Hitler and the Third Reich in American Magazines*, 140.

12. Quoted in Anthony Eden, *The Memoirs of Anthony Eden, Earl of Avon: Facing the Dictators* (Boston: Houghton Mifflin, 1962), 639.

13. Historians have paid insufficient attention to this decree and its timing. For details, see Gerald Reitlinger, *The SS: Alibi of a Nation, 1922–1945* (1956; Englewood, N.J.: Prentice Hall, 1981), 83–84; Heinz Höhne, *The Order of the Death's Head* (New York: Ballantine, 1971), 497–510; and George H. Stein, *The Waffen SS* (Ithaca, N.Y.: Cornell University Press, 1966), 9–26.

14. Wheeler-Bennett, *Munich*, 158.

15. On appeasement in Munich, see Martin Gilbert, *The Roots of Appeasement* (London: Weidenfeld and Nicolson, 1966); K. Eubanks, *Munich* (Norman: University of Oklahoma Press, 1963); R. A. C. Parker, *Chamberlain and Appeasement: British Policy and the Coming of the Second World War* (New York: St. Martin's Press, 1994); Andrew Rothstein, *The Munich Conspiracy* (London: Lawrence & Wishart, 1958); Wheeler-Bennett, *Munich: Prologue to Tragedy* (New York: Viking, 1964).

16. Quoted in Alan Bullock, *Hitler: A Study in Tyranny* (New York: Harper & Row, 1962), 469.

17. *Parliamentary Debates*, 5th ser., vol. 339 (October 5, 1938).

18. Domarus, *Reden*, 2:935–37.

19. Offner, *American Appeasement*, 246.

20. U.S. Department of State, *Foreign Relations of the United States: 1938*, 1:688.

21. Rosenman, *Public Papers*, 7:564.

22. Morgan, *FDR*, 489–90.

23. Domarus, *Reden*, 2:927–32.

24. Lucy Dawidowicz, *The War against the Jews, 1933–1945* (New York: Bantam, 1975), 134–35.

25. Klaus P. Fischer, *The History of an Obsession: German Judeophobia and the Holocaust* (New York: Continuum, 1998), 282.

26. Dorothy Thompson's broadcast, titled "We Are All on Trial Now," was printed in *Radio Guide*, week ending December 10, 1938. See also Marion K. Sanders, *Dorothy Thompson: A Legend in Her Time* (New York: Avon Books, 1974), 225ff

27. Morgan, *FDR*, 501.

28. Jonas, *United States and Germany*, 232.

29. Robert Dallek, *Franklin D. Roosevelt and American Foreign Policy, 1932–1945* (New York: Oxford University Press, 1979), 168.

30. Morgan, *FDR*, 498.

31. Ibid.

32. Robert N. Rosen, *Saving the Jews: Franklin D. Roosevelt and the Holocaust* (New York: Thunder's Mouth Press, 2006), 73–74.

33. Ibid., 78.

34. Ibid.

35. Noakes and Pridham, *Nazism*, 2:725.

36. Ian Kershaw, *Hitler*, vol. 2, *Nemesis* (New York: Norton, 2000), 123.

37. A. J. P. Taylor, *The Origins of the Second World War* (New York: Fawcett, 1961), 186.

38. Hull, *Memoirs*, 1:580.

39. Dallek, *Roosevelt and American Foreign Policy*, 164.

40. Elliott Roosevelt, *F.D.R., His Personal Letters, 1905–1928* (New York: Duell, Sloan and Pearce, 1950), 810.

41. Francis MacDonald, *Insidious Foes: The Axis Fifth Column and the American Home Front* (New York: Oxford University Press, 1995), 8.

42. Ibid., 136.

43. For Rumrich and Hitler's spies, see Leon G. Turrou, *Nazi Spies in America* (New York: Random House, 1939; William B. Breuer, *Hitler's Undercover War: The Nazi Espionage Invasion of the U.S.A.* (New York: St. Martin's Press, 1989); Ladislas Farrago, *The Game of the Foxes: The Untold Story of German Espionage in the United States and Great Britain during World War II* (New York: McKay,

1971); and David Kahn, *Hitler's Spies: German Military Intelligence in World War II* (New York: Macmillan, 1978).

44. MacDonald, *Insidious Foes*, 67.

45. Ibid.

46. Ibid.

47. On the Bund, see Joachim Remak, "Friends of the New Germany: The Bund and German-American Relations," *Journal of Modern History* 29 (March 1957): 38–41; Louis De Jong, *German Fifth Column in the Second World War* (Chicago: University of Chicago Press, 1956); Alton Frye, *Nazi Germany and the American Hemisphere, 1933–1941* (New Haven, Conn.: Yale University Press, 1967); and Sander A. Diamond, *The Nazi Movement in the United States, 1924–1941* (Ithaca, N.Y.: Cornell University Press, 1974).

48. Farrago, *Game of the Foxes*, 377. Also Joseph E. Persico, *Roosevelt's Secret War: FDR and World War II Espionage* (New York: Random House, 2001), 46–47.

49. Frye, *Nazi Germany and the American Hemisphere*, 81.

50. *DGFP*, series D, 1:664–78.

51. Wiedemann, *Feldherr*, 217.

52. *Akten zur Deutschen Auswärtigen Politik*, 4:591–93.

53. Diamond, *Nazi Movement in the United States*, 127.

54. Ibid., 256–57.

55. *DGFP*, series D, 1:648–51.

56. Adolf Hitler, *The Testament of Adolf Hitler: The Hitler-Bormann Documents*, introduction by H. R. Trevor-Roper (London: Cassell, 1961), 83.

57. Ibid., 46.

CHAPTER 4

1. Domarus, *Reden*, 3:1054–55. This reference to Ickes concerned a speech the secretary of the interior had given to the Zionist Society of Cleveland. In this speech Ickes accused Hitler of having taken Western civilization back to "a period when man was unlettered, benighted, and brutal." Ickes added that the German dictator counted the "day lost when he can commit no crime against humanity." Quoted in Zalampas, *Hitler and the Third Reich in American Magazines*, 171.

2. Domarus, *Reden*, 3:1058.

3. Ibid., 1066.

4. Ibid., 1066–67.

5. Rosenman, *Public Papers*, 8:1–3.

6. *The German White Paper: Full Text of the Polish Documents Issued by the Berlin Foreign Office* (New York: Howell, Soskin and Company, 1940), 20.

7. Joseph Goebbels, *The Secret Conferences of Dr. Goebbels: The Nazi Propaganda War, 1939–43*, ed. Willi A. Boelcke (New York: E. P. Dutton & Company, 1970), 27.

8. A German edition, consisting of seven issues, was published in 1940–41 by the Foreign Office (Auswärtige Amt).

9. Hamilton Fish introduced a resolution in the House that called for an investigation of the white paper's authenticity. See United States Congress, *Congressional Record* (1941): 4:3745. Daladier sent a letter to FDR assuring him that Bullitt had not made any promises to support France in a conflict with Germany.

10. *Time Magazine*, April 8, 1940.

11. FDRL, *PSF* 188.

12. Morgan, *FDR*, 505.

13. *DGFP*, series D, 4:270.

14. Quoted in Albert Zoller, *Hitler Privat: Erlebnisbericht seiner Geheimsekretärin* (Düsseldorf: Droste-Verlag, 1949), 84.

15. Domarus, *Reden*, 3:1167.

16. Ibid., 1172.

17. Ibid., 1177. ·

18. William L. Shirer, *Berlin Diary* (1941; New York: Popular Library, 1961), 127.

19. Joseph Goebbels, *Die Tagebücher von Joseph Goebbels*, vol. 6, pt. 1, ed. Elke Fröhlich (München: Saur, 1987), 332.

20. Zalampas, *Hitler and the Third Reich in American Magazines*, 203.

21. Domarus, *Reden*, 3:1197.

22. Ibid., 1196.

23. United States Congress, *Hearings before the Joint Committee on the Investigation of the Pearl Harbor Attack*, exhibit 4, Rainbow 5 (Washington, D.C.: U.S. Government Printing Office, 1946). On the background of Rainbow 5, see Henry G. Gole, *The Road to Rainbow* (Annapolis, Md.: Naval Institute Press, 2003).

24. Beck, *Hitler's Ambivalent Attaché*, 147.

25. Steven Casey, *Cautious Crusade: Franklin D. Roosevelt, American Public Opinion, and the War against Nazi Germany* (New York: Oxford University Press, 2001), 16.

26. *DGFP*, series D, 6:376.

27. *Trial of the Major War Criminals before the International Military Tribunal*, 26:798–PS.

28. Dallek, *Roosevelt and American Foreign Policy*, 196–97.

29. Morgan, *FDR*, 511.

30. Rosenman, *Public Papers*, 8:460–63.

31. *DGFP*, series D, 7:279–81.

32. H. L. Trefousse, ed., *Germany and American Neutrality, 1939–1941* (New York: Octagon Books, 1969), 36–37.

33. Robert Divine, *The Illusion of Neutrality* (Chicago: University of Chicago Press, 1962), 307.

34. For details on James D. Mooney's business interests in Germany on behalf of General Motors, see Henry Ashby Turner, Jr., *General Motors and the Nazis* (New Haven, Conn.: Yale University Press, 2005), chap. 7.

35. Quoted in Charles Callan Tansill, *Back Door to War: The Roosevelt Foreign Policy, 1933–1941* (Chicago: Henry Regnery, 1952), 560.

36. Warren F. Kimball, ed., *Churchill and Roosevelt: The Complete Correspondence* (Princeton, N.J.: Princeton University Press, 1984), 1:3.

37. For an excellent reconstruction of the atmosphere during these dark days for Britain, see Lukacs, *Duel*; and John Lukacs, *Five Days in London: May 1940* (New Haven, Conn.: Yale University Press, 1999).

38. Thomas A. Bailey, *A Diplomatic History of the American People* (Englewood, N.J.: Prentice Hall, 1980), 713.

39. *Fuehrer Conferences on Naval Affairs* (New York: Brassey's Naval Annual, 1948), 39.

40. Friedländer, *Prelude to Downfall*, 50.

41. *Akten zur Deutschen Auswärtigen Politik*, series D, 8: Nr. 144.

42. Thomas A. Bailey and Paul B. Ryan, *Hitler vs. Roosevelt: The Undeclared Naval War* (New York: Free Press, 1979), 38–40.

43. Trefousse, *Germany and American Neutrality*, 41–42; Bailey and Ryan, *Hitler vs. Roosevelt*, 42–46.

44. Baily and Ryan, *Hitler vs. Roosevelt*, 40. Ibid., 36; also Karl Dönitz, *Memoirs of Ten Years and Twenty Days*, trans. R. H. Stevens (Annapolis, Md.: Naval Institute Press, 1990), 184.

45. Hull, *Memoirs*, 1:738.

46. Sumner Welles, *The Time for Decision* (New York: Harper & Brothers Row, 1944), 92.

47. Ibid., 95.

48. Paul Schmidt, *Statist Auf Diplomatischer Bühne* (Bonn: Athenäum, 1952), 476. Schmidt said that Welles sat at the meeting like a "block of ice," telling Hitler he was merely a "pencil with two ears."

49. Welles, *Time for Decision*, 102.

50. Ibid., 108.

51. On the Nazi-U.S. business connections, see Charles Higham, *Trading with the Enemy: An Exposé of the Nazi-American Money Plot, 1933–1945* (New York: Delacorte Press, 1983); Antony C. Sutton, *Wall Street and the Rise of Hitler* (Seal

Beach, Calif.: '76 Press, 1976); and Turner, *General Motors* (New Haven, Conn.: Yale University Press, 2005).

52. Friedländer, *Prelude to Downfall*, 76–77.

53. *DGFP*, series D, 8:51.

54. Beck, *Hitler's Ambivalent Attaché*, 149–50.

55. Domarus, *Reden*, 3:1424.

56. Hitler, *Testament*, 96.

57. Franz Halder, *Kriegstagebuch: Tägliche Aufzeichnungen des Chefs des Generalstabs des Heeres, 1939–1942*, 3 vols., ed. Hans-Adolf Jacobsen (Stuttgart: Kohlhammer, 1962–64), 1:319.

58. Churchill, *Second World War*, 2:118.

59. Martin Gilbert, *The Churchill War Papers* (London: Heinemann, 1993–2000), 2:70–71.

60. Quoted in Lukacs, *Duel*, 117.

61. Hellmuth Günther Dahms, *Die Geschichte des Zweiten Weltkriegs* (München: Herbig, 1983), 164–65.

62. Andreas Hillgruber, *Hitlers Strategie: Politik und Kriegsführung, 1940–1941* (Frankfurt: Bernard und Graefe Verlag, 1965), 93–94.

63. For the details of this breach of security, Farrago, *Game of the Foxes*, 337–45.

64. Kimball, *Churchill and Roosevelt* Correspondence, 1:37.

65. James P. Duffy, *Target America: Hitler's Plan to Attack the United States* (Guilford, Conn.: Lyons Press, 2004), 47, 79.

66. Domarus, *Reden*, 3:1524.

67. This inconsistency did not escape Lukacs in *Duel*, 119–21.

68. Erich Raeder, *Grand Admiral*, trans. Henry W. Drexel (New York: De Capo Press, 2001), 366.

69. Hull, *Memoirs*, 1:855.

70. Persico, *Roosevelt's Secret War*, 43–49; also Farrago, *Game of the Foxes*, 369–75.

71. Tully, *F.D.R., My Boss*, 244.

72. Henry L. Stimson, *On Active Service in Peace and War* (New York: Harper & Brothers, 1947), 347.

73. *The Cambridge Modern History* (Cambridge: Cambridge University Press, 1968), 12:757.

74. Raeder, *Grand Admiral*, 335–36.

75. Hitler, *Monologe*, 57, 402.

76. Hitler's thinking on the topic of territorial expansion on land, especially in Eastern Europe, can be found in *Mein Kampf*, 949–50, and in *Hitler's Second Book*, 74.

77. I. C. B. Dear, ed., *The Oxford Companion to World War II* (New York: Oxford University Press, 1995), 472–73.

78. Raeder, *Grand Admiral*, 370.

79. Domarus, *Reden*, 3:1565; also *DGFP*, series D, 11:248.

80. Halder, *Kriegstagebuch*, 2:46–50.

81. Bailey and Ryan, *Hitler vs. Roosevelt*, 83–84.

82. Churchill, *Second World War*, 2:404.

83. Quoted in Bailey and Ryan, *Hitler vs. Roosevelt*, 87.

84. Ibid., 89.

85. Robert A. Divine, *The Reluctant Belligerent: American Entry into World War II* (New York: Wiley, 1965), 89–90.

86. Ibid., 90.

87. *DGFP*, series D, 11:639.

88. Hitler, *Testament*, 78.

89. Quoted in Bailey and Ryan, *Hitler vs. Roosevelt*, 98 and 282n.

90. Rosenman, *Public Papers*, 9:517.

91. Kimball, *Churchill and Roosevelt* Correspondence, 1:106.

92. Ibid., 108.

93. Robert E. Sherwood, *Roosevelt and Hopkins: An Intimate History* (New York: Harper & Brothers, 1948), 224.

94. Rosenman, *Public Papers*, 9:635.

95. James MacGregor Burns, *Roosevelt: Soldier of Freedom, 1940–1945* (New York: Harcourt Brace Jovanovich, 1970), 46.

96. Ibid., 44.

97. Quoted in Casey, *Cautious Crusade*, 38.

98. Ibid.

99. Lukacs, *Duel*, 213.

100. Churchill, *Second World War*, 2:569.

101. Hillgruber, *Hitlers Strategie*, 363.

102. Von Kotze, *Heeresadjutant bei Hitler*, 92.

CHAPTER 5

1. Domarus, *Reden*, 4:1650.

2. Ibid.

3. Morgan, *FDR*, 597.

4. Engel, *Heeresadjutant bei Hitler*, 99.

5. Andreas Hillgruber, *Staatsmänner und Diplomaten bei Hitler* (München: DTV, 1969), 243.

6. Ibid., 247.

7. Quoted in William L. Langer and S. Everett Gleason, *The Undeclared War, 1940–1941* (New York: Harper & Brothers, 1953), 354–55.

8. Ibid., 355; also John Lukacs, *June 1941: Hitler and Stalin* (New Haven, Conn.: Yale University Press, 2006), 67.

9. The belief that the Russians were planning to attack Germany in 1941 was widely held by members of the German High Command, including General Halder, who claimed in his book *Hitler als Feldherr* (München: Dom Verlag, 1949), 36, that "we know today from reliable sources that Hitler was right to suspect a Russian attack." Halder did not reveal what these reliable sources were. Some postwar German writers (Günther Gillessen, Joachim Hoffmann, Ernst Topitsch, and Werner Maser) have tried to make the same case. They have found support from anti-Stalin historians, particularly from Victor Suvorov, a Soviet defector, who wrote a controversial book on the origins of World War II, *Ice Breaker: Who Started the Second World War?* (London: Thomas B. Beattie, 1990).

10. Gerhard L. Weinberg, *A World at Arms: A Global History of World War II* (Cambridge: Cambridge University Press, 1994), 238–39.

11. Hitler, *Testament*, 78.

12. Two recent books on these matters pertaining to Hess's flight to Britain are worth noting because they are based on extensive archival material that was not available before: Martin Allen, *The Hitler/Hess Deception* (New York: Harper, 2003); and Rainer F. Schmidt, *Rudolf Heß: Botengang eines Toren? Der Flug nach Großbritannien vom 10, Mai 1941* (München: Econ Ullstein List Verlag, 2000).

13. Schmidt, *Rudolf Heß*, 278–79.

14. Hess allegedly had a discussion with Hitler in Berlin about the peace offer to Britain just a week before he flew to Scotland. On that occasion, according to Rüdiger Hess, Rudolf Hess's son, the conversation ended with Hess saying to Hitler, "and, if, my Führer, my plan . . . should fail, if fate should decide against me, it can have no evil consequences for you or Germany. You can drop me at any time—say that I am mad." Quoted in Allen, *Hitler/Hess Deception*, 244.

15. The secret files relating to the Hess affair are closed until 2018, much longer than the usual thirty-year restriction. See Schmidt, *Rudolf Heß*, 15. It is doubtful that even if *all* the documents were declassified the truth would emerge out of any of them. In this author's judgment, the really sensitive, perhaps even politically explosive, documents have long been destroyed.

16. Allen, *Hitler/Hess Deception*, 285–86.

17. Kimball, Correspondence, 1:187.

18. Ibid., 187–88.

19. Warren F. Kimball, *Forged in War: Roosevelt, Churchill and the Second World War* (New York: Morrow, 1997), 76, 352. The British did not share Ultra secrets until 1942, and then only selectively.

20. See the *New York Times* report of November 26, 1993, about the British

government releasing documents from Churchill's secret wartime intelligence archives. No smoking gun has been found to date among the 1,273 files representing the daily intelligence reports given to Churchill in 1941 and 1942. Conspiracy theories still abound. The evidence presented by cryptography experts shows at best that Churchill or Roosevelt *should* have known the facts, not that they *must* have known them. That they must have known about plans regarding the attack on Pearl Harbor, among other things, is the subject of two prominent revisionist works: James Rusbridger and Eric Nave, *Betrayal at Pearl Harbor: How Churchill Lured Roosevelt into World War II* (New York: Summit, 1991) and Robert Stinnett, *Day of Deceit: The Truth about FDR and Pearl Harbor* (New York: Touchstone, 2000).

21. Divine, *Roosevelt and World War II*, 43.

22. Persico, *Roosevelt's Secret War*, 43.

23. John Cudahy, *The Armies March: A Personal Report by John Cudahy* (New York: Charles Scribner's Sons, 1941), 181–83.

24. Frye, *Nazi Germany and the American Hemisphere*, 158ff.

25. MacDonald, *Insidious Foes*, 126–28.

26. Ibid., 138–39.

27. *Morgenthau Diaries* (May 20, 1940), FDRL.

28. Domarus, *Reden*, 4:1726.

29. *Nazi Conspiracy and Aggression*, ed., Office of the United States Chief of Counsel for Prosecution of Axis Criminality (Washington, D.C.: U.S. Government Printing Office, 1946–48), 8:645–46.

30. Bullock, *Hitler*, 652.

31. Hitler, *Monologe*, 110.

32. Rainer Zitelmann, "Zur Begründung des Lebensraum-Motivs in Hitlers Weltanschauung," in *Der Zweite Weltkrieg: Analysen, Grundzüge, Forschungsbilanz*, ed. Wolfgang Michalka (Weyarn, Austria: Seehamer Verlag, 1997), 551–67.

33. Ibid., 560.

34. Geoffrey Roberts, *Stalin's Wars* (New Haven, Conn.: Yale University Press, 2006), 15.

35. Susan Butler, ed., *Dear Mr. Stalin: The Complete Correspondence between Franklin D. Roosevelt and Joseph V. Stalin* (New Haven, Conn.: Yale University Press, 2005), 36.

36. Robert Conquest, *Reflections on a Ravaged Century* (New York: Norton, 2000), 123.

37. Davies, *Mission to Moscow*, 511.

38. Quoted in Lukacs, *Duel*, 215.

39. Hitler, *Testament*, 59.

40. Ibid., 64.

41. Hitler, *Monologe*, 110.

42. Raeder, *Grand Admiral*, 347.

43. Dönitz, *Memoirs*, 189.

44. Burns, *Soldier of Freedom*, 50–51.

45. Hillgruber, *Staatsmänner bei Hitler*, 299–300.

46. H. R. Trevor-Roper, ed., *Blitzkrieg to Defeat: Hitler's War Directives, 1933–1945* (New York: Holt, Rinehart and Winston, 1965), 82ff.

47. *Akten zur Deutschen Auswärtigen Politik* 13: 2:834; also Hillgruber, *Staatsmänner bei Hitler*, 291–303.

48. Lukacs, *Last European War*, 505–6.

49. Ian Kershaw, *Popular Opinion and Political Dissent in the Third Reich: Bavaria, 1933–1945* (New York: Oxford University Press, 1984), 340–41.

50. Bailey and Ryan, *Hitler vs. Roosevelt*, 165ff.

51. Kimball, *Forged in War*, 103; Orville H. Bullitt, ed., *For the President: Personal and Secret; Correspondence between Franklin Roosevelt and William C. Bullitt* (Boston: Houghton Mifflin, 1972), 512; Dallek, *Roosevelt and American Foreign Policy*, 285.

52. Bullitt, *For the President*, 512.

53. Bailey and Ryan, *Hitler vs. Roosevelt*, 200.

54. Morgan, *FDR*, 602–3.

55. Langer and Gleason, *Undeclared War*, 743.

56. FDRL, *Harry Hopkins Papers*, Box 308.

57. There is some evidence that Hitler was beginning to have qualms about defeating the Russians, and he wondered whether German reverses in Russia might convince the Japanese to bolt the Tripartite Pact. He wanted to string the Japanese along and show them that the German army was still invincible. A document entitled "Notebook of Hitler's Historiographer," put forward by Marianne Feuersenger, the former secretary of Major General Walter Scherff, who kept the official war diary of the Wehrmacht, indicates that Hitler was greatly concerned about Japan's reaction to German reverses, especially in late November and early December 1941. Marianne Feuersenger, *Im Vorzimmer der Macht: Aufzeichnungen aus dem Wehrmachtsführungsstab und Führerhauptquartier, 1940–1945* (München: Herbig, 1999), 106–10.

58. Domarus, *Reden*, 4:1756.

59. Ibid., 1778.

60. Roberts, *Stalin's Wars*, 88.

61. Andrew Nagorski, *The Greatest Battle: Stalin, Hitler, and the Desperate Struggle for Moscow That Changed the Course of World War II* (New York: Simon and Schuster, 2007), 213–15.

62. Quoted in Nagorski, *Greatest Battle*, 5.

63. ED 100, *Hewel Tagebuch* (December 8, 1941), Institut für Zeitgeschichte (hereafter cited as IfZ); also Kershaw, *Hitler: Nemesis*, 2:442.

64. *DGFP*, series D, 13:868–70.

65. Kershaw, *Hitler: Nemesis*, 2:444.

66. Waite, *Psychopathic God*, 468–76; also Eberhard Jäckel, *Hitler in History* (Hanover, N.H.: Brandeis University Press, 1984), chap. 4.

67. Domarus, *Reden*, 3:1794.

68. Ibid., 1800.

69. Ibid., 1803.

70. Ibid.

71. Christian Gerlach, *Krieg, Ernährung, Völkermord: Deutsche Vernichtungspolitik im Zweiten Weltkrieg* (Zürich: Pendo Verlag, 2001), 114–20.

72. For details of Hitler the dissembler, see Gerald Fleming, *Hitler and the Final Solution* (Berkeley: University of California Press, 1982), chap. 2.

73. Domarus, *Reden*, 4:2237.

74. Martin Gilbert, *The Holocaust: A History of the Jews of Europe during the Second World War* (New York: Holt, Rinehart and Winston, 1985), 239–40.

75. Goebbels, *Tagebücher*, pt. 2, 2:498–99.

76. Few historians have paid attention to Hitler's belief that the United States leadership had fallen prey to Jewish interests. Hitler increasingly believed that Roosevelt had surrounded himself with warmongering Jews and that one successful way of thwarting their influence was to threaten the Jews of Germany and Europe. Jeffrey Herf has marshaled some important evidence to illustrate this particular aspect of Hitler's Judeophobia in his book *The Jewish Enemy: Nazi Propaganda during World War II and the Holocaust* (Cambridge, Mass.: Harvard University Press, 2006), esp. chap. 4.

77. Gerlach, *Krieg, Ernährung, Völkermord*, 116–17.

78. For details of Kaufman's book, see Wolfgang Benz, "Judenvernichtung als Notwehr? Die Legenden um Theodore N. Kaufman," *Vierteljahreshefte für Zeitgeschichte* 29 (October 1981): 615–30.

79. Theodore N. Kaufman, *Germany Must Perish* (Newark, N.J.: Argyl Press, 1941), 5–6.

80. Goebbels, *Tagebücher*, pt. 1, 2:155.

81. Ibid., 271.

82. *Völkische Beobachter*, July 24, 1941.

83. Ibid., 117.

84. *Sammlung Irving*, IfZ; also Martin Broszat, "Hitler und die Genesis der Endlösung," *Vierteljahreshefte für Zeitgeschichte* 25 (October 1977): 749.

85. Richard Rhodes, *Masters of Death: The SS Einsatzgruppen and the Invention of the Holocaust* (New York: Knopf, 2002), 232–33.

86. Jäckel, *Hitler in History*, 58.

87. Walter Laqueur, *The Terrible Secret: Suppression of the Truth about Hitler's "Final Solution"* (New York: Penguin, 1982), 3.

88. Ibid., 9.

89. Gilbert, *Holocaust*, 186.

90. Ibid., 94–95.

91. Rosen, *Saving the Jews*, 5.

92. Ibid., xxiii.

93. Ian Kershaw, *Fateful Choices: Ten Decisions That Changed the World, 1940–1941* (New York: Penguin, 2007), 288–89.

94. *DGFP*, series D, 11:1062.

95. Kershaw, *Fateful Choices*, 198.

96. Gerhard L. Weinberg, "Germany's Declaration of War on the United States," in *Germany and American Neutrality, 1939–1941: Essays on Problems of International Relations and Immigration*, ed. Hans L. Trefousse (New York: Brooklyn College Press, 1980), 60–61.

97. Hillgruber, *Zweite Weltkrieg*, 89.

98. Halder, *Kriegstagebuch*, 3:295.

99. Quoted in Percy Ernst Schramm, *Hitler als militärischer Führer, Erkenntnisse und Erfahrungen aus dem Kriegstagebuch des Oberkommandos der Wehrmacht* (Frankfurt: Athenäum, 1962), 154.

100. Kershaw, *Hitler: Nemesis*, 440–41.

101. Hitler's private valet, Heinz Linge, and his pilot, Hans Baur, have left brief accounts of this curious event at Poltava. See Hans Baur, *Ich flog Mächtige der Erde* (Kempten, Allgäu: Pröpster Verlag, 1956), 212–13; for Heinz Linge's postwar testimony, see Domarus, *Reden*, 4:1788–89.

102. Domarus, *Reden*, 4:1788–89.

103. Lukacs, *Last European War*, 158.

CHAPTER 6

1. Thomas Fleming, *The New Dealers' War: F.D.R. and the War within World War II* (New York: Basic Books, 2001), 107. See also, Michael Gannon, *Drumbeat: The Dramatic True Story of Germany's First U-boat Attacks along the American Coast in World War II* (New York: Harper & Row, 1990).

2. Hitler, *Hitlers Tischgespräche*, 134.

3. Martin Vogt, ed., *Herbst 1941 im Führerhauptquartier: Berichte Werner Koeppens an seinen Minister Alfred Rosenberg* (Koblenz: Bundesarchiv, 2002), 30–31.

4. Ibid., 31.

5. Ibid., 98–99.

6. Quoted in Jean Edward Smith, *FDR* (New York: Random House, 2008), 572.

7. Hitler, *Monologe*, 179.

8. Hitler, *Hitlers Tischgespräche*, 155.

9. Hitler, *Monologe*, 255.

10. Hitler, *Hitlers Tischgespräche*, 141. See also *Time*, March 6 and May 8, 1939.

11. Hitler, *Hitlers Tischgespräche*, 141–42.

12. Ross described Roosevelt's condition at some length in his book *Amerikas Schickssalstunde*, 92.

13. A typical anti-American propaganda pamphlet was the widely circulated document "Amerika und Europa," published under the auspices of Robert Ley's Reichsorganisationsleitung NSDAP. Why the Americans were a nation without a cause (*Volk ohne Kampfziehl*), an army without a banner, was the topic of Helmut Mehringer, *Die Armee ohne Banner* (Dresden: Franz Müller Verlag, 1943). For one of many mass-produced propaganda pieces in picture form, juxtaposing contrasting images of decadent Amerika behind the façade of wealth and glitter, see Arnold Hammer, *USA hinter den Kulissen* (Berlin: Verlag Scherl, 1942).

14. Eric Linklater, *Juan in America* (Oxford: Alden Press, 1931).

15. Hitler, *Monologe*, 321.

16. Ibid.

17. Helmut Heiber and David M. Glantz, eds., *Hitler and His Generals: Military Conferences 1942–1945* (New York: Enigma Books, 2003), 92.

18. Siegfried Kracauer, *From Caligari to Hitler: A Psychological History of the German Film* (Princeton, N.J.: Princeton University Press, 1947), 149.

19. Joseph Goebbels, *Das Eherne Herz: Reden und Aufsätze aus den Jahren 1941/42* (München: Franz Eher Verlag, 1943), 99–104.

20. Ibid., 104. See also Kershaw, *Hitler: Nemesis*, 457.

21. Goebbels, *Das Eherne Herz*, 104.

22. Ibid.

23. Klaus-Dietmar Henke, *Die Amerikanische Besetzung Deutschlands* (München: Oldenbourg Verlag, 1996), 87ff.

24. Christof Mauch, *The Shadow War against Hitler: The Covert Operations of America's Wartime Intelligence Service*, trans. Jeremian Riemer (New York: Columbia University Press, 2003), 39.

25. Fleming, *New Dealers' War*, 45.

26. Quoted in Casey, *Cautious Crusade*, 57.

27. Ibid.

28. U.S. House of Representatives, Committee on Foreign Affairs, 78th Congress, 1st sess., "The German People: Testimony of Mr. Emil Ludwig" (March 26, 1943).

29. Casey, *Cautious Crusade*, 50.

30. On the anti-German campaign in the United States, see Benjamin Colby, 'Twas a Famous Victory: Deception and Propaganda in the War with Germany (New Rochelle, N.J.: Arlington House, 1974).

31. Henke, *Die Amerikanische Besetzung Deutschlands*, 72–73.

32. For details of the Morgenthau plan and what the secretary of the U.S. Treasury had in mind for the Germans, see Henry Morgenthau Jr., *Germany Is Our Problem* (New York: Harper & Brothers, 1945).

33. Casey, *Cautious Crusader*, 39.

34. George Kennan, *Memoirs, 1925–1950* (Boston: Little, Brown and Company, 1967), 123.

35. Walter C. Langer, *The Mind of Adolf Hitler* (New York: Basic Books, 1972), 240.

36. On the S-Project, see Steven Casey "Franklin Roosevelt, Ernst Putzi Hanfstaengl and the S-Project," *Journal of Contemporary History* 35 (2000): 339–59. Hanfstaengl left his own account in his book, *Hitler: Missing Years*, 287–99.

37. Conradi, *Hitler's Piano Player* (New York: Carroll & Graf Publishers, 2004), 283.

38. Mauch, *Shadow War*, 49.

39. Jonas, *United States and Germany*, 261.

40. Domarus, *Reden*, 4:1829.

41. Adam Tooze, *The Wages of Destruction: The Making and Breaking of the Nazi Economy* (New York: Penguin, 2006), 506–12.

42. Albert Speer, *Inside the Third Reich: Memoirs of Albert Speer*, trans. Richard and Clara Winston (New York: Macmillan, 1970), 225.

43. Mark Walker, *German National Socialism and the Quest for Nuclear Power* (Cambridge: Cambridge University Press, 1989), 51–52. See also Thomas Power, *Heisenberg's War: The Secret History of the German Bomb* (New York: Knopf, 1993), 478–84.

44. Speer, *Inside the Third Reich*, 225–26.

45. Power, *Heisenberg's War*, 95–97.

46. Speer, *Inside the Third Reich*, 227.

47. Morgan, *FDR*, 515.

48. Andreas Hillgruber, *Der 2. Weltkrieg: Kriegsziele und Strategie der großen Mächte* (Stuttgart: Kohlhammer, 1983), 97.

49. Goebbels recorded that the news from Stalingrad caused a shock wave among the public Joseph Goebbels, *Joseph Goebbels Tagebücher, 1943–1945*, ed. Ralf Georg Reuth (München: Piper Verlag, 2000), 5:1891.

50. Quoted in Simon Berthon and Joanna Potts, *Warlords* (New York: Da Capo Press, 2006), 149.

51. Sherwood, *Roosevelt and Hopkins*, 528.

52. Lukacs, *June 1941*, 51–52.

53. It was not until 1990 that the Russian government admitted that the Katyn atrocities were committed by the NKVD. That year two additional graves were discovered, bringing the total of murdered Polish officers to approximately 15,000. President Yeltsin turned over the documents that showed that the killings were ordered by Stalin.

54. Andreas Hillgruber, "Hitler und die USA 1933–1945," in *Europas Mitte*, ed. Otmar Franz (Göttingen: Muster-Schmidt, 1987), 139.

55. On the peace feelers between 1942 and 1945, see H. W. Koch, "The Specter of a Separate Peace in the East: Russo-German Peace Feelers, 1942–44," *Journal of Contemporary History* 10 (1975): 531–49; Vojtech Mastny, "Stalin and the Prospect of a Separate Peace in World War II *American Historical Review* 77 (February 1972): 1365–88; Ingeborg Fleischhauer, *Die Chance des Sonderfriedens: Deutsch-sowjetische Geheimgespräche, 1941–1945* (Berlin: Siedler Verlag, 1986); Richard Breitman, "A Deal with the Nazi Dictatorship? Himmler's Alleged Peace Emissaries in Autumn 1943," *Journal of Contemporary History* 30 (1995): 411–30.

56. Joachim Ribbentrop, *The Ribbentrop Memoirs*, intro. Alan Bullock (London: Weidenfeld and Nicolson, 1954), 169.

57. Hillgruber, *Der 2. Weltkrieg*, 98.

58. Mastny, "Stalin and the Prospects," 1365.

59. Roberts, *Stalin's Wars*, 12.

60. Evan Mawdsley, *Thunder in the East: The Nazi-Soviet War, 1941–1945* (London: Hodder Arnold, 2005), 247.

61. See Nisbet, *Roosevelt and Stalin*.

62. Butler, *Dear Mr. Stalin*, 87–90. Also Sherwood, *Roosevelt and Hopkins*, 639–40.

63. Nisbet, *Roosevelt and Stalin*, 11.

64. Anne Armstrong, *Unconditional Surrender: The Impact of the Casablanca Policy upon World War II* (New Brunswick, N.J.: Rutgers University Press, 1961), 6.

65. Sherwood, *Roosevelt and Hopkins*, 696–97.

66. Ibid., 697.

67. Fireside chat of December 29, 1940.

68. Alfred Vagts, "Unconditional Surrender: Vor und nach 1945," *Vierteljahreshefte für Zeitgeschichte*, no. 3 (July 1959): 288. Vagts shows how the concept of unconditional surrender was embraced by many American politicians, especially those who had played a role in World War I. He also shows that both the Germans and the Japanese pursued similar policies of unconditional surrender toward their enemies.

69. Ibid.

70. Von Below, *At Hitler's Side*, 161.

71. Ribbentrop, *Memoirs*, 154.

72. Halder, *Hitler als Feldherr*, 36.

73. Lukacs, *June 1941*, 28.

74. Roberts, *Stalin's Wars*, 11.

75. Quoted in Armstrong, *Unconditional Surrender*, 19.

76. Domarus, *Reden*, 3:1517, 4:1967.

77. Vagts, "Unconditional Surrender," 291.

78. Weizsäcker, *Erinnerungen*, 342.

79. Chester Wilmot, *The Struggle for Europe* (London: Collins, 1952), 123.

80. B. H. Liddell Hart, *The German Generals Talk* (New York: Morrow, 1948), 292-93.

81. Armstrong, *Unconditional Surrender*, 262.

82. Ibid., 11.

83. Ibid., 55.

84. Ibid., 56.

CHAPTER 7

1. Roy Jenkins, *Churchill: A Biography* (New York: Farrar, Strauss and Giroux, 2001), 700-701.

2. Churchill, *Second World War*, 4:478.

3. Ibid., 475.

4. Frances Perkins, *The Roosevelt I Knew* (New York: Viking, 1946), 87.

5. Kennan's views can be found in his introduction to Bullitt's memoirs, *For the President: Personal and Secret* (Boston: Houghton Mifflin Company, 1972), xiv.

6. Bullitt, *For the President*, 587.

7. Ibid., 579.

8. Fleming, *New Dealers' War*, 378.

9. Persico, *Roosevelt's Secret War*, 381-86.

10. Ibid., 386.

11. Ibid., 381.

12. Wolfgang Leonhard, *Die Revolution entlässt ihre Kinder* (1955; Köln: Kiepenheuer & Witsch, 2008), 362. For the whole episode, which Leonhard calls the "The Withdrawal of the Armistice Offer," see 360-63.

13. Ibid., 363.

14. In addition to his own account, there is a document dating to the fall of 1945 that concerns Kleist's interrogation by the Allies. It can be found in the National

Archives and Records Administration (NA) 226, entry 125, box 29, folder 407. The date of the interrogation was October 27, 1945.

15. Peter Kleist, *Zwischen Hitler und Stalin, 1939–1945* (Bonn: Athenäum Verlag, 1950), 241.

16. Ibid., 246.

17. Ribbentrop, *Memoirs*, 170.

18. Ibid., 171; also Koch, "The Specter of a Separate Peace in the East," 536.

19. Kleist, *Zwischen Hitler und Stalin*, 223.

20. Ibid., 224.

21. Ibid., 224–25.

22. Walter Görlitz, *History of the German General Staff* (New York: Praeger, 1953), 411.

23. Ribbentrop, *Memoirs*, 163.

24. Kleist, *Zwischen Hitler und Stalin*, 225.

25. Heinz Guderian, *Erinnerungen eines Soldaten* (Heidelberg: Kurt Vorwinckel Verlag, 1950), 279–80.

26. See Stalin's letter of June 11, 1943, in which he accused both Roosevelt and Churchill of going back on their word, given at the beginning of the year, that a second front would be opened in 1943. Butler, *Dear Mr. Stalin*, 138–39.

27. Roberts, *Stalin's Wars*, 72.

28. Sherwood, *Roosevelt and Hopkins*, 734.

29. Kahn, *Hitler's Spies*, 538.

30. Ibid., 176.

31. Ibid., 340–45. For Franz von Papen's account, see *Memoirs*, trans. Brian Connell (New York: E. P. Dutton, 1953), chap. 28.

32. Heiber and Glantz, *Hitler and His Generals*, 311–12.

33. Ibid., 314.

34. Ibid., 139.

35. Goebbels, *Joseph Goebbels Tagebücher*, 5:1949–50.

36. Ibid., 1959.

37. Gerhard Weinberg, *Visions of Victory: The Hopes of Eight World War II Leaders* (Cambridge: Cambridge University Press, 2005), 35–36.

38. Heinz Höhne, *Canaris: Patriot im Zwielicht* (München: C. Bertelsmann, n.d.), 536–37.

39. Ibid., 461–62.

40. Ibid., 462.

41. Ibid., 463–64; Agostino von Hassell and Sigrid MacRae, *Alliances of Enemies: The Untold Story of the Secret American and German Collaboration to End World War II* (New York: St. Martin's Press, 2006), 132–34.

42. Louis P. Lochner, *Always the Unexpected: A Book of Reminiscences* (New York: Macmillan, 1956), 294–95.

43. Papen, *Memoirs*, 504.

44. Walter Schellenberg, *Hitler's Secret Service*, trans. Louis Hagen with an introduction by Alan Bullock (New York: Pyramid Books, 1958), chap. 29.

45. Ibid., 308–12.

46. Felix Kersten, *The Kersten Memoirs, 1940–1945*, trans. Constantine Fitzgibbon and James Oliver with an introduction by H. R. Trevor-Roper (New York: Macmillan, 1957), 11.

47. See Höhne's account of the SS and the German resistance in *Order of the Death's Head*, chap. 17.

48. Dieter Ehlers, *Technik und Moral einer Verschwörung, 20, Juli 1944* (Frankfurt: Athenäum, 1964), 158–59. One day after the failed assassination on Hitler's life (July 21, 1944), Himmler made a revealing, even slightly amusing, comment. He said that "as Reichsführer SS, with all the news sources behind me and having a feeling for political developments, I was able [konnte ich] for a long time to expect an undertaking . . . by elements on the political scale. I knew that it would eventually come." Peter Longerich, *Himmler: Eine Biographie* (München: Siedler, 2008), 717. Did he know (*kennen*)? Perhaps. Was he able (*können*) to prevent the attempt on Hitler's life? Obviously not.

49. Schellenberg, *Hitler's Secret Service*, 338; Schellenberg's statement of August 6, 1945, NA 226, 125–A, box 2, folder 21.

50. Fleischhauer, *Die Chance des Sonderfriedens*, 90–97.

51. Breitman, "Deal with the Nazi Dictatorship?" 424.

52. Herbert Romerstein and Eric Breindel, *The Verona Secrets: Exposing Soviet Espionage and America's Traitors* (Washington, D.C.: Regnery, 2001), 192–93.

53. Sherwood, *Roosevelt and Hopkins*, 748.

54. Bohlen later wrote that FDR's remarks about reforming India from the bottom up revealed his ignorance about the Soviet Union. According to Bohlen, FDR undoubtedly viewed the Soviet coup d'état of 1917 as a genuine revolution rather than the seizure of power by a small Bolshevik minority. See Charles E. Bohlen, *Witness to History, 1929–1969* (New York: Norton, 1973), 140–41.

55. Quoted in Berthon and Potts, *Warlords*, 216–17.

56. Ibid., 223.

57. Ibid.

58. Ibid., 224.

59. John Lukacs, *The Great Powers and Eastern Europe* (New York: American Book Company, 1953), 557.

60. Nisbet, *Roosevelt and Stalin*, 46, goes too far when he says that Roosevelt

gave Stalin everything he wanted at Tehran; all he asked in return was that "Stalin showed some concern to the needs of his reelection campaign."

61. Hillgruber, *Der 2. Weltkrieg*, 128.

62. Trevor-Roper, *Blitzkrieg to Defeat*, 149.

CHAPTER 8

1. Domarus, *Reden*, 4:2072. In his Spandau diary, Speer reports Hitler as saying that German cities would not only be rebuilt in a few years but would be built on a more monumental scale than ever before. Albert Speer, *Spandauer Tagebücher* (Frankfurt: Propyläen, 1975), 309.

2. Heiber and Glantz, *Hitler and His Generals*, 415.

3. Ibid., 317.

4. On Hitler's west wall, see Alan F. Wilt, *The Atlantic Wall, 1941–1944: Hitler's Defenses for D-Day* (New York: Enigma Books, 2004)

5. Guderian, *Erinnerungen*, 295.

6. Erich Manstein, *Verlorene Siege* (Bonn: Athenäum, 1955), 571.

7. Britain protested this Soviet claim. See E. L. Woodward, *British Foreign Policy in the Second World War*, vol. 3 (London: H. M. Stationery Office, 1962), 106–8. Weizsäcker mentioned this Soviet report in a letter to his mother, dated January 29, 1944, in *Weizsäcker Papiere*, 367.

8. Goebbels, *Joseph Goebbels Tagebücher*, 5:2000ff.

9. One of the most revealing and rambling judgments that Hitler delivered on the Americans, including the upcoming election of 1944,occurred in late December 1943 at the Wolfsschanze. See Heiber and Glantz, *Hitler and His Generals*, 307–22.

10. Hull, *Memoirs*, 2:1573–74; also see Foreign Relations of the United States (FRUS), 1944, 1:582. FDR's reading of American history was not accurate. Grant did not demand that Lee surrender unconditionally at Appomattox. Grant had demanded unconditional surrender from the confederate commander at Fort Donelson in 1862, which journalists widely publicized because Grant's initials, Ulysses S., coincided with unconditional surrender. The term subsequently became a byword for Grant.

11. Papen, *Memoirs*, 522–23.

12. Kimball, *Churchill and Roosevelt*, 3:134.

13. FRUS, 1944, 1:521

14. Lukacs, *Hitler of History*, 166–68.

15. Domarus, *Reden*, 4:1915.

16. Ibid., 2104.

17. Von Below, *At Hitler's Side*, 203.

18. Gert Buchheit, *Hitler der Feldherr: Die Zerstörung einer Legende* (Rastatt: Grote, 1958), 396–97.

19. Hans Speidel, *Invasion 1944: Ein Beitrag zu Rommels und des Reiches Schicksal* (Tübingen: Wunderlich, 1949), 118; Buchheit, *Hitler der Feldherr*, 416–20.

20. Heiber and Glantz, *Hitler and His Generals*, 424.

21. Sherwood, *Roosevelt and Hopkins*, 830.

22. Ibid., 820.

23. Quoted in Robert H. Ferrell, *The Dying President: Franklin D. Roosevelt, 1944–1945* (Columbia: University of Missouri Press, 1998), 89.

24. Ibid., 151.

25. Goebbels, *Joseph Goebbels Tagebücher*, 5:2060.

26. Von Below, *At Hitler's Side*, 205–6.

27. Buchheit, *Hitler der Feldherr*, 425.

28. On Operation Valkyrie and the German Resistance, see Peter Hoffmann, *The History of the German Resistance, 1933–1945* (Cambridge, Mass.: MIT Press, 1977); and the same author's *Stauffenberg: A Family History, 1905–1944* (Cambridge: Cambridge University Press, 1995); Joachim Fest, *Staatsstreich: Der lange Weg zum 20. Juli* (Berlin: Siedler, 1999); Hans Rothfels, *Die deutsche Opposition gegen Hitler: Eine Würdigung* (Frankfurt: Fischer Verlag, 1958); Klemens von Klemperer, *German Resistance against Hitler: The Search for Allies Abroad* (Oxford: Clarendon Press, 1992); Gerhart Ritter, *The German Resistance: Carl Goerdeler's Struggle against Tyranny* (New York: Praeger, 1958); and Fabian von Schlabrendorff, *Offiziere gegen Hitler* (Zürich: Europa Verlag, 1946).

29. Armstrong, *Unconditional Surrender*, 210.

30. Ibid., 209.

31. Quoted in Casey, *Cautious Crusader*, 156.

32. Lochner, *Always the Unexpected*, 294.

33. Ibid., 294–95.

34. This comment was made at a midday situation conference on September 1, 1944. See Heiber and Glantz, *Hitler and His Generals*, 489.

35. Goebbels, *Joseph Goebbels, Tagebücher*, 5:2090.

36. Quoted in Max Hastings, *Overlord: D-Day and the Battle for Normandy* (New York: Simon & Schuster, 1984), 311.

37. Heiber and Glantz, *Hitler and His Generals*, 466ff.

38. Ibid., 467.

39. Ibid., 468.

40. Ibid.

41. Kershaw, *Hitler, 1936–1945*, 726–28; Fritz Redlich, *Hitler: Diagnosis of a Destructive Prophet* (New York: Oxford University Press, 1999), 204–20.

42. The pills were harmless. See Redlich, *Hitler*, 129, 209–13.

43. On the various medications Morell gave Hitler, the best source is Morell's diary, unearthed from the National Archives by David Irving and published under the title *The Secret Diaries of Hitler's Doctor* (New York: Macmillan, 1983). Other important works on Hitler's medical condition are Redlich, *Hitler*; and Ernst Günther Schenck, *Patient Hitler: Eine Medizinische Biographie* (Augsburg: Bechtermünz Verlag, 2000).

44. Werner Maser, *Hitler*, trans. Peter and Betty Ross (London: Allen Lane, 1973), 215.

45. This claim was made by Leonard L. Heston and Renate Heston in their book *The Medical Casebook of Adolf Hitler* (New York: Stein and Day, 1979), 121. The authors do not prove their remarkably reductionist argument that there was "one basic cause for Hitler's psychiatric disability, amphetamine toxicity, and no other diagnosis."

46. Fest, *Hitler*, 667.

47. Goebbels, *Goebbels Diaries*, 306–7.

48. Schenck, *Patient Hitler*, 415–16; Redlich, *Hitler*, 232–35.

49. Redlich, *Hitler*, 235–36, 230.

50. This was the thesis propounded by Waite, *Psychopathic God*, 176–77. Waite made this risky theory an intimate part of his psychological profile of Hitler. As a result, he was widely criticized, but this should not distract from the fact that his book was a pioneering effort to remind historians that private neuroses actually shape public policies.

51. Historians have almost entirely ignored Eric Voegelin's brilliant series of lectures delivered at the University of Munich in 1964. These lectures are now available in English under the title *Hitler and the Germans*, trans., ed., and with an introduction by Detlev Clemens and Brenda Purcell (Columbia: University of Missouri Press, 1999)

52. Redlich, *Hitler*, 256.

53. Ferrell, *Dying President*, esp. chap. 2. Ferrell has also written a briefer account of Roosevelt's illness in his book on presidential illnesses, titled *Ill-Advised: Presidential Health and Public Trust* (Columbia: University of Missouri Press, 1992), 28–48.

54. Ferrell, *Ill-Advised*, 33.

55. Berthon and Potts, *Warlords*, 256.

56. John Morton Blum, ed., *From the Morgenthau Diaries: Years of War, 1941–1945* (Boston: Houghton Mifflin, 1967), 342.

57. Fleming, *New Dealers' War*, 428.

58. For the relevant documentation and commentary on the Morgenthau plan, see Warren F. Kimball, *Swords into Ploughshares: The Morgenthau Plan for Defeated Nazi Germany, 1943–1946* (Philadelphia: J. B. Lippincott, 1976).

59. FRUS, 1944, 1:E466–67; Morgenthau, "Program to Prevent Germany from Starting a World War III," in Morgenthau, *Germany Is Our Problem,* 1–4; Kimball, *Swords into Ploughshares,* Documents 1 (*The Quebec Memorandum*) and Document 15 (*The Morgenthau Plan for Germany*).

60. Quoted in Morgan, *FDR,* 734.

61. For a lively re-creation of the Quebec Conference, see Michael Beschloss, *The Conquerors: Roosevelt, Truman and the Destruction of Hitler's Germany, 1941–1945* (New York: Simon and Schuster, 2002), chap. 13. Also Conrad Black, *Franklin Delano Roosevelt: Champion of Freedom* (New York: Public Affairs, 2003), 993.

62. Stimson, *On Active Service,* 573.

63. Ibid.

64. Ibid., 578.

65. Ibid., 581.

66. Ibid.

67. *Völkischer Beobachter,* September 28, 1944. Also see Speer, *Inside the Third Reich,* 433.

68. On the reaction of the German people to the American military successes, see Marlis Steinert, *Hitlers Krieg und die Deutschen* (Düsseldorf: Econ Verlag, 1970), chap. 4.

69. Domarus, *Reden,* 4:2185.

70. Ibid.

71. FDR, foreword to Morgenthau, *Germany Is Our Problem.*

72. Longerich, *Himmler,* 741.

73. Kershaw, *Hitler, 1936–1945,* 729–30.

74. Ibid., 730. The text can be found in Goebbels, *Die Tagebücher von Joseph Goebbels,* vol. 13, pt. 2, 536–42; also *BA Koblenz,* NL. 118/100.

75. Hillgruber, *Der 2. Weltkrieg,* 137.

76. Heiber and Glantz, *Hitler and His Generals,* 540.

77. Speer, *Inside the Third Reich,* 415.

78. Henke, *Die amerikanische Besetzung Deutschlands,* 339.

79. Ibid., 340.

80. Heiber and Glantz, *Hitler and His Generals,* 584.

81. On the Malmédy atrocities, see James J. Weingartner, *Crossroads to Death: The Story of the Malmédy Massacre and Trial* (Berkeley: University of California Press, 1979); and Henke, *Die amerikanische Besetzung Deutschlands,* 325–28.

82. O. D. Tolischus, *New York Times,* September 12, 1939.

CHAPTER 9

1. Quoted in Henke, *Die Amerikanische Besetzung Deutschlands*, 170.

2. Ibid., 90.

3. Ibid.

4. Domarus, *Reden*, 4:2181–82.

5. Quoted in Lukacs, *Hitler of History*, 258.

6. Domarus, *Reden*, 4:2185.

7. Quoted in Cornelius Ryan, *The Last Battle* (London: Collins, 1966), 87–94. Ryan first heard about the existence of this document from a remark Jodl made during his interrogation at the Nuremberg trials when he said that the reason he did not advise Hitler to capitulate was because of the Allied policy of unconditional surrender, a policy that was confirmed for the German leadership by the Eclipse documents. He told the court that "the gentlemen of the British delegation know what that is." They did not know because the documents were still kept so secret that they knew nothing about them. Frau Luise Jodl subsequently confirmed the story because she had seen the documents. Her story can be found in her book *Jenseits des Endes: Leben und Sterben des Generaloberst Alfred Jodl* (Vienna: Verlag Fritz Molden, 1976), 121.

8. *Das Reich*, February 23, 1945.

9. Fest, *Hitler*, 731.

10. Fritz Hesse, *Das Spiel um Deutschland* (München: Paul List Verlag, 1953), 387.

11. On Ribbentrop's peace initiative, see Reimer Hansen, "Ribbentrops Friedensfühler im Frühjahr 1945," *Geschichte in Wissenschaft und Unterricht 12* (1967): 716–30.

12. Hesse, *Spiel um Deutschland*, 393–97.

13. For a careful analysis of the *Sprachregelung* and German peace feelers extended to the Western powers, see Hansjakob Stehle, "Deutsche Friedensfühler bei den Westmächten im Februar/März 1945," in *Nationalsozialistische Diktatur, 1933–1945: Eine Bilanz*, ed. Karl Dietrich Bracher et al. (Düsseldorf: Droste Verlag, 1983), 509–28.

14. Ibid., 513.

15. Hesse, *Spiel um Deutschland*, 374–77.

16. Ibid., 377.

17. Schmidt, *Statist auf Diplomatischer Bühne*, 576.

18. Jochen von Lang, *Top Nazi: SS General Karl Wolff* (New York: Enigma Books, 2005), 274.

19. Ibid., 223.

20. Ibid., 245.

21. Lang, *Top Nazi*, 248.

22. Ibid., 268.

23. Henke, *Die amerikanische Besetzung Deutschlands,* 676. Also Lukacs, *Hitler of History,* 167; and Max Waibel, *1945: Kapitulation in Norditalien* (Basel: Helbing & Lichtenhahn Verlag, 1981).

24. On Operation Sunrise, see Bradley F. Smith and Elena Agarossi, *Operation Sunrise: The Secret Surrender* (New York: Basic Books, 1979).

25. Butler, *Dear Mr. Stalin,* 306.

26. Ibid., 308.

27. Quoted in John Lukacs, *1945: The Year Zero* (New York: Doubleday, 1978), 92.

28. Ribbentrop, *Memoirs,* 172.

29. Frank Manuel, *Scenes from the End: The Last Days of World War II* (London: Profile Books, 2000), 51.

30. Heiber and Glantz, *Hitler and His Generals,* 649.

31. Ibid.

32. Domarus, *Reden,* 4:2197–98.

33. Joseph Goebbels, *Final Entries 1945: The Diaries of Joseph Goebbels,* ed. H. R. Trevor-Roper (New York: Avon Books, 1979), 20.

34. Zoller, *Hitler Privat,* 204.

35. For the details of how the Hitler-Bormann documents were found and published, consult Trevor-Roper's introduction to Hitler, *Testament,* 1–26. Although doubts have been raised about the authenticity of the *Bormann-Vermerke* (Bormann records), no evidence has surfaced to disprove them. For recent updates, see Lukacs, *Hitler of History,* 47–48; Kershaw, *Hitler: 1936–1945,* 1024–25; and Richard C. Carrier, "Hitler's Table Talk: Troubling Finds," *German Studies Review* 26 (October 2003): 561–76.

36. Hitler, *Testament,* 87.

37. Ibid.

38. Ibid., 88. Hitler had made this point repeatedly in the past, claiming that FDR's New Deal was a dismal failure. See especially his speech to the Reichstag on December 11, 1942. Domarus, *Reden,* 4:1802–3.

39. Hitler, *Testament,* 90. In *Mein Kampf* and in his second book, Hitler had made reference to America as an international mishmash of peoples artificially glued together but lacking ethnic cohesion. His final testament thus repeats what he believed long before, another example of his mental rigidity.

40. Ibid.

41. Speer, *Spandauer Tagebücher,* 633.

42. Ibid., 634.

43. Hermann Giesler, *Ein anderer Hitler: Bericht seines Architekten Hermann*

Giesler; Erlebnisse, Gespräche, Reflexionen (Leoni am Starnberger See: Druffel-Verlag, 1977), 477.

44. Heiber and Glantz, *Hitler and His Generals*, 642.

45. Ibid., 726.

46. Smith, *FDR*, 634.

47. Morgan, *FDR*, 762.

48. Ibid., 635.

49. Bullock, *Hitler*, 781.

50. Speer, *Inside the Third Reich*, 463.

51. Bullock, *Hitler*, 781.

52. Dwight D. Eisenhower, *Crusade in Europe* (New York: Doubleday, 1948), 400–401. Eisenhower made it clear at the time that the future division or postwar occupation of Germany did not influence his military plans for the final conquest of the country (396–403).

53. Quoted in Lang, *Top Nazi*, 288.

54. Ibid., 289.

55. Zoller, *Hitler Privat*, 234.

56. Speer, *Inside the Third Reich*, 472. Those who saw Hitler during the last months of the war all gave similar descriptions of his physical deterioration. One of the most penetrating accounts comes from Bernd Freytag von Loringhoven, Guderian's adjutant, who was a frequent visitor to the führer bunker. *Mit Hitler im Bunker: Die letzten Monate im Führerhauptquartier Juli 1944–April 1945* (Berlin: Siedler, 2006), 147–72.

57. Kershaw, *Hitler, 1936–1945*, 803–5. Also Loringhoven, *Mit Hitler im Bunker*, 147–52; Gerhard Boldt, *Die letzten Tage der Reichskanzlei* (Hamburg: Rowohlt, 1964), 91ff; Karl Koller, *Der letzte Monat: Die Tagebuchaufzeichnungen des ehemaligen Chefs der deutschen Luftwaffe vom 14. April bis 27. Mai 1945* (Mannheim: Norbert Wohlgemuth Verlag, 1949), 21–23.

58. Heiber and Glantz, *Hitler and His Generals*, 733.

59. Domarus, *Reden*, 4:2236–37.

60. Hugh Trevor-Roper, *The Last Days of Hitler* (New York: Macmillan, 1947), 182.

61. Anton Joachimsthaler, *The Last Days of Hitler: Legend, Evidence and Truth* (London: Cassell, 2002), 144–45; Trevor-Roper, *Last Days of Hitler*, 196.

62. Joachimsthaler has convincingly argued that the "Russians have not presented a single piece of evidence that they found Hitler's corpse." Joachimsthaler, *Last Days of Hitler*, 222. Books about Hitler's body are all nonsense on stilts.

CONCLUSION

1. Domarus, *Reden*, 3:751.

2. For Hitler's war aims, see Norman Rich, *Hitler's War Aims: The Establishment of the New Order* (London: André Deutsch, 1974), 420–21.

3. Andreas Hillgruber, *Hitlers Strategie*; Klaus Hildebrandt, *The Foreign Policy of the Third Reich*, trans. Anthony Fothergill (Berkeley: University of California Press, 1970); Jochen Thies, *Architekt der Weltherrschaft: Die Endziele Hitlers* (Düsseldorf: Athenäeum Droste Taschenbücher, 1980).

4. Laurence Rees, *Behind Closed Doors: Stalin, the Nazis, and the West* (New York: Pantheon, 2009), 341. At Yalta, FDR told Churchill that "of one thing I am certain, Stalin is not an imperialist." Arthur Bryant, *Triumph in the West: Based on the Diaries of Lord Alanbrooke* (London: William Collins, 1959), 304.

5. Tooze, *Wages of Destruction*, xxiii.

6. Conversation with Ciano, October 25, 1941, *DGFP*, Series D, 13:424.

7. Goebbels, *Goebbels Diaries*, 145.

8. Churchill, *Second World War*, 2:225–26.

9. Steinert, *Hitlers Krieg*, 592; Henke, *Die Amerikanische Besetzung Deutschlands*, 89.

10. Koller, *Der Letzte Monat*, 40.

11. Hitler, *Testament*, 107.

12. Churchill, *Second World War*, 2:53.

13. Quoted in Mark Mazower, *Hitler's Empire: How the Nazis Ruled Europe* (New York: Penguin, 2008), 554. Mazower discusses this article at length in chapter 17 of his book. Also Lukacs, *Great Powers*, 655–56.

14. Domarus, *Reden*, 4:2237.

15. Hitler, *Second Book*, 118.

BIBLIOGRAPHY

PRIMARY SOURCES

Archives

Bundesarchiv Berlin-Lichterfelder
Bundesarchiv Koblenz
Bundesarchiv-Militärarchiv, Freiburg, Germany
Franklin D. Roosevelt Library, Hyde Park, New York
Hoover Institution on War, Revolution and Peace (HI), Stanford, California
Institut für Zeitgeschichte, München, Germany
Library of Congress, Washington, D.C.
National Archives and Records Administration, College Park, Maryland

Published Documents and Collections

Akten zur deutschen auswärtigen Politik, 1918–1945: Aus dem Archiv des Auswärtigen Amts. Series D, 10 vols. Baden-Baden/Frankfurt, 1950–70; Series E, 1841–1945. Göttingen, 1969–79.

Butler, Susan, ed. *My Dear Mr. Stalin: The Complete Correspondence between Franklin D. Roosevelt and Joseph V. Stalin.* New Haven, Conn.: Yale University Press, 2005.

Documents diplomatiques français. Paris: Imprimerie Nationale, 1963–86.

Documents on British Foreign Policy, 1919–1939. London: H. M. Stationery Office, 1949.

Fuehrer Conferences on Matters Dealing with the German Navy, 1939–1945. 8 vols. Washington, D.C.: U.S. Government Printing Office, 1946–47.

Fuehrer Conferences on Naval Affairs. New York: Brassey's Naval Annual, 1948.

The German White Paper: Full Text of the Polish Documents Issued by the Berlin Foreign Office. New York: Howell, Soskin and Company, 1940.

Heiber, Helmut, and David M. Glantz, eds. *Hitler and His Generals: Military Conferences, 1942–1945.* New York: Enigma Books, 2003.

International Military Tribunal, *Trial of the Major War Criminals before the International Military Tribunal: Proceedings and Documents.* 42 vols. Nuremberg, 1947–49.

Jacobson, Hans-Adolf, and Werner Jochmann, eds. *Ausgewählte Dokumente zur Geschichte des Nationalsozialismus.* Bielefeld: Verlag Neue Gesellschaft, 1961.

Kriegstagebuch des Oberkommandos der Wehrmacht, 1940–1945. Ed. Percy E. Schramm. 4 vols. Frankfurt: Bernard Graefe, 1961–65.

McJimsey, George, ed. *Documentary History of the Franklin D. Roosevelt Presidency.* 12 vols. Washington, D.C.: Congressional Information Service, 2003.

Meldungen aus dem Reich: Auswahl aus dem geheimen Lageberichten des Sicherheitsdienstes der SS, 1933 bis 1944. Ed. Heinz Boberach. Berlin: Luchterhand, 1965.

Nazi Conspiracy and Aggression. 8 vols. and two supplements. Washington, D.C.: U.S. Government Printing Office, 1946–48.

Noakes, J., and G. Pridham, eds. *Nazism: A History in Documents and Eyewitness Accounts, 1919–1945.* 2 vols. New York: Schocken Books, 1990.

Rosenman, Samuel I., ed. *The Public Papers and Address of Franklin D. Roosevelt, 1933–1945.* 13 vols. New York: Harper and Brothers, 1950.

Trevor-Roper, H. R., ed. *Blitzkrieg to Defeat: Hitler's War Directives, 1933–1945.* New York: Holt, Rinehart and Winston, 1965.

U.S. Congress. *Congressional Record: Proceedings and Debates of the 77th–79th Congress.* Washington, D.C.: U.S. Government Printing Office, 1942–45.

———. *Hearings between the Joint Committee of the Investigation of the Pearl Harbor Attack. Exhibit 4, Rainbow 5.* Washington, D.C.: U.S. Government Printing Office, 1946.

U.S. Department of State. *Documents on German Foreign Policy, 1918–1945.* Series C. 5 vols. Washington, D.C.: U.S. Government Printing Office, 1957–66.

———. *Documents on German Foreign Policy, 1918–1945.* Series D. 13 vols. Washington, D.C.: U.S. Government Printing Office, 1949–64.

———. *Foreign Relations of the United States.* Washington, D.C.: U.S. Government Printing Office, ongoing (consult relevant volumes for 1933–45).

———. *National Socialism: Basic Principles, Their Application by the Nazi Party's Foreign Organization and the Use of Germans Abroad for Nazi Aims.* Washington, D.C.: U.S. Government Printing Office, 1943.

Autobiographies, Diaries, Letters, Memoirs
American

Acheson, Dean. *Present at the Creation.* New York: Norton, 1969.

Berle, Adolf A. *Navigating the Rapids, 1918–1971: From the Papers of Adolf Berle.* Ed. Beatrice B. Berle and Francis Jacobs. New York: Harcourt Brace, 1973.

Biddle, Francis. *In Brief Authority.* New York: Doubleday, 1948.

Blum, John Morton, ed. *From the Morgenthau Diaries: Years of Crisis, 1933–1938.* Boston: Houghton Mifflin, 1959.

———. *From the Morgenthau Diaries: Years of Urgency, 1938–1941.* Boston: Houghton Mifflin, 1965.

———. *From the Morgenthau Diaries: Years of War, 1941–1945.* Boston: Houghton Mifflin, 1967.

Bohlen, Charles E. *Witness to History, 1929–1969.* New York: Norton, 1973.

Bradley, Omar N. *A General's Life: An Autobiography by General of the Army Omar Bradley and Clay Blair.* New York: Simon and Schuster, 1983.

Bullitt, Orville H., ed. *For the President: Personal and Secret: Correspondence between Franklin Roosevelt and William C. Bullitt.* Boston: Houghton Mifflin, 1972.

Cudahy, John. *The Armies March: A Personal Report by John Cudahy.* New York: Charles Scribner's Sons, 1941.

Davies, Joseph E. *Mission to Moscow.* New York: Simon and Schuster, 1941.

Dodd, William E., Jr., and Martha Dodd, eds. *Ambassador Dodd's Diary, 1933–1938.* New York: Harcourt, Brace and Company, 1941.

Eisenhower, Dwight D. *Crusade in Europe.* New York: Doubleday, 1948.

Hassett, William D. *Off the Record with FDR, 1942–1945.* London: George Allen & Unwin, 1960.

Harriman, W. Averell. *Special Envoy to Churchill and Stalin, 1941–1946.* New York: Random House, 1975.

Hull, Cordell. *The Memoirs of Cordell Hull.* 2 vols. New York: Macmillan, 1948.

Ickes, Harold L. *The Secret Diary of Harold Ickes.* New York: Simon and Schuster, 1953.

Kennan, George. *Memoirs, 1925–1950.* Boston: Little, Brown and Company, 1967.

Kimball, Warren F., ed. *Churchill and Roosevelt: The Complete Correspondence.* 3 vols. Princeton, N.J.: Princeton University Press, 1984.

Lindbergh, Charles A. *The Wartime Journals of Charles A. Lindbergh.* New York: Harcourt Brace, 1970.

Lochner, Louis P. *Always the Unexpected: A Book of Reminiscences.* New York: Macmillan, 1956.

Long, Breckenridge. *The War Diary of Breckenridge Long: Selections from the*

Years 1939–1944. Lincoln: University of Nebraska Press, 1966.

Marshall, George C. *The Papers of George Catlett Marshall.* 4 vols. Baltimore: Johns Hopkins University Press, 1986–96.

Perkins, Frances. *The Roosevelt I Knew.* New York: Viking, 1946.

Roosevelt, Elliott. *As He Saw It.* New York: Duell, Sloan and Pearce, 1946.

———, ed. *F.D.R., His Personal Letters: The Early Years.* New York: Duell, Sloan and Pearce, 1947.

———, ed. *F.D.R., His Personal Letters, 1905–1928.* New York: Duell, Sloan and Pearce, 1950.

———, ed., *F.D.R., His Personal Letters, 1928–1945.* New York: Duell, Sloan and Pearce, 1950.

Rosenman, Samuel I. *Working with Roosevelt.* New York: Harper & Brothers, 1945.

Shirer, William L. *Berlin Diary.* 1941. New York: Popular Library, 1961.

Stimson, Henry L. *On Active Service in Peace and War.* New York: Harper & Brothers, 1947.

Tully, Grace G. *F.D.R., My Boss.* New York: Charles Scribner's Sons, 1949.

Wallace, Henry A. *The Price of Vision: The Diary of Henry A. Wallace, 1942–1945.* Boston: Houghton Mifflin, 1973.

Welles, Sumner. *The Time for Decision.* New York: Harper & Brothers, 1944.

German

Below, Nicolaus von. *At Hitler's Side: The Memoirs of Hitler's Luftwaffe Adjutant, 1937–1945.* Trans. Geoffrey Brooks. London: Military Book Club, 2001.

Boldt, Gerhard. *Die letzten Tage der Reichskanzlei.* Hamburg: Rowohlt, 1964.

Bormann, Martin. *The Bormann Letters: The Private Correspondence between Martin Bormann and His Wife.* Ed. H. R. Trevor-Roper. London: Weidenfeld and Nicolson, 1954.

———. *Die letzten Notizen von Martin Bormann.* Ed. Lew Besymenski. Stuttgart: Deutsche Verlags-Anstalt, 1974.

The Bormann Letters. Ed. H. R. Trevor-Roper. London: Weidenfeld and Nicolson, 1954.

Dietrich, Otto. *Zwölf Jahre mit Hitler.* München: Isar, 1955.

Dönitz, Karl. *Memoirs of Ten Years and Twenty Days.* Trans. R. H. Stevens. Annapolis, Md.: Naval Institute Press, 1990.

Einsiedel, Heinrich Graf. *Tagebuch der Versuchung.* Berlin: Pontes-Verlag, 1950.

Feuersenger, Marianne. *Im Vorzimmer der Macht. Aufzeichnungen aus dem Wehrmachtsführungsstab und Führerhauptquartier, 1940–1945.* München: Herbig, 1999.

Frank, Hans. *Im Angesicht des Galgens.* München: Beck, 1953.

Fromm, Bella. *Blood and Banquets*. New York: Harper & Brothers, 1942.

Gerhard, Engel. *Heeresadjutant bei Hitler, 1938–1943*. Stuttgart: Deutsche Verlags-Anstalt, 1974.

Gisevius, Hans Bernd. *Bis zum Bitteren Ende*. 2 vols. Zürich: Fretz & Wasmuth Verlag, 1946.

Goebbels, Joseph. *Das Eherne Herz: Reden und Aufsätze aus den Jahren 1941/42*. München: Franz Eher Verlag, 1943.

———. *Final Entries, 1945: The Diaries of Joseph Goebbels*. Ed. H. R. Trevor-Roper. New York: Avon Books, 1979.

———. *The Goebbels Diaries*. Ed. Louis P. Lochner. New York: Popular Library, 1948.

———. *The Goebbels Diaries, 1939–41*. Trans. Fred Taylor. New York: G. P. Putnam's Sons, 1983.

———. *Goebbels Reden*. 2 vols. Ed. Helmut Heiber. Düsseldorf: Droste, 1971–72.

———. *Joseph Goebbels Tagebücher, 1924–1945*. Ed. Ralf Georg Reuth. 5 vols. München: Piper Verlag, 2000.

———. *The Secret Conferences of Dr. Goebbels: The Nazi Propaganda War, 1939–43*. Ed. Willi A. Boelcke. New York: E. P. Dutton & Co., 1970.

———. *Die Tagebücher von Joseph Goebbels: Sämtliche Fragmente*. Ed. Elke Fröhlich. 13 vols. München: Saur, 1987.

———. *Vom Kaiserhof zur Reichskanzlei*. München: Eher Verlag, 1937.

Guderian, Heinz. *Erinnerungen eines Soldaten*. Heidelberg: Kurt Vorwinckel Verlag, 1950.

Halder, Franz. *Hitler als Feldherr*. München: Dom Verlag, 1949.

———. *Kriegstagebuch: Tägliche Aufzeichnungen des Chefs des Generalstabs des Heeres, 1939–1942*. 3 vols. Ed. Hans-Adolf Jacobsen. Stuttgart: Kohlhammer, 1962–64.

Hanfstaengl, Ernst. *Unheard Witness*. Philadelphia: Lippincott, 1957.

Hassell, Ulrich von. *Vom anderen Deutschland: Aus den nachgelassenen Tagebüchern, 1938–1944*. Frankfurt: Fischer, 1946.

Hesse, Fritz. *Das Spiel um Deutschland*. München: Paul List Verlag, 1953.

Heusinger, Adolf. *Befehl im Widerstreit: Schicksalsstunden der deutschen Armee, 1923–1945*. Tübingen: R. Wunderlich, 1950.

Himmler, Heinrich. *Heinrich Himmler: Geheimreden, 1939–1945*. Ed. Bradley F. Smith and Agnes Peterson. Frankfurt: Propyläen, 1974.

———. *Reichsführer! Briefe an und von Himmler*. Ed. Helmut Heiber. Stuttgart: Deutsche Verlags-Anstalt, 1968.

Hitler, Adolf. *Adolf Hitler: Monologe im Führerhauptquartier, 1941–1944*. Ed. Werner Jochmann. München: Orbis Verlag, 2000.

————. *Hitler: Reden und Proklamationen, 1932–1945*. Ed. Max Domarus. 4 vols. Wiesbaden: R. Löwit, 1973.

————. *Hitler: Sämtliche Aufzeichnungen, 1905–1924*. Ed. Eberhard Jäckel. Stuttgart: Deutsche Verlags-Anstalt, 1980.

————. *Hitlers Briefe und Notizen*. Ed. Werner Maser. Düsseldorf: Econ Verlag, 1973.

————. *Hitlers Tischgespräche im Führerhauptquartier*. Ed. Henry Picker. Stuttgart: Goldmann Verlag, 1981.

————. *Hitler's Second Book*. Trans. Krista Smith and ed. Gerhard L. Weinberg. New York: Enigma Books, 2003.

————. *Mein Kampf*. 2 vols. München: Franz Eher, 1925–27.

————. *Mein Kampf*. Ed. William Langer et al. New York: Reynal & Hitchcock, 1941.

————. *The Speeches of Adolf Hitler: April 1922–August 1939*. Ed. Norman H. Baynes. 2 vols. London: Oxford University Press, 1942.

————. *The Testament of Adolf Hitler: The Hitler-Bormann Documents*. Introduction by H. R. Trevor-Roper. London: Cassell, 1961.

Hossbach, Friedrich. *Zwischen Wehrmacht und Hitler*. Wolfenbüttel: Wolfenbüttler Verlagsanstalt, 1949.

Jodl, Luise. *Jenseits des Endes: Leben und Sterben des Generaloberst Alfred Jodl*. Vienna: Verlag Fritz Molden, 1976.

Kersten, Felix. *The Kersten Memoirs, 1940–1945*. Trans. Constantine Fitzgibbon and James Oliver with an introduction by H. R. Trevor-Roper. New York: Macmillan, 1957.

Kleist, Peter. *Zwischen Hitler und Stalin, 1939–45*. Bonn: Athenäum Verlag, 1950.

Koeppen, Werner. *Herbst 1941 im Führerhauptquartier: Berichte Werner Koeppens an seinen Minister Alfred Rosenberg*. Ed. Martin Vogt. Koblenz: Bundesarchiv, 2002.

Koller, Karl. *Der Letzte Monat: Die Tagebuchaufzeichnungen des ehemaligen Chefs der deutschen Luftwaffe vom 14 April bis 27. Mai 1945*. Mannheim: Norbert Wohlgemuth Verlag, 1949.

Kordt, Erich. *Wahn und Wirklichkeit*. Stuttgart: Deutsche Union Verlagsgesellschaft, 1948.

Kubizek, August. *The Young Hitler I Knew*. Trans. E. V. Anderson. New York: Tower Publications, n.d.

Leonhard, Wolfgang. *Die Revolution entlässt ihre Kinder*. Köln: Kippenheuer & Witsch, 2008.

Linge, Heinz. *Bis zum Untergang: Als Chef des persönlichen Dienstes bei Hitler*. Ed. Werner Maser. München: Herbig, 1980.

Loringhoven, Bernd Freytag von. *Mit Hitler im Bunker: Die letzten Monate im Führerhauptquartier Juli 1944–April 1945*. Berlin: Siedler, 2006.

Lüdecke, Kurt G.W. *I Knew Hitler*. London: Jarrolds, 1938.

Manstein, Erich. *Verlorene Siege*. Bonn: Athenäum, 1955.

Morell, Theodor. *The Secret Diaries of Hitler's Doctor*. Ed. David Irving. New York: Macmillan, 1983.

Papen, Franz von. *Memoirs*. Trans. Brian Connell. New York: E. P. Dutton & Company, 1953.

Raeder, Erich. *Grand Admiral*. Trans. Henry W. Drexel. New York: Da Capo Press, 2001.

Ribbentrop, Joachim. *The Ribbentrop Memoirs*. Introduction by Alan Bullock. London: Weidenfeld and Nicolson, 1954.

Rommel, Erwin. *The Rommel Papers*. Ed. B. H. Liddell Hart. London: Collins, 1953.

Rosenberg, Alfred. *Letzte Aufzeichnungen*. Göttingen: Plesse, 1955.

———. *Das politische Tagebuch Alfred Rosenbergs*. Ed. Hans-Günther Seraphim. München: Deutscher Taschenbuchverlag, 1964.

Schacht, Hjalmar Greeley. *Account Settled*. London: Weidenfeld and Nicolson, 1949.

———. *Confessions of the Old Wizard*. Boston: Houghton Mifflin, 1956.

Schellenberg, Walter. *Memoirs of Walter Schellenberg*. Trans. Louis Hagen. New York: Pyramid Books, 1958.

Schmidt, Paul. *Statist Auf Diplomatischer Bühne, 1923–1945*. Bonn: Athenäum, 1952.

Schroeder, Christa. *Er war mein Chef*. München: Herbig, 1985.

Schuschnigg, Kurt von. *Austrian Requiem*. Trans. Franz von Hildebrand. London: Golancz, 1946.

———. *Im Kampf gegen Hitler*. Vienna: Molden, 1969.

Speer, Albert. *Inside the Third Reich: Memoirs by Albert Speer*. Trans. Richard and Clara Winston. New York: Macmillan, 1970.

———. *Spandauer Tagebücher*. Frankfurt: Propyläen, 1975.

Wagner, Eduard. *Der General-Quartiermeister: Briefe und Tagebuchaufzeichnungen des Generalquartiermeisters des Heeres General der Artillerie*. Ed. Elisabeth Wagner. München: Günther Olzog Verlag, 1963.

Wagner, Gerhard, ed. *Lagevorträge des Oberbefehlshabers der Kriegsmarine vor Hitler, 1939–1945*. München: J. F. Lehmanns, 1972.

Warlimont, Walter. *Inside Hitler's Headquarters*. London: Weidenfeld and Nicolson, 1954.

Weizsäcker, Ernst von. *Erinnerungen*. München: List Verlag, 1950.

————. *Die Weizsäcker-Papiere, 1933–1950*. Ed. Leonidas E. Hill. Frankfurt: Propyläen Verlag, 1974.

Wiedemann, Fritz. *Der Mann der Feldherr werden wollte*. Dortmund: blick+bild Verlag, 1964.

Zoller, Albert. *Hitler Privat: Erlebnisbericht seiner Geheimsekretärin*. Düsseldorf: Droste Verlag, 1949.

Bibliographic Aids

American Historical Association, Committee for the Study of War Documents. *Guides to German Documents Microfilmed at Alexandria, Virginia*. Washington, D.C.: National Archives, 1958–.

Aycoberry, Pierre. *The Nazi Question: An Essay on the Interpretations of National Socialism*. New York: Pantheon, 1988.

Dear, I. C. B., ed. *The Oxford Companion to World War II*. New York: Oxford University Press, 1995.

DeConde, Alexander, ed. *Encyclopedia of American Foreign Policy*. 3 vols. New York: Macmillan, 1978.

Encyclopedia of American History. 11 vols. New York: Facts on File, 2003.

Encyclopedia of German Resistance to the Nazi Movement. Ed. Wolfgang Benz and Walter H. Pehle. Trans. Lance W. Garmer. New York: Continuum, 1997.

Findling, John E. *Dictionary of American Diplomatic History*. New York: Greenwood Press, 1989.

Freidel, Frank, ed. *Harvard Guide to American History*. Rev. ed. 2 vols. Cambridge, Mass.: Harvard University Press, 1974.

Gassert, Philipp, and Daniel S. Mattern. *The Hitler Library: A Bibliography*. Westport, Conn.: Greenwood Press, 2001.

Hüttenberger, Peter. *Bibliographie zum Nationalsozialismus*. Göttingen: Vandenhoeck & Ruprecht, 1980.

Kehr, Helen, and Janet Langmaid. *The Nazi Era, 1919–1945: A Select Bibliography of Published Works from the Early Roots to 1980*. London: Mansell, 1980.

Kent, George O. *A Catalogue of the Files and Microfilms of the German Foreign Ministry Archives, 1920–1945*. 4 vols. Stanford, Calif.: Stanford University Press, 1962–72.

Klee, Ernst. *Das Personenlexikon zum dritten Reich*. Frankfurt: Fischer Verlag, 2005.

Krewson, Margrit B. *German-American Relations: A Selective Bibliography*. Washington, D.C.: Library of Congress, 1995.

Nicholls, David. *Adolf Hitler: A Biographical Companion*. Santa Barbara, Calif.: ABC-CLIO Press, 2000.

Snyder, Louis L. *Encyclopedia of the Third Reich*. New York: Paragon, 1976.

Wistrich, Robert S. *Who's Who in Nazi Germany.* London: Weidenfeld and Nicolson, 1982.

Zentner, Christian, and Friedemann Bedürftig, eds. *Das Grosse Lexikon des Dritten Reiches.* München: Südwest, 1985.

Newspapers and Magazines

American Mercury
American Scholar
Chicago Daily Tribune
Collier
The Nation
Nazionalsozialistische Monatsheft
Neues Deutschland
New Republic
New Yorker
New York Times
Saturday Evening Post
Time
Völkische Beobachter
Washington Post
Washington Times-Herald

SECONDARY SOURCES

General Studies

Allen, Martin. *The Hitler/Hess Deception.* New York: Harper, 2003.

Armstrong, Anne. *Unconditional Surrender: The Impact of the Casablanca Policy upon World War II.* New Brunswick, N.J.: Rutgers University Press, 1961.

Backer, John. *The Decision to Divide Germany: American Foreign Policy in Transition.* Durham, N.C.: Duke University Press, 1978.

Bailey, Thomas A. *A Diplomatic History of the American People.* Englewood, N.J.: Prentice Hall, 1980.

Berthon, Simon, and Joanna Potts. *Warlords.* New York: Da Capo Press, 2006.

Beschloss, Michael. *The Conquerors: Roosevelt, Truman and the Destruction of Hitler's Germany, 1941–1945.* New York: Simon and Schuster, 2002.

Beyerchen, A. D. *Scientists under Hitler: Politics and the Physics Community in the Third Reich.* New Haven, Conn.: Yale University Press, 1977.

Boyd, Carl. *Hitler's Japanese Confidant: General Ōshima and Magic Intelligence, 1942–1946.* Lawrence: University of Kansas Press, 1993.

Breitman, Richard. *The Architect of Genocide: Himmler and the Final Solution.* New York: Knopf, 1991.

———. "A Deal with the Nazi Dictatorship? Himmler's Alleged Peace Emissaries in Autumn 1943." *Journal of Contemporary History* 30 (1995): 411–30.

———. *Official Secrets: What the Nazis Planned, What the British and the Americans Knew.* New York: Hill and Wang, 1998.

Brook-Shepherd, Gordon. *The Anschluss.* Philadelphia: Lippincott, 1953.

Bukey, Evan Burr. *Hitler's Austria: Popular Sentiment in the Nazi Era, 1938–1945.* Chapel Hill: University of North Carolina Press, 2000.

Bytwerk, Randall L. *Bending Spines: The Propagandas of Nazi Germany and the German Democratic Republic.* East Lansing: Michigan State University Press, 2004.

Carrier, Richard C. "Hitler's Table Talk: Troubling Finds." *German Studies Review* 26, no. 3 (October 2003): 561–76.

Churchill, Winston S. *The Second World War.* 6 vols. Boston: Houghton Mifflin, 1948.

Clark, Alan. *Barbarossa: The Russian-German Conflict, 1941–1945.* New York: Signet, 1966.

Colby, Benjamin. *'Twas a Famous Victory: Deception and Propaganda in the War with Germany.* New Rochelle, N.J.: Arlington House, 1974.

Conquest, Robert. *Reflections on a Ravished Century.* New York: Norton, 2000.

Craig, Gordon A., and Felix Gilbert, eds. *The Diplomats.* 2 vols. New York: Atheneum, 1963.

Dahms, Helmuth Günther. *Die Geschichte des Zweiten Weltkriegs.* München: Herbig, 1983.

Dawidowicz, Lucy. *The War against the Jews, 1933–1945.* New York: Bantam, 1975.

De Jong, Louis. *The German Fifth Column in the Second World War.* Chicago: University of Chicago Press, 1956.

Dimbleby, David, and David Reynolds. *An Ocean Apart: The Relationship between Britain and America in the Twentieth Century.* New York: Random House, 1988.

Divine, Robert A. *The Reluctant Belligerent: American Entry into World War II.* New York: Wiley, 1965.

Dülffer, Jost. *Weimar, Hitler und die Marine. Reichspolitik und Flottenbau, 1920–1939.* Düsseldorf: Droste, 1973.

Eubanks, Keith. *Munich.* Norman: University of Oklahoma Press, 1963.

———. *The Origins of World War II.* New York: Crowell, 1963.

Feis, Herbert. *Churchill, Roosevelt, Stalin: The War They Waged and the Peace They Sought.* Princeton, N.J.: Princeton University Press, 1957.

Fischer, Klaus P. *The History of an Obsession: German Judeophobia and the Holocaust.* New York: Continuum, 1998.

————. *Nazi Germany: A New History.* New York: Continuum, 1995.

Fleischhauer, Ingeborg. *Die Chance des Sonderfriedens: Deutsch-sowjetische Geheimgespräche, 1941–1945.* Berlin: Siedler Verlag, 1986.

Franz, Otmar, et al. *Europas Mitte.* Göttingen: Muster-Schmidt, 1987.

Franz-Willig, Georg. *Ursprung der Hitlerbewegung: 1919–22.* Preussisch-Oldendorf: Schütz, 1974.

Friedländer, Saul. *Nazi Germany and the Jews.* Vol. 1, *The Years of Persecution, 1933–1939.* New York: HarperCollins, 1997. Vol. 2, *The Years of Extermination.* New York: Harper Perennial, 2007.

————. *Prelude to Downfall: Hitler and the United States, 1933–1941.* New York: Alfred A. Knopf, 1967.

Gellately, Robert. *Backing Hitler: Consent and Coercion in Nazi Germany.* New York: Oxford University Press, 2001.

Gerlach, Christian. *Krieg, Ernährung, Völkermord: Deutsche Vernichtungspolitik im Zweiten Weltkrieg.* Zürich: Pendo Verlag, 2001.

————. "The Wannsee Conference, the Fate of German Jews, and Hitler's Decision in Principle to Exterminate all European Jews." *Journal of Modern History* 70, no. 4 (December 1998): 759–812.

Gilbert, Martin. *Auschwitz and the Allies.* New York: Holt, Rinehart and Winston, 1981.

————. *The Holocaust: A History of the Jews in Europe during the Second World War.* New York: Holt, Rinehart and Winston, 1985.

Gole, Henry G. *The Road to Rainbow.* Annapolis, Maryland: Naval Institute Press, 2003.

Görlitz, Walter. *History of the German General Staff.* New York: Praeger, 1953

Hansen, Reimer. *Das Ende des Dritten Reiches.* Stuttgart: Klett, 1966.

————. "Ribbentrops Friedensfühler im Frühjahr 1945." *Geschichte in Wissenschaft und Unterricht* 12 (1967): 716–30.

Harper, John Lamberton. *American Visions of Europe: Roosevelt, George F. Kennan, and Dean G. Acheson.* New York: Cambridge University Press, 1994.

Hassell, Agostino, and Sigrid MacRae. *Alliances of Enemies: The Untold Story of the Secret American and German Collaboration to End World War II.* New York: St. Martin's Press, 2006.

Hastings, Max. *Armageddon: The Battle for Germany, 1944–1945.* New York: Knopf, 2004.

————. *Overlord: D-Day and the Battle of Normandy.* New York: Simon and Schuster, 1984.

Hearden, Patrick. *Roosevelt Confronts Hitler.* DeKalb: Northern Illinois University Press, 1987.

Heinrichs, Waldo. *The Threshold of War: Franklin Roosevelt and American Entry into World War II.* New York: Oxford University Press, 1988.

Henke, Klaus-Dietmar. *Die amerikanische Besetzung Deutschlands.* München: Oldenbourg Verlag, 1996.

Herf, Jeffrey. *The Jewish Enemy: Nazi Propaganda during World War II and the Holocaust.* Cambridge, Mass.: Harvard University Press, 2006.

———. *Reactionary Modernism: Technology, Culture and Politics in Weimar and the Third Reich.* New York: Cambridge University Press, 1984.

Hilberg, Raul. *The Destruction of the European Jews.* 3 vols. New York: Holmes and Meier, 1985.

———. *Perpetrators, Victims, Bystanders: The Jewish Catastrophe, 1933–1945.* New York: HarperCollins, 1993.

Hildebrand, Klaus. *The Foreign Policy of the Third Reich.* Trans. Anthony Fothergill. Berkeley: University of California Press, 1970.

———. "Monokratie oder Polykratie? Hitlers Herrschaft und das Dritte Reich," in Gerhard Hirschfeld and Lothar Kettenacker, eds., *Der Führerstaat: Mythos und Realität.* Stuttgart: Klett, 1981.

Hillgruber, Andreas. *Der 2. Weltkrieg: Kriegsziele und Strategie der großen Mächte.* Stuttgart: Kohlhammer, 1983.

———. "Hitler und die USA 1933–1945." In Otmar Franz, ed., *Europas Mitte.* Göttingen: Muster-Schmidt, 1987.

———. *Germany and the Two World Wars.* Trans. William C. Kirby. Cambridge, Mass.: Harvard University Press, 1981.

———. *Hitlers Strategie: Politik und Kriegsführung, 1940–1941.* Frankfurt: Bernard und Graefe Verlag, 1965.

———. *Kontinuität und Diskontinuität in der deutschen Aussenpolitik von Bismarck bis Hitler.* Düsseldorf: Droste Verlag, 1969.

———. *Staatsmänner und Diplomaten bei Hitler.* 2 vols. Frankfurt: Bernard und Graefe Verlag, 1967.

———. *Zweierlei Untergang: Die Zerschlagung des Deutschen Reiches und das Ende des europäischen Judentums.* Berlin: Corso bei Siedler, 1986.

Hoffmann, Peter. *The History of the German Resistance, 1933–1945.* Cambridge, Mass.: MIT Press, 1977.

———. *Stauffenberg: A Family History, 1905–1944.* Cambridge: Cambridge University Press, 1995.

Hofstadter, Richard. *The American Political Tradition and the Men Who Made It.* New York: Viking, 1948.

Höhne, Heinz. *Canaris: Patriot im Zwielicht.* München: C. Bertelsmann, 1976.

———. *Der Krieg im Dunkeln.* München: C. Bertelsmann, 1985.

———. *The Order of the Death's Head.* New York: Ballantine, 1971.

Jacobson, Hans-Adolf. *Nationalsozialistische Aussenpolitik, 1933–45*. Frankfurt: Alfred Metzner, 1968.

———. *Der Weg zur Teilung der Welt: Politik und Strategie, 1919–1945*. Koblenz: Wehr und Wissen, 1977.

Jenkins, Roy. *Churchill: A Biography*. New York: Farrar, Strauss and Giroux, 2001.

Johnson, Paul. "The Myth of American Isolationism: Reinterpreting the Past." *Foreign Affairs* 71 (May–June 1995): 159–64.

Kahn, David. *Hitler's Spies: German Military Intelligence in World War II*. New York: Macmillan, 1978.

Keegan, John. *The Second World War*. New York: Viking, 1990.

Kershaw, Ian. *Fateful Choices: Ten Decisions That Changed the World, 1940–1941*. New York: Penguin, 2007.

———. *The Germans and the Final Solution*. New Haven, Conn.: Yale University Press, 2008.

———. *Popular Opinion and Political Dissent in the Third Reich: Bavaria, 1933–1945*. New York: Oxford University Press, 1984.

Kimball, Warren F. "Dieckhoff and America: A German's View of German-American Relations, 1937–1941." *Historian* 27 (February 1965): 230–32.

———. *Swords into Ploughshares: The Morgenthau Plan for Defeated Germany, 1943–1946*. Philadelphia: J. B. Lippincott, 1976.

Kissinger, Henry. *Diplomacy*. New York: Simon and Schuster, 1994.

Klemperer, Klemens von. *German Resistance against Hitler: The Search for Allies Abroad*. Oxford: Clarendon Press, 1992.

Koch, H. W. "The Specter of a Separate Peace in the East: Russo-German Peace Feelers." *Journal of Contemporary History* 10 (1975): 531–49.

Kohn, Hans. *The Mind of Germany: The Education of a Nation*. New York: Harper and Row, 1960.

Kracauer, Siegfried. *From Caligari to Hitler: A Psychological History of the German Film*. Princeton, N.J.: Princeton University Press, 1947.

Kuklick, Bruce. *American Policy and the Division of Europe: The Clash with Russia over Reparations*. Ithaca, N.Y.: Cornell University Press, 1972.

Lang, Jochen von. *Top Nazi: SS General Karl Wolff*. New York: Enigma Books, 2005.

Langer, William L., and S. Everett Gleason. *The Undeclared War, 1940–1941*. New York: Harper & Brothers, 1953.

Laqueur, Walter. *The Terrible Secret: Suppression of the Truth about Hitler's Final Solution*. New York: Penguin, 1982.

Liddell Hart, B. H. *The German Generals Talk*. New York: Morrow, 1948.

———. *History of the Second World War*. New York: Putnam, 1970.

Longerich, Peter. *Himmler: Biographie*. Berlin: Siedler, 2008.

——. *Propagandisten im Krieg: Die Presseabteilung des Auswärtigen Amtes unter Ribbentrop.* München: Oldenbourg, 1987.

Low, Alfred D. *The Anschluss Movement, 1918–1938, and the Great Powers.* Boulder, Colo.: East European Monographs, 1985.

Lukacs, John. *The Duel: The Eighty-Day Struggle between Churchill and Hitler.* New Haven, Conn.: Yale University Press, 1990.

——. *Five Days in London: May 1940.* New Haven, Conn.: Yale University Press, 1999.

——. *The Great Powers and Eastern Europe.* New York: American Book Company, 1953.

——. "Herbert Hoover Meets Adolf Hitler." *American Scholar* (2000): 235–38.

——. *June 1941: Hitler and Stalin.* New Haven, Conn.: Yale University Press, 2006.

——. *The Last European War.* 1976. New Haven, Conn.: Yale University Press, 2001.

——. *1945: The Year Zero.* New York: Doubleday, 1978.

——. "The Transatlantic Duel: Hitler vs. Roosevelt." *American Heritage Magazine* (December 1991): 1–6.

MacDonald, Francis. *Insidious Foes: The Axis Fifth Column and the American Home Front.* New York: Oxford University Press, 1995.

Macdonough, Giles. *After the Reich: The Brutal History of the Allied Occupation.* New York: Basic Books, 2007.

Manuel, Frank. *Scenes from the End: The Last Days of World War II.* London: Profile Books, 2000.

Martin, Bernd. *Deutschland und Japan im Zweiten Weltkrieg.* Göttingen: Muster-Schmidt, 1969.

Mastny, Vojtech. "Stalin and the Prospect of a Separate Peace in World War II." *American Historical Review* 77 (February 1972): 1365–88.

Mauch, Christof. *The Shadow War against Hitler: The Covert Operations of America's Wartime Intelligence Service.* Trans. Jeremiah Riemer. New York: Columbia University Press, 2003.

Mazower, Mark. *Hitler's Empire: How the Nazis Ruled Europe.* New York: Penguin, 2008.

Michalka, Wolfgang, ed. *Nationalsozialistische Aussenpolitik.* Darmstadt: Wissenschaftliche Buchgesellschaft, 1978.

——, ed. *Der Zweite Weltkrieg: Analysen, Grundzüge, Forschungsbilanz.* Weyarn, Austria: Seehammer Verlag, 1997.

Militärgeschichtliches Forschungsamt: Das Deutsche Reich und der Zweite Weltkrieg. 10 vols. Stuttgart: Deutsche Verlags-Anstalt, 1979–.

Nagorski, Andrew. *The Greatest Battle: Stalin, Hitler, and the Desperate Struggle for Moscow That Changed the Course of World War II*. New York: Simon and Schuster, 2007.

Nave, Eric. *Betrayal at Pearl Harbor: How Churchill Lured Roosevelt into World War II. New York: Summit, 1991*.

Overy, Richard. *Why the Allies Won*. New York: Norton, 1995.

Parker, R. A. C. *Chamberlain and Appeasement: British Policy and the Coming of the Second World War*. New York: St. Martin's Press, 1994.

Pauley, Bruce F. *History and the Forgotten Nazis: A History of Austrian National Socialism*. Chapel Hill: University of North Carolina Press, 1981.

———. *The Habsburg Legacy, 1867–1938*. New York: Holt, Rinehart and Winston, 1972.

Power, Thomas. *Heisenberg's War: The Secret History of the German Bomb*. New York: Knopf, 1993.

Rees, Laurence. *Behind Closed Doors: Stalin, the Nazis, and the West*. New York: Pantheon, 2009.

Reitlinger Gerald. *The SS: Alibi of a Nation*. Englewood, N.J.: Prentice Hall, 1981.

Reynolds, David. *The Creation of the Anglo-American Alliance: 1937–1941*. Chapel Hill: University of North Carolina Press, 1982.

Rhodes, Richard. *Masters of Death: The SS Einsatzgruppen and the Invention of the Holocaust*. New York: Knopf, 2002.

Rich, Norman. *Hitler's War Aims: The Establishment of the New Order*. 2 vols. New York: Norton, 1973–74. Also published by André Deutsch, London, 1974.

Ritter, Gerhart. *The German Resistance: Carl Goerdeler's Struggle against Tyranny*. New York: Praeger, 1958.

Roberts, Andrew. *Hitler and Churchill: Secrets of Leadership*. London: Orion Books, 2004.

———. *Masters and Commanders: How Four Titans Won the War in the West, 1941–1945*. New York: HarperCollins, 2009.

Romerstein, Herbert and Eric Breiner. *The Verona Secrets: Exposing Soviet Espionage and America's Traitors*. Washington, D.C.: Regnery, 2001.

Rosen, Robert. *Saving the Jews: Franklin D. Roosevelt and the Jews*. New York: Thunder's Mouth Press, 2006.

Rothfels, Hans. *Die deutsche Opposition gegen Hitler: Eine Würdigung*. Frankfurt: Fischer Verlag, 1958.

Rothstein, Andrew. *The Munich Conspiracy*. London: Lawrence & Wishart, 1958.

Ryan, Cornelius. *The Last Battle*. London: Collins, 1966.

Ryback, Timothy W. *Hitler's Private Library: The Books that Shaped his Life.* London: Bodley Head, 2009.

Schivelbusch, Wolfgang. *Three New Deals: Reflections on Roosevelt's America, Mussolini's Italy, and Hitler's Germany, 1933–1939.* New York: Picador, 2007.

Schlabrendorff, Fabian von. *Offiziere gegen Hitler.* Zürich: Europa Verlag, 1946.

Schmidt, Rainer F. *Rudolf Heß: Botengang eines Toren? Der Flug nach Großbritannien vom 10. Mai 1941.* München: Econ, Ullstein, List Verlag, 2000.

Schustereit, Helmut. *Vabanque: Hitlers Angriff auf die Sowjetunion als Versuch durch den Sieg im Osten den Westen zu bezwingen.* 2nd ed. Selent, Austria: Pour le Mérite, 2000.

Seabury, Paul. *The Wilhelmstrasse: A Study of German Diplomats under the Nazi Regime.* Berkeley: University of California Press, 1954.

Smith, Bradley F., and Elena Agarossi. *Operation Sunrise: The Secret Surrender.* New York: Basic Books, 1979

Sontag, Raymond J. *A Broken World, 1919–1939.* New York: Harper & Row, 1971.

———. "The Last Months of Peace." *Foreign Affairs* 35 (1957): 507–24.

———. "The Origins of the Second World War." *Review of Politics* 25 (1963): 497–505.

Stehle, Hansjakob. "Deutsche Friedensfühler bei den Westmächten im Februar/ März 1945." In Dietrich Bracher et al., eds. *Nationalsozialistische Diktatur 1933–1945: Eine Bilanz.* Düsseldorf: Droste Verlag, 1983.

Stein, George H. *The Waffen SS.* Ithaca, N.Y.: Cornell University Press, 1966.

Stern, Fritz. *The Politics of Cultural Despair: A Study in the Rise of the German Ideology.* New York: Doubleday, 1965.

Suvorov, Victor. *Icebreaker: Who Started the Second World War?* London: Thomas B. Beattie, 1990.

Taylor, A. J. P. *The Origins of the Second World War.* New York: Fawcett, 1961.

Tooze, Adam. *The Wages of Destruction: The Making and Breaking of the Nazi Economy.* New York: Penguin, 2007.

Turner, Henry Ashby, Jr. *General Motors and the Nazis.* New Haven, Conn.: Yale University Press, 2005.

Waibel, Max. *1945: Kapitulation in Norditalien.* Basel: Helbing & Lichtenhahn Verlag, 1981.

Walker Mark. *Nazi Science: Myth, Truth, and the German Bomb.* Cambridge, Mass.: Perseus, 1995.

———. *German National Socialism and the Quest for Nuclear Power.* Cambridge: Cambridge University Press, 1989.

Waller, John H. *The Devil's Doctor: Felix Kersten and the Secret Plot to Turn Himmler against Hitler.* New York: Wiley, 2002.

Watt, Richard. *The Kings Depart. The Tragedy of Germany: Versailles and the German Revolution.* New York: Simon and Schuster, 1968.

Weinberg, Gerhard L. *The Foreign Policy of Hitler's Germany.* Vol. 1, *Diplomatic Revolution in Europe, 1933–36.* Chicago: University of Chicago Press, 1970.

———. *The Foreign Policy of Hitler's Germany.* Vol. 2, *Starting World War II, 1937–39.* Chicago: University of Chicago Press, 1980.

———. "Hitler's Image of the United States." *American Historical Review* 69 (July 1964): 1006–21.

———. *Visions of Victory: The Hopes of Eight World War II Leaders.* Cambridge: Cambridge University Press, 2005.

———. *A World at Arms: A Global History of World War II.* Cambridge: Cambridge University Press, 1994.

Weingartner, James J. *Crossroads to Death: The Story of the Malmédy Massacre and Trial.* Berkeley: University of California Press, 1979.

Wheeler-Bennett, J. W. *The Nemesis of Power: The German Army in Politics, 1918–1945.* London: Macmillan, 1964.

———. *Munich: Prologue to Tragedy.* New York: Viking, 1964.

Wilmot, Chester. *The Struggle for Europe.* London: Collins, 1952.

Wilt, Alan F. *The Atlantic Wall, 1941–1944: Hitler's Defenses for D-Day.* New York: Enigma Books, 2004.

Woodward, E. L. *British Foreign Policy in the Second World War.* 3 vols. London: H. M. Stationery Office, 1962.

Ziemke, Earl. *Stalingrad to Berlin: The German Defeat in the East.* New York: Dorset Press, 1986.

German-American Relations, 1933–45

Anthes Louis. "Publicly Deliberative Drama: The 1934 Mock Trial of Adolf Hitler for 'Crimes against Civilization." *Journal of Legal History* 42 (1998).

Barclay, David E., and Elisabeth Glaser-Schmidt, eds. *Transatlantic Images and Perceptions: Germany and America since 1776.* Cambridge: Cambridge University Press, 1997.

Beck, Alfred M. *Hitler's Ambivalent Attaché: Lt. Gen. Friedrich von Boetticher in America, 1933–1941.* Washington, D.C.: Potomac Books, 2005.

Benz, Wolfgang. "Judenvernichtung als Notwehr? Die Legenden um Theodore N. Kaufman." *Vierteljahreshefte für Zeitgeschichte* 29 (October 1981).

Breuer, William B. *Hitler's Undercover War: The Nazi Espionage Invasion of the U.S.A.* New York: St. Martin's Press, 1989.

Broszat, Martin. "Hitler und die Genesis der Endlösung." *Vierteljahreshefte für Zeitgeschichte* 25 (October 1977).

Canedy, Susan. *America's Nazis: A Democratic Dilemma: A History of the Ger-*

man-American Bund. Menlo Park, Calif.: Markgraf Publications Group, 1990.

Carter, John Franklin. *Catoctin Conversation.* New York: Charles Scribner's Sons, 1947.

Compton, James V. *The Swastika and the Eagle: Hitler, the United States, and the Origins of World War II.* Boston: Houghton Mifflin, 1967.

Conradi, Peter. *Hitler's Piano Player: The Rise and Fall of Ernst Hanfstaengl, Confidant of Hitler, Ally of FDR.* New York: Carroll and Graf Publishers, 2004

Dallek, Robert. *Democrat and Diplomat: The Life of William E. Dodd.* New York: Oxford University Press, 1968.

Davidson, Eugene. *The Death and Life of Germany: An Account of the American Occupation.* New York: Knopf, 1959.

De Bedts, Ralph F. *Ambassador Joseph Kennedy, 1938–1940.* New York: Peter Lang, 1985.

Diamond, Sander. *The Nazi Movement in the United States, 1924–1941.* Ithaca, N.Y.: Cornell University Press, 1974.

Dieckhoff, Hans Heinrich. *Roosevelt auf Kriegskurs: Amerikas Kreuzzug gegen den Frieden, 1933–1941.* Kiel: Arndt Verlag, 2003 (reprint of the author's 1943 book *Zur Vorgeschichte des Roosevelt-Krieges*).

Diner, Dan. *Feindbild Amerika: Über die Beständigkeit eines Resentiments.* München: Propyläen Verlag, 2002.

Doerries, Reinhard R. *Hitler's Intelligence Chief Walter Schellenberg.* New York: Enigma Books, 2009.

Duffy, James P. *Target America: Hitler's Plan to Attack the United States.* Guilford, Conn.: Lyons Press, 2004.

Eisele, Susanne Uta. "Das Deutschlandbild in der amerikanischen Literatur des Zweiten Weltkrieges." Diss., University of Erlangen, 1961.

Farrago, Ladislas. *The Game of the Foxes: The Untold Story of German Espionage in the United States and Great Britain during World War II.* New York: McKay, 1971.

Frye, Alton. *Nazi Germany and the American Hemisphere, 1933–1941.* New Haven, Conn.: Yale University Press, 1967.

Gannon, Michael. *Drumbeat: The Dramatic True Story of Germany's First U-boat Attacks along the American Coast in World War II.* New York: Harper & Row, 1990.

Gardener, Lloyd C. *Spheres of Influence: The Great Powers Partition Europe, from Munich to Yalta.* Chicago: Ivan R. Dee, 1993.

Gassert, Philipp. *Amerika im Dritten Reich.* Stuttgart: Steiner Verlag, 1977.

Halfeld, Adolf. *USA: greift in die Welt.* Hamburg: Verlag Broschek, 1941.

———. *Amerika und der Amerikanismus.* Jena: Eugen Diederichs, 1928.

Hammer, Arnold. *USA hinter den Kulissen.* Berlin: Verlag Scherl, 1942.

Hass, Gerhart. *Von München bis Pearl Harbor: Zur Geschichte der deutsch-amerikanischen Beziehungen, 1938–1941.* Berlin: Akademie Verlag, 1965.

Hedin, Sven. *Amerika im Kampf der Kontinente.* Leipzig: F. A. Brockhaus, 1942.

Heindl, Josef Engelbert. *Die diplomatischen Beziehungen zwischen Deutschland und den Vereinigten Staaten von Amerika von 1933 bis 1939.* Diss., University of Würzburg, 1963.

Herzstein, Robert E. *The War That Hitler Won: Goebbels and the Nazi Media Campaign.* New York: Paragon House, 1987.

Higham, Charles. *Trading with the Enemy: An Exposé of the Nazi-American Money Plot, 1933–1945.* New York: Delacorte Press, 1983.

Hoenicke-Moore, Michaela. *"Know Your Enemy": The American Response to Nazism, 1933–1945.* New York: Cambridge University Press, 2010.

Jonas, Manfred. *Isolationism in America, 1935–1941.* Ithaca, N.Y.: Cornell University Press, 1966.

———. *The United States and Germany: A Diplomatic History.* Ithaca, N.Y.: Cornell University Press, 1984.

Kaufman, Theodore N. *Germany Must Perish.* Newark, N.J.: Argyl Press, 1941.

Kipphahn, Klaus. *Deutsche Propaganda in den Vereinigten Staaten, 1933–1941.* Heidelberg: C. Winter, 1971.

Knapp, Manfred, et al. *Die USA und Deutschland, 1918–1975.* München: C. H. Beck, 1978.

Linklater, Eric. *Juan in America.* Oxford: Alden Press, 1931.

Lohe, Werner. *Roosevelt-Amerika.* München: Eher Verlag, 1943.

Ludwig, Emil. *How to Treat the Germans.* New York: Willard, 1944.

Mehringer, Helmut. *Die Armee ohne Banner.* Dresden: Franz Müller Verlag, 1943.

Miller, Douglas. *You Can't Do Business with Hitler: What a Nazi Victory Would Mean to Every American.* New York: Pocket Books, 1941.

Moltmann, Günter. *Amerikas Deutschlandpolitik im Zweiten Weltkrieg.* Heidelberg: C. Winter, 1958.

———. "Franklin D. Roosevelts Friedensappell vom 14. April 1939." *Jahrbuch für Amerikastudien* 9 (1964): 92109.

Morgenthau, Henry, Jr. *Germany Is Our Problem.* New York: Harper & Brothers, 1945.Offner, Arnold A. *American Appeasement: United States Foreign Policy and Germany, 1933–1938.* New York: Norton, 1968.

Persico, Joseph E. *Piercing the Reich: The Penetration of Nazi Germany by American Secret Agents during World War II.* New York: Viking Press, 1979.

———. *Roosevelt's Secret War: FDR and World War II Espionage.* New York: Random House, 2001.

Remak, Joachim. "Friends of the New Germany: The Bund and German-American Relations." *Journal of Modern History* 29 (March 1957): 38–41.

———. "Germany and the United States, 1933–1939." Diss., Stanford University, 1955.

Ross, Colin. *Amerikas Schicksalsstunde: Die Vereinigten Staaten zwischen Demokratie und Diktatur.* Leipzig: F. A. Brockhaus, 1936.

———. *Unser Amerika: Der deutsche Anteil an den Vereinigten Staaten.* Leipzig: F. A. Brockhaus, 1937.

———. *Von Chicago nach Chungking: Einem jungen Deutschen erschließt sich die Welt.* Berlin: Verlag der Heimbücherei, 1941.

———. *Die Westliche Hemisphäre als Programm und Phantom des amerikanischen Imperialismus.* Leipzig: F. A. Brockhaus, 1942.

Schad, Martha. *Hitlers Spionin: Das Leben der Stephanie von Hohenlohe.* München: Wilhelm Heyne, 2002.

Schröder, Hans-Jürgen. *Deutschland und die Vereinigten Staaten: Wirtschaft und Politik in der Entwicklung des deutsch-amerikanischen Gegensatzes.* Wiesbaden: Franz Steiner, 1970.

Smith, Arthur Lee. *The Deutschtum of Nazi Germany and the United States.* Hague: M. Nijhoff, 1965.

Trefousse, Hans Louis, ed. *Germany and American Neutrality, 1939–1941.* New York: Octagon Books, 1969.

Turrou, Leon G. *Nazi Spies in America.* New York: Random House, 1939.

Vagts, Alfred. *Deutschland und die Vereinigten Staaten in der Weltpolitik.* 2 vols. New York: Macmillan, 1935.

———. *The Military Attaché.* Princeton, N.J.: Princeton University Press, 1967.

———. "Unconditional Surrender: Vor und nach 1945." *Vierteljahreshefte für Zeitgeschichte* 3 (1959): 280–309.

Wette, Wolfram. *Die Wehrmacht: Feindbilder, Vernichtungskrieg, Legenden.* Frankfurt: S. Fischer Verlag, 2005.

Winkler, Allan M. *The Politics of Propaganda: The Office of War Information.* New Haven, Conn.: Yale University Press, 1978.

Wittke, Carl. *German-Americans and the World War.* Columbus: Ohio State Archeological and Historical Society, 1936.

Zalampas, Michael. *Adolf Hitler and the Third Reich in American Magazines, 1933–1939.* Bowling Green, Ohio: Bowling Green University Press, 1989.

Hitler

Baur, Hans. *Ich flog Mächtige der Erde.* Kempten, Allgäu: Pröpster Verlag, 1956.

Binion, Rudolph. *Hitler among the Germans.* New York: Elsevier, 1979.

Bromberg, Norbert, and Verna Volz Small. *Hitler's Psychopathology*. New York: International Universities Press, 1983.

Buchheit, Gert. *Hitler der Feldherr: Die Zerstörung einer Legende*. Rastatt: Grote, 1958.

Bullock, Alan. *Hitler: A Study in Tyranny*. New York: Harper & Row, 1962.

———. *Hitler and Stalin: Parallel Lives*. New York: Knopf, 1992.

Burrin, Philippe. *Hitler and the Jews: The Genesis of the Holocaust*. London: Edward Arnold, 1989.

Carr, William. *Hitler: A Study in Personality*. London: Edward Arnold, 1978.

Deuerlein, Ernst. *Hitler: Eine politische Biographie*. München: List Verlag, 1969.

Eitner, Hans-Jürgen. *Der Führer: Hitlers Persönlichkeit und Charakter*. München: Langen Müller, 1981.

Fest, Joachim. *Hitler*. Trans. Richard and Clara Winston. New York: Harcourt Brace Jovanovich, 1973.

———. *Der Untergang: Hitler und das Ende des Dritten Reiches: Eine historische Skizze*. Hamburg: Rowolt Taschenbuch Verlag, 2005.

———. *Staatsstreich: Der lange Weg zum 20. Juli*. Berlin: Siedler, 1999.

Fleming, Gerald. *Hitler and the Final Solution*. Berkeley: University of California Press, 1982.

Funke, Manfred. *Starker oder schwacher Diktator? Hitlers Herrschaft und die Deutschen*. Düsseldorf: Droste Verlag, 1989.

Giesler, Hermann. *Ein anderer Hitler: Bericht seines Architekten Hermann Giesler: Erlebnisse, Gespräche, Reflexionen*. Leoni am Starnberger See: Druffel-Verlag, 1977.

Görlitz, Walter. *Adolf Hitler*. Göttingen: Musterschmidt Verlag, 1960.

Haffner, Sebastian. *The Meaning of Hitler*. Trans. Ewald Osers. Cambridge, Mass.: Harvard University Press, 1983.

Hamann, Brigitte. *Hitlers Wien: Lehrjahre eines Diktators*. München: Piper, 1998.

Hauner, Milan. *Hitler: A Chronology of His Life and Times*. New York: St. Martin's Press, 1983.

Heer, Friedrich. *Der Glaube des Adolf Hitler: Anatomie einer politischen Religiosität*. München: Bechtle Verlag, 1968.

Heiber, Helmut. *Adolf Hitler: Eine Biographie*. Berlin: Colloquium, 1960.

Heiden, Konrad. *Adolf Hitler: Das Zeitalter der Verantwortungslosigkeit. Eine Biographie*. Zürich: Europa Verlag, 1936.

———. *Der Führer: Hitler's Rise to Power*. Boston: Houghton Mifflin, 1944.

Heston, Leonard L., and Renate Heston. *The Medical Casebook of Adolf Hitler*. New York: Stein & Day, 1979.

Irving, David. *Hitler's War*. 2 vols. New York: Viking, 1977.

Jäckel, Eberhard. *Hitler in History*. Hanover, N.H.: Brandeis University Press, 1984.

———. *Hitlers Herrschaft: Vollzug einer Weltanschauung*. Stuttgart: Deutsche Verlags-Anstalt, 1986.

———. *Hitlers Weltanschauung: Entwurf einer Herrschaft*. Stuttgart: Deutsche Verlags-Anstalt, 1983.

Jenks, W. A. *Vienna and the Young Hitler*. New York: Columbia University Press, 1960.

Jetzinger, Franz. *Hitler's Youth*. Trans. Lawrence Wilson. Westport, Conn.: Greenwood Press, 1976.

Joachimsthaler, Anton. *Hitlers Liste: Ein Dokument persönlicher Beziehungen*. München: F. A. Herbig, 2003.

———. *Hitlers Weg begann in München, 1913–1923*. München: F. A. Herbig, 2000.

———. *Korrektur einer Biographie: Adolf Hitler, 1908–1920*. München: F. A. Herbig, 1989.

——— *The Last Days of Hitler: Legend, Evidence, and Truth*. London: Cassell, 2002.

Kallenbach, Hans. *Mit Hitler auf Festung Landsberg*. München: Kress & Hornung, 1939.

Kershaw, Ian. *Hitler, 1889–1936: Hubris*. New York: Norton, 1999.

———. *Hitler, 1936–1945: Nemesis*. New York: Norton, 2000.

———. *The "Hitler Myth": Image and Reality in the Third Reich*. New York: Oxford University Press, 1987.

———. *Hitler, the Germans, and the Final Solution*. New Haven, Conn.: Yale University Press, 2008.

Langer, Walter C. *The Mind of Adolf Hitler*. New York: Basic Books, 1972.

Large, David Clay. *Hitlers München: Aufstieg und Fall der Hauptstadt der Bewegung*. München: C. H. Beck, 1998.

Lukacs, John. *The Hitler of History*. New York: Knopf, 1997.

Maser, Werner. *Hitler*. Trans. Peter and Betty Ross. London: Allen Lane, 1973.

———. *Mein Kampf: Der Fahrplan eines Welteroberers*. Esslingen: Bechtle, 1974.

O'Donnell, James R. *The Bunker*. New York: Bantam, 1979.

Peterson, Edward N. *The Limits of Hitler's Power*. Princeton, N.J.: Princeton University Press, 1969.

Redlich, Fritz. *Hitler: Diagnosis of a Destructive Prophet*. New York: Oxford University Press, 1999.

Roberts, Geoffrey. *Stalin's Wars*. New Haven, Conn.: Yale University Press, 2006.

Rosenbaum, Ron. *Explaining Hitler*. New York: Random House, 1998.

Rosenfeld, Alvin. *Imagining Hitler*. Bloomington: University of Indiana Press, 1985.

Schenck, Ernst Günther. *Patient Hitler: Eine Medizinische Biographie*. Augsburg: Bechtermünz Verlag, 2000.

Schramm, Percy Ernst. *Hitler: The Man and the Military Leader*. Trans. Donald S. Detweiler. Chicago: Quadrangle, 1971.

Schreiber, Gerhard. *Hitler Interpretationen*. Darmstadt: Wissenschaftliche Buchgesellschaft, 1984.

Smith, Bradley F. *Adolf Hitler: His Family, Childhood, and Youth*. Stanford, Calif.: Hoover Institution Press, 1967.

Steinert, Marlis. *Hitler*. München: C. C. Beck, 1994.

———. *Hitlers Krieg und die Deutschen*. Düsseldorf: Econ Verlag, 1970.

Stern, J. P. *The Führer and the People*. Glasgow: William Collins Sons, 1975.

Stierlin, Helm. *Adolf Hitler: A Family Perspective*. New York: Psychohistory Press, 1976.

Tallgren, Vappu. *Hitler und die Helden: Heroismus und Weltanschauung*. Helsinki: Suomalainen Tiedeakatemia, 1981.

Thies, Jochen. *Architekt der Weltherrschaft: Die Endziele Hitlers*. Düsseldorf: Athenäum Droste Taschenbücher, 1980.

Toland, John. *Hitler*. 2 vols. New York: Doubleday, 1976.

Trevor-Roper, H. R. *The Last Days of Adolf Hitler*. New York: Macmillan, 1947.

Tyrell, Albrecht. *Vom Trommler zum Führer*. München: Wilhelm Fink, 1975.

Voegelin, Eric. *Hitler and the Germans*. Translated, edited, and with an introduction by Detlev Clemens and Brenda Purcell. Columbia: University of Missouri Press, 1999.

Wagner, Eduard. *Der General-Quartiermeister: Briefe und Tagebuchaufzeichnungen des Generalquartiermeisters des Heeres General der Artillerie*. Ed. Elisabeth Wagner. München: Günther Olzog Verlag, 1963.

Wagner, Otto. *Hitler: Memoirs of a Confidant*. Ed. Henry Ashby Turner Jr. New Haven, Conn.: Yale University Press, 1985.

Waite, Robert G. L. *The Psychopathic God: Adolf Hitler*. New York: Basic Books, 1977.

Wistrich, Robert. *Hitler and the Holocaust*. New York: Modern Library, 2001.

———. *Hitler's Apocalypse: Jews and the Nazi Legacy*. New York: St. Martin's Press, 1985.

Zitelmann, Rainer. *Adolf Hitler: Eine politische Biographie*. Göttingen: Muster-Schmidt Verlag, 1998.

———. *Hitler: Selbstverständnis eines Revolutionärs*. Stuttgart: Klett , 1987.

———. "Zur Begründung des Lebensraum-Motivs in Hitlers Weltanschauung." In Wolfgang Michalka, ed., *Der Zweite Weltkrieg: Analysen, Grundzüge, Forschungsbilanz*. Weyarn: Seehamer Verlag, 1997.

Roosevelt

Aga Rossi, Elena. *Origins of the Bipolar World: Roosevelt's Policy toward Europe and the Soviet Union: A Reevaluation.* Berkeley: Center for German and European Studies, University of California, 1993.

Bailey, Thomas A., and Paul B. Ryan. *Hitler vs. Roosevelt: The Undeclared Naval War.* New York: Free Press, 1979.

Barnes, Harry Elmer. *Perpetual War for Perpetual Peace.* Caldwell, Idaho: Caxton Printers Ltd., 1953.

Beard, Charles A. *President Roosevelt and the Coming of the War.* New Haven, Conn.: Yale University Press, 1948.

Bell, Michael. "The World View of Franklin D. Roosevelt: France, Germany and the United States' Involvement in World War II." Ph.D. diss., University of Maryland, 2004.

Beschloss, Michael. *Kennedy and Roosevelt: The Uneasy Alliance.* New York: Norton, 1980.

Bishop, Jim. *F.D.R.'s Last Year.* New York: Pocket Books, 1975.

Black, Conrad. *Franklin Delano Roosevelt: Champion of Freedom.* New York: Public Affairs, 2003.

Blum, John Morton. *Roosevelt and Morgenthau.* Boston: Houghton Mifflin, 1970.

Brinkley, Alan. *The End of Reform: New Deal Liberalism in Recession and War.* New York: Knopf, 1995.

Brinkley, David. *Washington Goes to War.* New York: Knopf, 1988.

Burns, James MacGregor. *Roosevelt: The Lion and the Fox.* New York: Harcourt Brace, 1956.

———. *Roosevelt: The Soldier of Freedom, 1940–1945.* New York: Harcourt Brace Jovanovich, 1970.

Burns, James MacGregor, and Susan Dunn. *The Three Roosevelts: Patrician Leaders Who Transformed America.* New York: Atlantic Monthly Press, 2001.

Butler, Susan, ed. *Dear Mr. Stalin: The Complete Correspondence between Franklin D. Roosevelt and Joseph Stalin.* New Haven, Conn.: Yale University Press, 2005.

Casey, Steven. *Cautious Crusade: Franklin D. Roosevelt, American Public Opinion, and the War against Nazi Germany.* New York: Oxford University Press, 2001.

———. "Franklin D. Roosevelt, Ernst 'Putzi' Hanfstaengl and the 'S-Project,' June 1942–June 1944." *Journal of Contemporary History* 35 (2000): 339–59.

Collier, Peter, and David Horowitz. *The Roosevelts: An American Saga.* New York: Simon and Schuster, 1994.

Dallek, Robert. *Franklin D. Roosevelt and American Foreign Policy, 1932–1945.* New York: Oxford University Press, 1979.

Davis, Kenneth Sidney. *F.D.R.* 5 vols. New York: Random House, 1972–2000.

Divine, Robert A. *The Illusion of Neutrality.* Chicago: University of Chicago Press, 1962.

———. *Roosevelt and World War II.* Baltimore: Johns Hopkins University Press, 1969.

———. *Second Chance: The Triumph of Internationalism during World War II.* New York: Atheneum, 1967.

Evans, Hugh E. *The Hidden Campaign: FDR's Health and the 1944 Campaign.* Armonk, N.Y.: M. E. Sharpe, 2002.

Feis, Herbert. *Churchill-Roosevelt-Stalin: The War They Waged and the Peace They Sought.* Princeton, N.J.: Princeton University Press, 1957.

Ferrell, Robert H. *The Dying President: Franklin D. Roosevelt, 1944–1945.* Columbia: University of Missouri Press, 1998.

———. *Ill-Advised: Presidential Health and Public Trust.* Columbia: University of Missouri Press, 1992.

Fleming, Thomas. *The New Dealers' War: F.D.R. and the War within World War II.* New York: Basic Books, 2001.

Flynn, John. *The Roosevelt Myth.* New York: Devlin-Adair, 1956.

Freidel, Frank. *Franklin D. Roosevelt.* 5 vols. New York: Little, Brown, 1952–90.

Goodwin, Doris Kearns. *Franklin D. Roosevelt: A Rendezvous with Destiny.* New York: Little, Brown, 1990.

———. *No Ordinary Time: Franklin and Eleanor Roosevelt: The Home Front in World War II.* New York: Simon and Schuster, 1994.

Graham, Otis L., Jr. *Franklin D. Roosevelt: His Life and Times: An Encyclopedic View.* New York: Da Capo Press, 1991.

Gunther, John. *Roosevelt in Retrospect: A Profile in History.* New York: Harper & Brothers, 1950.

Herzstein, Robert Edwin. *Roosevelt and Hitler: Prelude to War.* New York: Paragon House, 1989.

Jenkins, Roy. *Franklin Roosevelt.* New York: Times Books, 2003.

Kimball, Warren F. *Forged in War: Roosevelt, Churchill and the Second World War.* New York: Morrow, 1997.

———. *The Juggler: Franklin Roosevelt as Wartime Statesman.* Princeton, N.J.: Princeton University Press, 1991.

Lash, Joseph P. *Eleanor and Franklin: The Story of Their Relationship.* New York: Norton, 1971.

———. *Roosevelt and Churchill, 1939–1941: The Partnership That Saved the West.* New York: Norton, 1976.

Leuchtenberg, William. *Franklin D. Roosevelt and the New Deal.* New York: Harper, 1960.

———. *In the Shadow of FDR.* Ithaca, N.Y.: Cornell University Press, 2001.

Morgan, Ted. *FDR: A Biography.* New York: Simon and Schuster, 1985.

Newton, Verne W., ed. *FDR and the Holocaust.* New York: St. Martin's Press, 1996.

Nisbet, Robert. *Roosevelt and Stalin: The Failed Courtship.* Washington, D.C.: Regnery Gateway, 1988.

O'Connor, Raymond Gish. *Diplomacy for Victory: FDR and Unconditional Surrender.* New York: Norton, 1971.

Roosevelt, Franklin D. *Looking Forward.* New York: John Day Company, 1933.

Schlesinger, Arthur, Jr. *The Age of Roosevelt.* 3 vols. Boston: Houghton Mifflin, 1957–60.

Sherwood, Robert E. *Roosevelt and Hopkins: An Intimate History.* New York: Harper, & Brothers, 1948.

Smith, Jean Edward. *FDR.* New York: Random House, 2008.

Stinnett, Robert B. *Day of Deceit: The Truth about FDR and Pearl Harbor.* New York: Touchstone, 1999.

Tansill, Charles Callan. *Back Door to War: The Roosevelt Foreign Policy, 1933–1945.* Chicago: Henry Regnery, 1952.

Tugwell, Rexford G. *The Democratic Roosevelt: A Biography of Franklin D. Roosevelt.* New York: Doubleday, 1957.

———. *In Search of Roosevelt.* Cambridge, Mass.: Harvard University Press, 1972.

———. *Roosevelt's Revolution.* New York: Macmillan, 1977.

Ward, Geoffrey. *Before the Trumpet: Young Franklin Roosevelt.* New York: Harper & Row, 1964.

———. *A First Class Temperament: The Emergence of Franklin Roosevelt.* New York: Harper & Row, 1989.

White, Graham J. *FDR and the Press.* Chicago: University of Chicago Press, 1979.

Winfield, Betty Houdin. *FDR and the News Media.* New York: Columbia University Press, 1994.

INDEX

ACKNOWLEDGMENTS

In checking about a dozen acknowledgments by various authors who had written books in recent years, I noticed a disconcerting trend of name-dropping, which I swore I would avoid in my own case, limiting myself strictly to those people who had a significant hand in helping me get this topic off my chest. In that spirit, I would like to thank, above all, John Lukacs, who encouraged me to undertake this project and then alerted me to a number of potential land mines. He also reminded me to cut unnecessary verbiage and to avoid those distempers of what Francis Bacon called "fantastical learning." His counsel proved that even at my age one can still learn from someone still older and wiser. This is also true of my former Ph.D. mentor and good friend Leonard Marsak, whose memories of his own experiences in World War II were rekindled by my research on Hitler and America, revealing just how fresh the events of that gruesome war were to him even now, some sixty-five years afterward. Len read every chapter with great care and made invaluable suggestions. The same is true of Jeffrey Russell. Although a medievalist by training, Jeff is also a generalist who knows and can speak with great expertise about topics outside his specialty, a skill that is not always encouraged by professional academics. As with my previous two books, Jeff read the whole manuscript with meticulous care, raising questions and correcting mistakes. In keeping with my promise to avoid unnecessary name-dropping, I cannot neglect to mention my debt to my wife, Ann. She was not a long-suffering wife who resented the fact that I spent more time on Hitler than on her or the family. She willingly typed the manuscript despite her obligations as a school psychologist, but I must add that she now hopes that I will permanently retire Hitler to the broom closet.